Networking
FOR
DUMMIES®
8TH EDITION

by Doug Lowe

BICENTENNIAL
1807
WILEY
2007
BICENTENNIAL

Wiley Publishing, Inc.

Networking For Dummies®, 8th Edition

Published by
Wiley Publishing, Inc.
111 River Street
Hoboken, NJ 07030-5774

www.wiley.com

Copyright © 2007 by Wiley Publishing, Inc., Indianapolis, Indiana

Published by Wiley Publishing, Inc., Indianapolis, Indiana

Published simultaneously in Canada

No part of this publication may be reproduced, stored in a retrieval system or transmitted in any form or by any means, electronic, mechanical, photocopying, recording, scanning or otherwise, except as permitted under Sections 107 or 108 of the 1976 United States Copyright Act, without either the prior written permission of the Publisher, or authorization through payment of the appropriate per-copy fee to the Copyright Clearance Center, 222 Rosewood Drive, Danvers, MA 01923, (978) 750-8400, fax (978) 646-8600. Requests to the Publisher for permission should be addressed to the Legal Department, Wiley Publishing, Inc., 10475 Crosspoint Blvd., Indianapolis, IN 46256, (317) 572-3447, fax (317) 572-4355, or online at http://www.wiley.com/go/permissions.

Trademarks: Wiley, the Wiley Publishing logo, For Dummies, the Dummies Man logo, A Reference for the Rest of Us!, The Dummies Way, Dummies Daily, The Fun and Easy Way, Dummies.com, and related trade dress are trademarks or registered trademarks of John Wiley & Sons, Inc. and/or its affiliates in the United States and other countries, and may not be used without written permission. All other trademarks are the property of their respective owners. Wiley Publishing, Inc., is not associated with any product or vendor mentioned in this book.

For general information on our other products and services, please contact our Customer Care Department within the U.S. at 800-762-2974, outside the U.S. at 317-572-3993, or fax 317-572-4002.

For technical support, please visit www.wiley.com/techsupport.

Wiley also publishes its books in a variety of electronic formats. Some content that appears in print may not be available in electronic books.

Library of Congress Control Number: 2007924234

ISBN: 978-0-470-05620-2

Manufactured in the United States of America

10 9 8 7 6 5 4 3 2 1

About the Author

Doug Lowe has written a whole bunch of computer books, including more than 40 *For Dummies* books (such as *PowerPoint 2007 For Dummies, Word 2007 All-In-One Desk Reference For Dummies,* and *Networking All-In-One Desk Reference For Dummies*). He lives in that sunny All-American city of Fresno, California, which isn't nearly as close to San Francisco as most people think, with his wife and his youngest daughter (the other two have flown the coop), and a couple of crazy dogs. He manages the network for an engineering firm in Clovis, CA, and in his free time creates computer-controlled Halloween decorations that rival Disney's Haunted Mansion. Maybe his next book should be *Computer-Controlled Halloween Props For Dummies.* (For pictures, check out his Web site at www.LoweWriter.com/halloween.)

Dedication

To Debbie, Rebecca, Sarah, and Bethany.

Author's Acknowledgments

The list of thank-yous for this book is long and goes back several years. I'd like to first thank John Kilcullen, David Solomon, Janna Custer, Erik Dafforn, Grag Robertson, and Ray Marshall for all of their help with the first edition. Those who worked on subsequent editions include Christopher Morris, Dan DiNicolo, Barry Childs-Helton, Tim Gallan, Mary Goodwin, Joe Salmeri, Jennifer Ehrlich, Constance Carlisle, Jamey L. Marcum, Jeanne S. Criswell, Ted Cains, Dana Lesh, Rebekah Mancilla, Becky Huehls, Amy Pettinella, Suzanne Thomas, Garret Pease, and Andrea Boucher. Each of these people made valuable contributions to the content, readability, and accuracy that have paved the way for the current edition.

Now, for the eighth edition, I'd like to thank project editor Pat O'Brien, who did a great job overseeing all the editorial work that was required to put this book together. I'd also like to thank Srinath Sitaraman, who gave the entire manuscript a thorough technical look-through, and copy editors Jen Riggs and Becky Whitney, who maid sure there whir know spelling hair ores. And, as always, thanks to all the behind-the-scenes people who chipped in with help I'm not even aware of.

Publisher's Acknowledgments

We're proud of this book; please send us your comments through our online registration form located at www.dummies.com/register/.

Some of the people who helped bring this book to market include the following:

Acquisitions, Editorial, and Media Development

Project Editor: Pat O'Brien

Acquisitions Editor: Melody Layne

Copy Editor: Jennifer Riggs

Technical Editor: Srinath Sitaraman

Editorial Manager: Kevin Kirschner

Media Development Manager: Laura VanWinkle

Editorial Assistant: Amanda Foxworth

Sr. Editorial Assistant: Cherie Case

Cartoons: Rich Tennant (www.the5thwave.com)

Composition Services

Coordinator: Heather Kolter

Layout and Graphics: Carl Byers, Joyce Haughey, Stephanie D. Jumper, Barbara Moore, Laura Pence, Ronald Terry

Proofreaders: Aptara, Todd Lothery, Susan Moritz

Indexer: Aptara

Anniversary Logo Design: Richard Pacifico

Publishing and Editorial for Technology Dummies

Richard Swadley, Vice President and Executive Group Publisher

Andy Cummings, Vice President and Publisher

Mary Bednarek, Executive Acquisitions Director

Mary C. Corder, Editorial Director

Publishing for Consumer Dummies

Diane Graves Steele, Vice President and Publisher

Joyce Pepple, Acquisitions Director

Composition Services

Gerry Fahey, Vice President of Production Services

Debbie Stailey, Director of Composition Services

Contents at a Glance

Introduction *1*

Part I: Let's Network! *7*
Chapter 1: Networks Will Not Take Over the World, and Other Network Basics.......9
Chapter 2: Life on the Network..21
Chapter 3: More Ways to Use Your Network...41

Part II: Building Your Own Network *61*
Chapter 4: Planning Your Network...63
Chapter 5: Oh, What a Tangled Web We Weave: Cables, Adapters, and Other Stuff...81
Chapter 6: Dealing with TCP/IP 107
Chapter 7: Setting Up a Server...133
Chapter 8: Configuring Windows XP and Vista Clients....................................155
Chapter 9: Wireless Networking 169

Part III: Getting Connected *187*
Chapter 10: Connecting Your Network to the Internet......................................189
Chapter 11: Running a Mail Server...195
Chapter 12: Creating an Intranet 207
Chapter 13: Is It a Phone or a Computer? (Or, Understanding VoIP
  and Convergence)..217
Chapter 14: Connecting from Home..221

Part IV: Network Management For Dummies *225*
Chapter 15: Welcome to Network Management 227
Chapter 16: Managing User Accounts with Active Directory 237
Chapter 17: Managing Network Storage 251
Chapter 18: Network Performance Anxiety 265
Chapter 19: Solving Network Problems 279
Chapter 20: How to Stay on Top of Your Network
  and Keep Its Users Off Your Back 293

Part V: Protecting Your Network *299*
Chapter 21: Backing Up Your Data 301
Chapter 22: Securing Your Network 313
Chapter 23: Hardening Your Network...327

Part VI: Beyond Windows 339

Chapter 24: Networking with Linux 341
Chapter 25: Macintosh Networking 363

Part VII: The Part of Tens 371

Chapter 26: More Than Ten Big Network Mistakes 373
Chapter 27: Ten Networking Commandments 381
Chapter 28: Ten Things You Should Keep in Your Closet 387
Chapter 29: Layers of the OSI Model 391

Index 397

Table of Contents

Introduction *1*

About This Book...1
How to Use This Book 2
What You Don't Need to Read 3
Foolish Assumptions 3
How This Book Is Organized..3
    Part I: Let's Network! 4
    Part II: Building Your Own Network 4
    Part III: Getting Connected 4
    Part IV: Network Management For Dummies.................4
    Part V: Protecting Your Network 5
    Part VI: Beyond Windows 5
    Part VII: The Part of Tens 5
Icons Used in This Book...5
Where to Go from Here...6

Part 1: Let's Network! *7*

**Chapter 1: Networks Will Not Take Over the World,
and Other Network Basics** 9

What Is a Network? 10
Why Bother with a Network?...12
    Sharing files...12
    Sharing resources...12
    Sharing programs 13
Servers and Clients 13
Dedicated Servers and Peers...14
What Makes a Network Tick? 15
It's Not a Personal Computer Anymore!................................17
The Network Administrator..18
What Have They Got That You Don't Got?.............................19

Chapter 2: Life on the Network 21

Distinguishing between Local Resources and Network Resources.........21
What's in a Name?..22
Logging On to the Network..24
Understanding Shared Folders..26

Four Good Uses for a Shared Folder..26
        Store files that everybody needs...27
        Store your own files 27
        Make a pit stop for files on their way to other users...........28
        Back up your local hard drive 28
Oh, the Network Places You'll Go 29
Mapping Network Drives...31
Using a Network Printer 34
        Adding a network printer 35
        Printing to a network printer 37
        Playing with the print queue..37
Logging Off the Network 39

Chapter 3: More Ways to Use Your Network **41**

Sharing Your Stuff...41
        Enabling File and Printer Sharing (Windows XP)...............42
        Enabling File and Printer Sharing (Windows Vista)...........44
Sharing a Folder 45
        Sharing a folder in Windows XP 45
        Sharing a folder in Windows Vista 47
Using the Public Folder in Windows Vista 48
Sharing a Printer 50
        Sharing a printer in Windows XP..51
        Sharing a printer in Windows Vista......................................52
Using Microsoft Office on a Network..53
        Installing Office on a network — some options.................54
        Accessing network files 55
        Using workgroup templates 55
        Networking an Access database...58
Working with Offline Files 59

Part II: Building Your Own Network *61*

Chapter 4: Planning Your Network **63**

Making a Network Plan..63
Being Purposeful 64
Taking Stock...65
        What you need to know 65
        Programs that gather information for you..........................68
To Dedicate, or Not to Dedicate: That Is the Question 69
Looking at Different Types of Servers 70
        File servers..70
        Print servers 70
        Web servers...70
        Mail servers...71
        Database servers...71

Choosing a Server Operating System 71
Planning the Infrastructure..71
Drawing Diagrams 72
Sample Network Plans...73
    Building a small network: California Sport Surface, Inc. 74
    Connecting two networks: Creative Course Development, Inc. 76
    Improving network performance: DCH Accounting.......................78

Chapter 5: Oh, What a Tangled Web We Weave:
Cables, Adapters, and Other Stuff **81**
What Is Ethernet?..81
All about Cable 84
    Cable categories 85
    What's with the pairs? 86
    To shield or not to shield 86
    When to use plenum cable 87
    Sometimes solid, sometimes stranded...............................87
    Installation guidelines...88
    The tools you need..89
    Pinouts for twisted-pair cables.......................................90
    RJ-45 connectors 91
    Crossover cables 93
    Wall jacks and patch panels 93
Hubs and Switches..95
    Hubs or switches? 95
    Working with switches...96
    Daisy-chaining switches 97
Network Interface Cards 98
    Picking a network interface card......................................98
    Installing a network card 99
Other Network Devices 101
    Repeaters..101
    Bridges...103
    Routers 104

Chapter 6: Dealing with TCP/IP **107**
Understanding Binary 107
    Counting by ones...108
    Doing the logic thing 109
Introducing IP Addresses 110
    Networks and hosts 110
    The dotted-decimal dance 110
Classifying IP Addresses 111
    Class A addresses..112
    Class B addresses..113
    Class C addresses..113

Subnetting 114
    Subnets 115
    Subnet masks 116
    The great subnet roundup 117
    Private and public addresses 118
Understanding Network Address Translation.............................118
Configuring Your Network for DHCP 119
    Understanding DHCP 120
    DHCP servers..120
    Understanding scopes 121
    Feeling excluded? 122
    Reservations suggested...123
    How long to lease?..124
Managing a Windows Server 2003 DHCP Server 124
Configuring a Windows DHCP Client 126
Using DNS..127
    Domains and domain names..127
    Fully qualified domain names 129
Working with the Windows DNS Server 130
Configuring a Windows DNS Client 131

Chapter 7: Setting Up a Server **133**
Network Operating System Features...133
    Network support 133
    File-sharing services 134
    Multitasking...135
    Directory services 135
    Security services 137
Understanding Windows Server 2003 Versions..........................138
Other Server Operating Systems 139
The Many Ways to Install a Network Operating System 140
    Full install versus upgrade..140
    Installation over the network..141
    Automated and remote installations 142
Gathering Your Stuff..142
    A capable server computer..142
    The server operating system 143
    Other software 144
    A working Internet connection 144
    A good book 144
Making Informed Decisions 145
Making Final Preparations 146
Installing a Network Operating System 146
    Phase 1: Collecting Information...147
    Phase 2: Dynamic Update...147
    Phase 3: Preparing Installation 147
    Phase 4: Installing Windows..148
    Phase 5: Finalizing Installation 149

Life after Setup 149
 Logging on 149
 Activating Windows 149
 Downloading service packs 152
 Testing the installation 152
Configuring Server Roles..152

Chapter 8: Configuring Windows XP and Vista Clients **155**

Configuring Network Connections..155
 Configuring Windows XP network connections 156
 Configuring Windows Vista network connections 160
Configuring Client Computer Identification........................162
 Configuring Windows XP computer identification........163
 Configuring Windows Vista computer identification....164
Configuring Network Logon 166

Chapter 9: Wireless Networking **169**

Diving into Wireless Networking...169
A Little High School Electronics..170
 Waves and frequencies 171
 Wavelength and antennas 171
 Spectrums and the FCC 173
Eight-Oh-Two-Dot-Eleventy Something? (Or, Understanding
 Wireless Standards) 174
Home on the Range...175
Wireless Network Adapters 176
Wireless Access Points..177
 Infrastructure mode 179
 Multifunction WAPs..179
Roaming..179
 Wireless bridging 180
 Ad hoc networks...180
Configuring a Wireless Access Point 180
 Basic configuration options 181
 DHCP configuration...183
Configuring Windows for Wireless Networking..................183

Part III: Getting Connected **187**

Chapter 10: Connecting Your Network to the Internet **189**

Connecting to the Internet...189
 Connecting with cable or DSL..190
 Connecting with high-speed private lines: T1 and T3 191
 Sharing an Internet connection 191
Securing Your Connection with a Firewall 192
 Using a firewall..192
 The built-in Windows firewall 193

Chapter 11: Running a Mail Server **195**

Using the Exchange System Manager Console 195
Managing Mailboxes 196
The Exchange General tab 196
The E-mail Addresses tab 197
The Exchange Features tab 197
The Exchange Advanced tab 199
Configuring Outlook for Exchange 200
Viewing Another Mailbox 202

Chapter 12: Creating an Intranet **207**

What Is an Intranet? 207
What Do You Use an Intranet For? 208
What You Need to Set Up an Intranet 209
How to Set Up an IIS Web Server 210
How to Create a Simple Intranet Page 212
Managing IIS 214

Chapter 13: Is It a Phone or a Computer? (Or, Understanding VoIP and Convergence) **217**

Understanding VoIP 217
Advantages of VoIP 219
Disadvantages of VoIP 220
Popular VoIP Providers 220

Chapter 14: Connecting from Home **221**

Using Outlook Web Access 221
Using a Virtual Private Network 224

Part IV: Network Management For Dummies ***225***

Chapter 15: Welcome to Network Management **227**

What a Network Administrator Does 227
Picking a Part-Time Administrator and Providing the Right Resources . . .229
Documenting the Network 230
Performing Routine Chores 231
Managing Network Users 232
Acquiring Software Tools for Network Administrators 233
Building a Library 234
Pursuing Certification 236

Chapter 16: Managing User Accounts with Active Directory **237**

Basics of Windows User Accounts 237
Local accounts versus domain accounts 238
User account properties 238

Creating a New User..239
Setting User Properties 241
    Changing a user's contact information.................242
    Setting account options.......................................242
    Setting a user's profile information....................244
Resetting User Passwords...245
Disabling and Enabling User Accounts 246
Deleting a User 247
Working with Groups..247
    Creating a group 247
    Adding a member to a group 248
Creating a Logon Script..249

Chapter 17: Managing Network Storage 251

Understanding Network Storage...............................251
    File servers...251
    Storage appliances 252
Understanding Permissions......................................252
Understanding Shares 254
Configuring the File Server Role...............................256
Managing Your File Server 259
    Sharing a folder from the File Server Manager......259
    Granting permissions..262

Chapter 18: Network Performance Anxiety 265

Why Administrators Hate Performance Problems 265
What Exactly Is a Bottleneck?...................................266
The Five Most Common Network Bottlenecks...........268
    The hardware inside your servers......................268
    The server's configuration options.....................268
    Servers that do too much....................................269
    The network infrastructure.................................270
    Malfunctioning components.................................270
Tune Your Network the Compulsive Way 271
Monitor Network Performance..................................272
Creating Performance Logs.......................................275
More Performance Tips..278

Chapter 19: Solving Network Problems 279

When Bad Things Happen to Good Computers 280
How to Fix Dead Computers 281
Ways to Check a Network Connection 282
A Bunch of Error Messages Just Flew By! 283
Double-Check Your Network Settings........................283
Time to Experiment 284
Who's on First...285
How to Restart a Client Computer............................285

How to Restart Network Services 287
How to Restart a Network Server 288
Look at Event Logs..290
Document Your Trials and Tribulations.......................................291

**Chapter 20: How to Stay on Top of Your Network
and Keep Its Users Off Your Back** **293**

Train Your Users..293
Organize a Library 294
Keep Up with the Computer Industry 295
Remember That the Guru Needs a Guru.....................................296
Spew Helpful Bluffs and Excuses 296

Part V: Protecting Your Network..................................299

Chapter 21: Backing Up Your Data **301**

Backing Up Your Data..301
All about Tapes and Tape Drives 302
Backup Software..303
Types of Backups 304
    Normal backups...305
    Copy backups 306
    Daily backups 306
    Incremental backups...306
    Differential backups 307
Local versus Network Backups 308
How Many Sets of Backups Should You Keep?...........................309
A Word about Tape Reliability..310
About Cleaning the Heads...311
Backup Security...312

Chapter 22: Securing Your Network **313**

Do You Need Security? 314
Two Approaches to Security 315
Physical Security: Locking Your Doors 315
Securing User Accounts 317
    Obfuscating your usernames...317
    Using passwords wisely..318
    Generating passwords for dummies 319
    Secure the Administrator account 320
Managing User Security...320
    User accounts 321
    Built-in accounts 321
    User rights 322
    Permissions (who gets what) 323

Group therapy..324
User profiles..325
Logon scripts 325
Securing Your Users...326

Chapter 23: Hardening Your Network 327

Firewalls 327
The Many Types of Firewalls 329
Packet filtering...329
Stateful packet inspection (SPI) 331
Circuit-level gateway..331
Application gateway..332
The Built-In Firewall in Windows XP and Windows Vista 333
Virus Protection 334
What is a virus? 334
Antivirus programs 335
Safe computing 336
Patching Things Up 337

Part VI: Beyond Windows 339

Chapter 24: Networking with Linux 341

Comparing Linux with Windows 342
Choosing a Linux Distribution..344
Installing Linux 345
On Again, Off Again..346
Logging on (or is that in?)...346
Logging off..348
Shutting down 348
Using GNOME 348
Getting to a Command Shell 350
Managing User Accounts...351
Network Configuration 352
Using the Network Configuration Program 353
Restarting your network...354
Doing the Samba Dance...355
Understanding Samba..356
Installing Samba..357
Starting and stopping Samba 357
Using the Samba Server Configuration tool...................358

Chapter 25: Macintosh Networking 363

What You Need to Know to Hook Up a Macintosh Network..................363
AppleTalk and Open Transport 363
Mac OS X Server 364

What You Need to Know to Use a Macintosh Network 365
  Configuring a Mac for networking..366
  Accessing a network printer 366
  Sharing files with other users 367
  Accessing shared files...367
What You Need to Know to Network Macintoshes with PCs................368

Part VII: The Part of Tens.................................371

Chapter 26: More Than Ten Big Network Mistakes 373
Skimping on Cable..373
Turning Off or Restarting a Server Computer While
  Users Are Logged On..374
Deleting Important Files on the Server 375
Copying a File from the Server, Changing It, and Then Copying It Back ...375
Sending Something to the Printer Again Just Because
  It Didn't Print the First Time 376
Assuming That the Server Is Safely Backed Up............................376
Connecting to the Internet without Considering Security Issues 376
Plugging In a Wireless Access Point without Asking 377
Thinking You Can't Work Just Because the Network Is Down...............377
Running Out of Space on a Server 378
Always Blaming the Network...378

Chapter 27: Ten Networking Commandments 381
I. Thou Shalt Back Up Thy Hard Drive Religiously....................381
II. Thou Shalt Protect Thy Network from Infidels 382
III. Thou Shalt Keepeth Thy Network Drive Pure
  and Cleanse It of Old Files 382
IV. Thou Shalt Not Tinker with Thine Network Configuration
  Unless Thou Knowest What Thou Art Doing............................382
V. Thou Shalt Not Covet Thy Neighbor's Network....................383
VI. Thou Shalt Schedule Downtime before Working
  upon Thy Network..383
VII. Thou Shalt Keep an Adequate Supply of Spare Parts.....................383
VIII. Thou Shalt Not Steal Thy Neighbor's Program without a License....384
IX. Thou Shalt Train Thy Users in the Ways of the Network 384
X. Thou Shalt Write Down Thy Network Configuration
  upon Tablets of Stone 384

Chapter 28: Ten Things You Should Keep in Your Closet 387

Chapter 29: Layers of the OSI Model 391

Index..397

Introduction

Welcome to the eighth edition of *Networking For Dummies,* the book that's written especially for people who have this nagging feeling in the back of their minds that they should network their computers but haven't a clue about how to start or where to begin.

Do you often burn a spreadsheet file to a CD-R disc just so you can give it to someone else in your office? Are you frustrated because you can't use the fancy color laser printer that's on the financial secretary's computer? Do you wait in line to use the computer that has the customer database? You need a network!

Or maybe you already have a network, but you have just one problem: They promised that the network would make your life easier, but instead it has turned your computing life upside down. Just when you had this computer thing figured out, someone popped into your office, hooked up a cable, and said, "Happy networking!" Makes you want to scream.

Either way, you've found the right book. Help is here, within these humble pages.

This book talks about networks in everyday — and often irreverent — terms. The language is friendly; you don't need a graduate education to get through it. And the occasional potshot helps unseat the hallowed and sacred traditions of networkdom, bringing just a bit of fun to an otherwise dry subject. The goal is to bring the lofty precepts of networking down to earth, where you can touch them and squeeze them and say, "What's the big deal? I can do this!"

About This Book

This isn't the kind of book you pick up and read from start to finish, as if it were a cheap novel. If I ever see you reading it at the beach, I'll kick sand in your face. This book is more like a reference, the kind of book you can pick up, turn to just about any page, and start reading. It has 29 chapters, each one covering a specific aspect of networking — such as printing on the network, hooking up network cables, or setting up security so that bad guys can't break in. Just turn to the chapter you're interested in and start reading.

Each chapter is divided into self-contained chunks, all related to the major theme of the chapter. For example, the chapter on hooking up the network cable contains nuggets like these:

- ✔ What is Ethernet?
- ✔ All about cable
- ✔ To shield or not to shield
- ✔ Wall jacks and patch panels
- ✔ Hubs and switches

You don't have to memorize anything in this book. It's a need-to-know book: You pick it up when you need to know something. Need to know what 100BaseT is? Pick up the book. Need to know how to create good passwords? Pick up the book. Otherwise, put it down and get on with your life.

How to Use This Book

This book works like a reference. Start with the topic you want to find out about. Look for it in the table of contents or in the index to get going. The table of contents is detailed enough that you should be able to find most of the topics you're looking for. If not, turn to the index, where you can find even more detail.

After you find your topic in the table of contents or the index, turn to the area of interest and read as much as you need or want. Then close the book and get on with it.

Of course, this book is loaded with information, so if you want to take a brief excursion into your topic, you're more than welcome. If you want to know the big security picture, read the whole chapter on security. If you just want to know how to create a decent password, read just the section on passwords. You get the idea.

If you need to type something, you see the text you need to type like this: **Type this stuff**. In this example, you type **Type this stuff** at the keyboard and then press Enter. An explanation usually follows, just in case you're scratching your head and grunting, "Huh?"

Whenever I describe a message or information that you see on the screen, I present it this way:

```
A message from your friendly network
```

This book rarely directs you elsewhere for information — just about everything that you need to know about networks is right here. If you find the need for additional information, plenty of other _For Dummies_ books can help. If you have a networking question that isn't covered in this book, allow me to suggest my own _Networking All-in-One Desk Reference For Dummies,_ 2nd Edition (Wiley) — this much-expanded reference book goes deeper into specific network operating systems and TCP/IP protocols. You can also find plenty of other _For Dummies_ books that cover just about every operating system and application program known to humanity.

What You Don't Need to Read

Aside from the topics you can use right away, much of this book is skippable. I carefully placed extra-technical information in self-contained sidebars and clearly marked them so that you can steer clear of them. Don't read this stuff unless you're really into technical explanations and want to know a little of what's going on behind the scenes. Don't worry: My feelings won't be hurt if you don't read every word.

Foolish Assumptions

I'm making only two assumptions about who you are: You're someone who works with a PC, and you either have a network or you're thinking about getting one. I hope that you know (and are on speaking terms with) someone who knows more about computers than you do. My goal is to decrease your reliance on that person, but don't throw away his or her phone number yet.

Is this book useful for Macintosh users? Absolutely. Although the bulk of this book is devoted to showing you how to link Windows-based computers to form a network, you can find information about how to network Macintosh computers as well.

Windows Vista? Gotcha covered. You'll find plenty of information about how to network with the latest and greatest Microsoft operating system.

How This Book Is Organized

Inside this book, you find chapters arranged in seven parts. Each chapter breaks down into sections that cover various aspects of the chapter's main subject. The chapters are in a logical sequence, so reading them in order (if you want to read the whole thing) makes sense. But the book is modular enough that you can pick it up and start reading at any point.

Here's the lowdown on what's in each of the seven parts.

Part I: Let's Network!

The chapters in this part present a layperson's introduction to what networking is all about. This part is a good place to start if you're clueless about what a network is and why you're suddenly expected to use one. It's also a great place to start if you're a hapless network user who doesn't give a whit about "optimizing network performance" but you want to know what the network is and how to get the most out of it.

The best thing about this part is that it focuses on how to use a network without getting into the technical details of setting up a network or maintaining a network server. In other words, this part is aimed at ordinary network users who have to know how to get along with a network.

Part II: Building Your Own Network

Uh-oh. The boss just gave you an ultimatum: Get a network up and running by Friday or pack your things. The chapters in this section cover everything you need to know to build a network, from picking the network operating system to installing the cable.

Part III: Getting Connected

After you get a basic network up and running, the chapters in this part show you how to connect it to the world. You find out all about safely connecting your network to the Internet, setting up an e-mail server, and even connecting your network to computers at home and on the road.

Part IV: Network Management For Dummies

I hope that the job of managing the network doesn't fall on your shoulders, but in case it does, the chapters in this part can help you out. You find out all about backup, security, performance, dusting, mopping, changing the oil, and all the other stuff that network managers have to do.

Part V: Protecting Your Network

This part is all about network security: backing up your data, protecting your network from evil people who want to break your network's back, and hardening your network against threats, such as viruses and spyware.

Part VI: Beyond Windows

There's more to networking than Windows. That's why this part focuses on the two most popular alternatives: Linux and Macintosh.

Part VII: The Part of Tens

This wouldn't be a *For Dummies* book without a collection of lists of interesting snippets: ten networking commandments, ten things you should keep in your closet, ten big network mistakes, and more!

Icons Used in This Book

Those nifty little pictures in the margin aren't there just to pretty up the place. They also have practical functions:

Hold it — technical details lurk just around the corner. Read on only if you have a pocket protector.

Pay special attention to this icon; it lets you know that some particularly useful tidbit is at hand — perhaps a shortcut or a little-used command that pays off big.

Did I tell you about the memory course I took?

Danger, Will Robinson! This icon highlights information that may help you avert disaster.

Where to Go from Here

Yes, you can get there from here. With this book in hand, you're ready to plow right through the rugged networking terrain. Browse through the table of contents and decide where you want to start. Be bold! Be courageous! Be adventurous! Above all, have fun!

Part I
Let's Network!

The 5th Wave   By Rich Tennant

"Oh, Arthur is very careful about security on the Web. He never goes online in the same room on consecutive days."

In this part . . .

One day the Network Thugs barge into your office and shove a gun in your face. "Don't move until we hook you up to the network!" one of them says while the other one connects one end of a suspicious-looking cable to the back of your computer and shoves the other end into a hole in the wall. "It's done," they say as they start to leave. "Now, don't you say nuttin' to nobody — or we'll be back!"

If this has happened to you, you'll appreciate the chapters in this part. They provide a gentle introduction to computer networks written especially for the reluctant network user.

What if you don't have a network yet and you're the one who's supposed to do the installing? Then the chapters in this part clue you in to what a network is all about. That way, you're prepared for the (unfortunately more technical) chapters in Part II and beyond.

Chapter 1

Networks Will Not Take Over the World, and Other Network Basics

In This Chapter
▶ Getting a handle on networks
▶ Considering why networking is useful (and is everywhere)
▶ Telling the difference between servers and clients
▶ Looking under the hood at the network operating system
▶ Asking "How does it work when a network works if a network works for me?" (Say what?)
▶ Assessing how networks change computing life
▶ Identifying (and offering sympathy to) the network administrator
▶ Comparing servers to clients: What have they got that you don't got?

Computer networks get a bad rap in the movies. In the *Terminator* movies, Skynet (a computer network of the future) takes over the planet, builds deadly terminator robots, and sends them back through time to kill everyone unfortunate enough to have the name Sarah Connor. In *The Matrix* movies, a vast and powerful computer network enslaves humans and keeps them trapped in a simulation of the real world. And in one of Matthew Broderick's first movies, *War Games,* a computer whiz kid nearly starts World War III by connecting to a Defense Department network and playing the game Global Thermonuclear War.

Fear not. These bad networks exist only in the dreams of science fiction writers. Real-world networks are much more calm and predictable. They don't think for themselves, they can't evolve into something you don't want them to be, and they won't hurt you — even if your name is Sarah Connor.

Now that you're over your fear of networks, you're ready to breeze through this chapter. It's a gentle, even superficial, introduction to computer networks, with a slant toward the concepts that can help you use a computer that's attached to a network. This chapter goes easy on the details; the detailed and boring stuff comes later.

What Is a Network?

A *network* is nothing more than two or more computers connected by a cable (or in some cases by radio connection) so that they can exchange information.

Of course, computers can exchange information in ways other than networks. Most of us have used what computer nerds call the *sneakernet.* That's where you copy a file to a diskette, a CD-RW disc, or a removable flash drive, and then walk the data over to someone else's computer. (The term *sneakernet* is typical of computer nerds' feeble attempts at humor, and why not? As a way to transfer information, sneakernet *is* feeble.)

The whole problem with the sneakernet is that it's slow — plus, it wears a trail in your carpet. One day, some penny-pinching computer geeks discovered that connecting computers with cables was cheaper than replacing the carpet every six months. Thus, the modern computer network was born.

You can create a computer network by hooking together all the computers in your office with cables and using the computer's *network interface* (an electronic circuit that resides inside your computer and has a special jack on the computer's backside). Then you set up your computer's operating system software to make the network *work,* and — *voilà* — you have a working network. That's all there is to it.

If you don't want to mess with cables, you can create a *wireless network* instead. In a wireless network, each computer is equipped with a special wireless network adapter that has little rabbit-ear antennas. Thus, the computers can communicate with each other without the need for cables.

Figure 1-1 shows a typical network with four computers. You can see that all four computers are connected by a network cable to a central network device: the *hub.* You can also see that Ward's computer has a fancy laser printer attached to it. Because of the network, June, Wally, and the Beaver can also use this laser printer. (Also, you can see that the Beaver stuck yesterday's bubble gum to the back of his computer. Although the bubble gum isn't recommended, it shouldn't adversely affect the network.)

Computer networking has its own, strange vocabulary. Fortunately, you don't have to know every esoteric networking term. Here are a few basic buzzwords to get you by:

- **LAN:** Networks are often called LANs. The acronym *LAN* stands for *local-area network.* It's the first *TLA,* or *three-letter acronym,* that you see in this book. You don't really need to remember it, or any of the many TLAs that follow. In fact, the only three-letter acronym you need to remember is TLA.

- **FLA:** You may guess that a four-letter acronym is an *FLA.* Wrong! A four-letter acronym is an *ETLA,* which stands for *extended three-letter* *acronym.* (After all, it just wouldn't be right if the acronym for *four-letter acronym* had only three letters.)

✔ **On the network:** Every computer connected to the network is said to be *on the network*. The technical term (which you can forget) for a computer that's on the network is a *node*.

✔ **Online:** When a computer is turned on and can access the network, the computer is said to be *online*. When a computer can't access the network, it's *offline*. A computer can be offline for several reasons. The computer can be turned off, the user may have disabled the network connection, the computer may be broken, the cable that connects it to the network can be unplugged, or a wad of gum can be jammed into the disk drive.

✔ **Up:** When a computer is turned on and working properly, it's said to be *up*. When a computer is turned off, broken, or being serviced, it's said to be *down*. Turning off a computer is sometimes called *taking it down*. Turning it back on is sometimes called *bringing it up*.

Don't confuse local-area networks with the Internet. The *Internet* is a huge amalgamation of computer networks strewn about the entire planet. Networking the computers in your home or office so that they can share information with one another and connecting your computer to the worldwide Internet are two separate, but related, tasks. If you want to use your local-area network to connect your computers to the Internet, you can consult Chapter 10 for instructions.

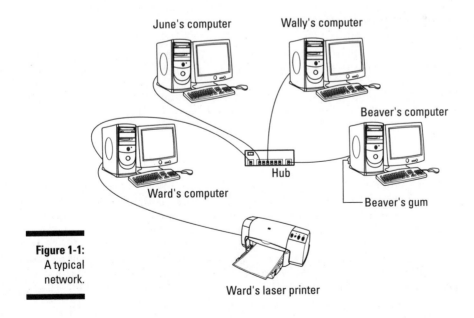

Figure 1-1:
A typical
network.

Why Bother with a Network?

Frankly, computer networks are a bit of a pain to set up. So, why bother? Because the benefits of having a network make the pain of setting up one bearable. You don't have to be a PhD to understand the benefits of networking. In fact, you learned everything you need to know in kindergarten: Networks are all about sharing. Specifically, networks are about sharing three things: files, resources, and programs.

Sharing files

Networks enable you to share information with other computers on the network. Depending on how you set up your network, you can share files with your network friends in several different ways. You can send a file from your computer directly to a friend's computer by attaching the file to an e-mail message and then mailing it. Or, you can let your friend access your computer over the network so that your friend can retrieve the file directly from your hard drive. Yet another method is to copy the file to a disk on another computer and then tell your friend where you put the file so that he can retrieve it later. One way or the other, the data travels to your friend's computer over the network cable, and not on a floppy disk, CD-RW, or flash drive, as it would in a sneakernet.

Sharing resources

You can set up certain computer resources — such as hard drives or printers — so that all computers on the network can access them. For example, the laser printer attached to Ward's computer in Figure 1-1 is a *shared resource,* which means that anyone on the network can use it. Without the network, June, Wally, and the Beaver would have to buy their own laser printers.

Hard drives can be shared resources, too. In fact, you must set up a hard drive as a shared resource to share files with other users. Suppose that Wally wants to share a file with the Beaver, and a shared hard drive has been set up on June's computer. All Wally has to do is copy his file to the shared hard drive in June's computer and tell the Beaver where he put it. Then when the Beaver gets around to it, he can copy the file from June's computer to his own (unless, of course, Eddie Haskell deletes the file first).

You can share other resources, too, such as an Internet connection. In fact, sharing an Internet connection is one of the main reasons many networks are set up.

Sharing programs

Rather than keep separate copies of programs on each person's computer, putting programs on a drive that everyone shares is sometimes best. For example, if ten computer users all use a particular program, you can purchase and install ten copies of the program — one for each computer. Or, you can purchase a ten-user license for the program and then install just one copy of the program on a shared drive. Each of the ten users can then access the program from the shared hard drive.

In most cases, however, running a shared copy of a program over the network is unacceptably slow. A more common way of using a network to share programs is to copy the program's installation disks or CDs to a shared network drive. Then you can use that copy to install a separate copy of the program on each user's local hard drive. For example, Microsoft Office enables you to do this if you purchase a license from Microsoft for each computer on which you install Office.

The advantage of installing Office from a shared network drive is that you don't have to lug around the installation disks or CDs to each user's computer. And, the system administrator can customize the network installation so that the software is installed the same way on each user's computer. (However, these benefits are significant only for larger networks. If your network has fewer than about ten computers, you're probably better off installing the program separately on each computer directly from the installation disks or CDs.)

Remember that purchasing a single-user copy of a program and then putting it on a shared network drive — so that everyone on the network can access it — is illegal. If five people use the program, you need to either purchase five copies of the program or purchase a *network license* that specifically allows five or more users.

Another benefit of networking is that networks enable computer users to communicate with one another over the network. The most obvious way networks allow computer users to communicate is by passing messages back and forth, using e-mail or instant-messaging programs. Networks also offer other ways to communicate: For example, you can hold online meetings over the network. Network users who have inexpensive video cameras *(Webcams)* attached to their computers can have videoconferences. You can even play a friendly game of Hearts over a network — during your lunch break, of course.

Servers and Clients

The network computer that contains the hard drives, printers, and other resources that are shared with other network computers is a *server.* This term comes up repeatedly, so you have to remember it. Write it on the back of your left hand.

Any computer that's not a server is a *client.* You have to remember this term, too. Write it on the back of your right hand.

Only two kinds of computers are on a network: servers and clients. Look at your left hand and then look at your right hand. Don't wash your hands until you memorize these terms.

The distinction between servers and clients in a network has parallels in sociology — in effect, a sort of class distinction between the "haves" and "have-nots" of computer resources:

- ✔ Usually, the most powerful and expensive computers in a network are the servers. There's a good technical reason: Every user on the network shares the server's resources.

- ✔ The cheaper and less powerful computers in a network are the clients. *Clients* are the computers used by individual users for everyday work. Because clients' resources don't have to be shared, they don't have to be as fancy.

- ✔ Most networks have more clients than servers. For example, a network with ten clients can probably get by with one server.

- ✔ In many networks, a clean line of demarcation exists between servers and clients. In other words, a computer functions as either a server or a client, and not both. For the sake of an efficient network, a server can't become a client, nor can a client become a server.

- ✔ Other (usually smaller) networks can be more evenhanded by allowing any computer in the network to be a server and allowing any computer to be both server and client at the same time.

Dedicated Servers and Peers

In some networks, a server computer is a server computer and nothing else. It's dedicated to the sole task of providing shared resources, such as hard drives and printers, to be accessed by the network client computers. This type of server is a *dedicated server* because it can perform no other task than network services.

Some smaller networks take an alternative approach by enabling any computer on the network to function as both a client and a server. Thus, any computer can share its printers and hard drives with other computers on the network. And, while a computer is working as a server, you can still use that same computer for other functions, such as word processing. This type of network is a *peer-to-peer network* because all the computers are thought of as *peers,* or equals.

Here are some points to ponder concerning the differences between dedicated server networks and peer-to-peer networks while you're walking the dog tomorrow morning:

✔ Peer-to-peer networking features are built into Windows. Thus, if your computer runs Windows, you don't have to buy any additional software to turn your computer into a server. All you have to do is enable the Windows server features.

✔ The network server features that are built into desktop versions of Windows (such as Windows XP and Vista) aren't efficient because these versions of Windows weren't designed primarily to be network servers.

If you dedicate a computer to the task of being a full-time server, use a special network operating system rather than the standard Windows operating system. A *network operating system,* also known as a *NOS,* is specially designed to handle networking functions efficiently.

- The most commonly used network operating systems are the server versions of Windows.

  At the time of publication, the current server version of Windows was *Windows Server 2003,* and a newer version, probably to be called *Windows Server 2007,* was on the way.

- Other network operating systems include *Linux* and *Novell NetWare.*

✔ Many networks are both peer-to-peer *and* dedicated-server networks at the same time. These networks have

- At least one *server* computer that runs a NOS, such as Windows Server 2003.

- *Client* computers that use the server features of Windows to share their resources with the network.

✔ Besides being dedicated, your servers should also be sincere.

What Makes a Network Tick?

To use a network, you don't really have to know much about how it works. Still, you may feel a little bit better about using the network if you realize that it doesn't work by voodoo. A network may seem like magic, but it isn't. The following list describes the inner workings of a typical network:

- ✔ **Network interface card:** Inside any computer attached to a network is a special electronic circuit card: the *network interface card.* The TLA for network interface card is *NIC.*

Using your network late into the evening isn't the same as watching NIC at night. If the network is set up to use that time to update software and back up data, the NIC has to be robust enough to handle all-day-all-night use.

Although you can also use an external network interface that connects to the computer by using the computer's USB (universal serial bus) port, most networked computers use a built-in network interface card.

Nearly all computers built these days have a network interface built into the computer's motherboard. This network interface is still commonly called the NIC, even though it isn't technically a separate card.

- ✔ **Network cable:** The network cable physically connects the computers. It plugs into the network interface card on the back of your computer.

Nearly all networks now use a type of cable that looks something like telephone cable. However, appearances can be deceiving. Most phone systems are wired using a lower grade of cable that doesn't work for networks. For a computer network, each pair of wires in the cable must be twisted in a certain way. That's why this type of cable is called *twisted-pair cable.* (Standard phone cable doesn't do the twist.)

For the complete lowdown on networking cables, refer to Chapter 5.

You can do away with network cable by creating a wireless network, although that option has some challenges of its own. For more information about wireless networking, see Chapter 9.

- ✔ **Network switch:** Networks built with twisted-pair cabling require one or more switches. A *switch* is a box with a bunch of cable connectors. Each computer on the network is connected by cable to the switch. The switch, in turn, connects all the computers to each other.

In the early days of twisted-pair networking, devices known as *hubs* were used rather than switches. The term *hub* is sometimes used to refer to switches, but true hubs went out of style sometime around the turn of the century.

- ✔ **Network software:** Of course, the software makes the network work. To make any network work, a whole bunch of software has to be set up just right. For peer-to-peer networking with Windows, you have to play with the Control Panel to get networking to work. And, a network operating system (such as Windows Server 2003) requires a substantial amount of tweaking to get it to work just right.

For more information about choosing which network software to use for your network, refer to Chapter 7.

It's Not a Personal Computer Anymore!

If I had to choose one point that I want you to remember from this chapter more than anything else, it's this: After you hook up your personal computer (PC) to a network, it's not a "personal" computer anymore. You are now part of a network of computers, and in a way, you've given up one of the key concepts that made PCs so successful in the first place: independence.

I got my start in computers back in the days when mainframe computers ruled the roost. *Mainframe computers* are big, complex machines that used to fill entire rooms and had to be cooled with chilled water. My first computer was a water-cooled Binford Power-Proc Model 2000. Argh, argh, argh. (I'm not making up the part about the water. A plumber was often required to install a mainframe computer. In fact, the really big ones were cooled by liquid nitrogen. I *am* making up the part about the Binford 2000.)

Mainframe computers required staffs of programmers and operators in white lab coats just to keep them going. The mainframes had to be carefully managed. A whole bureaucracy grew up around managing them.

Mainframe computers used to be the dominant computers in the workplace. Personal computers changed all that: They took the computing power out of the big computer room and put it on the user's desktop, where it belongs. PCs severed the tie to the centralized control of the mainframe computer. With a PC, a user could look at the computer and say, "This is mine — all mine!" Mainframes still exist, but they're not nearly as popular as they once were.

Networks are changing everything all over again. In a way, it's a change back to the mainframe-computer way of thinking: central location, distributed resources. True, the network isn't housed in the basement and doesn't have to be installed by a plumber. But you can no longer think of "your" PC as your own. You're part of a network — and, like the mainframe, the network has to be carefully managed.

Here are several ways in which a network robs you of your independence:

> ✔ **You can't just indiscriminately delete files from the network.** They may not be yours.

✔ **You're forced to be concerned about network security.** For example, a server computer has to know who you are before it lets you access its files. So, you have to know your user ID and password to access the network. This precaution prevents some 15-year-old kid from hacking his way into your office network by using its Internet connection and stealing all your computer games.

✔ **You may have to wait for shared resources.** Just because Wally sends something to Ward's printer doesn't mean that it immediately starts to print. The Beav may have sent a two-hour print job before that. Wally just has to wait.

✔ **You may have to wait for access to documents.** You may try to retrieve an Excel spreadsheet file from a network drive, only to discover that someone else is using it. Like Wally, you just have to wait.

✔ **You don't have unlimited storage space.** If you copy a 600MB database file to a server's drive, you may get calls later from angry co-workers complaining that no room is left on the server's drive for their important files.

✔ **Your files can become infected from viruses given to you by someone over the network.** You may then accidentally infect other network users.

✔ **You have to be careful about saving sensitive files on the server.** If you write an angry note about your boss and save it on the server's hard drive, your boss may find the memo and read it.

✔ **The server computer must be up and running at all times.** For example, if you turn Ward's computer into a server computer, Ward can't turn his computer off when he's out of the office. If he does, you can't access the files stored on his computer.

✔ **If your computer is a server, you can't just turn it off when you're finished using it.** Someone else may be accessing a file on your hard drive or printing on your printer.

Why does Ward always get the best printer? If *Leave It to Beaver* were made today, I would bet that the good printer would be on June's computer.

The Network Administrator

Because so much can go wrong — even with a simple network — designating one person as the *network administrator* is important. This way, someone is responsible for making sure that the network doesn't fall apart or get out of control.

The network administrator doesn't have to be a technical genius. In fact, some of the best network administrators are complete idiots when it comes to technical stuff. What's important is that the administrator is organized. That person's job is to make sure that plenty of space is available on the file server, that the file server is backed up regularly, that new employees can access the network, and other tasks.

The network administrator's job also includes solving basic problems that the users themselves can't solve — and knowing when to call in an expert when something really bad happens. It's a tough job, but somebody's got to do it. Here are a few tips that might help:

- Part IV of this book is devoted entirely to the hapless network administrator. So, if you're nominated, read the chapters in that part. If you're lucky enough that someone *else* is nominated, celebrate by buying her a copy of this book.

- In small companies, picking the network administrator by drawing straws is common. The person who draws the shortest straw loses and becomes administrator.

- Of course, the network administrator can't be a *complete* technical idiot. I was lying about that. (For those of you in Congress, the word is *testifying.*) I exaggerated to make the point that organizational skills are more important than technical skills. The network administrator needs to know how to do various maintenance tasks. Although this knowledge requires at least a little technical know-how, the organizational skills are more important.

What Have They Got That You Don't Got?

With all this technical stuff to worry about, you may begin to wonder whether you're smart enough to use your computer after it's attached to the network. Let me assure you that you are. If you're smart enough to buy this book because you know that you need a network, you're more than smart enough to use the network after it's put in. You're also smart enough to install and manage a network yourself. It isn't rocket science.

I know people who use networks all the time. They're no smarter than you are, but they do have one thing that you don't have: a certificate. And so, by the powers vested in me by the International Society for the Computer Impaired, I present you with the certificate in Figure 1-2, confirming that you've earned the coveted title Certified Network Dummy, better known as CND. This title is considered much more prestigious in certain circles than the more stodgy CNE or MCSE badges worn by real network experts.

Congratulations, and go in peace.

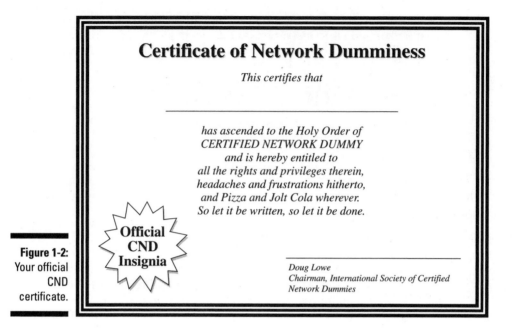

Certificate of Network Dumminess

This certifies that

_____

has ascended to the Holy Order of
CERTIFIED NETWORK DUMMY
and is hereby entitled to
all the rights and privileges therein,
headaches and frustrations hitherto,
and Pizza and Jolt Cola wherever.
So let it be written, so let it be done.

Official
CND
Insignia

_____

Doug Lowe
Chairman, International Society of Certified
Network Dummies

Figure 1-2:
Your official
CND
certificate.

Chapter 2

Life on the Network

In This Chapter

▶ Using local resources and network resources

▶ Playing the name game

▶ Mapping network drives

▶ Logging on to the network

▶ Using shared folders

▶ Using a network printer

▶ Logging off the network

After you hook up your PC to a network, it's not an island any more — separated from the rest of the world like some kind of isolationist fanatic waving a "Don't tread on me" flag. The network connection changes your PC forever. Now your computer is part of a system, connected to other computers on the network. You have to worry about annoying network details, such as using local and shared resources, logging on and accessing network drives, using network printers, logging off, and who knows what else.

Oh, bother.

This chapter brings you up to speed on what living with a computer network is like. Unfortunately, this chapter gets a little technical at times, so you may need your pocket protector.

Distinguishing between Local Resources and Network Resources

In case you don't catch this statement in Chapter 1, one of the most important differences between using an isolated computer and using a network computer lies in the distinction between local resources and network resources. *Local resources* are items, such as hard drives, printers, and CD-ROM or DVD drives, that are connected directly to your computer. You can use local resources whether you're connected to the network or not. *Network resources,* on the other hand, are the hard drives, printers, modems, and CD-ROM or DVD drives that are connected to the network's server computers. You can use network resources only after your computer is connected to the network.

The whole trick to using a computer network is to know which resources are *local* resources (they belong to you) and which are *network* resources (they belong to the network). In most networks, your C drive is a local drive. If a printer is sitting next to your PC, it's probably a local printer. You can do anything you want with these resources without affecting the network or other users on the network (as long as the local resources aren't shared on the network).

✔ You can't tell just by looking at a resource whether it's a local resource or a network resource. The printer that sits right next to your computer is probably your local printer, but then again, it may be a network printer. The same statement is true for hard drives: The hard drive in your PC is probably your own, but it may be a network drive, which can be used by others on the network.

✔ Because dedicated network servers are full of resources, you may say that they're not only dedicated (and sincere) but also resourceful. (Groan. Sorry, this is yet another in a tireless series of bad computer-nerd puns.)

What's in a Name?

Just about everything on a computer network has a name: The computers themselves have names, the people that use the computers have names, the hard drives and printers that can be shared on the network have names, and the network itself has a name. Knowing all the names used on your network isn't essential, but you do need to know some of them.

Here are some additional details about network names:

✔ **Every person who can use the network has a *username* (sometimes called a *user ID*).** You need to know your username to log on to the network. You also need to know the usernames of your buddies, especially if you want to steal their files or send them nasty notes.

You can find more information about usernames and logging on in the section "Logging On to the Network," later in this chapter.

✔ **Letting folks on the network use their first names as their usernames is tempting but not a good idea.** Even in a small office, you eventually run into a conflict. (And, what about Mrs. McCave — made famous by Dr. Seuss — who had 23 children and named them all Dave?)

Create a consistent way of creating usernames. For example, you may use your first name plus the first two letters of your last name. Then Wally's username is `wallycl`, and Beaver's is `beavercl`. Or, you may use the first letter of your first name followed by your complete last name. Then Wally's username is `wcleaver`, and Beaver's is `bcleaver`. (In most networks, capitalization doesn't matter in usernames. Thus, `bcleaver` is the same as `BCleaver`.)

✔ **Every computer on the network must have a unique computer name.**

You don't have to know the names of all the computers on the network, but it helps if you know your own computer's name and the names of any server computers you need to access.

The computer's name is sometimes the same as the username of the person who uses the computer, but that's usually a bad idea because in many companies, people come and go more often than computers. Sometimes the names indicate the physical location of the computer, such as `office-12` or `back-room`. Server computers often have names that reflect the group that uses the server most, like `acctng-server` or `cad-server`.

Some network nerds like to assign techie-sounding names, like `BL3K5-87a`. And some like to use names from science fiction movies — `HAL`, `Colossus`, `M5`, and `Data` come to mind. Cute names like `Herbie` aren't allowed. (However, `Tigger` and `Pooh` are entirely acceptable — recommended, in fact. Tiggers like networks.)

Usually, the sensible approach to computer naming is to use names that have numbers, such as `computer001` or `computer002`.

✔ **Network resources, such as shared disk folders and printers, have names.** For example, a network server may have two printers, named `laser` and `inkjet` (to indicate the type of printer), and two shared disk folders, named `AccountingData` and `MarketingData`.

✔ **Server-based networks have a username for the network administrator.**

If you log on with a username that has administrator's rights, you can do anything you want: add new users, define new network resources, change Wally's password — anything. The administrator's username is usually something clever, such as `Administrator`.

✔ **The network itself has a name.**

The Windows world has two basic types of networks:

- *Domain networks* are the norm for large corporate environments that have dedicated servers with IT staff to maintain them.

- *Workgroup networks* are more common in homes or in small offices that don't have dedicated servers or IT staff.

A domain network is known by — you guessed it — a *domain name*. And a workgroup network is identified by — drum roll, please — a *workgroup name*. Regardless of which type of network you use, you need to know this name to gain access to the network.

Logging On to the Network

To use network resources, you must connect your computer to the network, and you must go through the supersecret process of logging on. The purpose of *logging on* is to let the network know who you are so that it can decide whether you're one of the good guys.

Logging on is a little bit like cashing a check — the process requires two forms of identification:

✔ **Your *username:*** The name by which the network knows you.

Your username is usually some variation of your real name, like Beav for the Beaver. Everyone who uses the network must have a username.

✔ **Your *password:*** A secret word that only you and the network know. If you type the correct password, the network believes that you are who you say you are.

Every user has a different password, and the password should be a secret.

In the early days of computer networking, you had to type a logon command at a stark MS-DOS prompt and then supply your user ID and password. Nowadays, the glory of Windows is that you get to log on to the network through a special network logon dialog box that appears when you start your computer. Figure 2-1 shows the Windows XP version of this dialog box.

Here are some more logon points to ponder:

✔ The terms *user ID* and *logon name* are sometimes used instead of *username*. They mean the same thing.

✔ As long as we're talking about words that mean the same thing, *log in* and *log on* mean the same thing, as do (respectively) *log out* and *log off* as ways of saying, "I'm outta here." Although you see both out there in the world, this book uses *log on* and *log off* throughout — and if there's any exception, the book says why and grouses about it a bit.

✔ As far as the network's concerned, you and your computer aren't the same thing. Your username refers to you, not to your computer. That's why you have a username, and your computer has a computer name. You can log on to the network by using your username from any computer that's attached to the network. Other users can log on at your computer by using their own usernames.

When others log on at your computer by using their own usernames, they can't access any of your network files that are protected by your password. However, they *can* access any local files that you haven't protected. Be careful which people you allow to use your computer.

✔ Windows XP and Vista have a cool feature that displays icons for each of the users registered on your computer. When this feature is enabled, you can log on by clicking your name's icon and then typing your password.

✔ If you're logging on to a domain network, the Windows XP Logon dialog box has a field in which you can enter the domain name you want to log on to. Normally, a suitable default value appears for the domain name, so you can safely ignore this field. If not, your network administrator will be happy to tell you how to enter this information.

✔ Windows Vista doesn't include a field in which you can enter the domain name. Instead, you must type the domain name before your username, separated from it by a backslash. For example:

```
lowewriter\dlowe
```

Here, the domain name is `lowewriter`, and the username is `dlowe`.

✔ Your computer may be set up so that it logs you on automatically whenever you turn it on. In that case, you don't have to type your username and password. This setup makes the task of logging on more convenient but takes the sport out of it. And, it's a terrible idea if you're the least bit worried about bad guys getting into your network or personal files.

✔ Guard your password with your life. I'd tell you mine, but then I'd have to shoot you.

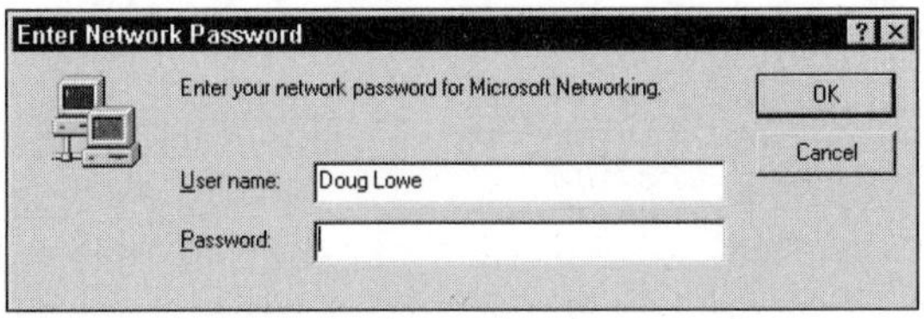

Figure 2-1:
You have to enter your user ID and password to access the network.

Understanding Shared Folders

Long ago, in the days Before Network (B.N.), your computer probably had just one hard drive, known as C: drive. Maybe it had two — C: and D:. The second drive might be another hard disk, or possibly a CD-ROM or DVD-ROM drive. Even to this day, the descendants of those drives are physically located inside your PC. They're your *local drives*.

Now that you're on a network, however, you probably have access to drives that aren't located inside your PC but are located instead in one of the other computers on the network. These network drives can be located on a dedicated server computer or, in the case of a peer-to-peer network, on another client computer.

In some cases, you can access an entire network drive over the network. But in most cases, you can't access the entire drive. Instead, you can access only certain folders (*directories,* in old MS-DOS lingo) on the network drives. Either way, the shared drives or folders are known in Windows terminology as *shared folders*. A shared folder is commonly referred to as a *network drive* because the shared folder can be accessed as though it were a separate drive, complete with its own drive letter.

Shared folders can be set up with restrictions on how you can use them. For example, you may be granted full access to some shared folders so that you can copy files to or from them, delete files on them, or create or remove folders on them. On other shared folders, your access may be limited in certain ways. For example, you may be able to copy files to or from the shared folder but not delete files, edit files, or create new folders. You may also be asked to enter a password before you can access a protected folder. The amount of disk space you're allowed to use on a shared folder may also be limited. For more information about file-sharing restrictions, refer to Chapter 17.

In addition to accessing shared folders that reside on other people's computers, you can designate your computer as a server to enable other network users to access folders that you share. To find out how to share folders on your computer with other network users, see Chapter 3.

Four Good Uses for a Shared Folder

After you know which shared network folders are available, you may wonder what you're supposed to do with them. This section describes four good uses for a network folder.

Store files that everybody needs

A shared network folder is a good place to store files that more than one user needs to access. Without a network, you have to store a copy of the file on everyone's computer, and you have to worry about keeping the copies synchronized (which you can't do, no matter how hard you try). Or, you can keep the file on a disk and pass it around. Or, you can keep the file on one computer and play musical chairs — whenever someone needs to use the file, he goes to the computer that contains the file.

On a network, you can keep one copy of the file in a shared folder on the network, and everyone can access it.

Store your own files

You can also use a shared network folder as an extension of your own hard drive storage. For example, if you filled up all the free space on your hard drive with pictures, sounds, and movies that you downloaded from the Internet, but the network server has billions and billions of gigabytes of free space, you have all the drive space you need. Just store your files on the network drive!

Here are a few guidelines for storing files on network drives:

- ✔ Using the network drive for your own files works best if the network drive is set up for private storage that other users can't access. That way, you don't have to worry about the nosy guy down in Accounting who likes to poke around in other people's files.

- ✔ Don't overuse the network drive. Remember that other users have probably filled up their own hard drives, so they want to use the space on the network drive, too.

- ✔ Before you store personal files on a network drive, make sure that you have permission. A note from your mom will do.

- ✔ On domain networks, a drive (typically drive H) is commonly mapped to a user's home folder. The *home folder* is a network folder that's unique for each user. You can think of it as a network version of My Documents. If your network is set up with a home folder, you should use it rather than My Documents for any important work-related files. That's because the home folder is usually included in the network's daily backup schedule. In contrast, most networks do *not* back up data you store in My Documents.

Make a pit stop for files on their way to other users

"Hey, Wally, could you send me a copy of last month's baseball stats?"

"Sure, Beav." But how? If the baseball stats file resides on Wally's local drive, how does Wally send a copy of the file to Beaver's computer? Wally can do it by copying the file to a network folder. Then Beaver can copy the file to his local hard drive.

Here are some tips to keep in mind when you use a network drive to exchange files with other network users:

- **Remember to delete files that you saved to the network folder after they're picked up!** Otherwise, the network folder quickly fills up with unnecessary files.

- **Create a folder on the network drive specifically intended for holding files en route to other users.** Name this folder PITSTOP or something similar to suggest its function.

In many cases, it's easier to send files to other network users by e-mail than by using a network folder. Just send a message to the other network user and attach the file you want to share. The advantage of sending a file by e-mail is that you don't have to worry about details like where to leave the file on the server and who's responsible for deleting the file.

Back up your local hard drive

If enough drive space is available on the file server, you can use it to store backup copies of the files on your hard drive. Just copy the files that you want to back up to a shared network folder.

Obviously, if you copy *all* your data files to the network drive — and everybody else follows suit — it can quickly fill up. Check with the network manager before you start storing backup copies of your files on the server. The manager may have already set up a special network drive that's designed just for backups. And, if you're lucky, your network manager may be able to set up an automatic backup schedule for your important data so that you don't have to remember to back it up manually.

I hope that your network administrator also routinely backs up the contents of the network server's disk to tape. (Yes, *tape* — see Chapter 21 for details.) That way, if something happens to the network server, the data can be recovered from the backup tapes.

Oh, the Network Places You'll Go

Windows enables you to access network resources, such as shared folders, by browsing the network. In Windows XP, you do this by double-clicking the My Network Places icon that resides on your desktop. In Windows Vista, choose Network from the Start menu. Figure 2-2 shows the Vista version of the network browser.

Figure 2-2:
Browsing
the network
in Windows
Vista.

The network shown in Figure 2-2 consists of just two computers, named WK07-001 and LSERVER01, and a router named Linksys BEFW11S4 V2/V3. You can open either of the computers by double-clicking their icons to reveal a list of shared resources available on the computer. For example, Figure 2-3 shows the resources shared by the LSERVER01 computer.

You can also browse the network from any Windows application program. For example, you may be working with Microsoft Word 2007 and want to open a document file that's stored in a shared folder on your network. All you have to do is use the Open command to bring up the dialog box. (In Office 2003, this command is on the File menu. In Office 2007, you'll find it by clicking the Office button.) Choose Network in the list that appears in the pane on the left side of the Open dialog box to browse the network, as shown in Figure 2-4.

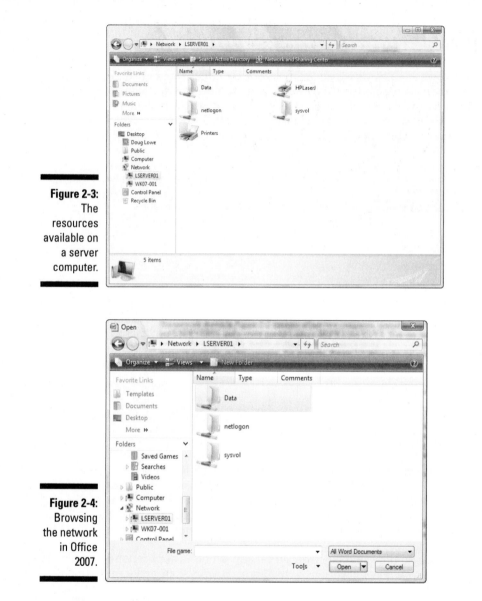

Figure 2-3:
The
resources
available on
a server
computer.

Figure 2-4:
Browsing
the network
in Office
2007.

If you're using Windows 95 or Windows 98, My Network Places is referred to as Network Neighborhood. When you call up the Network Neighborhood in Windows 95 or Windows 98, you're immediately greeted by a list of computers available on your network. You can then click one of the computers to access its shared drives and folders.

Mapping Network Drives

If you often access a particular shared folder, you may want to use the special trick known as *mapping* to access the shared folder more efficiently. Mapping assigns a drive letter to a shared folder. Then you can use the drive letter to access the shared folder as though it were a local drive. In this way, you can access the shared folder from any Windows program without having to browse the network.

For example, you can map a shared folder named Data on the server named LSERVER01 Files to drive K on your computer. Then, to access files stored in the shared Data folder, you look on drive K.

To map a shared folder to a drive letter in Windows Vista, follow these steps:

1. **Choose Start⇨Computer.**

   This step opens the Computer window.

2. **Click the Map Network Drive button located on the toolbar.**

   This action summons the Map Network Drive dialog box, as shown in Figure 2-5.

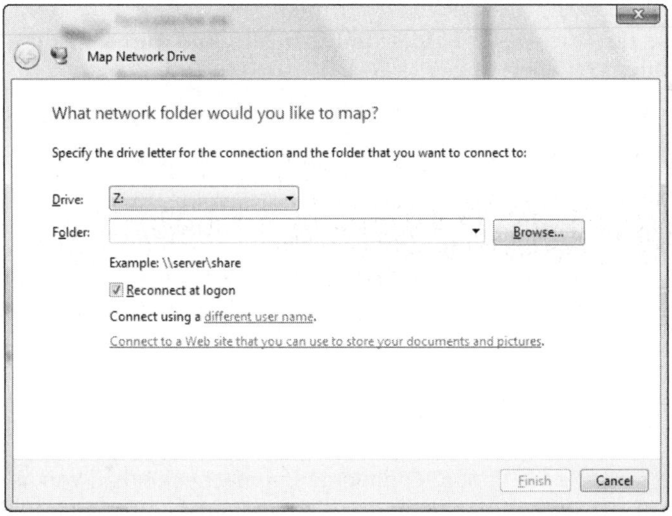

Figure 2-5:
The Map Network Drive dialog box.

3. **Change the drive letter in the Drive drop-down list, if you want.**

   You probably don't have to change the drive letter that Windows selects (in Figure 2-5, drive Z). If you're picky, though, you can select the drive letter from the Drive drop-down list.

4. **Click the Browse button.**

   This step summons the dialog box, as shown in Figure 2-6.

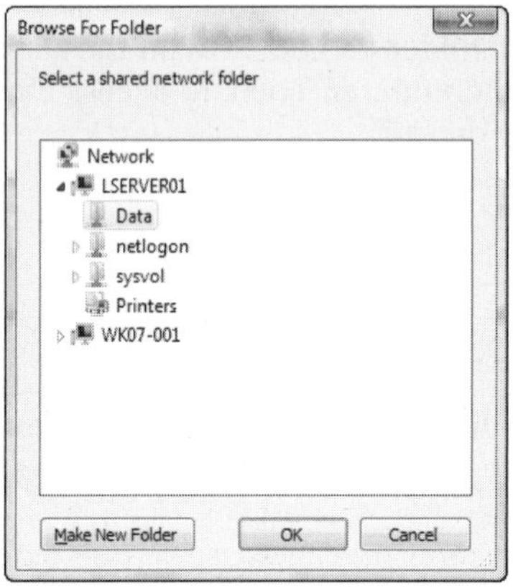

Browse For Folder

Select a shared network folder

- Network
  - LSERVER01
    - Data
    - netlogon
    - sysvol
    - Printers
  - WK07-001

Make New Folder   OK   Cancel

Figure 2-6:
Browsing
for the
folder to
map.

5. **Use the Browse for Folder dialog box to find and select the shared folder you want to use.**

   You can navigate to any shared folder on any computer in the network.

6. **Click OK.**

   The Browse for Folder dialog box is dismissed, and you return to the Map Network Drive dialog box (refer to Figure 2-5).

7. **If you want this network drive to be automatically mapped each time you log on to the network, select the Reconnect at Logon check box.**

   If you leave the Reconnect at Logon check box deselected, the drive letter is available only until you shut down Windows or log off the network. If you select this option, the network drive reconnects automatically each time you log on to the network.

   Be sure to select the Reconnect at Logon check box if you use the network drive often.

8. **Click OK.**

   You return to the Computer folder, as shown in Figure 2-7. Here, you can see the newly mapped network drive.

Figure 2-7:
The
Computer
folder
shows a
mapped
network
drive.

Your network administrator may have already set up your computer with one or more mapped network drives. If so, you can ask her to tell you which network drives have been mapped. Or, you can just open the Computer folder (My Computer on Windows XP) and have a look.

Here are a few additional tips:

✔ If you're using Windows XP, the procedure for mapping a network drive is similar to the one for Windows Vista. Start by opening My Computer and choosing Tools⇨Map Network drive. Then follow the preceding set of steps starting at Step 3.

✔ Assigning a drive letter to a network drive is called *mapping the drive,* or *linking the drive,* by network nerds. "Drive H is mapped to a network drive," they say.

✔ Network drive letters don't have to be assigned the same way for every computer on the network. For example, a network drive that's assigned drive letter H on your computer may be assigned drive letter Q on someone else's computer. In that case, your drive H and the other computer's drive Q refer to the same data. This arrangement can be confusing. If your network is set up this way, put pepper in your network administrator's coffee.

✔ Accessing a shared network folder through a mapped network drive is much faster than accessing the same folder by browsing the network. That's because Windows has to browse the entire network to list all available computers whenever you browse the network. In contrast, Windows doesn't have to browse the network to access a mapped network drive.

✓ If you select the Reconnect at Logon option for a mapped drive, you receive a warning message if the drive isn't available when you log on. In most cases, the problem is that the server computer isn't turned on. Sometimes, however, this message is caused by a broken network connection. For more information about fixing network problems such as this one, refer to Chapter 19.

Using a Network Printer

Using a network printer is much like using a network hard drive: You can print to a network printer from any Windows program by choosing the Print command to call up a Print dialog box from any program and choosing a network printer from the list of available printers. (In Office XP, this command is under the File menu. In Office 2007, you can reach it by clicking the Office button.)

Keep in mind, however, that printing on a network printer isn't exactly the same as printing on a local printer — you have to take turns. When you print on a local printer, you're the only one using it. When you print to a network printer, however, you are (in effect) standing in line behind other network users, waiting to share the printer. This line complicates the situation in several ways:

✓ **If several users print to the network printer at the same time, the network has to keep the print jobs separate from one another.** If it didn't, the result would be a jumbled mess, with your 168-page report getting mixed in with the payroll checks. That would be bad. Fortunately, the network takes care of this situation by using the fancy *print spooling* feature.

✓ **Network printing works on a first-come, first-served basis (unless you know some of the tricks that I discuss in Chapter 3).** Invariably, when I get in line at the hardware store, the person in front of me is trying to buy something that doesn't have a product code on it. I end up standing there for hours waiting for someone in Plumbing to pick up the phone for a price check. Network printing can be like that. If someone sends a two-hour print job to the printer before you send your half-page memo, you have to wait.

✓ **You may have access to a local printer and several network printers.** Before you were forced to use the network, your computer probably had just one printer attached to it. You may want to print some documents on your cheap (oops, I mean *local*) inkjet printer but use the network laser printer for important stuff. To do that, you have to find out how to use your programs' functions for switching printers.

Adding a network printer

Before you can print to a network printer, you have to configure your computer to access the network printer that you want to use. From the Start menu, open the Control Panel and then double-click the Printers icon. If your computer is already configured to work with a network printer, an icon for the network printer (see the icon in the margin) appears in the Printers folder. You can tell a network printer from a local printer by the shape of the printer icon. Network printer icons have a pipe attached to the bottom of the printer.

If you don't have a network printer configured for your computer, you can add one by using the Add Printer Wizard. Just follow these steps for Windows Vista:

1. **Choose Start⇨Control Panel and then double-click the Printers icon.**

2. **Click the Add a Printer button on the toolbar.**

   This step starts the Add Printer Wizard, as shown in Figure 2-8.

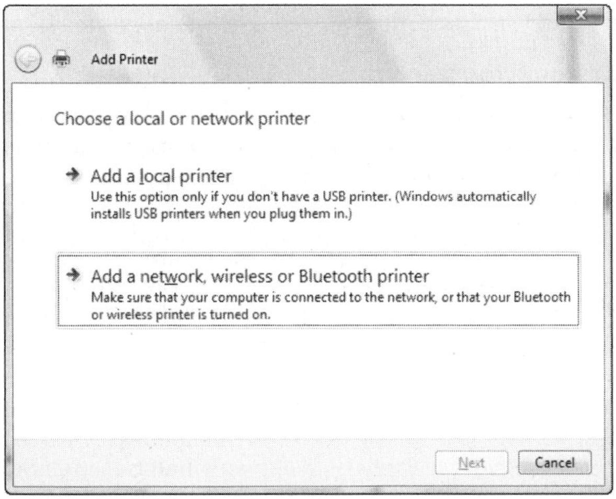

Figure 2-8:
The Add
Printer
Wizard
comes
to life.

3. **Select the Add a Network, Wireless or Bluetooth Printer option.**

   The wizard searches the network for available printers and displays a list of the printers it finds, as shown in Figure 2-9.

4. Click the printer you want to use.

If you can't find the printer you want to use, ask your network adminis-trator for the printer's UNC path, which is the name used to identify the printer on the network, or its IP address. Then click The Printer That I Want Isn't Listed and enter the UNC or IP address for the printer when prompted.

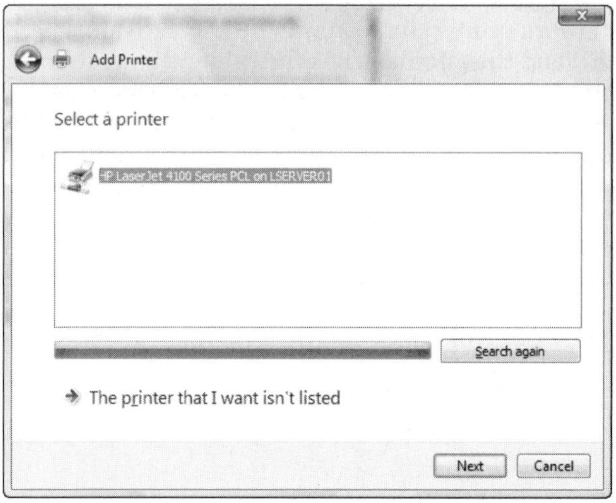

Figure 2-9:
The Add
Printer
Wizard asks
you to pick
a printer.

Add Printer

Select a printer

HP LaserJet 4100 Series PCL on LSERVER01

Search again

→ The printer that I want isn't listed

Next   Cancel

5. Click Next to add the printer.

The wizard copies to your computer the correct printer driver for the network printer. (You may be prompted to confirm that you want to add the driver. If so, click Install Driver to proceed.)

The Add Printer Wizard displays a screen that shows the printer's name and asks whether you want to designate the printer as your default printer.

6. If you want, designate the printer as your default printer.

7. Click Next to continue.

A final confirmation dialog box is displayed.

8. Click Finish.

You're done!

Many network printers, especially newer ones, are connected directly to the network by using a built-in Ethernet card. Setting up these printers can be tricky. You may need to ask the network administrator for help in setting up this type of printer. (Some printers that are connected directly to the network have their own Web addresses, such as `Printer.CleaverFamily.com`. If that's the case, you can often set up the printer in a click or two: Use your Web browser to go to the printer's Web page and then click a link that lets you install the printer.)

Printing to a network printer

After you install the network printer in Windows, printing to the network printer is a snap. You can print to the network printer from any Windows program by using the Print command to summon the Print dialog box, found under the File menu in Office 2003 or the Office button in Office 2007. For example, Figure 2-10 shows the Print dialog box for WordPad — the free text-editing program that comes with Windows. The available printers are listed near the top of this dialog box. Choose the network printer from this list and then click OK to print your document. That's all there is to it!

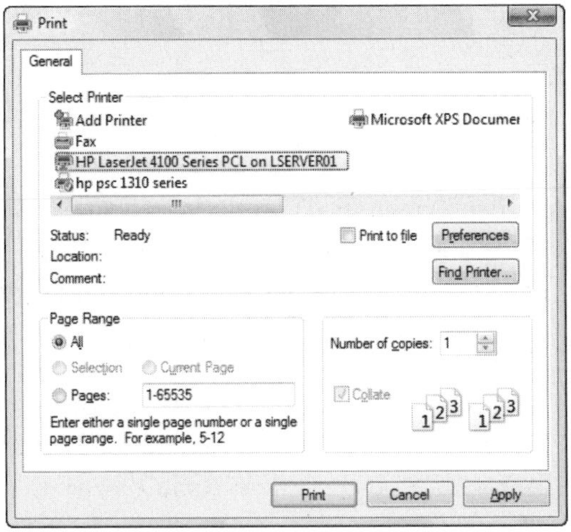

Figure 2-10:
A typical
Print dialog
box.

Playing with the print queue

After you send your document to a network printer, you usually don't have to worry about it. You just go to the network printer and — *voilà!* — your printed document is waiting for you.

That's what happens in the ideal world. In the real world, where you and I
live, all sorts of things can happen to your print job between the time you
send it to the network printer and the time it prints:

- You discover that someone else already sent a 50-trillion-page report
  ahead of you that isn't expected to finish printing until the national debt
  is paid off.

- The price of a framis valve suddenly goes up by $2, rendering foolish the
  recommendations you made in your report.

- Your boss calls and tells you that his brother-in-law will be attending the
  meeting, so won't you please print an extra copy of the proposal for him.
  Oh, and a photocopy won't do. Originals only, please.

- You decide to take lunch, so you don't want the output to print until you
  get back.

Fortunately, your print job isn't totally beyond your control just because you
already sent it to the network printer. You can easily change the status of
jobs that you already sent. You can change the order in which jobs print,
hold a job so that it doesn't print until you say so, or cancel a job.

You can probably make your network print jobs do other tricks, too — such
as shake hands, roll over, and play dead. But the basic tricks — hold, cancel,
and change the print order — are enough to get you started.

To play with the printer queue, open the Control Panel (choose Start➪
Control Panel) and click Printers. Then double-click the icon for the printer
that you want to manage. A window similar to the one shown in Figure 2-11
appears. You can see the bad news: Some clown named `dlowe` has just
started a 308-page report from Microsoft Word. You have to wait for this
report to finish before you can print your little 1-page memo.

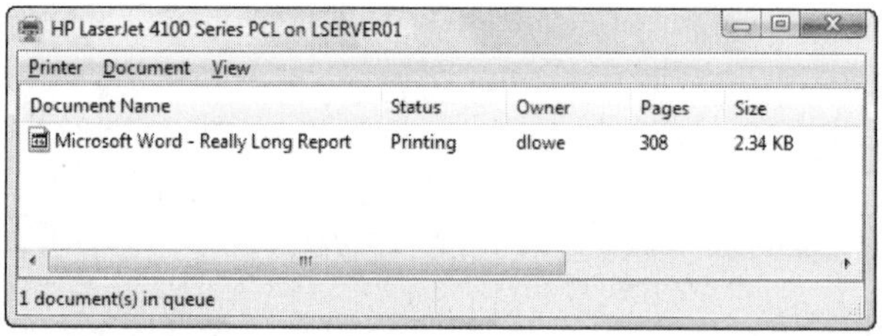

Figure 2-11:
Managing a
print queue.

HP LaserJet 4100 Series PCL on LSERVER01				
Printer Document View				
Document Name	Status	Owner	Pages	Size
Microsoft Word - Really Long Report	Printing	dlowe	308	2.34 KB
1 document(s) in queue				

To manipulate the print jobs that appear in the print queue or in the printer
itself, use these tricks:

- **To temporarily stop a job from printing:** Select the job and choose the
  Document➪Pause Printing command. Choose the same command again
  to release the job from its state of frustration and print it out, already.

✔ **To delete a print job:** Select the job and choose the Document⇨ Cancel Printing command.

✔ **To stop the printer:** Choose the Printer⇨Pause Printing command. To resume, choose the command again.

✔ **To delete all print jobs:** Choose the Printer⇨Purge Print Documents command.

✔ **To cut to the front of the line:** Drag to the top of the list the print job that you want to print.

All these tips apply to only your own print jobs. Unfortunately, you can't capriciously delete other people's print jobs.

The best thing about Windows printer management is that it shelters you from the details of working with different network operating systems. Whether you print on a NetWare printer, a Windows 2003 network printer, or a shared Windows printer, the Printer window icon manages all print jobs in the same way.

Logging Off the Network

After you finish using the network, you should log off. Logging off the network makes the network drives and printers unavailable. Your computer is still physically connected to the network (unless you cut the network cable with pruning shears; it's a bad idea — don't do it!), but the network and its resources are unavailable to you.

Here are a few other tips to keep in mind when you log off:

✔ After you turn off your computer, you're automatically logged off the network. After you start your computer, you have to log on again.

Logging off the network is a good idea if you're going to leave your computer unattended for a while. As long as your computer is logged in to the network, anyone can use it to access the network. And, because unauthorized users can access it under your user ID, you get the blame for any damage they do.

✔ In Windows, you can log off the network by clicking the Start button and choosing the Log Off command. This process logs you off the network without restarting Windows:

• In Windows XP, you can reach this command directly from the Start menu.

• In Windows Vista, click Start and then click the right-facing arrow that appears next to the little padlock icon.

Chapter 3

More Ways to Use Your Network

In This Chapter

▶ Transforming your computer into a network server

▶ Sharing folders with network users

▶ Using the Public Folder in Windows Vista

▶ Sharing your printer

▶ Using Microsoft Office on a network

▶ Working with offline files

Chapter 2 introduces you to the basics of using a network: logging on, accessing data on shared network folders, printing, and logging off. In this chapter, we go beyond these basics. You'll find out how to turn your computer into a server that shares its own files and printers, how to use one of the most popular network computer applications — e-mail — and how to work with Office on a network.

Sharing Your Stuff

As you probably know, networks consist of two types of computers: client computers and server computers. In the economy of computer networks, *client computers* are the consumers — the ones that use network resources, such as shared printers and disk drives. *Servers* are the providers — the ones that offer their own printers and hard drives to the network so that the client computers can use them.

This chapter shows you how to turn your humble Windows client computer into a server computer so that other computers on your network can use your printer and any folders that you decide you want to share. In effect, your computer functions as both a client and a server at the same time. A couple of examples show how:

- ✔ It's a **client** when you send a print job to a network printer or when you access a file stored on another server's hard drive.

- ✔ It's a **server** when someone else sends a print job to your printer or accesses a file stored on your computer's hard drive.

Enabling File and Printer Sharing (Windows XP)

Before you can share your files or your printer with other network users, you must set up a Windows feature known as *File and Printer Sharing*. Without this feature installed, your computer can be a network client but not a server. This section shows you how to enable this feature for Windows XP. For Windows Vista, refer to the next section, "Enabling File and Printer Sharing (Windows Vista)."

If you're lucky, the File and Printer Sharing feature is already set up on your computer. To find out, double-click the My Computer icon on your desktop. Select the icon for your C drive and then click File on the menu bar to reveal the File menu. If the menu includes a Sharing command, File and Printer Sharing is already set up, so you can skip the rest of this section. If you can't find a Sharing command on the File menu, you have to install File and Printer Sharing before you can share a file or printer with other network users.

To enable File and Printer Sharing on a Windows XP system, follow these steps:

1. **From the Start menu, choose Settings⇨Control Panel.**

   The Control Panel comes to life.

2. **Double-click the Network icon.**

   The Network dialog box appears, as shown in Figure 3-1.

3. **Click the File and Print Sharing button.**

   This action summons the File and Print Sharing dialog box.

4. **Click the File and Print Sharing options you want to enable for your computer.**

   The first option enables you to share your files with other network users; the second allows you to share your printer. To share both your files and your printer, select both check boxes.

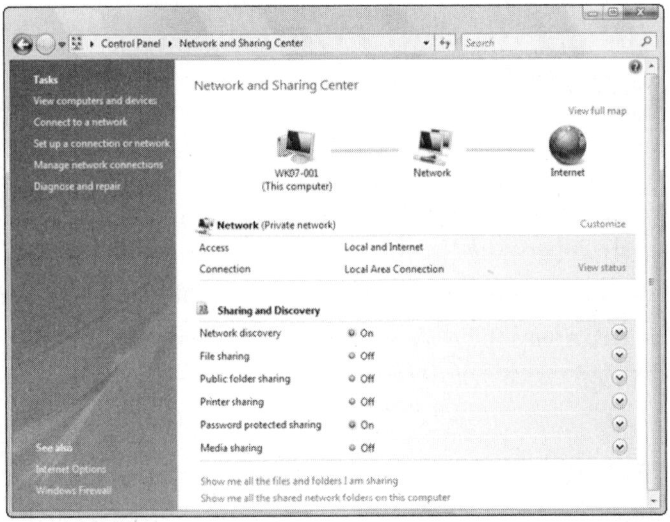

Figure 3-1:
The
Network
dialog box.

5. **Click OK to dismiss the File and Print Sharing dialog box.**

   You return to the Network dialog box.

6. **Click OK to dismiss the Network dialog box.**

   The Network dialog box vanishes, and a Copy Progress dialog box appears and lets you know that Windows is copying the files required to enable File and Print Sharing. If you're prompted to insert the Windows CD-ROM, do so with a smile.

   After all the necessary files have been copied, you see a dialog box informing you that you must restart your computer for the new settings to take effect.

7. **Click Yes to restart your computer.**

   Your computer shuts down and then restarts. Your computer may take a minute or so to restart, so be patient. When your computer comes back to life, you're ready to share files or your printer.

While you're working in the Network dialog box, don't mess around with any of the other network settings. You can safely change the File and Print Sharing options, but you should leave the rest of the settings in the Network dialog box well enough alone.

Enabling File and Printer Sharing (Windows Vista)

To enable file and printer sharing in Windows Vista, follow these steps:

1. **Choose Start⇨Network.**

   This step opens the Network folder.

2. **Click the Network and Sharing Center button on the toolbar.**

   This step opens the Network and Sharing Center, as shown in Figure 3-2.

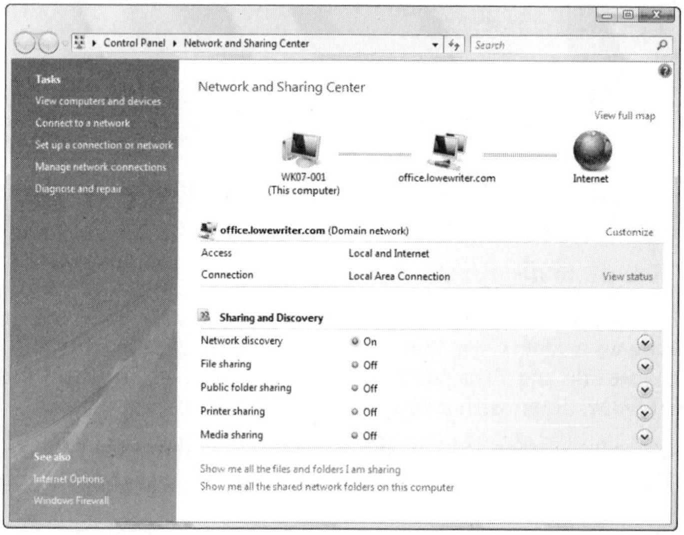

Figure 3-2:
The
Network
and Sharing
Center.

3. **Click File Sharing.**

   This step reveals the controls that enable you to activate file sharing, as shown in Figure 3-3.

4. **Select the Turn On File Sharing option and then click Apply.**

   This file sharing feature is activated.

5. **Select the Printer Sharing option.**

   This step reveals the controls that enable you to activate printer sharing.

6. **Select the Turn On Printer Sharing option and then click Apply.**

   This file sharing feature is activated.

7. **Close the Network and Sharing Center folder.**

   You're done; you can now share your files and printers.

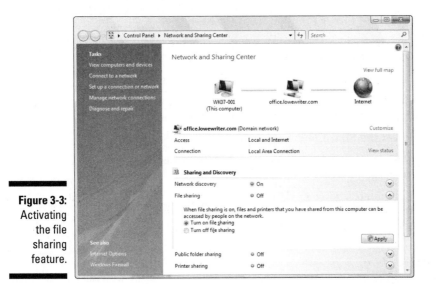

Figure 3-3:
Activating
the file
sharing
feature.

Sharing a Folder

To enable other network users to access files that reside on your hard drive, you must designate a folder on the drive as a *shared* folder. Note that you can also share an entire drive, if you so desire. If you share an entire drive, other network users can access all the files and folders on the drive. If you share a folder, network users can access only those files that reside in the folder you share. (If the folder you share contains other folders, network users can access files in those folders, too.)

Don't share an entire hard drive, unless you want to grant *everyone on the network* the freedom to sneak a peek at every file on your hard drive. Instead, you should share just the folder or folders containing the specific documents that you want others to be able to access. For example, if you store all your Word documents in the My Documents folder, you can share your My Documents folder so that other network users can access your Word documents.

Sharing a folder in Windows XP

To share a folder on a Windows XP computer, follow these steps:

1. **Double-click the My Computer icon on your desktop.**

   The My Computer window comes to center stage.

2. **Select the folder that you want to share.**

   Click the icon for the drive that contains the folder you want to share, and then find the folder itself and click it.

3. **Choose the File⇨Sharing and Security command.**

   The Properties dialog box for the folder that you want to share appears. Notice that the sharing options are grayed out.

4. **Select the Share This Folder on the Network option.**

   After you select this option, the rest of the sharing options come alive, as shown in Figure 3-4.

   If you prefer, you can skip Steps 2 through 4. Instead, just right-click the folder you want to share and then choose Sharing and Security from the pop-up menu that appears.

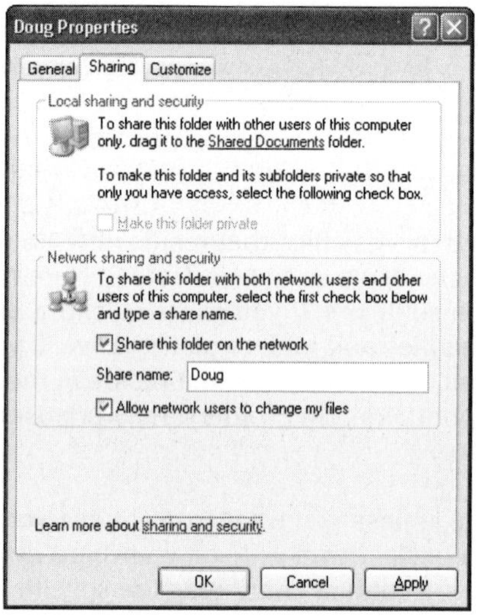

Figure 3-4:
The Sharing
options
come to life
when you
select the
Share This
Folder on
the Network
check box
(in Windows
XP).

5. **Change the share name if you don't like the name that Windows proposes.**

   The *share name* is the name that other network users use to access the shared folder. You can give it any name you want, but the name can be no more than 12 characters long. Uppercase and lowercase letters are treated the same in a share name, so the name My Documents is the same as MY DOCUMENTS.

Windows proposes a share name for you, based on the actual folder name. If the folder name has 12 or fewer characters, the proposed share name is the same as the folder name. If the folder name is longer than 12 characters, however, Windows abbreviates it. For example, the name Multimedia Files becomes MULTIMEDIA F.

If the name that Windows chooses doesn't make sense or seems cryptic, you can change the share name to something better. For example, I would probably use MEDIA FILES rather than MULTIMEDIA F.

6. **If you want to allow other network users to change the files in this folder, select the Allow Network Users to Change My Files check box.**

   If you leave this option deselected, other network users can open your files, but they can't save any changes they make.

7. **Click OK.**

   The Properties dialog box vanishes, and a hand is added to the icon for the folder to show that the folder is shared.

If you change your mind and decide that you want to stop sharing a folder, double-click the My Computer icon, select the folder or drive that you want to stop sharing, and choose the File⇨Sharing command to summon the Properties dialog box. Deselect the Share This Folder on the Network check box and then click OK.

Sharing a folder in Windows Vista

To share a folder in Windows Vista, follow these steps:

1. **Choose Start⇨Computer.**

   The Computer folder comes to center stage.

2. **Select the folder that you want to share.**

   Click the icon for the drive that contains the folder you want to share, and then find the folder itself and click it.

3. **Click the Sharing button on the toolbar.**

   The File Sharing dialog box appears, as shown in Figure 3-5.

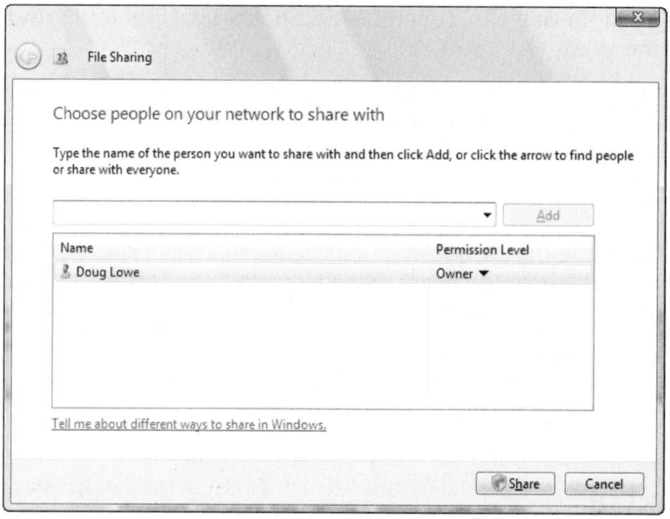

Figure 3-5:
The File
Sharing
dialog box
(in Windows
Vista).

4. **Click the arrow in the drop-down list and choose Everyone, and then click Add.**

   This action designates that anyone on your network can access the shared folder.

   If you prefer, you can limit access to just certain users. To do so, select each person you want to grant access to and then click Add.

5. **Select the level of access you want to grant each user.**

   You can choose from three levels of access:

   - **Reader:** A reader can open files but can't modify or create new files or folders.

   - **Contributor:** A contributor can add files to the share but can change or delete only her own files.

   - **Co-owner:** A co-owner has full access to the shared folder. He can create, change, or delete any file in the folder.

6. **Click Share.**

   The dialog box shown in Figure 3-6 is displayed to confirm that the folder has been shared.

Using the Public Folder in Windows Vista

Windows Vista introduces a new way of sharing files on the network: the Public folder. The *Public folder* is simply a folder that's designated for public access. Files you save in this folder can be accessed by other users on the network and by any user who logs on to your computer.

Before you can use the Public folder, you must enable it by following these steps:

1. **Choose Start⊅Network.**

   This step brings up the Network folder.

2. **Click the Network and Sharing Center button on the toolbar.**

   This step brings up the Network and Sharing Center. (Refer to Figure 3-2.)

3. **Select the Public Folder Sharing option.**

   This step reveals the controls that enable you to activate Public folder sharing. You have three options for sharing the Public folder:

   - **Turn on sharing so that anyone with network access can open files.** This option shares the Public folder as read-only, so other users can open files but can't modify or delete them or create their own files.

   - **Turn on sharing so that anyone with network access can open, change, or create files.** This option grants full access to the Public folder.

   - **Turn off sharing.** This option turns off Public folder sharing.

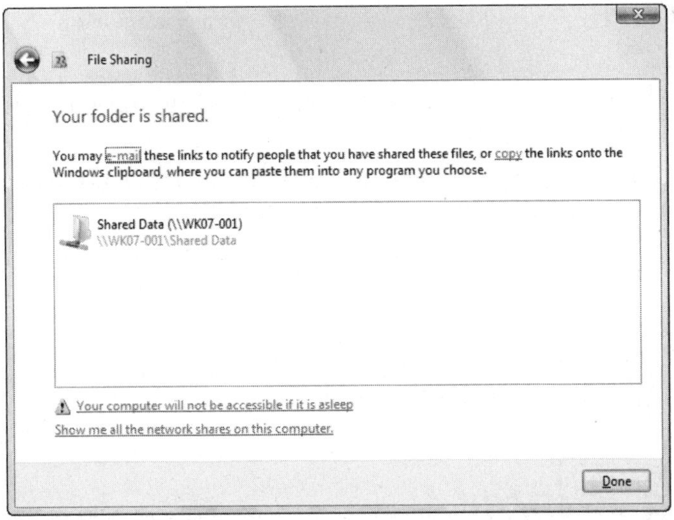

Figure 3-6: The folder has been shared.

4. **Select the level of sharing you want to use and then click Apply.**

   The Public Folder sharing feature is activated.

5. **Close the Network and Sharing Center folder.**

   You're done; you can now share your files and printers.

After you enable Public folder sharing, you can access the Public folder on your own computer by choosing Start➪Computer and then clicking the Public icon in the pane on the left side of the window. This action opens the Public folder, as shown in Figure 3-7.

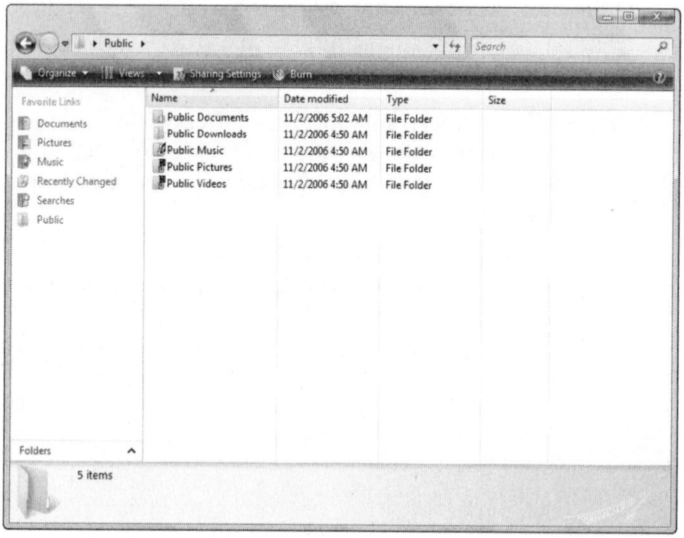

Public
Search
Organize
Views
Sharing Settings
Burn
Favorite Links
Documents
Pictures
Music
Recently Changed
Searches
Public
Name
Date modified
Type
Size
Public Documents 11/2/2006 5:02 AM File Folder
Public Downloads 11/2/2006 4:50 AM File Folder
Public Music 11/2/2006 4:50 AM File Folder
Public Pictures 11/2/2006 4:50 AM File Folder
Public Videos 11/2/2006 4:50 AM File Folder
Folders
5 items

Figure 3-7: The Public folder.

As you can see, the Public folder includes several predefined subfolders designed for sharing documents, downloaded files, music, pictures, and videos. You can use these subfolders if you want, or you can create your own subfolders to help organize the data in your Public folder.

TIP

To access the Public folder of another computer, use the techniques described in Chapter 2 to either browse to the Public folder or map it to a network drive.

Sharing a Printer

Sharing a printer is much more traumatic than sharing a hard drive. When you share a hard drive, other network users access your files from time to time. When they do, you hear your drive click a few times, and your computer may hesitate for a half-second or so. The interruptions caused by other users accessing your drive are sometimes noticeable, but rarely annoying.

When you share a printer, you get to see Murphy's Law in action: Your coworker down the hall is liable to send a 140-page report to your printer just moments before you try to print a 1-page memo that has to be on the boss's desk in two minutes. The printer may run out of paper or, worse, jam during someone else's print job — and you're expected to attend to the problem.

Although these interruptions can be annoying, sharing your printer makes a lot of sense in some situations. If you have the only decent printer in your office or workgroup, everyone will bug you to let them use it anyway. You may as well share the printer on the network. At least this way, they won't line up at your door to ask you to print their documents for them.

Sharing a printer in Windows XP

The following procedure shows you how to share a printer in Windows XP:

1. **From the Start menu, choose Printers and Faxes.**

   The Printers and Faxes folder appears, as shown in Figure 3-8. In this example, the Printers folder lists a single printer, named HP PSC 750.

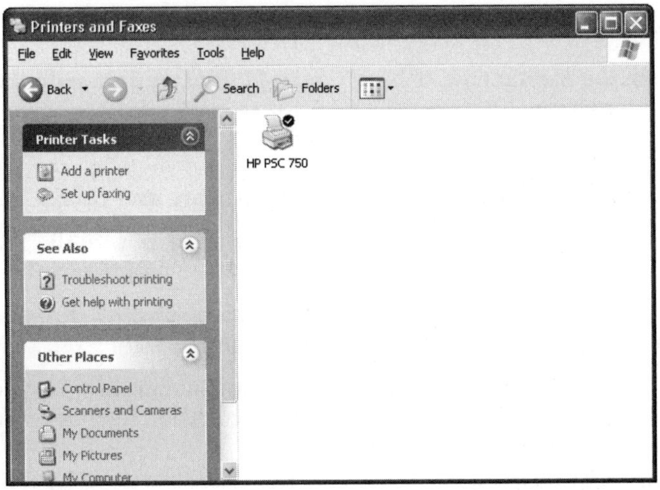

Figure 3-8:
The Printers
and Faxes
folder.

2. **Select the printer that you want to share.**

   Click the icon for the printer to select the printer.

3. **Choose File⇨Sharing.**

   You're right: This command doesn't make sense. You're sharing a *printer,* not a file, but the Sharing command is on the File menu. Go figure.

   When you choose the File⇨Sharing command, the Properties dialog box for the printer appears.

4. **Select the Share This Printer option.**

5. **Change the share name if you don't like the name suggested by Windows.**

   Other computers use the share name to identify the shared printer, so choose a meaningful or descriptive name.

6. **Click OK.**

   You return to the Printers folder, where a hand is added to the printer icon to show that the printer is now a shared network printer.

To take your shared printer off the network so that other network users can't access it, follow Steps 1 through 3 in the preceding set of steps to open the Printer Properties dialog box. Select the Do Not Share This Printer option and then click OK. The hand disappears from the printer icon, to indicate that the printer is no longer shared.

Sharing a printer in Windows Vista

To share a printer in Windows Vista, follow these steps:

1. **From the Start menu, choose Control Panel, and then double-click the Printers icon.**

   The Printers folder appears.

2. **Right-click the printer that you want to share and choose Sharing.**

   The Properties dialog box for the printer appears with the Sharing tab selected, as shown in Figure 3-9. Notice that the options for sharing the printer are disabled.

3. **Click the Change Sharing Options button.**

   Because Windows Vista's is annoyingly suspicious of what you're doing, a dialog box appears, asking for your permission to change the printer sharing settings.

4. **Click Continue.**

   You return to the Properties dialog box, this time with the printer sharing options enabled.

5. **Select the Share This Printer option.**

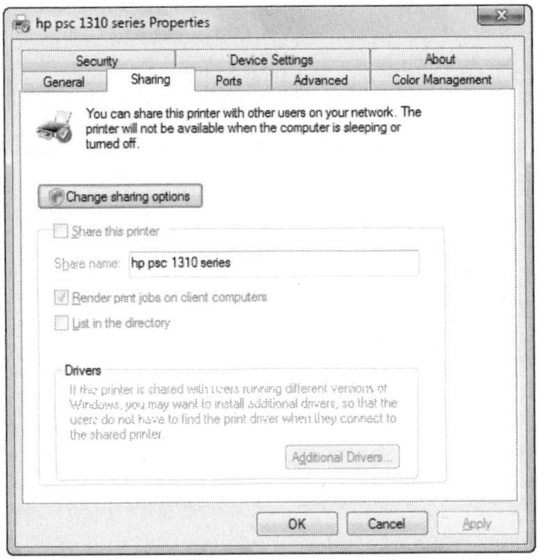

Figure 3-9:
Sharing a
printer in
Windows
Vista.

6. **Change the share name if you don't like the name suggested by Windows.**

   Because other computers will use the share name to identify the shared printer, pick a descriptive name.

7. **Click OK.**

   You return to the Printers folder. The icon for the printer is modified to indicate that it has been shared.

To take your shared printer off the network so that other network users can't access it, follow Steps 1 through 6 in the preceding set of steps. Uncheck the Share This Printer check box and then click OK.

Using Microsoft Office on a Network

Microsoft Office is far and away the most popular suite of application programs used on personal computers, and it includes the most common types of application programs used in an office: a word processing program (Word), a spreadsheet program (Excel), a presentation program (PowerPoint), and an excellent e-mail program (Outlook). Depending on the version of Office you purchase, you may also get a database program (Access), a Web-site development program (FrontPage), a desktop publishing program (Publisher), a set of Ginsu knives (KnifePoint), and a slicer and dicer (ActiveSalsa).

This section describes the networking features of Microsoft Office System 2007, the latest and greatest version of Office. Most of these features also work with previous versions of Office.

To get the most from using Office on a network, you should purchase the Microsoft Office Resource Kit. The Office Resource Kit, also known as *ORK*, contains information about installing and using Office on a network and comes with a CD that has valuable tools. If you don't want to purchase the ORK, you can view it online and download the ORK tools from the Microsoft TechNet Web site (`www.microsoft.com/technet`). Nanoo-nanoo, earthling.

Installing Office on a network — some options

You need to make some basic decisions when you prepare to install Microsoft Office on a network. In particular, here are some possible approaches to installing Microsoft Office on your network clients:

✔ You can simply ignore the fact that you have a network and purchase a separate copy of Office for each user on the network. Then you can install Office from the CD on each computer. This option works well if

- Your network is small.

- Each computer has ample disk space to hold the necessary Office files.

- Each computer has its own CD-ROM drive.

✔ On a larger network, you can use the Office Setup program in Administrative Setup mode. This option lets you create a special type of setup on a network server disk from which you can install Office on network computers. Administrative Setup enables you to control the custom features selected for each network computer and reduce the amount of user interaction required to install Office on each computer.

If you choose to use Administrative Setup, you can use the Network Installation Wizard, which comes with the Office Resource Kit. The Network Installation Wizard lets you customize settings for installing Office on client computers. For example, you can choose which Office components to install, provide default answers to yes/no questions that Setup asks the user while installing Office, and select the amount of interaction you want the Setup program to have with the user while installing Office.

No matter which option you choose for installing Office on your network, you must purchase either a copy of Office or a license to install Office for every computer that uses Office. Purchasing a single copy of Office and installing it on more than one computer is illegal.

Accessing network files

Opening a file that resides on a network drive is almost as easy as opening a file on a local drive. All Office programs use the File➪Open command to summon the Open dialog box, as shown in its Excel incarnation in Figure 3-10. (The Open dialog box is nearly identical in other Office programs.)

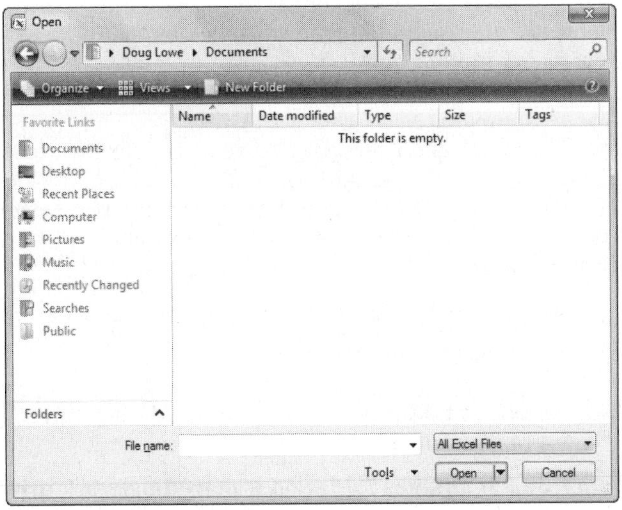

Figure 3-10: The Open dialog box in Excel 2007.

To access a file that resides on a network volume that's mapped to a drive letter, all you have to do is use the drop-down list at the top of the dialog box to select the network drive. If the network volume isn't mapped to a drive, click Folders near the lower-left corner of the Open dialog box, select Network, and then browse to the file you want to open.

You can map a network drive directly from the Open dialog box by navigating to the folder you want to map, right-clicking the folder, and choosing Map Network Drive.

If you try to open a file that another network user has opened already, Office tells you that the file is already in use and offers to let you open a read-only version of the file. You can read and edit the read-only version, but Office doesn't let you overwrite the existing version of the file. You have to use the Save As command instead to save your changes to a new file.

Using workgroup templates

A template isn't a place of worship, although an occasional sacrifice to the Office gods may make your computing life a bit easier. Rather, a *template* is a special type of document file that holds formatting information, boilerplate text, and other customized settings that you can use as the basis for new documents.

Three Office programs — Word, Excel, and PowerPoint — enable you to specify a template whenever you create a new document. When you create a new document in Word, Excel, or PowerPoint by choosing the File⇨New command, you see a dialog box that lets you choose a template for the new document.

Office comes with a set of templates for the most common types of documents. These templates are grouped under the various tabs that appear across the top of the New dialog box.

In addition to the templates that come with Office, you can create your own templates in Word, Excel, and PowerPoint. Creating your own templates is especially useful if you want to establish a consistent look for documents prepared by your network users. For example, you can create a Letter template that includes your company's letterhead, or a Proposal template that includes a company logo.

Office enables you to store templates in two locations. Where you put them depends on what you want to do with them:

- **The User Templates folder on each user's local disk drive:** If a particular user needs a specialized template, put it here.

- **The Workgroup Templates folder on a shared network drive:** If you have templates that you want to make available to all network users on the network server, put them here. This arrangement still allows each user to create templates that aren't available to other network users.

When you use both a User Templates folder and a Workgroup Templates folder, Office combines the templates from both folders and lists them in alphabetical order in the New dialog box. For example, the User Templates folder may contain templates named Blank Document and Web Page, and the Workgroup Templates folder may contain a template named Company Letterhead. In this case, three templates appear in the New dialog box, in this order: Blank Document, Company Letterhead, and Web Page.

To set the location of the User Templates and Workgroup Templates folders, follow these steps in Microsoft Word:

1. **Click the Office button and then click Word Options.**

   The Word Options dialog box opens.

2. **Click the Advanced tab.**

   The Advanced options appear.

3. **Scroll down to the General section and then click the File Locations button.**

   The File Locations dialog box appears, as shown in Figure 3-11.

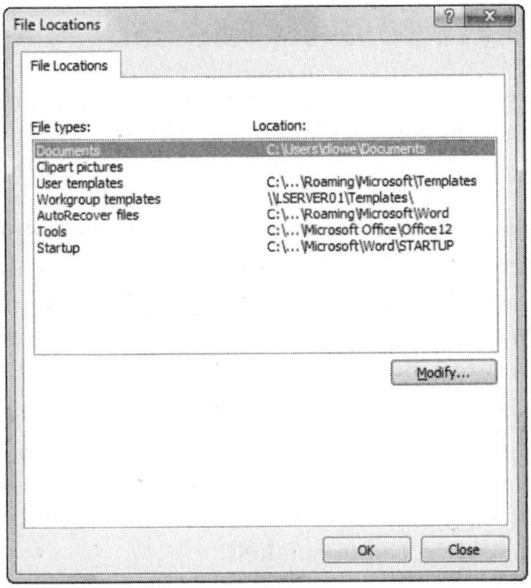

Figure 3-11:
Setting
the file
locations in
Word 2007.

4. **Double-click the Workgroup Templates item.**

   This step opens a dialog box that lets you browse to the location of your template files.

5. **Browse to the template files and then click OK.**

   You return to the File Locations dialog box.

6. **Click OK to dismiss the File Locations dialog box.**

   You return to the Word Options dialog box.

7. **Click OK again.**

   The Word Options dialog box is dismissed.

Although the User Templates and Workgroup Templates settings affect Word, Excel, and PowerPoint, you can change these settings only from Word. The Options dialog boxes in Excel and PowerPoint don't show the User Templates or Workgroup Templates options.

When you install Office, the standard templates that come with Office are copied into a folder on the computer's local disk drive, and the User Templates option is set to this folder. The Workgroup Templates option is left blank. You can set the Workgroup Templates folder to a shared network folder by click-ing Network Templates, clicking the Modify button, and specifying a shared network folder that contains your workgroup templates.

Networking an Access database

If you want to share a Microsoft Access database among several network users, you should be aware of a few special considerations. Here are the more important ones:

✔ When you share a database, more than one user may try to access the same record at the same time. This situation can lead to problems if two or more users try to update the record. To handle this potential traffic snarl, Access locks the record so that only one user at a time can update it. Access uses one of three methods to lock records:

- **Edited Record:** This method locks a record whenever a user begins to edit a record. For example, if a user retrieves a record in a form that allows the record to be updated, Access locks the record while the user edits it so that other users can't edit the record until the first record is finished.

- **No Locks:** This method doesn't really mean that the record isn't locked. Instead, No Locks means that the record isn't locked until a user writes a change to the database. This method can be confus-ing to users because it enables one user to overwrite changes made by another user.

- **All Records:** All Records locks an entire table whenever a user edits any record in the table.

✔ Access lets you split a database so that the forms, queries, and reports are stored on each user's local disk drive, but the data itself is stored on a network drive. This feature can make the database run more efficiently on a network, but it's a little more difficult to set up. (To split a database, use the Tools➪Database Utilities➪Database Splitter command.)

✔ Access includes built-in security features that you should use if you share an Access database from a Windows client computer, such as one running Windows XP or Windows Vista. If you store the database on a domain server, you can use the server's security features to protect the database.

✔ Access automatically refreshes forms and datasheets every 60 seconds. That way, if one user opens a form or datasheet and another user changes the data a few seconds later, the first user sees the changes within one minute. If 60 seconds is too long (or too short) an interval, you can change the refresh rate by using the Advanced tab in the Options dialog box.

Working with Offline Files

Desktop computers are by nature stationary beasts. As a result, they're almost always connected to their networks. Notebook computers, however, are more transitory. If you have a notebook computer, you're likely to tote it around from place to place. If you have a network at work, you probably connect to the network when you're at work. But then you take the notebook computer home for the weekend, where you aren't connected to your network.

Of course, your boss wants you to spend your weekends working, so you need a way to access your important network files while you're away from the office and disconnected from the network. That's where the offline files feature comes in. It lets you access your network files even while you're disconnected from the network.

It sounds like magic, but it isn't really. Imagine how you would work away from the network without this feature. You simply copy the files you need to work on to your notebook computer's local hard disk. Then, when you take the computer home, you work on the local copies. When you get back to the office, you connect to the network and copy the modified files back to the network server.

That's essentially how the offline files feature works, except that Windows does all the copying automatically. Windows also uses smoke and mirrors to make it look like the copies are actually on the network, even though you're not connected to the network. For example, if you map a drive (drive M, for example) and make it available offline, you can still access the offline copies of the file on the M drive. That's because Windows knows that when you aren't connected to the network, it should redirect drive M to its local copy of the drive M files.

The main complication of working with offline files, of course, is what happens when two or more users want to access the same offline files. Windows can attempt to straighten that mess out for you, but it doesn't do a great job of it. Your best bet is to not use the offline files feature with network resources that other users may want available offline too. In other words, it's okay to make your home drive available offline because that drive is accessible only to you. But I don't recommend making shared network resources available offline, unless they're read-only resources that don't contain files you intend to modify.

Using the offline files feature is easy:

✓ **In Windows Vista,** open the Computer folder, right-click the mapped network drive you want to make available offline, and then choose Always Available Offline.

✓ **In Windows XP,** open My Computer, right-click the mapped drive, and choose Make Available Offline.

If you don't want to designate an entire mapped drive for offline access, you can designate individual folders within a mapped drive by using the same technique: Right-click the folder, and then choose Always Available Offline (Windows Vista) or Make Available Offline (Windows XP).

When you first designate a drive or folder as available offline, Windows copies all the files on the drive or folder to local storage. Depending on how many files are involved, this process can take awhile, so plan accordingly.

After you designate a drive as available offline, Windows takes care of the rest. Each time you log on or off the network, Windows synchronizes your offline files. Windows compares the time stamp on each file on both the server and the local copy and then copies any files that have changed.

Here are a few other thoughts to consider about offline files:

- ✔ If you want, you can force Windows to synchronize your offline files by right-clicking the drive or folder and choosing Sync.

- ✔ The Properties dialog box for mapped drives includes an Offline Files tab, as shown in Figure 3-12.

- ✔ Employers love the offline files feature because it encourages their employees to work at home during evenings and weekends. In fact, every time you use the offline files feature to work at home, your boss sends Bill Gates a nickel. That's how he got so rich.

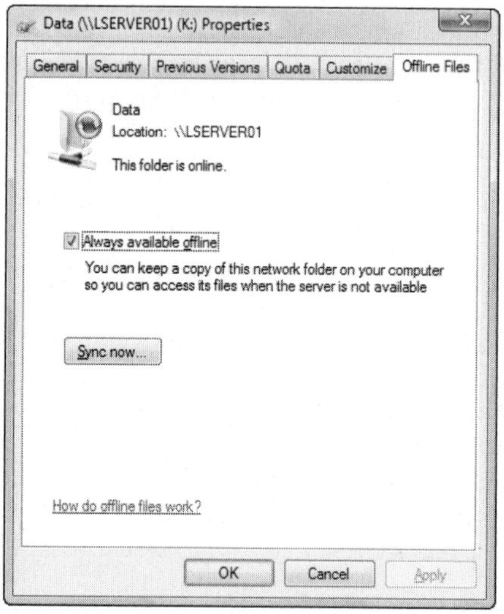

Figure 3-12:
Offline file
properties.

Part II
Building Your Own Network

The 5th Wave   By Rich Tennant

©RICHTENNANT

"That's it! We're getting a wireless network
for the house."

In this part . . .

You discover how to build a network yourself, which includes planning it and installing it. And you find out what choices are available for cable types, network operating systems, and all the other bits and pieces that you have to contend with.

Yes, some technical information is included in these chapters. Fear not! I bring you tidings of great joy! Lo, a working network is at hand, and you — yea, even you — can design it and install it yourself.

Chapter 4

Planning Your Network

. . . .

In This Chapter

▶ Creating a network plan

▶ Taking stock of your computer stock

▶ Making sure that you know why you need a network

▶ Making the three basic network decisions you can't avoid

▶ Using a starter kit

▶ Looking at a sample network

. . . .

*O*kay, so you're convinced that you need to network your computers. What now? Do you stop by Computers-R-Us on the way to work, install the network before morning coffee, and expect the network to be fully operational by noon?

I don't think so.

Networking your computers is just like any other worthwhile endeavor: To do it right requires a bit of planning. This chapter helps you think through your network before you start spending money. It shows you how to come up with a networking plan that's every bit as good as the plan that a network consultant would charge $1,000 for.

This book is already saving you money!

Making a Network Plan

Before you begin any networking project, whether it's a new network installation or an upgrade of an existing network, first make a detailed plan. If you make technical decisions too quickly, before studying all the issues that affect the project, you'll regret it. You'll discover too late that a key application doesn't run over the network, that the network has unacceptably slow performance, or that key components of the network don't work together.

Here are some general thoughts to keep in mind while you create your network plan:

- ✔ **Don't rush the plan.** The most costly networking mistakes are the ones you make *before* you install the network. Think things through and consider alternatives.

- ✔ **Write down the network plan.** The plan doesn't have to be a fancy, 500-page document. If you want to make it look good, pick up a ½-inch three-ring binder — big enough to hold your network plan with room to spare.

- ✔ **Ask someone else to read your network plan before you buy anything.** Preferably, ask someone who knows more about computers than you do.

- ✔ **Keep the plan up-to-date.** If you add to the network, dig up the plan, dust it off, and update it.

"The best-laid schemes of mice and men gang oft agley, and leave us not but grief and pain for promised joy." Robert Burns lived a couple hundred years before computer networks, but his famous words ring true. A network plan isn't chiseled in stone. If you discover that something doesn't work the way you thought it would, that's okay. You can always adjust your plan for unforeseen circumstances.

Being Purposeful

One of the first steps in planning your network is making sure that you understand why you want the network in the first place. Here are some of the more common reasons for needing a network, all of them quite valid:

- ✔ My co-worker and I exchange files using a flash drive just about every day. With a network, we could trade files without using the flash drive.

- ✔ I don't want to buy everyone a printer when I know that the one we have now just sits there taking up space most of the day. Wouldn't buying a network be better than buying a printer for every computer?

- ✔ I want to provide an Internet connection for all my computers. Many networks, especially smaller ones, exist solely for the purpose of sharing an Internet connection.

- ✔ Someone figured out that we're destroying seven trees a day by printing interoffice memos on paper, so we want to give the rainforest a break by setting up an e-mail system and trying to print less of the routine stuff.

It won't work! One of the inescapable laws of business is that the more you try to eliminate paperwork, the more paperwork you end up creating.

✔ Business is so good that one person typing in orders eight hours each day can't keep up. With a network, I can have two people entering orders, and I don't have to pay overtime to either person.

✔ My brother-in-law just put in a network at his office, and I don't want him to think that I'm behind the times.

Make sure that you identify all the reasons why you think you need a network and then write them down. Don't worry about winning the Pulitzer Prize for your stunning prose. Just make sure that you write down what you expect a network to do for you.

If you were making a 500-page networking proposal, you would place the description of why a network is needed in a tabbed section labeled Justification. In your ½-inch network binder, file the description under Purpose.

When you consider the reasons why you need a network, you may conclude that you don't need a network after all. That's okay. You can always use the binder for your stamp collection.

Taking Stock

One of the most challenging parts of planning a network is figuring out how to work with the computers you already have — how do you get from here to there? Before you can plan how to get "there," you have to know where "here" is: Take a thorough inventory of your current computers.

What you need to know

You need to know the following information about each of your computers:

✔ **The processor type and, if possible, its clock speed:** Hope that all your computers are 2GHz Pentium 4s or better. But in most cases, you find a mixture of computers — some new, some old, some borrowed, some blue. You may even find a few archaic pre-Pentium computers, which should be converted to beehives as soon as possible.

You can't usually tell what kind of processor a computer has just by looking at the computer's case. Most computers, however, display the processor type when you turn them on or reboot them. If the information on the startup screen scrolls too quickly for you to read it, try pressing the Pause key to freeze the information. After you finish reading it, press the Pause key again so that your computer can continue booting.

✔ **The size of the hard drive and the arrangement of its partitions:** In Windows, you can find out the size of your computer's hard drive by opening the My Computer window, right-clicking the drive icon, and choosing the Properties command from the shortcut menu that appears. Figure 4-1 shows the Properties dialog box for a 149GB hard drive that has 137GB of free space.

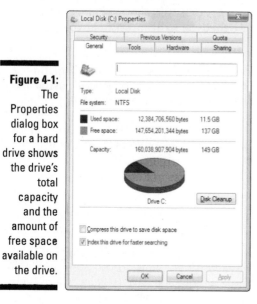

Figure 4-1: The Properties dialog box for a hard drive shows the drive's total capacity and the amount of free space available on the drive.

If your computer has more than one hard drive or partition, Windows lists an icon for each drive or partition in the My Computer window. Jot down the size and amount of free space available on each of the drives. (A *partition* is a section of a hard drive that's treated as though it were a separate drive. But that won't be on the test.)

✔ **The amount of memory:** In Windows, you can find out this information easily enough by right-clicking the My Computer desktop icon and choosing the Properties command. The amount of memory on your computer appears in the dialog box that appears. For example, Figure 4-2 shows the System Properties dialog box for a computer running Windows XP Professional with 2GB of RAM.

✔ **The version of the operating system that's installed:** You can determine the version by checking the System Properties dialog box. For example, Figure 4-2 shows the System Properties dialog box for a computer running Windows Vista Business Edition.

Figure 4-2:
The System
Properties
dialog
box for a
computer
running
Windows
Vista with
2GB of
RAM.

✔ **The type of network interface installed in the computer:** To find out
the exact name of the network interface, open the Control Panel and
double-click the System icon. Then click the Hardware tab and click the
Device Manager button. This action opens the Device Manager dialog
box, as shown in Figure 4-3. In this case, you can see that the computer's
network interface is an Intel(R) Pro/100 VE Network Connection.

The Device Manager is also useful for tracking down other hardware
devices attached to the computer or for checking which device drivers
are being used for the computer's devices.

Figure 4-3:
Using the
Device
Manager to
probe for
hardware
devices.

- ✓ **The network protocols that are in use:** To determine this information, open the Control Panel, double-click the Network Connections icon to open the Network Connections dialog box, and then right-click the network connection and choose the Properties command.

- ✓ **The kind of printer, if any, that's attached to the computer:** Usually, you can tell just by looking at the printer itself. You can also tell by examining the Printers and Faxes folder.

- ✓ **Any other devices connected to the computer:** A CD, DVD, or CD-RW drive? Scanner? Zip or Jaz drive? Tape drive? Video camera? Battle droid? Hot tub?

- ✓ **Whether driver and installation disks are available:** Hopefully, you can locate the disks or CDs required by hardware devices, such as the network card, printers, and scanners. If not, you may be able to locate the drivers on the Internet.

- ✓ **Which software is used on the computer:** Microsoft Office? QuickBooks? AutoCAD? Make a complete list and include version numbers.

Programs that gather information for you

Gathering information about your computers is a lot of work if you have more than a few computers to network. Fortunately, several available software programs can automatically gather the information for you. These programs inspect various aspects of a computer, such as the CPU type and speed, amount of RAM, and size of the computer's hard drives. Then they show the information on the screen and give you the option of saving the information to a hard drive file or printing it.

Windows comes with just such a program: Microsoft System Information. This program gathers and prints information about your computer. You can start Microsoft System Information by choosing Start➪Programs➪Accessories➪ System Tools➪System Information.

When you fire up Microsoft System Information, you see the window shown in Figure 4-4, which displays basic information about your computer, such as your version of Microsoft Windows, the processor type, the amount of memory on the computer, and the free space on each of the computer's hard drives. You can obtain more detailed information by clicking any of the following options on the left side of the window: Hardware Resources, Components, Software Environment, or Applications.

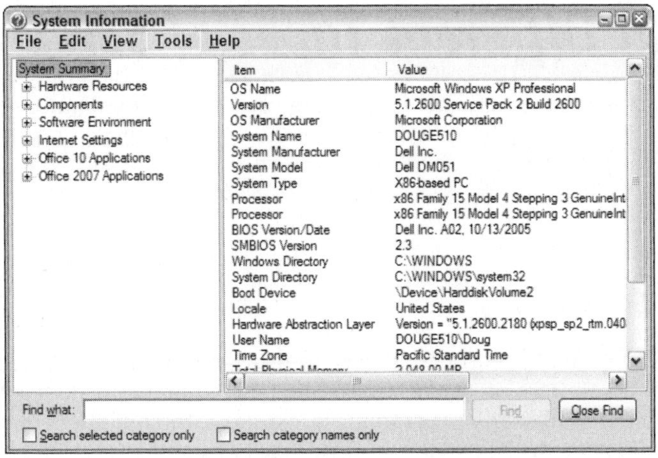

Figure 4-4:
Displaying
system
information.

To Dedicate, or Not to Dedicate: That Is the Question

One of the most basic questions that a network plan must answer is whether the network will have one or more dedicated servers or whether it will rely completely on peer-to-peer networking, with no single computer acting as a dedicated server. If the only reason for purchasing your network is to share a printer and exchange an occasional file, you may not need a dedicated server computer. In that case, you can create a peer-to-peer network by using the computers you already have. However, all but the smallest networks benefit from having a separate, dedicated server computer.

Here are a few points to ponder regarding dedicated versus nondedicated servers:

✔ Using a dedicated server computer makes the network faster, easier to work with, and more reliable. Consider what happens when the user of a server computer, which doubles as a workstation, decides to turn off the computer, not realizing that someone else is accessing files on her hard drive.

✔ You don't necessarily have to use your biggest and fastest computer as your server computer. I've seen networks where the slowest computer on the network is the server. This is especially true when the server is mostly used to share a printer or to store a small number of shared files. If you need to buy a computer for your network, consider promoting one of your older computers to be the server and using the new computer as a client.

Looking at Different Types of Servers

Assuming that your network will require one or more dedicated servers, you should consider which types of servers the network needs. In some cases, a single server computer can fill one or more of these roles. Whenever possible, try to limit each server computer to a single server function.

File servers

File servers provide centralized disk storage that can be conveniently shared by client computers on the network. The most common task of a file server is to store shared files and programs. For example, the members of a small workgroup can use disk space on a file server to store their Microsoft Office documents.

File servers must ensure that two users don't try to update the same file at the same time. The file servers do this by *locking* a file while a user updates the file so that other users can't access the file until the first user finishes. For document files (for example, word processing or spreadsheet files), the whole file is locked. For database files, the lock can be applied just to the portion of the file that contains the record or records being updated.

Print servers

Sharing printers is one of the main reasons that many small networks exist. Although it isn't often necessary to do so, you can dedicate a server computer for use as a *print server,* whose sole purpose is to collect information being sent to a shared printer by client computers and print it in an orderly fashion.

- ✔ A single computer may double as both a file server and a print server, but performance is better if you use separate print and file server computers.

- ✔ With an inexpensive inkjet printer running about $100 or less, just giving each user his own printer is tempting. However, you get what you pay for. Rather than buy a cheap inkjet printer for each user, you may be better off buying one good laser printer and sharing it.

Web servers

A *Web server* is a server computer that runs software that enables the computer to host an Internet Web site. The two most popular Web server programs are Microsoft IIS (Internet Information Services) and Apache, an open-source Web server program managed by the Apache Software Foundation.

Mail servers

A *mail server* is a server computer that handles the network's e-mail needs. It's configured with e-mail server software, such as Microsoft Exchange Server. Your mail-server software must be compatible with your e-mail program; Exchange Server, for example, is designed to work with Microsoft Outlook, the e-mail client software that comes with Microsoft Office.

Database servers

A *database server* is a server computer that runs database software, such as Microsoft SQL Server 2005. Database servers are usually used along with customized business applications, such as accounting or marketing systems.

Choosing a Server Operating System

If you determine that your network needs one or more dedicated servers, the next step is to determine what network operating system those servers should use. If possible, all the servers should use the same NOS so you don't find yourself awash in the conflicting requirements of different operating systems.

Although you can choose from many network operating systems, from a practical point of view, your choices are limited to the following:

- ✔ Windows Server 2003 (or its forthcoming replacement, Windows Server 2007)
- ✔ Novell NetWare
- ✔ Linux or another version of UNIX

For more information, see Chapter 7.

Planning the Infrastructure

You also need to plan the details of how you'll connect the computers in the network. You have to determine which network topology the network will use, which type of cable will be used, where the cable will be routed, and which other devices — most likely, network switches and perhaps a router — will be needed.

Although you have many cabling options to choose from, you'll probably use Cat5e or better UTP for most — if not all — of the desktop client computers on the network. However, you have many questions to answer beyond this basic choice:

- ✔ Where will you place workgroup switches — on a desktop somewhere within the group or in a central wiring closet?

- ✔ How many client computers will you place on each switch, and how many switches will you need?

- ✔ If you need more than one switch, which type of cabling will you use to connect the switches to one another?

For more information about network cabling, see Chapter 5.

If you're installing new network cable, don't scrimp on the cable itself. Because installing network cable is a labor-intensive task, the cost of the cable itself is a small part of the total cable-installation cost. And, if you spend a little extra to install higher-grade cable now, you don't have to replace the cable in a few years when it's time to upgrade the network.

Drawing Diagrams

One of the most helpful techniques for creating a network plan is to draw a picture of it. The diagram can be a detailed floor plan, showing the actual location of each network component. This type of diagram is sometimes called a *physical map.* If you prefer, the diagram can be a *logical map,* which is more abstract and Picasso-like. Anytime you change the network layout, update the diagram. Also include a detailed description of the change, the date that the change was made, and the reason for the change.

You can diagram very small networks on the back of a napkin, but if the network has more than a few computers, use a drawing program to help you create the diagram. One of the best programs for this purpose is Microsoft Visio, as shown in Figure 4-5.

Here's a rundown of some of the features that make Visio useful:

- ✔ Smart shapes and connectors maintain the connections you draw between network components, even if you rearrange the layout of the components on the page.

✔ Stencils provide dozens of useful shapes for common network components — not just client and server computers, but also routers, hubs, switches, and just about anything else you can imagine. If you're picky about the diagrams, you can even purchase stencil sets that have accurate drawings of specific devices, such as Cisco routers or IBM mainframe computers.

✔ You can add information to each computer or device in the diagram, such as the serial number or physical location. Then you can quickly print an inventory that lists this information for each device in the diagram.

✔ You can easily create large diagrams that span multiple pages.

Sample Network Plans

In what's left of this chapter, I present some network plans drawn from real-life situations. These examples illustrate many of the network-design issues I cover earlier in this chapter. The stories you're about to read are true. The names have been changed to protect the innocent.

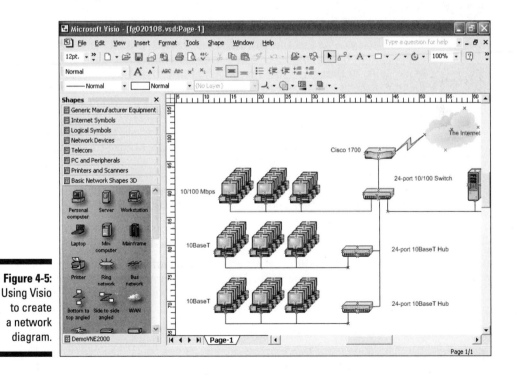

Figure 4-5:
Using Visio to create a network diagram.

Building a small network: California Sport Surface, Inc.

California Sport Surface, Inc. (CSS) is a small company specializing in the installation of outdoor sports surfaces, such as tennis courts, running tracks, and football fields. CSS has an administrative staff of just four employees who work out of a home office. The company has three computers:

- ✔ A brand-new Dell desktop computer running Windows XP Home Edition, shared by the president (Mark) and vice president (Julie) to prepare proposals and marketing brochures, handle correspondence, and do other miscellaneous chores. This computer has a built-in 10/100 Mbps Ethernet network port.

- ✔ An older Gateway computer running Windows 98 Second Edition, used by the bookkeeper (Erin), who uses QuickBooks to handle the company's accounting needs. This computer doesn't have a network port.

- ✔ A notebook that runs Windows XP Media Edition, used by the company's chief engineer (Daniel), who often takes it to job sites to help with engineering needs. This computer has a built-in 10/100/1000 Mbps Ethernet port.

The company owns just one printer, a moderately priced inkjet printer that's connected to Erin's computer. The computers aren't networked, so whenever Mark, Julie, or Daniel needs to print something, that person must copy the file to a diskette and give it to Erin, who then prints the document. The computer shared by Mark and Julie is connected to the Internet by using a residential DSL connection.

The company wants to install a network to support these three computers. Here are the primary goals of the network:

- ✔ Provide shared access to the printer so that users don't have to exchange diskettes to print their documents.

- ✔ Provide shared access to the Internet connection so that users can access the Internet from any of the computers.

- ✔ Allow for the addition of another desktop computer, which the company expects to purchase within the next six months, and potentially another notebook computer. (If business is good, the company hopes to hire another engineer.)

- ✔ The network should be intuitive to the users and shouldn't require any extensive upkeep.

CSS's networking needs can be met with the simple peer-to-peer network diagrammed in Figure 4-6.

Here's what the network requires:

✔ A 10/100 Mbps Ethernet adapter card for the Gateway computer, which is the only computer that doesn't have a network port. (A better alternative is to replace this computer with a newer computer that runs Windows Vista and has a built-in network interface.)

✔ A combination DSL router and 4-port 10/100 Mbps switch, such as the LinkSys BEFSR41W or the Belkin F5D5231-4. The company may outgrow this device when it adds a laptop, but if and when that happens, another 4- or 8-port 10/100 Mbps switch can be added then.

✔ The firewall features of the DSL router need to be enabled to protect the network from Internet hackers.

✔ File and Printer Sharing needs to be activated on Erin's computer, and the printer needs to be shared.

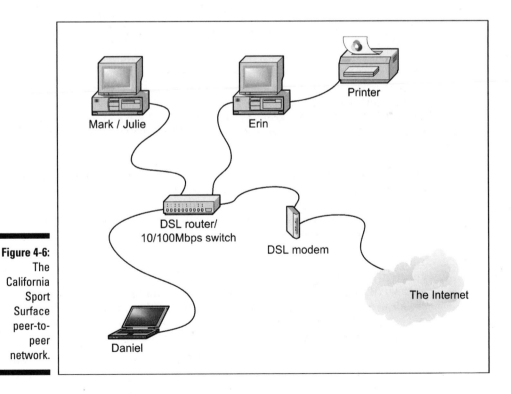

Figure 4-6: The California Sport Surface peer-to-peer network.

Connecting two networks: Creative Course Development, Inc.

Creative Course Development, Inc. (CCD) is a small educational publisher located in central California that specializes in integrated math and science curriculums for primary and secondary grades. The company publishes a variety of course materials, including textbooks, puzzle books, and CD-ROM software.

CCD leases two adjacent office buildings, separated only by a small court-yard. The creative staff, which consists of a dozen writers and educators, works in Building A. The sales, marketing, and administrative staff — all six employees of it — works in Building B.

The product development and marketing staff has 14 relatively new personal computers, all running Windows XP Professional, and a server computer running Windows 2000 Server. These computers are networked by a 100 Mbps UTP network, which utilizes a single 24-port 100 Mbps switch. A fractional T1 line that's connected to the network through a small Cisco router provides Internet access.

The administrative staff has a hodgepodge of computers, some running Windows 98 Second Edition, some running Windows XP, and one still running Windows 95. The staff has a small Windows NT server that meets everyone's needs. The older computers have 10BaseT network cards; the newer ones have 10/100 Mbps cards. However, the computers are all connected to a fairly old 10 Mbps Ethernet hub with 12 ports. Internet access is provided by an ISDN connection.

Both groups are happy with their computers and networks. The problem is that the networks can't communicate with each other. For example, the marketing team in Building A relies on daily printed reports from the sales system in Building B to keep track of sales, and employees frequently go to the other building to follow up on important sales or to look into sales trends.

Although several solutions to this problem exist, the easiest is to bridge the networks with a pair of wireless switches. To do this, CCD will purchase two wireless access points: one to be plugged into the 100 Mbps switch in Building A and the other to be plugged into the hub in Building B. After the access points are configured, the two networks will function as a single net-work. Figure 4-7 shows a logical diagram for the completed network.

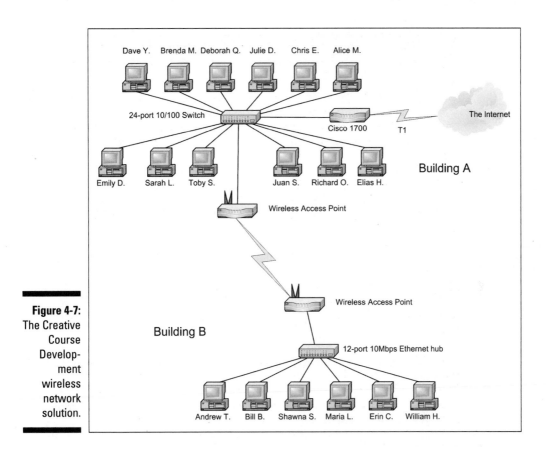

Figure 4-7:
The Creative
Course
Develop-
ment
wireless
network
solution.

Although the wireless solution to this problem sounds simple, a number of complications still need to be dealt with — specifically:

- ✔ Depending on the environment, the wireless access points may have trouble establishing a link between the buildings. It may be necessary to locate the devices on the roof. In that case, CCD will have to spend a little extra money for weatherproof enclosures.

- ✔ Because the wireless access point in Building A will be connected to a switch rather than to a hub, the switch will provide some degree of isolation between the networks. As a result, overall network performance shouldn't be affected.

✔ Before the networks were connected, each network had its own DHCP server to assign IP addresses to users as needed. Unfortunately, both DHCP servers have the same local IP address (192.168.0.1). When the networks are combined, one of these DHCP servers will have to be disabled.

✔ In addition, both networks had their own Internet connections. With the networks bridged, CCD can eliminate the ISDN connection. Users in both buildings can get their Internet access by using the shared T1 connection.

✔ The network administrator also has to determine how to handle directory services for the network. Previously, each network had its own domain. With the networks bridged, CCD may opt to keep these domains separate, or it may decide to merge them into a single domain. (Doing so requires considerable work, so it will probably leave the domains separate.)

Improving network performance: DCH Accounting

DCH Accounting is an accounting firm that has grown in two years from 15 to 35 employees, all located in one building. Here's the lowdown on the existing network:

✔ The network consists of 35 client computers and three servers running Windows 2000 Server.

✔ The 35 client computers all run Windows XP Professional.

✔ The client computers all have 10/100 Mbps Ethernet interfaces; a few have 10/100/1000 interfaces.

✔ The servers have 10/100 Mbps cards.

✔ All offices in the building are wired with Category 5 wiring to a central wiring closet, where a small equipment rack holds two 24-port 10BaseT hubs.

✔ Internet access is provided through a T1 connection with a Cisco 1700 router.

Lately, network performance has been noticeably slow, particularly Internet access and large file transfers between client computers and the servers. Users have started to complain that sometimes the network seems to crawl.

The problem is twofold:

✔ The network has outgrown the old 10BaseT hubs. All network traffic must flow through them, and they're limited to the speed of 10 Mbps. As a result, the new computers with the 10/100 Mbps Ethernet cards are connecting to the network at 10 Mbps, not at 100 Mbps. In addition, the hubs treat the entire network as a single Ethernet segment. With 35 users, the network is saturated.

✔ The network has outgrown the capabilities of Windows 2000 Server. The server computers themselves are old, and the operating system is outdated.

The performance of this network can be dramatically improved in two steps:

1. **Upgrade the network infrastructure.**

   Replace the old network hubs with three 24-port 10/100/1000 Mbps switches.

2. **Replace the aging servers with faster servers running Windows Server 2003.**

   The network is reconfigured, as shown in Figure 4-8.

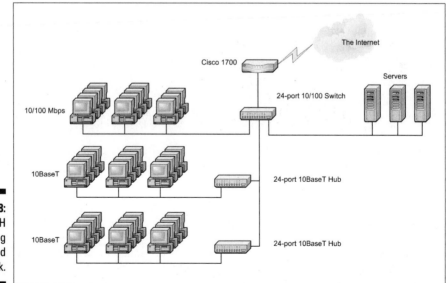

Figure 4-8: The DCH Accounting upgraded network.

Chapter 5

Oh, What a Tangled Web We Weave: Cables, Adapters, and Other Stuff

In This Chapter

▶ Getting a whiff of Ethernet

▶ Checking out the different types of network cable

▶ Installing twisted-pair cable

▶ Working with hubs and switches

▶ Installing network interface cards

▶ Adding professional touches to your cabling

▶ Mulling over other devices (such as repeaters, bridges, and routers)

Cable is the plumbing of your network. In fact, working with network cable is a lot like working with pipe: You have to use the right pipe (cable), the right valves and connectors (switches and routers), and the right fixtures (network interface cards).

Network cables have one more advantage over pipes: You don't get wet when they leak.

This chapter tells you far more about network cables than you probably need to know. I introduce you to *Ethernet,* the most common system of network cabling for small networks. Then you find out how to work with the cables used to wire an Ethernet network. You also find out how to install a network interface card, which enables you to connect the cables to your computer.

What Is Ethernet?

Ethernet is a standardized way of connecting computers to create a network.

Worthless filler about network topology

A networking book wouldn't be complete without the usual textbook description of the three basic *network topologies.* One type of network topology is a *bus,* in which network nodes (that is, computers) are strung together in a line, like this:

A *bus* is the simplest type of topology, but it has some drawbacks. If the cable breaks somewhere in the middle, the whole network breaks.

A second type of topology is the *ring:*

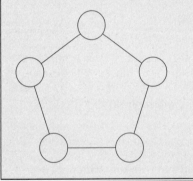

A *ring* is very much like a bus except with no end to the line: The last node on the line is connected to the first node, forming an endless loop.

A third type of topology is a *star:*

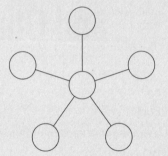

In a star network, all the nodes are connected to a central hub. In effect, each node has an independent connection to the network, so a break in one cable doesn't affect the others.

Ethernet networks are based on a bus design. However, fancy cabling tricks make an Ethernet network appear to be wired like a star when twisted-pair cable is used.

You can think of Ethernet as a kind of municipal building code for networks: It specifies what kind of cables to use, how to connect the cables, how long the cables can be, how computers transmit data to one another by using the cables, and more.

Although Ethernet is now the overwhelming choice for networking, that wasn't always the case. In ye olde days, Ethernet had two significant competitors:

- ✔ **Token Ring:** This IBM standard for networking is still in some organizations (especially where IBM mainframe or midrange systems are in use).
- ✔ **ARCnet:** This standard is still commonly used for industrial network applications, such as building automation and factory robot control.

But the vast majority of business networks use Ethernet. You can purchase inexpensive Ethernet components and cables at almost any store that sells electronics. It's really the only choice for new networks — small or large.

Here are a few tidbits you're likely to run into at parties where the conversation is about Ethernet standards:

✔ Ethernet is a set of standards for the infrastructure on which a network is built. All the network operating systems that I discuss in this book — including all versions of Windows, NetWare, Linux, and Macintosh OS/X — can operate on an Ethernet network. If you build your network on a solid Ethernet base, you can change network operating systems later.

✔ Ethernet is often referred to by network gurus as 802.3 (pronounced "eight-oh-two-dot-three"), which is the official designation used by the *IEEE* (pronounced "eye-triple-e," not "aieeee!"), a group of electrical engineers who wear bow ties and have nothing better to do than argue all day long about things like inductance and cross-talk — and it's a good thing they do. If not for them, you couldn't mix and match Ethernet components made by different companies.

✔ The original vintage Ethernet transmits data at a rate of 10 million bits per second, or 10 Mbps. (*Mbps* is usually pronounced "megabits per second.") Because 8 bits are in a byte, that translates into roughly 1.2 million bytes per second. In practice, Ethernet can't move information that fast because data must be transmitted in packages of no more than 1,500 bytes, called *packets*. So, 150KB of information has to be split into 100 packets.

Ethernet's transmission speed has nothing to do with how fast electrical signals move on the cable. The electrical signals travel at about 70 percent of the speed of light, or as Captain Picard would say, "Warp factor point-seven-oh."

✔ The newer version of Ethernet, and now the most common, is *Fast Ethernet,* or *100 Mbps Ethernet,* moves data ten times as fast as normal Ethernet. Because Fast Ethernet moves data at a whopping 100 Mbps and uses twisted-pair cabling, it's often called *100BaseT* (and sometimes *100BaseT*X).

✔ An even faster version of Ethernet, known as *Gigabit Ethernet,* is also available. Gigabit Ethernet components were once expensive enough that they were used only for speed-critical parts of the network, such as connecting servers to the network switches. However, gigabit Ethernet has dropped in price enough that many desktop computers are connected to the network at gigabit speed.

✔ Most networking components that you can buy these days support both 10 Mbps and 100 Mbps Ethernet. These components are called *10/100 Mbps components* because they support both speeds. Network components that support all three speeds are called *10/100/1000 Mbps components*.

All about Cable

Although you can use wireless technology to create networks without cables, most networks still use cables to physically connect each computer to the network. Over the years, various types of cables have been used with Ethernet networks. Almost all networks are now built with *twisted-pair cable*. In this type of cable, pairs of wires are twisted around each other to reduce electrical interference. (You almost need a PhD in physics to understand why twisting the wires helps to reduce interference, so don't feel bad if this concept doesn't make sense.)

You may encounter other types of cable in an existing network; for example, on older networks, you may encounter two types of *coaxial* cable (also known as *coax,* pronounced "COE-ax"). The first type resembles television cable and is known as RG-58 cable. The second type is a thick, yellow cable that used to be the only type of cable used for Ethernet. You may also encounter fiber-optic cables that span long distances at high speeds or thick twisted-pair bundles that carry multiple sets of twisted-pair cable between wiring closets in a large building. Most networks, however, use simple twisted-pair cable.

Twisted-pair cable is sometimes called *UTP.* (The *U* stands for *u*nshielded, but "twisted-pair" is the standard name.) Figure 5-1 shows a twisted-pair cable.

Figure 5-1:
Twisted-pair
cable.

When you use UTP cable to construct an Ethernet network, you connect the computers in a star arrangement, as Figure 5-2 illustrates. In the center of this star is a device called a *switch.* Depending on the model, Ethernet hubs enable you to connect from 4 to 48 computers (or more) by using twisted-pair cable.

In the UTP star arrangement, if one cable goes bad, only the computer attached to that cable is affected. The rest of the network continues to chug along.

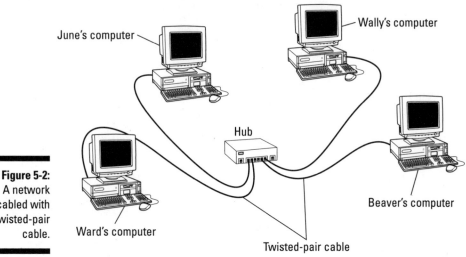

Figure 5-2:
A network cabled with twisted-pair cable.

Labels in figure: June's computer · Wally's computer · Hub · Beaver's computer · Ward's computer · Twisted-pair cable

Cable categories

Twisted-pair cable comes in various grades called *categories*. These categories are specified by the ANSI/EIA Standard 568. (ANSI stands for American National Standards Institute; EIA stands for Electronic Industries Association). The standards indicate the data capacity — or *bandwidth* — of the cable. Table 5-1 lists the various categories of twisted-pair cable.

Although higher-category cables are more expensive, the real cost of installing Ethernet cabling is the labor required to pull the cables through the walls. You should never install anything less than Category 5e cable. And, if at all possible, invest in Category 6 cable, to allow for future upgrades to your network.

To sound like the cool kids, say "Cat 6" rather than "Category 6."

Table 5-1	Twisted-Pair Cable Categories	
Category	*Maximum Data Rate*	*Intended Use*
1	1 Mbps	Voice only
2	4 Mbps	4 Mbps Token Ring
3	16 Mbps	10BaseT Ethernet
4	20 Mbps	16 Mbps Token Ring

(continued)

Table 5-1 *(continued)*

Category	Maximum Data Rate	Intended Use
5	100 Mbps (2-pair)	100BaseT Ethernet
	1000 Mbps (4-pair)	1000BaseTX
5e	1000 Mbps (2-pair)	1000BaseT
6	1000 Mbps (2-pair)	1000BaseT and faster broadband applications
6a	10000 Mbps (2-pair)	Future standard that will provide for 10 Gbps Ethernet

What's with the pairs?

Most twisted-pair cable has four pairs of wires, for a total of eight wires. Standard Ethernet uses only two of the pairs, so the other two pairs are unused. You may be tempted to save money by purchasing cable with just two pairs of wires, but that's a bad idea. If a network cable develops a problem, you can sometimes fix it by switching over to one of the extra pairs. If you use two-pair cable, though, you don't have any spare pairs to use.

Don't use the extra pairs for some other purpose, such as a *voice line* or *a second data line.* The electrical "noise" in the extra wires can interfere with your network.

To shield or not to shield

Unshielded twisted-pair cable, or *UTP,* is designed for normal office environments. When you use UTP cable, you must be careful not to route cable close to fluorescent light fixtures, air conditioners, or electric motors (such as automatic door motors or elevator motors). UTP is the least expensive type of cable.

In environments that have a lot of electrical interference (such as factories), you may want to use *shielded twisted-pair* cable, also known as *STP.* Because STP can be as much as three times more expensive than regular UTP, you don't want to use STP unless you have to. With a little care, UTP can withstand the amount of electrical interference found in a normal office environment.

Most STP cable is shielded by a layer of aluminum foil. For buildings with unusually high amounts of electrical interference, the more expensive braided-copper shielding offers even more protection.

When to use plenum cable

The outer sheath of shielded and unshielded twisted-pair cable comes in two kinds:

- *PVC cable* is the most common and least expensive type.

- *Plenum cable* is a special type of fire-retardant cable designed for use in the plenum space (definition coming right up) of a building. Plenum cable has a special Teflon coating that not only resists heat but also gives off fewer toxic fumes if it does burn. Unfortunately, plenum cable costs more than twice as much as ordinary PVC cable.

Most local building codes require plenum cable when the wiring is installed in the building's *plenum space* (a compartment that's part of the building's air-distribution system, usually the space above a suspended ceiling or under a raised floor).

The area above a suspended ceiling is *not* a plenum space *if* both the delivery and return lines of the air-conditioning and heating systems are ducted. Plenum cable is required only if the air-conditioning and heating systems are not ducted. When in doubt, have the local inspector look at your facility before you install cable.

Sometimes solid, sometimes stranded

The actual copper wire that comprises the cable comes in two varieties: solid and stranded. Your network will have some of each:

- In *stranded cable,* each conductor is made from a bunch of very small wires that are twisted together. Stranded cable is more flexible than solid cable, so it doesn't break as easily. However, stranded cable is more expensive than solid cable and isn't very good at transmitting signals over long distances. Stranded cable is best used for *patch cables* (such as patch panels to hubs and switches).

  Strictly speaking, the cable that connects your computer to the wall jack is a *station cable* — not a patch cable — but it's an appropriate use for stranded cable. (It's not technically correct, but most people refer to the cables that connects a computer to a wall jack as a patch cable.)

- In *solid cable,* each conductor is a single, solid strand of wire. Solid cable is less expensive than stranded cable and carries signals farther, but it isn't very flexible. If you bend it too many times, it breaks. Normally you find solid cable in use as permanent wiring within the walls and ceilings of a building.

Installation guidelines

The hardest part of installing network cable is the physical task of pulling the cable through ceilings, walls, and floors. This job is just tricky enough that I recommend you don't attempt it yourself, except for small offices. For large jobs, hire a professional cable installer. You may even want to hire a professional for small jobs if the ceiling and wall spaces are difficult to access.

Keep these pointers in mind if you install cable yourself:

- You can purchase twisted-pair cable in prefabricated lengths, such as 50 feet, 75 feet, and 100 feet. You can also special-order prefabricated cables in any length you need. But attaching connectors to bulk cable isn't very difficult.

 Use prefabricated cables only for very small networks and only when you don't need to route the cable through walls or ceilings.

- Always use a bit more cable than you need, especially if you're running cable through walls. For example, when you run a cable up a wall, leave a few feet of slack in the ceiling above the wall. That way, you have plenty of cable if you need to make a repair later on.

- When running cable, avoid sources of interference, such as fluorescent lights, big motors, and X-ray machines.

 Fluorescent lights are the most common source of interference for cables behind ceiling panels. Give light fixtures a wide berth. Three feet should do it.

- The maximum allowable cable length between the hub and the computer is 100 meters (about 328 feet).

- If you must run cable across the floor where people walk, cover the cable so no one trips over it. Cable protectors are available at most hardware stores.

- When running cables through walls, label each cable at both ends. Most electrical supply stores carry pads of cable labels that are perfect for the job. These pads contain 50 sheets or so of precut labels with letters and numbers. They look much more professional than wrapping a loop of masking tape around the cable and writing on the tape with a marker.

 Alternatively, you can just write directly on the label with a permanent marker.

- If you're installing cable in new construction, label each end of the cable at least three times, leaving about a foot of space between the labels. The drywallers or painters will probably spray mud or paint all over your cables, making the labels difficult to find.

✔ When several cables come together, tie them with plastic cable ties. Avoid masking tape if you can; the tape doesn't last, but the sticky glue stuff does. It's a mess a year later. Cable ties are available at electrical supply stores.

✔ Cable ties have all sorts of useful purposes. Once, on a backpacking trip, I used a pair of cable ties to attach an unsuspecting buddy's hat to a high tree limb. He wasn't impressed with my innovative use of the cable ties, but my other hiking companions were.

✔ When you run cable above suspended ceiling panels, use cable ties, hooks, or clamps to secure the cable to the ceiling or to the metal frame that supports the ceiling tiles. Don't just lay the cable on top of the panels.

The tools you need

Of course, to do a job right, you must have the right tools:

✔ Start with a basic set of computer tools, which you can get for about $15 from any computer store and most office-supply stores. These kits include socket wrenches and screwdrivers to open your computers and insert adapter cards.

The computer tool kit probably contains everything you need if

- All your computers are in the same room.
- You're running the cables along the floor.
- You're using prefabricated cables.

If you don't have a computer tool kit, make sure that you have several flat-head and Phillips screwdrivers of various sizes.

✔ If you're using bulk cable and plan on attaching your own connectors, you also need the following tools in addition to the basic computer tool kit:

- **Wire cutters:** You need big ones for coax, smaller ones work for twisted-pair cable. For yellow cable, you need the Jaws of Life.

- **A crimp tool:** You need the crimp tool to attach the connectors to the cable. Don't use a cheap $25 crimp tool. A good crimp tool costs $100 and will save you many headaches in the long run.

   When you crimp, you mustn't scrimp.

- **Wire stripper:** You need this tool only if the crimp tool doesn't include a wire stripper.

✔ If you plan on running cables through walls, you need these additional tools:

- **A hammer.**
- **A keyhole saw.** This one is useful if you plan on cutting holes through walls to route your cable.
- **A flashlight.**
- **A ladder.**
- **Someone to hold the ladder.**
- **Possibly a fish tape.**

A *fish tape* is a coiled-up length of stiff metal tape. To use it, you feed the tape into one wall opening and fish it toward the other opening, where a partner is ready to grab it when the tape arrives. Next, your partner attaches the cable to the fish tape and yells something like "Let 'er rip!" or "Bombs away!" Then you reel in the fish tape and the cable along with it. (You can find fish tape in the electrical section of most well-stocked hardware stores.)

If you plan on routing cable through a concrete subfloor, you need to rent a jackhammer and a backhoe and hire someone to hold a yellow flag while you work. Better yet, find some other route for the cable.

Pinouts for twisted-pair cables

Each pair of wires in a twisted-pair cable is one of four colors: orange, green, blue, or brown. The two wires that make up each pair are complementary: one is white with a colored stripe; the other is colored with a white stripe. For example, the orange pair has an orange wire with a white stripe (the *orange wire*) and a white wire with an orange stripe (the *white/orange wire*). Likewise, the blue pair has a blue wire with a white stripe (the *blue wire*) and a white wire with a blue stripe (the *white/blue wire*).

When you attach a twisted-pair cable to a modular connector or jack, you must match up the right wires to the right pins. It's harder than it sounds; you can use any of several different standards to wire the connectors. To confuse matters further, you can use one of the two popular standard ways of hooking up the wires: EIA/TIA 568A or EIA/TIA 568B, also known as AT&T 258A. Both these wiring schemes are shown in Table 5-2.

It doesn't matter which of these wiring schemes you use, but pick one and stick with it. If you use one wiring standard on one end of a cable and the other standard on the other end, the cable doesn't work.

Table 5-2		Pin Connections for Twisted-Pair Cable	
Pin	*Function*	*EIA/TIA 568A*	*EIA/TIA568B AT&T 258A*
1	Transmit +	White/Green	White/orange wire
2	Transmit −	Green	Orange wire
3	Receive +	White/Orange	White/green wire
4	Unused	Blue	Blue wire
5	Unused	White/Blue	White/blue wire
6	Receive -	Orange	Green wire
7	Unused	White/Brown	White/brown wire
8	Unused	Brown	Brown wire

The 10BaseT and 100BaseT standards use only two of the four pairs, connected to Pins 1, 2, 3, and 6. One pair transmits data; the other receives data. The only difference between the two wiring standards is which pair transmits and which receives. In the EIA/TIA 568A standard, the green pair is used for transmit and the orange pair is used for receive. In the EIA/TIA 568B and AT&T 258A standards, the orange pair is used for transmit and the green pair for receive.

If you want, you can get away with connecting only Pins 1, 2, 3, and 6. However, I suggest that you connect all four pairs, as indicated in Table 5-2.

RJ-45 connectors

RJ-45 connectors for twisted-pair cables aren't too difficult to attach if you have the right crimping tool. The only trick is making sure that you attach each wire to the correct pin and then pressing the tool hard enough to ensure a good connection.

Here's the procedure for attaching an RJ-45 connector:

1. **Cut the end of the cable to the desired length.**

   Make sure that you make a square cut — not a diagonal cut.

2. **Insert the cable into the stripper portion of the crimp tool so that the end of the cable is against the stop.**

   Squeeze the handles and slowly pull out the cable, keeping it square. This strips off the correct length of outer insulation without puncturing the insulation on the inner wires.

3. Arrange the wires so that they lie flat and line up according to Table 5-2.

You have to play with the wires a little bit to get them to lay out in the right sequence.

4. Slide the wires into the pinholes on the connector.

Double-check to make sure all the wires are slipped into the correct pinholes.

5. Insert the plug and wire into the crimping portion of the tool and then squeeze the handles to crimp the plug.

Squeeze it tight!

6. Remove the plug from the tool and double-check the connection.

You're done!

Here are a few other points to remember when dealing with RJ-45 connectors and twisted-pair cable:

✔ The pins on the RJ-45 connectors aren't numbered.

You can tell which is Pin 1 by holding the connector so that the metal conductors are facing up, as shown in Figure 5-3. Pin 1 is on the left.

✔ Some people wire 10BaseT cable differently — using the green-and-white pair for Pins 1 and 2, and the orange-and-white pair for Pins 3 and 6. Doing it this way doesn't affect the operation of the network (the network is color blind) *as long as the connectors on both ends of the cable are wired the same way!*

✔ If you're installing cable for a Fast Ethernet system, be extra careful to follow the rules of Category 5 cabling. Among other things, make sure that you use Category 5 components throughout. The cable and all the connectors must be up to Category 5 specs. When you attach the connectors, don't untwist more than half an inch of cable. And, don't try to stretch the cable runs beyond the 100-meter maximum. When in doubt, have cable for a 100 Mbps Ethernet system professionally installed.

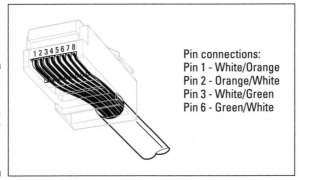

Figure 5-3: Attaching an RJ-45 connector to twisted-pair cable.

Pin connections:
Pin 1 - White/Orange
Pin 2 - Orange/White
Pin 3 - White/Green
Pin 6 - Green/White

Crossover cables

A *crossover cable* can directly connect two devices without a hub or switch. You can use a crossover cable to connect two computers directly to each other, but crossover cables are more often used to daisy-chain hubs and switches to each other.

If you want to create your own crossover cable, you must reverse the wires on one end of the cable, as shown in Table 5-3. This table shows how you should wire both ends of the cable to create a crossover cable. Connect one of the ends according to the Connector A column and the other according to the Connector B column.

Note that you don't need to use a crossover cable if one of the switches or hubs that you want to connect has a crossover port, usually labeled Uplink or Daisy-chain. If the hub or switch has an Uplink port, you can daisy-chain it by using a normal network cable. For more information about daisy-chaining hubs and switches, see the section "Hubs and Switches," later in this chapter.

If you study Table 5-3 long enough and then compare it with Table 5-2, you may notice that a crossover cable is a cable that's wired according to the 568A standard on one end and the 568B standard on the other end.

Table 5-3	Creating a Crossover Cable	
Pin	*Connector A*	*Connector B*
1	White/Green	White/orange
2	Green	Orange
3	White/Orange	White/green
4	Blue	Blue
5	White/Blue	White/blue
6	Orange	Green
7	White/Brown	White/brown
8	Brown	Brown

Wall jacks and patch panels

If you want, you can run a single length of cable from a network hub or switch in a wiring closet through a hole in the wall, up the wall to the space above the ceiling, through the ceiling space to the wall in an office, down the wall, through a hole, and all the way to a desktop computer. That's not a good idea. For example, every time someone moves the computer or even cleans behind it, the cable will get moved a little bit. Eventually, the connection will fail and the RJ-45 plug will have to be replaced. Then the cables in the wiring closet will quickly become a tangled mess.

The alternative is to put a *wall jack* in the wall at the user's end of the cable and connect the other end of the cable to a *patch* panel. Then the cable itself is completely contained within the walls and ceiling spaces. To connect a computer to the network, you plug one end of a patch cable (properly called a *station cable*) into the wall jack and plug the other end into the computer's network interface. In the wiring closet, you use a patch cable to connect the wall jack to the network hubs or switches. Figure 5-4 shows how this arrangement works.

Connecting a twisted-pair cable to a wall jack or a patch panel is similar to connecting it to an RJ-45 plug. However, you don't usually need any special tools. Instead, the back of the jack has a set of slots that you lay each wire across. You then snap a removable cap over the top of the slots and press it down. This action forces the wires into the slots, where little metal blades pierce the insulation and establish the electrical contact.

When you connect the wire to a jack or a patch panel, be sure to untwist as little of the wire as possible. If you untwist too much of the wire, the signals that pass through the wire may become unreliable.

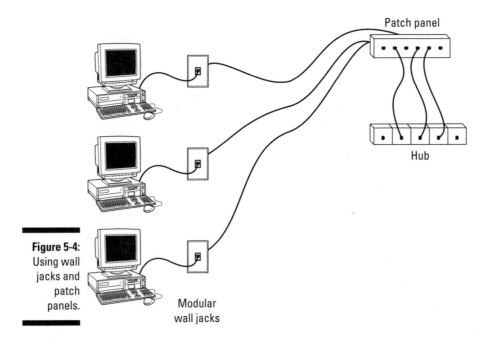

Figure 5-4:
Using wall jacks and patch panels.

Hubs and Switches

When you use twisted-pair cable to wire a network, you don't plug the computers into each other. Instead, each computer plugs into a separate device called a *hub*. Years ago, hubs were expensive devices — expensive enough that most do-it-yourself networkers who were building *small* networks opted for coax cable rather than twisted-pair because networks wired with coax cable don't require hubs.

Nowadays, the cost of hubs has dropped so much that the advantages of using twisted-pair cabling outweigh the hassle and cost of using hubs. With twisted-pair cabling, you can more easily add new computers to the network, move computers, find and correct cable problems, and service the computers that you need to remove from the network temporarily.

Hubs or switches?

A *switch* is simply a more sophisticated type of hub.

Because the cost of switches has come down dramatically in the past few years, new networks are built with switches rather than hubs. (You probably have to find a hub at a garage sale or on eBay.) If you have an older network that uses hubs and seems to run slowly, you can probably improve the network's speed by replacing the older hubs with newer switches.

Switches are more efficient than hubs, but not just because they're faster:

✔ In a hub, every packet that arrives at the hub on any of its ports is automatically sent out on every other port. The hub has to do this because it doesn't keep track of which computer is connected to each port.

Suppose that Wally's computer is connected to Port 1 on an 8-port hub and Ward's computer is connected to Port 5. If Ward's computer sends a packet of information to Wally's computer, the hub receives the packet on Port 1 and then sends it out on Ports 2 through 8. All the computers connected to the hub get to see the packet and determine whether the packet was intended for them.

✔ A switch keeps track of which computer is connected to each port.

If Wally's computer on Port 1 sends a packet to Ward's computer on Port 5, the switch receives the packet on Port 1 and then sends the packet out only on Port 5. This system is faster and also improves the security of the system because other computers aren't shown packets that aren't meant for them.

Ten base what?

The IEEE, in its infinite wisdom, has decreed that the following names shall be used to designate the various types of cable used with 802.3 networks (in other words, with Ethernet):

✔ **10Base5:** Old-fashioned thick coaxial cable (the yellow stuff)

The number *5* in 10Base5 is the maximum length of a yellow cable segment: 500 meters.

✔ **10Base2:** Thin coaxial cable *(Thinnet)*.

The number *2* in 10Base2 stands for 200 meters, which is about the 185-meter maximum segment length for Thinnet cable. (For engineers, the IEEE is an odd bunch; I didn't know that the word *about* could be part of an engineer's vocabulary.)

✔ **10BaseT:** Unshielded twisted-pair cable (UTP).

The letter *T* in 10BaseT stands for *twisted.*

In each name, the number *10* means that the cable operates at 10 Mbps, and *Base* means that the cable is used for baseband networks as opposed to broadband networks. (Don't ask.) Of these three official monikers, 10BaseT is the only one used frequently; 10Base5 and 10Base2 are usually just called *thick* and *thin,* respectively.

Fast Ethernet running over 10BaseT cabling uses the designation 100BaseT.

Working with switches

You need to know only a few details when working with switches. Here they are:

✔ Installing a switch is usually very simple. Just plug in the power cord and then plug in patch cables to connect the network.

✔ Each port on the switch has an RJ-45 jack and a single LED indicator, labeled *Link,* that lights up when a connection is made on the port.

If you plug one end of a cable into the port and the other end into a computer or other network device, the Link light should come on. If it doesn't, something is wrong with the cable, the hub or switch port, or the device on the other end of the cable.

✔ Each port may have an LED indicator that flashes to indicate network activity.

If you stare at a switch for a while, you can find out who uses the network most by noting which activity indicators flash the most.

✔ The ports may also have a collision indicator that flashes whenever a packet collision occurs on the port.

It's perfectly acceptable for the collision indicator to flash now and then, but if it flashes a lot, you may have a problem with the network:

- Usually, the flashing means that the network is overloaded and should be segmented with a switch to improve performance.

- In some cases, the flashing may be caused by a faulty network node that clogs the network with bad packets.

Daisy-chaining switches

If a single switch doesn't have enough ports for your entire network, you can connect switches by *daisy-chaining* them, as shown in Figure 5-5. If one of the switches has an uplink port, you can use a normal patch cable to connect the uplink port to one of the regular ports on the other hub or switch. If neither device has an uplink port, use a crossover cable to connect them. (For instructions on making a crossover cable, see the section, "Crossover cables," earlier in this chapter.)

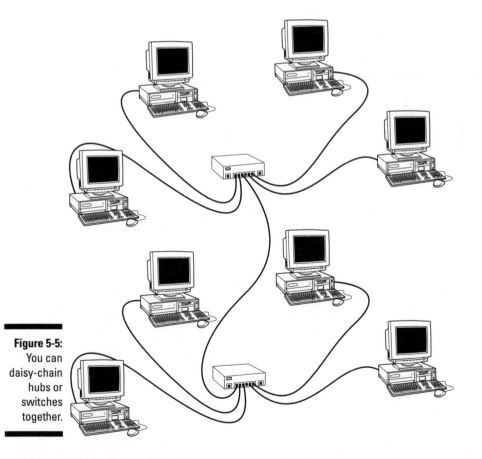

Figure 5-5:
You can daisy-chain hubs or switches together.

On many newer switches, each port on the switch can automatically detect whether it is connected to another switch. In that case, you don't have to use special uplink ports or crossover cables. You can use a standard patch cable to connect the switches by using any available port.

You can often increase the overall performance of your network by using two (or more) connections between switches. For example, you may use two patch cables to create two connections between a pair of switches.

Keep in mind these two simple rules when daisy-chaining hubs:

✔ The number of hubs that you can chain together is limited:

- For 10BaseT networks, don't connect more than three hubs together.

- For 100BaseT, you can chain only two hubs together.

You can get around this rule by using *stackable hubs* (hubs with a special cable connector that connects two or more hubs so that they function as a single hub). Stackable hubs are a must for large networks.

✔ The cable to daisy-chain a 100BaseT hub can't be longer than 5 meters.

If your building is prewired and has a network jack near each desk, you can use a small hub or switch to connect two or more computers to the network by using a single jack. Just use one cable to plug the daisy-chain port of the hub into the wall jack and then plug each computer into one of the hub's ports.

Network Interface Cards

Every computer that connects to your network must have a network interface. Most new computers come with a built-in network interface. But you may need to add a separate network interface card to older computers that don't have built-in interfaces. The following sections show you what you need to know to purchase and install a network interface card.

Picking a network interface card

You can buy inexpensive network interface cards at any computer supply store, and most large office supply stores also carry them. The following pointers should help you pick the right card for your system:

✔ The network interface cards that you use must have a connector that matches the type of cable you use. If you plan on wiring your network with Thinnet cable, make sure that the network cards have a BNC connector. For twisted-pair wiring, make sure that the cards have an RJ-45 connector.

✔ Some network cards provide two or three connectors. I see them in every combination: BNC and AUI, RJ-45 and AUI, BNC and RJ-45, and all three. AUI connectors are pretty much obsolete. As for BNC connectors, get them only if your network has existing coax wiring. If it doesn't, cards that have just RJ-45 connectors are adequate.

✔ Most newer network cards are designated as 10/100/1000 Mbps cards, which means that they work at 10 Mbps, 100 Mbps, or 1000 Mbps. These cards automatically detect the network speed and switch accordingly. Ah, progress.

✔ When you purchase a network card, make sure that you get one that's compatible with your computer. Many older computers can accommodate cards designed for the standard 16-bit ISA bus. Newer computers can accommodate cards that use the PCI bus. If your computer supports PCI, purchase a PCI card. PCI cards are not only faster than ISA cards but are also easier to configure. Use ISA cards only for older computers that can't accommodate PCI cards.

✔ Network cards can be a bit tricky to set up. Each different card has its own nuances. You can simplify your life a bit if you use the same card for every computer in your network. Try not to mix and match network cards.

✔ Some computers come with network interfaces built in. In that case, you don't have to worry about adding a network card.

Installing a network card

Installing a network interface card is a manageable task, but you have to be willing to roll up your sleeves. If you've installed one adapter card, you've installed them all. In other words, installing a network interface card is just like installing a modem, a new video controller card, a sound card, or any other type of card. If you've ever installed one of these cards, you can probably install a network interface card blindfolded.

Here's the step-by-step procedure for installing a network interface card:

1. **Shut down Windows and then turn off the computer and unplug it.**

   Never work in your computer's insides with the power on or the power cord plugged in!

2. **Remove the cover from your computer.**

   Figure 5-6 shows the screws that you must typically remove to open the cover. Put the screws someplace where they won't wander off.

Remove these screws

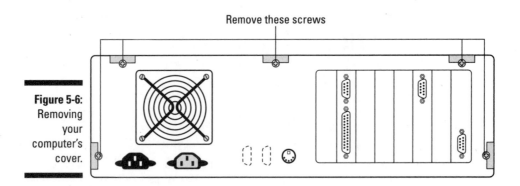

Figure 5-6:
Removing
your
computer's
cover.

3. **Find an unused expansion slot inside the computer.**

   The expansion slots are lined up in a neat row near the back of the computer; you can't miss 'em:

   - Most newer computers have at least two slots known as *PCI slots.*

   - Many older computers also have several slots known as *ISA slots.*

   You can distinguish ISA slots from PCI slots by noting the size of the slots. PCI slots are smaller than ISA slots, so you can't accidentally insert a PCI card in an ISA slot or vice versa.

   - Some computers also have other types of slots — mainly *VESA* and *EISA* slots.

   Standard ISA or PCI networking cards don't fit into these types of slots, so don't try to force them.

4. **When you find the right type of slot that doesn't have a card in it, remove the metal slot protector from the back of the computer's chassis:**

   a. If a small retaining screw holds the slot protector in place, remove the screw and keep it in a safe place.

   b. Pull out the slot protector.

   c. Put the slot protector in a box with all your other old slot protectors.

   After a while, you collect a whole bunch of slot protectors. Keep them as souvenirs, or use them as Christmas-tree ornaments.

5. **Insert the network interface card into the slot.**

   Line up the connectors on the bottom of the card with the connectors in the expansion slot and then press the card straight down. Sometimes you have to press uncomfortably hard to get the card to slide into the slot.

6. **Secure the network interface card with the screw you remove in Step 4.**

7. **Put the computer's case back together.**

Network starter kits

Often, the easiest way to buy the equipment that you need to build a network is to purchase a network starter kit. A typical network starter kit includes everything that you need to network two computers. To add computers, you purchase add-on kits that include everything you need to add one computer to the network.

Suppose that you want to network three computers in a small office. You can start with a two-computer network starter kit, which includes these items:

✔ Two 10/100 Mbps auto-switching PCI Ethernet cards

✔ One 4-port Ethernet 100 Mbps switch

✔ Two 25-foot-long 10BaseT twisted-pair cables

✔ Software for the cards

✔ Instructions

This kit should set you back about $75. It connects two of the three computers. To connect the third computer, purchase an add-on kit that includes a 10/100 auto-switching PCI Ethernet card, another 25-foot-long twisted-pair cable, software, and instructions — all for about $40.

Watch out for the loose cables inside the computer. You don't want to pinch them with the case as you slide it back on.

Secure the case with the screws you remove in Step 2.

8. Turn the computer back on.

If you're using a Plug and Play card with Windows, the card is configured automatically after you start the computer again.

If you're working with an older computer or an older network interface card, you may need to run an additional software installation program. See the installation instructions that come with the network interface card for details.

Other Network Devices

In addition to network interface cards, cables, and hubs or switches, some networks may require one or more of the devices described in the following sections.

Repeaters

A *repeater* is a gizmo that gives your network signals a boost so that the signals can travel farther. It's kind of like the Gatorade stations in a marathon. As the signals travel past the repeater, they pick up a cup of Gatorade, take a sip, splash the rest of it on their heads, toss the cup, and hop in a cab when they're sure that no one is looking.

You need a repeater when the total length of a single span of network cable is larger than the maximum allowed for your cable type:

Cable	Maximum Length
10Base2 (coaxial)	185 meters or 606 feet
10/100BaseT (twisted-pair)	100 meters or 328 feet

For coaxial cable, the cable lengths given here apply to cable segments — not to individual lengths of cable. A *segment* is the entire run of cable from one terminator to another and may include more than one computer. In other words, if you connect ten computers with 25-foot lengths of thin coaxial cable, the total length of the segment is 225 feet. (Made you look! Only nine cables are required to connect ten computers — that's why it's not 250 feet.)

For 10BaseT or 100BaseT cable, the 100-meter length limit applies to the cable that connects a computer to the hub or the cable that connects hubs to each other when hubs are daisy-chained with twisted-pair cable. In other words, you can connect each computer to the hub with no more than 100 meters of cable, and you can connect hubs to each other with no more than 100 meters of cable.

Figure 5-7 shows how you can use a repeater to connect two groups of computers that are too far apart to be strung on a single segment. When you use a repeater like this, the repeater divides the cable into two segments. The cable length limit still applies to the cable on each side of the repeater.

Ponder these points when you lie awake tonight thinking about repeaters:

- ✔ Repeaters are used only with Ethernet networks wired with coaxial cable; twisted-pair networks don't use repeaters.

  Actually, that's not quite true: twisted-pair *does* use repeaters. It's just that the repeater isn't a separate device. In a twisted-pair network, the switch is a multiport repeater. That's why the cable used to attach each computer to the switch is considered a separate segment.

- ✔ Some 10/100BaseT switches have a BNC connector on the back. This BNC connector is a Thinnet repeater that enables you to attach a full 185-meter Thinnet segment. The segment can attach other computers, 10BaseT hubs, or a combination of both.

- ✔ A basic rule of Ethernet life is that a signal can't pass through more than three repeaters on its way from one node to another.

  You can have more than three repeaters or switches. If you do, you have to carefully plan the network cabling so that the three-repeater rule isn't violated.

✔ A two-port 10Base2 repeater costs about $200. (Sheesh! I guess that's one of the reasons few people use coaxial cable anymore.)

✔ Repeaters are legitimate components of a by-the-book Ethernet network. They don't extend the maximum length of a single segment; they just enable you to tie two segments together.

WARNING!

Beware of the little black boxes that claim to extend the segment limit beyond the 185-meter limit for Thinnet or the 100-meter limit for 10/100BaseT cable. These products usually work, but playing by the rules is better.

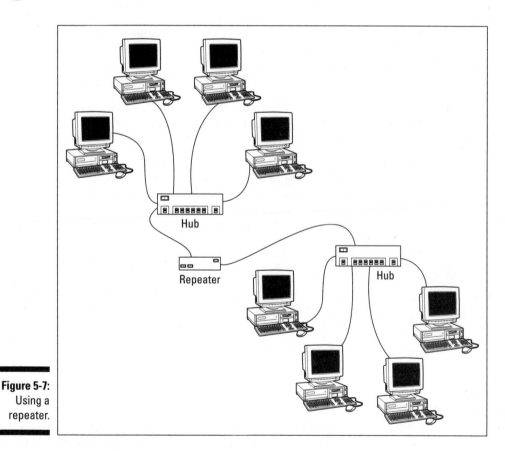

Figure 5-7:
Using a
repeater.

Bridges

A *bridge* is a device that connects two networks. Bridges are used to partition one large network into two smaller networks for performance reasons.

Think of a bridge as a kind of *smart repeater*. Repeaters listen to signals coming down one network cable, amplify them, and send them down the other cable. They do this blindly, paying no attention to the content of the messages they repeat.

In contrast, a bridge is a little smarter about the messages that come down the pike. For starters, most bridges can listen to the network and automatically figure out the address of each computer on both sides of the bridge. Then the bridge can inspect each message that comes from one side of the bridge and broadcast it on the other side of the bridge, but only if the message is intended for a computer that's on the other side.

This key feature enables bridges to partition a large network into two smaller, more efficient networks. Bridges work best in networks that are highly segregated. For example, your network may consist of two distinct groups of users: the Marketing department and the Accounting department, each with its own servers.

A bridge lets you partition this network so that the Marketing side of the network isn't bogged down by Accounting, and vice versa. The bridge automatically learns which computers are on each side of the bridge and forwards messages from the one side to the other only when necessary. The overall performance of both networks improves, although the performance of any network operation that has to travel over the bridge slows down a bit.

Here are a few additional thoughts to consider about bridges:

✔ Some bridges can translate the messages from one format to another.

 For example, if the Marketing folks build their network with Ethernet and the accountants use Token Ring, a bridge can tie the two together.

✔ You can get a basic bridge to partition two Ethernet networks for about $500. More-sophisticated bridges can cost $5,000 or more.

Routers

A *router* is like a bridge, but with a key difference: Bridges use actual hardware addresses (known as *MAC addresses*) to tell which network node each message is sent to so that it can forward the message to the appropriate segment. However, a bridge can't look inside the message to see what type of information is being sent. A router can. As a result, routers work at a higher level than bridges. Thus, routers can perform additional tasks, such as filtering packets based on their content. (Many routers also have built-in bridging functions, so routers are often used as bridges.)

You can configure a network with several routers that can work cooperatively together. For example, some routers can monitor the network to determine the most efficient path for sending a message to its ultimate destination. If a part of the network is extremely busy, a router can automatically route messages along a less-busy route. In this respect, the router is kind of like a traffic reporter flying in a helicopter. The router knows that the 101 is bumper to bumper all the way through Sunnyvale, so it sends the message on the 280 instead.

Here's some additional information about routers:

✔ Routers used to be expensive and used only on large networks. However, the price of small routers has dropped substantially in recent years, so they're now becoming common even on small networks.

✔ The functional distinctions between bridges and routers — and switches and hubs, for that matter — get blurrier all the time. *Multifunction routers* (which combine the functions of routers, bridges, hubs, and switches) are often used to handle some chores that used to require separate devices.

✔ Some routers are nothing more than computers with delusions of grandeur — along with several network interface cards and special software to perform the router functions.

✔ Routers can also connect networks that are geographically distant from each other by using a phone line (using modems) or ISDN.

✔ One of the main reasons for using routers is to connect a LAN to the Internet. Figure 5-8 shows a router used for this purpose.

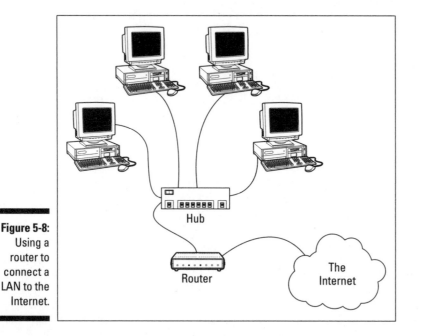

Figure 5-8:
Using a
router to
connect a
LAN to the
Internet.

Chapter 6

Dealing with TCP/IP

In This Chapter

▶ Getting a handle (or two) on the binary system

▶ Digging into IP addresses

▶ Finding out how subnetting works

▶ Understanding private and public IP addresses

▶ Looking at network address translation

▶ Finding out how DHCP works

▶ Understanding how DNS works

*T*CP/IP is the basic *protocol* by which computers on a network talk to each other. Without TCP/IP, networks wouldn't work. In this chapter, I introduce you to the most important concepts of TCP/IP.

This chapter is far and away the most technical chapter in this book. It helps you examine the binary system, the details of how IP addresses are constructed, how subnetting works, and how two of the most important TCP/IP services — DHCP and DNS — work. You don't need to understand every detail in this chapter to set up a simple TCP/IP network. However, the more you understand the information in this chapter, the more TCP/IP will start to make sense. Be brave.

Understanding Binary

Before you can understand the details of how TCP/IP — in particular, IP — addressing works, you need to understand how the binary numbering system works because binary is the basis of IP addressing. If you already understand binary, please skip right over this section to the next main section, "Introducing IP Addresses." I don't want to bore you with stuff that's too basic.

Counting by ones

The *binary* counting system uses only two numerals: 0 and 1. In the decimal system to which most people are accustomed, you use ten numerals: 0 through 9. In an ordinary decimal number, such as 3,482, the rightmost digit represents ones; the next digit to the left, tens; the next, hundreds; the next, thousands; and so on. These digits represent powers of ten: first 10^0 (which is 1); next, 10^1 (10); then 10^2 (100); then 10^3 (1,000); and so on.

In binary, you have only two numerals rather than ten, which is why binary numbers look somewhat monotonous, as in 110011, 101111, and 100001.

The positions in a binary number (called *bits* rather than *digits*) represent powers of two rather than powers of ten: 1, 2, 4, 8, 16, 32, and so on. To figure the decimal value of a binary number, you multiply each bit by its corresponding power of two and then add the results. The decimal value of binary 10101, for example, is calculated as follows:

```
  1 _ 2⁰ = 1 _  1 =   1
+ 0 _ 2¹ = 0 _  2 =   0
+ 1 _ 2² = 1 _  4 =   4
+ 0 _ 2³ = 0 _  8 =   0
+ 1 _ 2⁴ = 1 _ 16 =  16
                     21
```

Fortunately, a computer is good at converting a number between binary and decimal — so good, in fact, that you're unlikely ever to need to do any conversions yourself. The point of knowing binary isn't to be able to look at a number, such as 1110110110110, and say instantly, "Ah! Decimal 7,606!" (If you could do that, Barbara Walters would probably interview you, and they would even make a movie about you — starring Dustin Hoffman and a vintage Buick.)

Instead, the point is to have a basic understanding of how computers store information and — most important — to understand how the hexadecimal counting system works (which is described in the following section).

Here are some of the more interesting characteristics of binary and how the system is similar to and differs from the decimal system:

- ✔ The number of bits allotted for a binary number determines how large that number can be. If you allot eight bits, the largest value that number can store is 11111111, which happens to be 255 in decimal.

- ✔ To quickly determine how many different values you can store in a binary number of a given length, use the number of bits as an exponent of two. An eight-bit binary number, for example, can hold 2^8 values. Because 2^8 is 256, an 8-bit number can have any of 256 different values — which is why a byte, which is eight bits, can have 256 different values.

✔ This powers-of-two concept is why computers don't use nice, even, round numbers in measuring such values as memory or disk space. A value of 1K, for example, isn't an even 1,000 bytes — it's 1,024 bytes because 1,024 is 2^{10}. Similarly, 1MB isn't an even 1,000,000 bytes but rather is 1,048,576 bytes, which happens to be 2^{20}.

Doing the logic thing

One of the great things about binary is that it is very efficient at handling special operations called *logical operations*. Four basic logical operations exist, although additional operations are derived from the basic four operations. Three of the operations — AND, OR, and XOR — compare two binary digits (bits). The fourth (NOT) works on just a single bit.

The following list summarizes the basic logical operations:

✔ AND: An AND operation compares two binary values. If both values are 1, the result of the AND operation is 1. If one or both of the values are 0, the result is 0.

✔ OR: An OR operation compares two binary values. If at least one of the values is 1, the result of the OR operation is 1. If both values are 0, the result is 0.

✔ XOR: An XOR operation compares two binary values. If exactly one of them is 1, the result is 1. If both values are 0 or if both values are 1, the result is 0.

✔ NOT: The NOT operation doesn't compare two values. Instead, it simply changes the value of a single binary value. If the original value is 1, NOT returns 0. If the original value is 0, NOT returns 1.

Logical operations are applied to binary numbers that have more than one binary digit by applying the operation one bit at a time. The easiest way to do this manually is to

1. **Line one of the two binary numbers on top of the other.**

2. **Write the result of the operation beneath each binary digit.**

The following example shows how you calculate `10010100` AND `11011101`:

```
        10010100
AND     11011101
        10010100
```

As you can see, the result is `10010100`.

Introducing IP Addresses

An *IP address* is a number that uniquely identifies every host on an IP network. IP addresses operate at the Network layer of the TCP/IP protocol stack, so they're independent of lower-level Data Link layer MAC addresses, such as Ethernet MAC addresses.

IP addresses are 32-bit binary numbers, which means that, theoretically, a maximum of something in the neighborhood of 4 billion unique host addresses can exist throughout the Internet. You'd think that'd be enough, but TCP/IP places certain restrictions on how IP addresses are allocated. These restrictions severely limit the total number of usable IP addresses, and about half of the total available IP addresses have already been assigned. However, new techniques for working with IP addresses have helped to alleviate this problem, and a new standard for 128-bit IP addresses (known as *IPv6*) is on the verge of winning acceptance.

Networks and hosts

IP stands for *Internet Protocol,* and its primary purpose is to enable communications between networks. As a result, a 32-bit IP address consists of two parts:

- ✔ **The network ID (or network address):** Identifies the network on which a host computer can be found.
- ✔ **The host ID (or host address):** Identifies a specific device on the network indicated by the network ID.

Most of the complexity of working with IP addresses has to do with figuring out which part of the complete 32-bit IP address is the network ID and which part is the host ID. The original IP specification uses the *address classes* system to determine which part of the IP address is the network ID and which part is the host ID. A newer system, known as *classless IP addresses,* is rapidly taking over the address classes system. You come to grips with both systems later in this chapter.

The dotted-decimal dance

IP addresses are usually represented in a format known as *dotted-decimal notation.* In dotted-decimal notation, each group of eight bits, known as an *octet,* is represented by its decimal equivalent. For example, consider the following binary IP address:

```
11000000101010001000100000011100
```

The dotted-decimal equivalent to this address is

```
192.168.136.28
```

Here, 192 represents the first eight bits (11000000); 168, the second set of eight bits (10101000); 136, the third set of eight bits (10001000); and 28, the last set of eight bits (00011100). This is the format in which you usually see IP addresses represented.

Classifying IP Addresses

When the original designers of the IP protocol created the IP addressing scheme, they could have assigned an arbitrary number of IP address bits for the network ID. The remaining bits would then be used for the host ID. For example, the designers may have decided that half of the address (16 bits) would be used for the network and the remaining 16 bits would be used for the host ID. The result of that scheme would be that the Internet could have a total of 65,536 networks and each of those networks could have 65,536 hosts.

In the early days of the Internet, this scheme probably seemed like several orders of magnitude more than would ever be needed. However, the IP designers realized from the start that few networks would actually have tens of thousands of hosts. Suppose that a network of 1,000 computers joins the Internet and is assigned one of these hypothetical network IDs. Because that network uses only 1,000 of its 65,536 host addresses, more than 64,000 IP addresses would be wasted.

As a solution to this problem, the idea of IP address *classes* was introduced. The IP protocol defines five different address classes: A, B, C, D, and E. Each of the first three classes, A through C, uses a different size for the network ID and host ID portion of the address. Class D is for a special type of address called a *multicast address*. Class E is an experimental address class that isn't used.

The first four bits of the IP address are used to determine into which class a particular address fits:

- ✔ If the first bit is a zero, the address is a Class A address.
- ✔ If the first bit is one and the second bit is zero, the address is a Class B address.
- ✔ If the first two bits are both one and the third bit is zero, the address is a Class C address.
- ✔ If the first three bits are all one and the fourth bit is zero, the address is a Class D address.
- ✔ If the first four bits are all one, the address is a Class E address.

Because Class D and E addresses are reserved for special purposes, I focus the rest of this discussion on Class A, B, and C addresses. Table 6-1 summarizes the details of each address class.

Table 6-1			IP Address Classes		
Class	Address Range	Starting Bits	Length of Network ID	Number of Networks	Number of Hosts
A	1-126.x.y.z	0	8	126	16,777,214
B	128-191.x.y.z	10	16	16,384	65,534
C	192-223.x.y.z	110	24	2,097,152	254

Class A addresses

Class A addresses are designed for very large networks. In a Class A address, the first octet of the address is the network ID, and the remaining three octets are the host ID. Because only eight bits are allocated to the network ID, and the first of these bits is used to indicate that the address is a Class A address, only 126 Class A networks can exist in the entire Internet. However, each Class A network can accommodate more than 16 million hosts.

Only about 40 Class A addresses are assigned to companies or organizations. The rest are either reserved for use by the IANA (Internet Assigned Numbers Authority) or are assigned to organizations that manage IP assignments for geographic regions, such as Europe, Asia, and Latin America.

Just for fun, Table 6-2 lists some of the better-known Class A networks. You probably recognize many of them. In case you're interested, you can find a complete list of all the Class A address assignments at www.iana.org/assignments/ipv4-address-space.

Table 6-2	Some Well-Known Class A Networks		
Net	Description	Net	Description
3	General Electric Company	20	Computer Sciences Corporation
6	Army Information Systems Center	22,26, 29, 30	Defense Information Systems Agency
9	IBM	34	Halliburton

Net	Description	Net	Description
11	DoD Intel Information Systems	38	Performance Systems International
12	AT&T Bell Laboratories	40	Eli Lilly and Company
13	Xerox Corporation	43	Japan Inet
15	Hewlett-Packard Company	45	Interop Show Network
16	Digital Equipment Corporation	47	Bell-Northern Research
17	Apple Computer, Inc.	48	Prudential Securities Inc.
18	MIT	54	Merck and Co., Inc.
19	Ford Motor Company	56	U.S. Postal Service

Class B addresses

In a Class B address, the first two octets of the IP address are used as the network ID, and the second two octets are used as the host ID. Thus, a Class B address comes close to my hypothetical scheme of splitting the address down the middle, using half for the network ID and half for the host ID. It isn't identical to this scheme, however, because the first two bits of the first octet are required to be 10, to indicate that the address is a Class B address. Thus, a total of 16,384 Class B networks can exist. All Class B addresses fall within the range 128.x.y.z to 191.x.y.z. Each Class B address can accommodate more than 65,000 hosts.

The problem with Class B networks is that even though they're much smaller than Class A networks, they still allocate far too many host IDs. Very few networks have tens of thousands of hosts. Thus, the careless assignment of Class B addresses can lead to a large percentage of the available host addresses being wasted on organizations that don't need them.

Class C addresses

In a Class C address, the first three octets are used for the network ID, and the fourth octet is used for the host ID. With only eight bits for the host ID, each Class C network can accommodate only 254 hosts. However, with 24 network ID bits, Class C addresses allow for more than 2 million networks.

What about IPv6?

Most of the current Internet is based on version 4 of the Internet Protocol, also known as IPv4. IPv4 has served the Internet well for more than 20 years. However, the growth of the Internet has put a lot of pressure on IPv4's limited 32-bit address space. This chapter describes how IPv4 has evolved to make the best possible use of 32-bit addresses, but eventually all the addresses will be assigned — the IPv4 address space will be filled to capacity. When that happens, the Internet will have to migrate to the next version of IP, known as IPv6.

IPv6 is also called *IP next generation,* or *IPng,* in honor of the favorite television show of most Internet gurus, *Star Trek: The Next Generation.*

IPv6 offers several advantages over IPv4, but the most important is that it uses 128 bits for Internet addresses rather than 32 bits. The number of host addresses possible with 128 bits is a number so large that it would make Carl Sagan proud. It doesn't just double or triple the number of available addresses. Just for the fun of it, here's the number of unique Internet addresses provided by IPv6:

340,282,366,920,938,463,463,374,607,431,768, 211,456

This number is so large that it defies understanding. If the IANA had been around at the creation of the universe and started handing out IPv6 addresses at a rate of one per millisecond, it would now, 15 billion years later, have not yet allocated even 1 percent of the available addresses.

Unfortunately, the transition from IPv4 to IPv6 has been a slow one. Thus, the Internet will continue to be driven by IPv4 for at least a few more years.

The problem with Class C networks is that they're too small. Although few organizations need the tens of thousands of host addresses provided by a Class B address, many organizations need more than a few hundred. The large discrepancy between Class B networks and Class C networks led to the development of subnetting, which is described in the next section.

Subnetting

Subnetting is a technique that lets network administrators use the 32 bits available in an IP address more efficiently by creating networks that aren't limited to the scales provided by Class A, B, and C IP addresses. With subnetting, you can create networks with more realistic host limits.

Subnetting provides a more flexible way to designate which portion of an IP address represents the network ID and which portion represents the host ID.

With standard IP address classes, only three possible network ID sizes exist: 8 bits for Class A, 16 bits for Class B, and 24 bits for Class C. Subnetting lets you select an arbitrary number of bits to use for the network ID.

Two reasons compel us to use subnetting. The first is to allocate the limited IP address space more efficiently. If the Internet were limited to Class A, B, or C addresses, every network would be allocated 254, 65,000, or 16 million IP addresses for host devices. Although many networks with more than 254 devices exist, few (if any) exist with 65,000, let alone 16 million. Unfortunately, any network with more than 254 devices would need a Class B allocation and probably waste tens of thousands of IP addresses.

The second reason for subnetting is that even if a single organization has thousands of network devices, operating all those devices with the same network ID would slow the network to a crawl. The way TCP/IP works dictates that all the computers with the same network ID must be on the same physical network. The physical network comprises a single *broadcast domain,* which means that a single network medium must carry all the traffic for the network. For performance reasons, networks are usually segmented into broadcast domains that are smaller than even Class C addresses provide.

Subnets

A *subnet* is a network that falls within another (Class A, B, or C) network. Subnets are created by using one or more of the Class A, B, or C host bits to extend the network ID. Thus, rather than the standard 8-, 16-, or 24-bit network ID, subnets can have network IDs of any length.

Figure 6-1 shows an example of a network before and after subnetting has been applied. In the unsubnetted network, the network has been assigned the Class B address 144.28.0.0. All the devices on this network must share the same broadcast domain.

In the second network, the first four bits of the host ID are used to divide the network into two small networks, identified as subnets 16 and 32. To the outside world (that is, on the other side of the router), these two networks still appear to be a single network identified as 144.28.0.0. For example, the outside world considers the device at 144.28.16.22 to belong to the 144.28.0.0 network. As a result, a packet sent to this device is delivered to the router at 144.28.0.0. The router then considers the subnet portion of the host ID to decide whether to route the packet to subnet 16 or subnet 32.

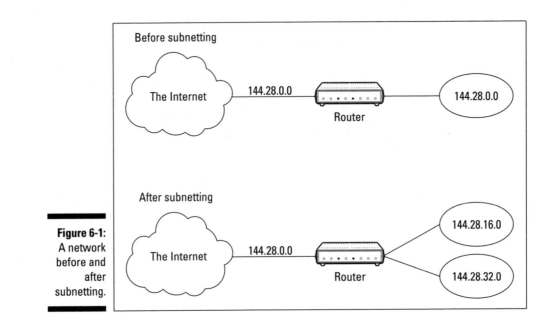

Figure 6-1:
A network
before and
after
subnetting.

Subnet masks

For subnetting to work, the router must be told which portion of the host ID to use for the subnet's network ID. This little sleight of hand is accomplished by using another 32-bit number, known as a *subnet mask*. Those IP address bits that represent the network ID are represented by a 1 in the mask, and those bits that represent the host ID appear as a 0 in the mask. As a result, a subnet mask always has a consecutive string of ones on the left, followed by a string of zeros.

For example, the subnet mask for the subnet, as shown in Figure 6-1, where the network ID consists of the 16-bit network ID plus an additional 4-bit subnet ID, would look like this:

```
11111111 11111111 11110000 00000000
```

In other words, the first 20 bits are ones; the remaining 12 bits are zeros. Thus, the complete network ID is 20 bits in length, and the actual host ID portion of the subnetted address is 12 bits in length.

To determine the network ID of an IP address, the router must have both the IP address and the subnet mask. The router then performs a bitwise operation called a *logical AND* on the IP address to extract the network ID. To perform a logical AND, each bit in the IP address is compared to the corresponding bit in the subnet mask. If both bits are 1, the resulting bit in the network ID is set to 1. If either of the bits is 0, the resulting bit is set to 0.

For example, here's how the network address is extracted from an IP address using the 20-bit subnet mask from the previous example:

```
                144  .   28   .   16  .   17
IP address:   10010000 00011100 00100000 00001001
Subnet mask:  11111111 11111111 11110000 00000000
Network ID:   10010000 00011100 00100000 00000000
                144  .   28   .   16  .    0
```

Thus, the network ID for this subnet is 144.28.16.0.

The subnet mask itself is usually represented in dotted-decimal notation. As a result, the 20-bit subnet mask used in the previous example would be represented as 255.255.240.0:

```
Subnet mask:  11111111 11111111 11111111 11111111
                255  .   255  .   240  .   0
```

Don't confuse a subnet mask with an IP address. A subnet mask doesn't represent any device or network on the Internet. It's just a way of indicating which portion of an IP address should be used to determine the network ID. (You can spot a subnet mask right away because the first octet is always 255, and 255 isn't a valid first octet for any class of IP address.)

The great subnet roundup

You should know about a few additional restrictions that are placed on subnet masks — in particular:

✔ The minimum number of network ID bits is eight. As a result, the first octet of a subnet mask is always 255.

✔ The maximum number of network ID bits is 30. You have to leave at least two bits for the host ID portion of the address, to allow for at least two hosts. If you used all 32 bits for the network ID, that would leave no bits for the host ID. Obviously, that doesn't work. Leaving just one bit for the host ID doesn't work, either. That's because a host ID of all ones is reserved for a broadcast address — and all zeros refers to the network itself. Thus, if you used 31 bits for the network ID and left only one for the host ID, host ID 1 would be used for the broadcast address and host ID 0 would be the network itself, leaving no room for actual hosts. That's why the maximum network ID size is 30 bits.

✔ Because the network ID is always composed of consecutive bits set to 1, only nine values are possible for each octet of a subnet mask (including counting 0). For your reference, these values are listed in Table 6-3.

Table 6-3		The Eight Subnet Octet Values	
Binary Octet	*Decimal*	*Binary Octet*	*Decimal*
00000000	0	11111000	248
10000000	128	11111100	252
11000000	192	11111110	254
11100000	224	11111111	255
11110000	240		

Private and public addresses

Any host with a direct connection to the Internet must have a globally unique IP address. However, not all hosts are connected directly to the Internet. Some are on networks that aren't connected to the Internet. Some hosts are hidden behind firewalls, so their Internet connection is indirect.

Several blocks of IP addresses are set aside just for this purpose — for use on private networks that aren't connected to the Internet or to use on networks hidden behind a firewall. Three such ranges of addresses exist, as summarized in Table 6-4. Whenever you create a private TCP/IP network, use IP addresses from one of these ranges.

Table 6-4		Private Address Spaces
CIDR	*Subnet Mask*	*Address Range*
10.0.0.0/8	255.0.0.0	10.0.0.1–10.255.255.254
172.16.0.0/12	255.255.240.0	172.16.1.1–172.31.255.254
192.168.0.0/16	255.255.0.0	192.168.0.1–192.168.255.254

Understanding Network Address Translation

Many firewalls use a technique called *network address translation* (or *NAT*) to hide the actual IP address of a host from the outside world. When that's the case, the NAT device must use a globally unique IP to represent the host to the Internet; behind the firewall, however, the host can use any IP address it wants. As packets cross the firewall, the NAT device translates the private IP address to the public IP address and vice versa.

One of the benefits of NAT is that it helps to slow down the rate at which the IP address space is assigned. That's because a NAT device can use a single public IP address for more than one host. It does this by keeping track of outgoing packets so that it can match up incoming packets with the correct host. To understand how this process works, consider this sequence of steps:

1. A host whose private address is 192.168.1.100 sends a request to 216.239.57.99, which happens to be www.google.com. The NAT device changes the source IP address of the packet to 208.23.110.22, the IP address of the firewall. That way, Google will send its reply back to the firewall router. The NAT records that 192.168.1.100 sent a request to 216.239.57.99.

2. Now another host, at address 192.168.1.107, sends a request to 207.46.134.190, which happens to be www.microsoft.com. The NAT device changes the source of this request to 208.23.110.22 so that Microsoft will reply to the firewall router. The NAT records that 192.168.1.107 sent a request to 207.46.134.190.

3. A few seconds later, the firewall receives a reply from 216.239.57.99. The destination address in the reply is 208.23.110.22, the address of the firewall. To determine to whom to forward the reply, the firewall checks its records to see who is waiting for a reply from 216.239.57.99. It discovers that 192.168.1.100 is waiting for that reply, so it changes the destination address to 192.168.1.100 and sends the packet on.

Actually, the process is a little more complicated than that because it's very likely that two or more users may have pending requests from the same public IP. In that case, the NAT device uses other techniques to figure out to which user each incoming packet should be delivered.

Configuring Your Network for DHCP

Every host on a TCP/IP network must have a unique IP address. Each host must be properly configured so that it knows its IP address. When a new host comes online, it must be assigned an IP address within the correct range of addresses for the subnet — one that's not already in use. Although you can manually assign IP addresses to each computer on your network, that task quickly becomes overwhelming if the network has more than a few computers.

That's where DHCP, the Dynamic Host Configuration Protocol, comes into play. *DHCP* automatically configures the IP address for every host on a network, thus ensuring that each host has a valid, unique IP address. DHCP even automatically reconfigures IP addresses as hosts come and go. As you can imagine, DHCP can save a network administrator many hours of tedious configuration work.

In this section, you discover the ins and outs of DHCP: what it is, how it works, and how to set it up.

Understanding DHCP

DHCP allows individual computers on a TCP/IP network to obtain their configuration information — in particular, their IP addresses — from a server. The DHCP server keeps track of which IP addresses have already been assigned so that when a computer requests an IP address, the DHCP servers offer it an IP address that isn't already in use.

The alternative to DHCP is to assign each computer on your network a *static IP address:*

- ✔ Static IP addresses are okay for networks with a handful of computers.

- ✔ For networks with more than a few computers, using static IP addresses is a huge mistake. Eventually, some poor, harried administrator (guess who) will make the mistake of assigning two computers the same IP address. Then you have to manually check each computer's IP address to find the conflict. DHCP is a must for any but the smallest networks.

Although the primary job of DHCP is to assign IP addresses, DHCP provides more configuration information than just the IP address to its clients. The additional configuration information is referred to as *DHCP options.* The following list describes some common DHCP options that can be configured by the server:

- ✔ Router address, also known as the default gateway address
- ✔ Expiration time for the configuration information
- ✔ Domain name
- ✔ DNS server address
- ✔ WINS server address

DHCP servers

A DHCP server can be a server computer located on the TCP/IP network. Fortunately, all modern server operating systems have a built-in DHCP server capability. To set up DHCP on a network server, all you have to do is enable the server's DHCP function and configure its settings. In the section, "Managing a Windows Server 2003 DHCP Server," later in this chapter, I show you how to configure a DHCP server for Windows 2003.

A server computer running DHCP doesn't have to be devoted entirely to DHCP unless the network is very large. For most networks, a file server can share duty as a DHCP server, especially if you provide long leases for your IP addresses. (I explain the idea of leases later in this chapter.)

Many multifunction routers also have built-in DHCP servers. So, if you don't want to burden one of your network servers with the DHCP function, you can enable the router's built-in DHCP server. An advantage of allowing the router to be your network's DHCP server is that you rarely need to power down a router. In contrast, you occasionally need to restart or power down a file server to perform system maintenance, to apply upgrades, or to do some needed troubleshooting.

Most networks require only one DHCP server. Setting up two or more servers on the same network requires that you carefully coordinate the IP address ranges (known as scopes) for which each server is responsible. If you accidentally set up two DHCP servers for the same scope, you may end up with duplicate address assignments if the servers attempt to assign the same IP address to two different hosts. To prevent this situation from happening, set up just one DHCP server unless your network is so large that one server can't handle the workload.

Understanding scopes

A *scope* is simply a range of IP addresses that a DHCP server is configured to distribute. In the simplest case, where a single DHCP server oversees IP configuration for an entire subnet, the scope corresponds to the subnet. However, if you set up two DHCP servers for a subnet, you can configure each one with a scope that allocates only one part of the complete subnet range. In addition, a single DHCP server can serve more than one scope.

You must create a scope before you can enable a DHCP server. When you create a scope, you can provide it with these properties:

- ✔ A **scope name,** which helps you to identify the scope and its purpose.
- ✔ A **scope description,** which lets you provide additional details about the scope and its purpose.
- ✔ A **starting IP address** for the scope.
- ✔ An **ending IP address** for the scope.

✔ A **subnet mask** for the scope. You can specify the subnet mask with dotted decimal notation or with Classless Inter Domain Routing (CIDR) notation.

✔ **One or more ranges of excluded addresses.** These addresses aren't assigned to clients. (For more information, see the section, "Feeling excluded?," later in this chapter.)

✔ **One or more reserved addresses.** These addresses are always assigned to particular host devices. (For more information, see the section, "Reservations suggested," later in this chapter.)

✔ The **lease duration,** which indicates how long the host is allowed to use the IP address. The client attempts to renew the lease when half of the lease duration has elapsed. For example, if you specify a lease duration of eight days, the client attempts to renew the lease after four days have passed. The host then has plenty of time to renew the lease before the address is reassigned to some other host.

✔ The **router address** for the subnet.

This value is also known as the *default gateway address.*

✔ The **domain name and the IP address** of the network's DNS servers and WINS servers.

Feeling excluded?

We all feel excluded once in a while. With a wife and three daughters, I know how that feels. Sometimes, however, being excluded is a good thing. In the case of DHCP scopes, exclusions can help you to prevent IP address conflicts and can enable you to divide the DHCP workload for a single subnet among two or more DHCP servers.

An *exclusion* is a range of addresses not included in a scope but falling within the range of the scope's starting and ending addresses. In effect, an exclusion range lets you punch a hole in a scope: The IP addresses that fall within the hole aren't assigned.

Here are a couple of reasons to exclude IP addresses from a scope:

✔ **The computer that runs the DHCP service itself must usually have a static IP address assignment.** As a result, the address of the DHCP server should be listed as an exclusion.

✔ **You may want to assign static IP addresses to your other servers.** In that case, each server IP address should be listed as an exclusion.

Reservations are often a better solution to this problem, as described in the next section.

Reservations suggested

In some cases, you may want to assign a specific IP address to a particular host. One way to do this is to configure the host with a static IP address so that the host doesn't use DHCP to obtain its IP configuration. However, two major disadvantages to that approach exist:

- ✔ **TCP/IP configuration supplies more than just the IP address.** If you use static configuration, you must manually specify the subnet mask, default gateway address, DNS server address, and other configuration information required by the host. If this information changes, you have to change it not only at the DHCP server but also at each host that you configured statically.

- ✔ **You must remember to exclude the static IP address from the DHCP server's scope.** Otherwise, the DHCP server doesn't know about the static address and may assign it to another host. Then comes the problem: You have two hosts with the same address on your network.

A better way to assign a fixed IP address to a particular host is to create a DHCP reservation. A *reservation* simply indicates that whenever a particular host requests an IP address from the DHCP server, the server should provide it the address that you specify in the reservation. The host doesn't receive the IP address until the host requests it from the DHCP server, but whenever the host does request IP configuration, it always receives the same address.

To create a reservation, you associate the IP address that you want assigned to the host with the host's MAC address. Accordingly, you need to get the MAC address from the host before you create the reservation:

- ✔ Usually, you can get the MAC address by running the command `ipconfig /all` from a command prompt.

- ✔ If TCP/IP has not yet been configured on the computer, you can get the MAC address by choosing the System Information command:

   Choose Start➪All Programs➪Accessories➪System Tools➪System Information.

If you set up more than one DHCP server, be sure to specify the same reservations on each server. If you forget to repeat a reservation on one of the servers, that server may assign the address to another host.

How long to lease?

One of the most important decisions that you make when you configure a DHCP server is the length of time to specify for the lease duration. The default value is eight days, which is appropriate in many cases. However, you may encounter situations in which a longer or shorter interval may be appropriate.

✔ The more stable your network, the longer the lease duration can safely exist. If you only periodically add new computers to your network (or replace existing computers), you can safely increase the lease duration past eight days.

✔ The more volatile the network, the shorter the lease duration should be. For example, you may have a wireless network in a university library, used by students who bring their laptop computers into the library to work for a few hours at a time. For this network, a duration as short as one hour may be appropriate.

Don't configure your network to allow leases of infinite duration. Although some administrators feel that this duration cuts down the workload for the DHCP server on stable networks, no network is permanently stable. Whenever you find a DHCP server that's configured with infinite leases, look at the active leases. I guarantee that you'll find IP leases assigned to computers that no longer exist.

Managing a Windows Server 2003 DHCP Server

The exact steps to follow when you configure and manage a DHCP server depend on the network operating system or router you're using. The following procedures show you how to work with a DHCP server in Windows Server 2003. The procedures for other operating systems are similar.

If you haven't already installed the DHCP server on the server, open the Manage Your Server application (choose Start➪Administrative Tools➪ Manage Your Server), click Add or Remove a Role, select DHCP Server from the list of roles, click Next, and then complete the New Scope Wizard to create the first scope for the DHCP server. This wizard asks you to enter a name and description for the scope. Then it asks for the basic IP address range information for the scope, as shown in Figure 6-2.

After you enter the starting and ending IP addresses for the range and the subnet mask used for your network, click Next. The wizard then asks for any IP addresses you want to exclude from the scope, the lease duration (the default is 8 days), the IP address of your gateway router, the domain name for your network, and the IP addresses for the DNS servers you want the client computers to use. After you complete the wizard, the DHCP server is properly configured. It doesn't start running, however, until you authorize it, as described in the next section.

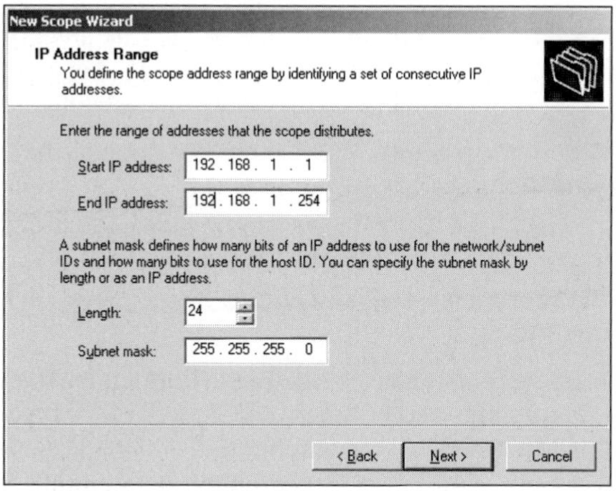

Figure 6-2:
Specifying
the scope's
address
range and
subnet
mask.

After you set up a DHCP server, you can manage it from the DHCP management console by choosing Start⇨Administrative Tools⇨DHCP or by clicking Manage This DHCP Server from the Manage Your Server application. Either way, the DHCP management console appears, as shown in Figure 6-3.

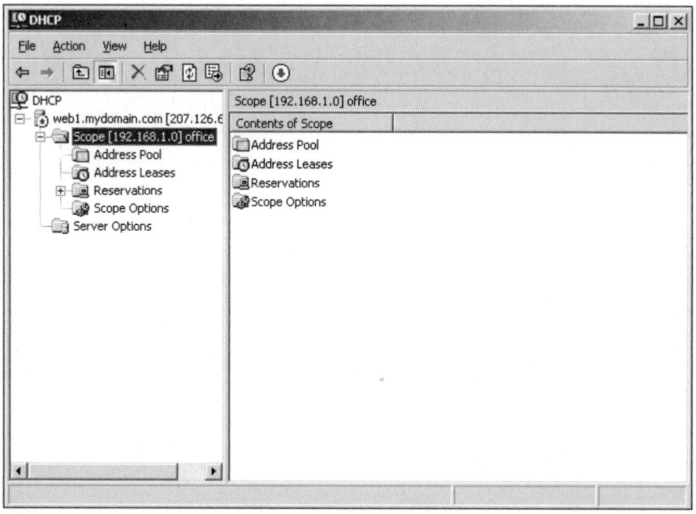

Figure 6-3:
The DHCP
management
console.

From the DHCP console, you have complete control over the DHCP server's configuration and operation. The following paragraphs summarize some of the things you can do from the DHCP console:

- **Authorize the DHCP server, which allows it to begin assigning client IP addresses:** To authorize a server, select the server, choose Action⇨ Manage Authorized Servers, and click Authorize.

- **Add another scope:** Right-click the server in the tree and choose the New Scope command from the menu that appears. This action opens the New Scope Wizard so that you can create a new scope.

- **Activate or deactivate a scope:** Right-click the scope in the tree and choose the Activate or Deactivate command.

- **Change scope settings:** Right-click the scope and choose the Properties command. This action opens the Scope Properties dialog box, which lets you change the scope's starting and ending IP addresses, subnet mask, and DNS configuration.

- **Change the scope exclusions:** Click Address Pool under the scope in the tree. This action lists each range of addresses that's included in the scope. You can add or delete a range by right-clicking the range and choosing the Delete command from the menu that appears. You can also add a new exclusion range by right-clicking Address Pool in the tree and choosing Add New Exclusion from the pop-up menu.

- **View or change reservations:** Click Reservations in the tree.

- **View a list of the addresses that are currently assigned:** Click Address Leases in the tree.

Configuring a Windows DHCP Client

Configuring a Windows client for DHCP is easy. The DHCP client is included automatically when you install the TCP/IP protocol, so all you have to do is configure TCP/IP to use DHCP. To do this, open the Network Properties dialog box by choosing Network or Network Connections in the Control Panel (depending on which version of Windows the client is running). Then select the TCP/IP protocol and click the Properties button. This action opens the TCP/IP Properties dialog box, as shown in Figure 6-4. To configure the computer to use DHCP, select the Obtain an IP Address Automatically and Obtain DNS Server Address Automatically check boxes.

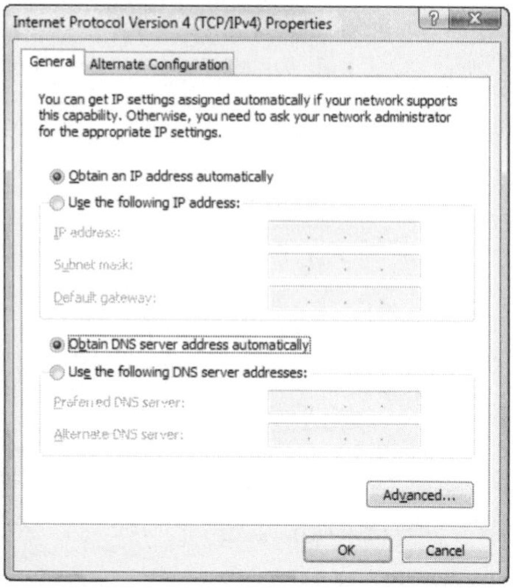

Figure 6-4:
Configuring
a Windows
client to use
DHCP.

Using DNS

DNS, which stands for *domain name system,* is the TCP/IP facility that lets you use names rather than numbers to refer to host computers. Without DNS, you'd buy books from `207.171.182.16` rather than from `www.amazon.com`, you'd sell your used furniture at `66.135.192.87` rather than on `www.ebay.com`, and you'd search the Web at `216.239.51.100` rather than at `www.google.com`.

Understanding how DNS works and how to set up a DNS server is crucial to setting up and administering a TCP/IP network. The rest of this chapter introduces you to the basics of DNS, including how the DNS naming system works and how to set up a DNS server.

Domains and domain names

To provide a unique DNS name for every host computer on the Internet, DNS uses a time-tested technique: divide and conquer. DNS uses a hierarchical naming system that's similar to the way folders are organized hierarchically on a Windows computer. Instead of folders, however, DNS organizes its names into *domains.* Each domain includes all the names that appear directly beneath it in the DNS hierarchy.

For example, Figure 6-5 shows a small portion of the DNS domain tree. At the top of the tree is the *root domain,* which is the anchor point for all domains. Directly beneath the root domain are four *top-level domains,* named `edu`, `com`, `org`, and `gov`.

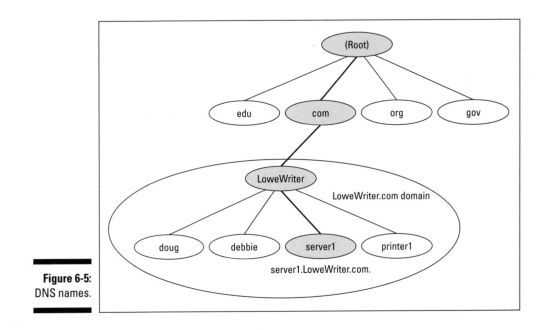

Figure 6-5:
DNS names.

In reality, many more top-level domains than this exist in the Internet's root domain. In fact, at the time I wrote this, there were more than 87 million of them.

Beneath the com domain in Figure 6-5 is another domain named LoweWriter, which happens to be my own, personal domain. (Pretty clever, eh?) To completely identify this domain, you have to combine it with the name of its *parent domain* (in this case, com) to create the complete domain name: LoweWriter.com. Notice that the parts of the domain name are separated from each other by periods, which are pronounced "dot." As a result, when you read this domain name, you should pronounce it "LoweWriter dot com."

Beneath the LoweWriter node are four host nodes, named doug, debbie, server1, and printer1. These nodes correspond to three computers and a printer on my home network. You can combine the host name with the domain name to get the complete DNS name for each of my network's hosts. For example, the complete DNS name for my server is server1.LoweWriter.com. Likewise, my printer is printer1.LoweWriter.com.

Here are a few additional details that you need to remember about DNS names:

✔ DNS names aren't case sensitive. As a result, LoweWriter and Lowewriter are treated as the same name, as are LOWEWRITER, LOWEwriter, and LoWeWrItEr. When you use a domain name, you can use capitalization to make the name easier to read, but DNS ignores the difference between capital and lowercase letters.

✔ The name of each DNS node can be up to 63 characters long (not including the dot) and can include letters, numbers, and hyphens. No other special characters are allowed.

✔ A *subdomain* is a domain that's beneath an existing domain. For example, the com domain is a subdomain of the root domain. Likewise, LoweWriter is a subdomain of the com domain.

✔ DNS is a hierarchical naming system that's similar to the hierarchical folder system used by Windows. However, one crucial difference exists between DNS and the Windows naming convention. When you construct a complete DNS name, you start at the bottom of the tree and work your way up to the root. Thus, doug is the lowest node in the name doug. LoweWriter.com. In contrast, Windows paths are the opposite: They start at the root and work their way down. For example, in the path \Windows\System32\dns, dns is the lowest node.

✔ The DNS tree can be up to 127 levels deep. However, in practice, the DNS tree is pretty shallow. Most DNS names have just three levels (not counting the root), and although you sometimes see names with four or five levels, you rarely see more levels than that.

✔ Although the DNS tree is shallow, it's very broad. In other words, each of the top-level domains has a huge number of second-level domains immediately beneath it. For example, at the time I wrote this book, the com domain had more than two million second-level domains beneath it.

Fully qualified domain names

If a domain name ends with a trailing dot, that trailing dot represents the root domain, and the domain name is said to be a *fully qualified domain name* (also known as an *FQDN*). A fully qualified domain name is also called an *absolute name*. A fully qualified domain name is unambiguous because it identifies itself all the way back to the root domain. In contrast, if a domain name doesn't end with a trailing dot, the name may be interpreted in the context of some other domain. Thus, DNS names that don't end with a trailing dot are *relative names*.

This concept is similar to the way relative and absolute paths work in Windows. For example, if a path begins with a backslash, such as \Windows\ System32\dns, the path is absolute. However, a path that doesn't begin with a backslash, such as System32\dns, uses the current folder as its starting point. If the current folder happens to be \Windows, \Windows\System32\ dns and System32\dns refer to the same location.

In many cases, relative and fully qualified domain names are interchangeable because the software that interprets them always interprets relative names in the context of the root domain. That's why, for example, you can type www. wiley.com — without the trailing dot — rather than www.wiley.com. to go to the Wiley home page in a Web browser. Some applications, such as DNS servers, may interpret relative names in the context of a domain other than the root.

Working with the Windows DNS Server

The procedure for installing and managing a DNS server depends on the network operating system you're using. This section is specific to working with a DNS server in Windows 2003. Working with BIND in a Linux or Unix environment is similar but without the help of a graphical user interface.

You can install the DNS server on Windows Server 2003 from the Manage Your Server application. (Choose Start⇨Administrative Tools⇨Manage Your Server.) Click the Add or Remove a Role link, select DNS Server from the list of server roles, and then click Next to install the DNS server. The Configure a DNS Server Wizard appears, as shown in Figure 6-6. This wizard guides you through the process of configuring the first zone for your DNS server.

Figure 6-6:
The
Configure a
DNS Server
Wizard.

After you set up a DNS server, you can manage the DNS server from the DNS management console. Here, you can perform common administrative tasks, such as adding additional zones, changing zone settings, or adding A or MX records to an existing zone. The DNS management console hides the details of the resource records from you, thus allowing you to work with a friendly graphical user interface instead.

To add a new host (that is, an A record) to a zone, right-click the zone in the DNS management console and choose the Add New Host command. This action opens the New Host dialog box, as shown in Figure 6-7.

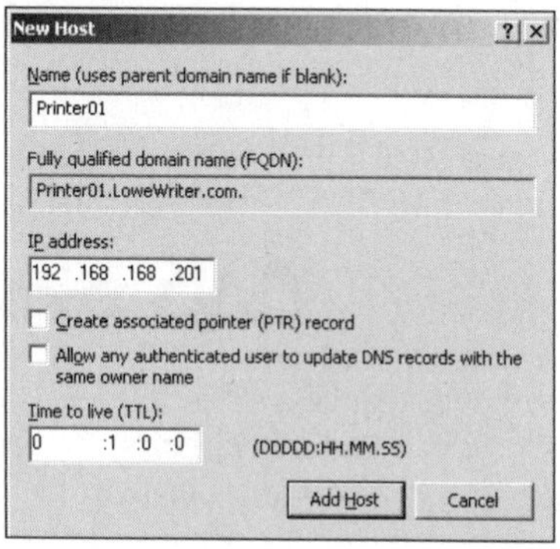

Figure 6-7:
The New
Host dialog
box.

This dialog box lets you specify the following information:

- ✔ **Name:** The host name for the new host.

- ✔ **IP Address:** The host's IP address.

- ✔ **Create Associated Pointer (PTR) Record:** Automatically creates a PTR record in the reverse lookup zone file. Select this option if you want to allow reverse lookups for the host.

- ✔ **Allow Any Authenticated User to Update:** Select this option if you want to allow other users to update this record or other records with the same host name. You should usually leave this option unchecked.

- ✔ **Time to Live:** The TTL value for this record.

You can add other records, such as MX or CNAME records, in the same way.

Configuring a Windows DNS Client

Client computers don't need much configuration to work properly with DNS. The client must have the address of at least one DNS server. Usually, this address is supplied by DHCP, so if the client is configured to obtain its IP address from a DHCP server, it also obtains the DNS server address from DHCP.

To configure a client computer to obtain the DNS server location from DHCP, open the Network Properties dialog box by choosing Network or Network Connections in the Control Panel (depending on which version of Windows the client is running). Then select the TCP/IP protocol and click the

Properties button. This action summons the TCP/IP Properties dialog box, as shown in Figure 6-8:

- ✓ **To configure the computer to use DHCP,** select the Obtain an IP Address Automatically and the Obtain DNS Server Address Automatically options.

- ✓ **If the computer doesn't use DHCP,** you can use this same dialog box to manually enter the IP address of your DNS server.

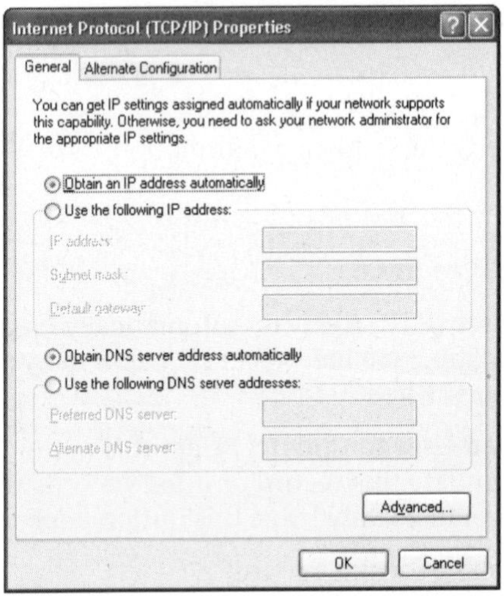

Figure 6-8: Configuring a Windows client to obtain its DNS address from DHCP8m.

Chapter 7

Setting Up a Server

- -

In This Chapter

▶ Thinking about the different ways to install a network operating system

▶ Getting ready for the installation

▶ Installing a network operating system

▶ Figuring out what to do after you install the network operating system

- -

*O*ne of the basic choices that you must make before you proceed any further in building your network is to decide which *network operating system (NOS)* to use as the foundation for your network. This chapter begins with a description of several important features found in all network operating systems. Next, it provides an overview of the advantages and disadvantages of the most popular network operating systems.

Of course, your work doesn't end with the selection of an NOS. You must then install and configure the NOS to get it working. This chapter provides an overview of what's involved with installing and configuring the most popular NOS choice, Windows Server 2003.

Network Operating System Features

All network operating systems must provide certain core functions, such as connecting to other computers on the network, sharing files and other resources, and providing for security. In the following sections, I describe some core NOS features in general terms.

Network support

It goes without saying that a network operating system should support networks. (I can picture Mike Myers in his classic *Saturday Night Live* role as Linda Richman, host of *Coffee Talk,* saying "I'm getting a little *verklempt* . . . talk amongst yourselves . . . I'll give you a topic: Network operating systems do not network, nor do they operate. Discuss.")

That requires a range of technical capabilities:

- ✔ A network operating system must support a wide variety of *networking protocols* to meet the needs of its users.

  A large network typically consists of a mixture of various versions of Windows, as well as Macintosh and Linux computers. As a result, the server may need to simultaneously support TCP/IP, NetBIOS, and AppleTalk protocols.

- ✔ Many servers have more than one network interface card installed. In that case, the NOS must be able to support *multiple network connections:*

  - Ideally, the NOS should be able to balance the network load among its network interfaces.

  - If one of the connections fails, the NOS should be able to seamlessly switch to another connection.

- ✔ Most network operating systems include a built-in capability to function as a *router* that connects two networks.

  The NOS router functions should also include *firewall* features to keep unauthorized packets from entering the local network.

File-sharing services

One of the most important functions of a network operating system is to share resources with other network users. The most common resource that's shared is the server's *file system* — organized disk space that a network server must be able to share (in whole or in part) with other users. In effect, those users can treat the server's disk space as an extension of their own computers' disk space.

The NOS allows the system administrator to determine which portions of the server's file system to share.

Although an entire hard drive can be shared, it isn't commonly done. Instead, individual directories or folders are shared. The administrator can control which users are allowed to access each shared folder.

Because file sharing is the reason many network servers exist, network operating systems have more sophisticated disk management features than are found in desktop operating systems. For example, most network operating systems can manage two or more hard drives as though they were a single drive. In addition, most can create a *mirror* — an automatic backup copy of a drive — on a second drive.

Multitasking

Only one user at a time uses a desktop computer; however, multiple users simultaneously use server computers. As a result, a network operating system must provide support for multiple users who access the server remotely via the network.

At the heart of multiuser support is *multitasking* — a technique that slices processing time microthin and juggles the pieces lightning fast among running programs. It's how an operating system can execute more than one program (a *task* or a *process*) at a time. Multitasking operating systems are like the guy who used to spin plates balanced on sticks on the old *Ed Sullivan Show*. He'd run from plate to plate, trying to keep them all spinning so that they wouldn't fall off the sticks. To make it challenging, he'd do it blindfolded or riding on a unicycle. Substitute programs for the plates and file management for the unicycle, and there you are.

Although multitasking creates the *appearance* that two or more programs are executing on the computer at the same time, in reality a computer with a single processor can execute only one program at a time. The operating system switches the CPU from one program to another to create the appearance that several programs are executing simultaneously, but at any given moment, only one of the programs is processing commands. The others are patiently waiting their turns. (However, if the computer has more than one CPU, the CPUs *can* execute programs simultaneously — but that's another kettle of fish.)

To see multitasking in operation on a Windows Server 2003 computer, press Ctrl+Alt+Delete to bring up the Windows Task Manager and then click the Processes tab. This displays all tasks that are active on the computer, as shown in Figure 7-1.

Directory services

Directories are everywhere — and were, even in the days when they were all hard copy. When you needed to make a phone call, you looked up the number in a phone directory. When you needed to find the address of a client, you looked her up in your Rolodex. And then there were the nonbook versions: When you needed to find the Sam Goody store at a shopping mall (for example), you looked for the mall directory — usually, a lighted sign showing what was where.

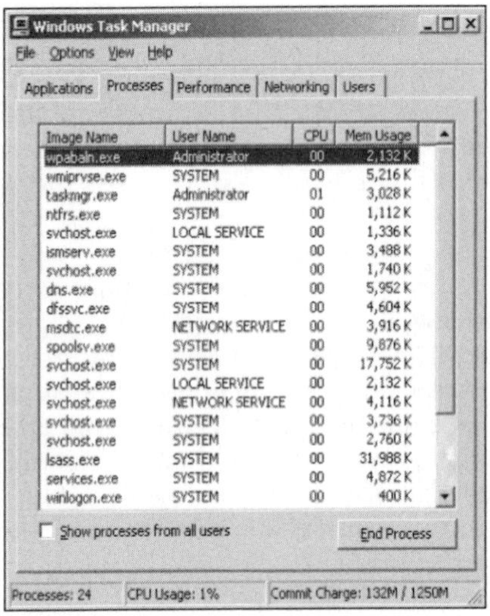

Figure 7-1:
Displaying
active tasks
on a
Windows
Server 2003
computer.

Networks have directories, too, providing information about the resources that are available on the network — such as users, computers, printers, shared folders, and files. Directories are an essential part of any network operating system.

In early network operating systems (such as Windows NT 3.1 and NetWare 3.*x*), each server computer maintained its own *directory database* — a file that contained an organized list of the resources available just on that server. The problem with that approach was that network administrators had to maintain each directory database separately. That wasn't too bad for networks with just a few servers, but maintaining the directory on a network with dozens or even hundreds of servers was next to impossible.

In addition, early *directory services* (programs that made the directory databases usable) were application specific. For example, a server had one directory database for user logons, another for file sharing, and yet another for e-mail addresses. Each directory had its own tools for adding, updating, and deleting directory entries.

The most popular modern directory service is *Active Directory,* which is standard with Windows-based server operating systems. Active Directory provides a single directory of all network resources. It drops the old-style 15-character domain and computer names that were used by Windows NT Server in favor of Internet-style DNS-style names, such as `Marketing.MyCompany.com` or `Sales.YourCompany.com`. Figure 7-2 shows the *Active Directory Users and Computers* tool, which is used to manage Active Directory user and computer accounts on Windows Server 2003.

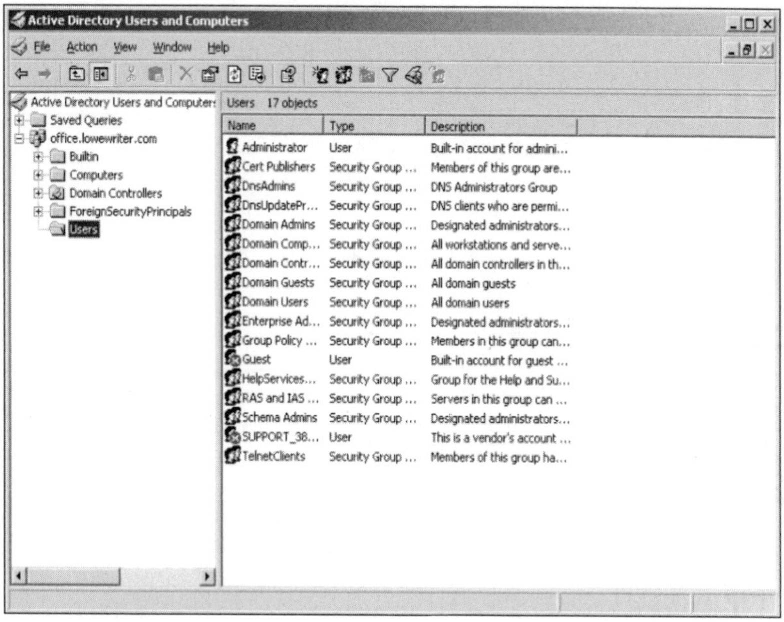

Figure 7-2:
Active
Directory
Users and
Computers.

Security services

All network operating systems must provide some measure of security to protect the network from unauthorized access. Hacking seems to be the national pastime these days. With most computer networks connected to the Internet, anyone anywhere in the world can — and probably will — try to break into your network.

The most basic type of security is handled through *user accounts,* which grant individual users the right to access the network resources and govern which resources the user can access. User accounts are secured by passwords; therefore, good password policy is a cornerstone of any security system. Most network operating systems give you some standard tools for maintaining network security:

- ✔ **Establish password policies,** such as requiring that passwords have a minimum length and include a mix of letters and numerals.

- ✔ **Set passwords to expire after a certain number of days.** Doing so forces network users to change their passwords frequently.

- ✔ **Encrypt network data.** A data-encryption capability scrambles data before it's sent over the network or saved on disk, making unauthorized use a lot more difficult.

Good encryption is the key to setting up a *virtual private network,* or *VPN,* which enables network users to securely access a network from a remote location by using an Internet connection.

✔ **Issue digital certificates.** These special codes are used to ensure that users are who they say they are and files are what they claim to be.

Understanding Windows Server 2003 Versions

The current version of Windows for network servers is Windows Server 2003. Windows Server 2003 builds on Windows 2000 Server, with many new features. Here are just a few of its new features:

✔ A new and improved version of Active Directory with tighter security, an easier-to-use interface, and better performance.

✔ A better and easier-to-use system-management interface: the Manage My Server window. On the flip side — for those who prefer brute-force commands — Windows Server 2003 includes a more comprehensive set of command-line management tools than is offered by Windows 2000 Server. Of course, the familiar Microsoft Management Console tools from Windows 2000 Server are still there.

✔ A built-in Internet firewall to secure your Internet connection.

✔ A new version of the Microsoft Web server, Internet Information Services (IIS) 6.0.

Windows Server 2003 comes in several versions — four, to be specific:

✔ **Windows Server 2003, Standard Edition:** This is the basic version of Windows 2003. If you're using Windows Server 2003 as a file server or to provide other basic network services, this version is the one you use. Standard Edition can support servers with up to four processors and 4GB of RAM.

✔ **Windows Server 2003, Web Edition:** This version of Windows 2003 is optimized for use as a Web server.

✔ **Windows Server 2003, Enterprise Edition:** Designed for larger networks, this version can support servers with up to eight processors, 32GB of RAM, server clusters, and advanced features designed for high performance and reliability.

✔ **Windows Server 2003, Datacenter Edition:** This is the most powerful version of Windows 2003, with support for servers with 64 processors, 64GB of RAM, and server clusters, as well as advanced fault-tolerance features designed to keep the server running for mission-critical applications.

The pricing for Windows Server 2003 is based on the number of clients that will use each server. Each server must have a server license — *and* an appropriate number of client licenses. When you buy Windows Server 2003, you get a server license and (depending on the size of your network) a bundle of 5, 10, or 25 client licenses. You can then purchase additional client licenses 5 or 20 at a time. Table 7-1 lists the prices for the various types of Windows Server 2003 and client licenses.

Table 7-1	Windows 2003 Server Pricing
Product	*Price*
Windows Server 2003, 5 clients	$999
Windows Server 2003, 10 clients	$1,199
Windows Server 2003 Enterprise Edition, 25 clients	$3,999
Client license 5-pack	$199
Client license 20-pack	$799
Windows Server 2003, Web Edition	$399

Other Server Operating Systems

Although Windows Server 2003 is the most popular choice for network operating systems, it isn't the only available choice. The following sections briefly describe two other server choices: Linux and the Macintosh OS X Server.

Linux

Perhaps the most interesting operating system now available is Linux. The free *Linux* operating system is based on *Unix,* a powerful network operating system often used on large networks. Linux was started by Linus Torvalds, who thought it'd be fun to write a version of Unix in his free time — as a hobby. He enlisted help from hundreds of programmers throughout the world, who volunteered their time and efforts via the Internet. Today, Linux is a full-featured version of Unix; its users consider it to be as good as or better than Windows. In fact, almost as many people now use Linux as use Macintosh computers.

Linux offers the same networking benefits of Unix and can be an excellent choice as a server operating system.

Apple Mac OS X Server

All the other server operating systems I describe in this chapter run on Intel-based PCs with Pentium or Pentium-compatible processors. But what about

Macintosh computers? After all, Macintosh users need networks, too. For Macintosh networks, Apple offers a special network server operating system known as Mac OS X Server. Mac OS X Server has all the features you expect in a server operating system: file and printer sharing, Internet features, e-mail, and others.

The Many Ways to Install a Network Operating System

Regardless of which network operating system you choose to use for your network servers, you can use any of several common ways to install the NOS software on the server computer. The following sections describe these alternatives.

Full install versus upgrade

One of your basic NOS installation choices is whether you want to perform a full installation or an upgrade installation. In some cases, you may be better off performing a full installation even if you're installing the NOS on a computer that already has an earlier version of the NOS installed. Here are your choices:

- ✔ If you're installing the NOS on a brand-new server, you're performing a *full installation* that installs the operating system and configures it with default settings.

- ✔ If you're installing the NOS on a server computer that already has a server operating system installed, you can perform an *upgrade installation* that replaces the existing operating system with the new one but retains as many of the settings as possible from the existing operating system.

- ✔ You can also perform a full installation on a computer that already has an operating system installed. In that case, you have these two options:

  - *Delete* the existing operating system.

  - Perform a *multiboot installation,* which installs the new server operating system alongside the existing operating system. When you restart the computer, you can choose which operating system you want to run.

Although multiboot installation may sound like a good idea, it's fraught with peril. I suggest that you avoid the multiboot option unless you have a specific reason to use it. For more information about multiboot setups, see the nearby sidebar "Giving multiboot the boot."

✔ You can't *upgrade* a client version of Windows to a server version. Instead, you must perform either

- *A full installation,* which deletes the existing Windows operating system.

- *A multiboot installation,* which leaves the existing client Windows intact.

Either way, you can preserve existing data on the Windows computer when you install the server version.

Installation over the network

Normally, you install the NOS directly from the distribution discs on the server's CD-ROM drive. However, you can also install the operating system from a shared drive located on another computer, if the server computer already has access to the network. You can either use a shared CD-ROM drive or copy the entire contents of the distribution disc onto a shared hard drive.

Giving multiboot the boot

Multiboot installations enable you to have more than one operating system on a single computer. Of course, only one of these operating systems can be running at any time. When you boot the computer, a menu appears with each of the installed operating systems listed. You can choose which operating system to boot from this menu.

Multiboot is most useful for software developers or network managers who want to make sure that software is compatible with a wide variety of operating systems. Rather than set up a bunch of separate computers with different operating system versions, you can install several operating systems on a single PC and use that one PC to test the software. For production network servers, however, you probably don't need to have more than one operating system installed.

If you still insist on loading two or more operating systems on a network server, be sure to install each operating system into its own disk partition. Although most network operating systems let you install two (or more) operating systems into a single partition, doing so is not a good idea. To support two operating systems in a single partition, the operating systems have to play a risky shell game with key system files — moving or renaming them each time you restart the computer. Unfortunately, things can go wrong. For example, if lightning strikes and the power goes out just as the NOS is switching the startup files around, you may find yourself with a server that can't boot to any of its installed operating systems.

The best way to set up a multiboot system is to install each operating system into its own partition. Then you can use a boot manager program to choose the partition you want to boot from when you start the computer.

Obviously, the server computer must have network access for this technique to work. If the server already has an operating system installed, it probably already has access to the network. If not, you can boot the computer from a floppy that has basic network support.

If you're going to install the NOS on more than one server, you can save time by first copying the distribution CD to a shared hard drive. That's because even the fastest CD-ROM drives are slower than the network. Even with a basic 10/100 Mbps network, access to hard drive data over the network is much faster than access to a local CD-ROM drive.

Automated and remote installations

In case you find yourself in the unenviable position of installing a NOS on several servers, you can use a few tricks to streamline the process:

- ✔ **Automated setup:** Lets you create a setup script that provides answers to all the questions asked by the installation program. After you create the script, you can start the automated setup, leave, and come back when the installation is finished.

    Creating the setup script is a bit of work, so automated setup makes sense only if you have more than a few servers to install.

- ✔ **Remote Installation Services (RIS):** The Microsoft feature that lets you install Windows 2000 Server or Windows Server 2003 from a remote network location without even going to the server computer.

    This feature is tricky to set up, so it's worth it only if you have to install operating systems on a lot of servers. (RIS can also install client operating systems.)

Gathering Your Stuff

Before you install a network operating system, you should gather up everything you need so that you don't have to look for something in the middle of the setup. The following sections describe the items you're most likely to need.

A capable server computer

Obviously, you have to have a server computer on which to install the NOS. Each NOS has a list of the minimum hardware requirements supported by the operating system. Table 7-2 lists two kinds of minimum requirements for Windows Server 2003:

✔ Microsoft's extremely inadequate published requirements

✔ Your author's realistic recommendations for acceptable performance

Table 7-2	Windows Server 2003 Hardware Requirements	
Hardware	*Microsoft's Published Minimum*	*Doug's Realistic Minimum*
CPU	133 MHz Pentium	1 GHz Pentium
RAM	128MB	2GB
Free disk space	1.5GB	20GB

Computer components are inexpensive enough that you shouldn't scrimp on hardware costs.

You should also check your server hardware against the list of compatible hardware published by the maker of your NOS. For example, Microsoft publishes a list of hardware that it has tested and certified as compatible with Windows servers. This list is the *Hardware Compatibility List,* or *HCL* for short. You can check the HCL for your specific server by going to the Microsoft Web site at `www.microsoft.com/whdc/hcl/default.mspx`. You can also test your computer's compatibility by running the Check System Compatibility option from the Windows distribution disc.

The server operating system

You also need a server operating system to install. You need either the distribution discs or access to a copy of them over the network. In addition to the discs, you should have these items:

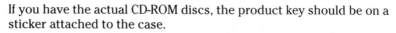

✔ **The product key:** The installation program asks you to enter the product key during the installation to prove that you have a legal copy of the software.

If you have the actual CD-ROM discs, the product key should be on a sticker attached to the case.

✔ **Manuals:** If the operating system came with printed manuals, keep them handy.

✓ **A startup diskette:** If you're installing on a brand-new server, you need some way to boot the computer. Depending on the NOS version you're installing and the capabilities of the server computer, you may be able to boot the computer directly from the distribution disc. If not, you need a floppy disk from which to boot the server.

✓ **Your license type:** You can purchase Microsoft operating systems on a per-server or per-user basis. You need to know which plan you have when you install the NOS.

Check the CD-ROM distribution disc for product documentation and additional last-minute information. For example, Windows servers have a \docs folder that contains several files that have useful setup information.

Other software

In most cases, the installation program should be able to automatically configure your server's hardware devices and install appropriate drivers. Just in case, though, you should dig out the driver discs that came with your devices, such as network interface cards, SCSI devices, CD-ROM drives, printers, and scanners.

A working Internet connection

This item isn't an absolute requirement, but the installation goes much more smoothly if you have a working Internet connection before you start. The installation process may use this Internet connection for several tasks:

✓ **Downloading late-breaking updates or fixes to the operating system:** This can eliminate the need to install a service pack after you finish installing the NOS.

✓ **Locating drivers for nonstandard devices:** This one can be a big plus if you can't find the driver disk for your obscure SCSI card.

✓ **Activating the product after you complete the installation (for Microsoft operating systems):** For more information, see the section "Activating Windows," later in this chapter.

A good book

You spend lots of time watching progress bars during installation, so you may as well have something to do while you wait.

Making Informed Decisions

When you install a NOS, you have to make some decisions about how you want the operating system and its servers to be configured. Most of these decisions aren't cast in stone, so don't worry if you're not 100 percent sure how you want everything configured. You can always go back and reconfigure things. However, you can save yourself time if you make the right decisions up front rather than just guess when the Setup program starts asking you questions.

The following list details most of the decisions that you need to make:

- ✔ **The existing operating system:** If you want to retain the existing operating system, the installation program can perform a multiboot setup, which allows you to choose which operating system to boot to each time you start the computer.

   This is rarely a good idea for server computers. I recommend that you *delete* the existing operating system.

- ✔ **Partition structure:** Most of the time, you want to treat the entire server disk as a single partition. However, if you want to divide the disk into two or more partitions, you should do so during setup. (Unlike most of the other setup decisions, this one is hard to change later.)

- ✔ **Computer name:** During the operating system setup, you're asked to provide the computer name used to identify the server on the network.

   If your network has only a few servers, you can just pick a name, such as Server01 or MyServer. If your network has more than a few servers, follow an established guideline for creating server names.

- ✔ **Administrator password:** Okay, this one is tough. You don't want to pick something obvious, like Password, Administrator, or your last name. On the other hand, you don't want to type something random that you'll later forget, because you'll be in a big pickle if you forget the administrator password.

   Make up a complex password consisting of a mix of uppercase and lowercase letters, some numerals, and a special symbol or two; then write it down and keep it in a secure location where you know that it won't get lost.

- ✔ **Networking protocols:** You almost always need to install the TCP/IP protocol, the Microsoft network client protocol, and file and printer sharing. Depending on how the server will be used, you may want to install other protocols as well.

- ✔ **TCP/IP configuration:** You need to know which IP address to use for the server. Even if your network has a DHCP server to dynamically assign IP addresses to clients, most servers use static IP addresses.

- ✔ **Domain name:** You need to know the domain name for the network.

Making Final Preparations

Before you begin the installation, you should take a few more steps:

- ✔ Clean up the server's disk by uninstalling any software that you don't need and removing any old data that's no longer needed. This step is especially important if you're converting a computer that has been in use as a client computer to a server. You probably don't need Microsoft Office or a bunch of games on the computer after it becomes a server.

- ✔ Do a complete backup of the computer. Operating system setup programs are almost flawless, so the chances of losing data during installation are minimal. But you still face the chance that something may go wrong.

- ✔ If the computer is connected to an Uninterruptible Power Supply (UPS) that has a serial or USB connection to the computer, unplug the serial or USB connection. In some cases, this control connection can confuse the operating system's Setup program when it tries to determine which devices are attached to the computer.

- ✔ Light some votive candles, take two Tylenol, and put on a pot of coffee.

Installing a Network Operating System

The following sections present an overview of a typical installation of Windows Server 2003. Although the details vary, the overall installation process for other network operating systems is similar.

The method you use to begin the installation depends on whether the computer already has a working operating system:

- ✔ If the computer already has a working operating system, simply insert the Windows 2003 Setup disc in the computer's CD-ROM drive. After a moment, a dialog box appears, asking whether you want to install Windows Server 2003. Click Yes to proceed.

- ✔ If you're installing Windows Server 2003 from a network drive, open a My Network Places window, navigate to the shared folder that contains the distribution files, and run `Winnt32.exe`.

- ✔ If the computer doesn't already have a working operating system but can boot from a CD-ROM disc, insert the distribution disc into the CD-ROM drive and restart the computer.

- ✔ If the computer doesn't have a working operating system and can't boot from its CD-ROM drive, insert a bootable floppy disk that has CD-ROM support into drive A and restart the computer. When the MS-DOS command prompt appears, type **d:** to switch to the CD-ROM drive (assuming that drive D is the CD-ROM), type **cd \i386**, and then type **winnt**.

As the Setup program proceeds, it leads you through five distinct installation phases: Collecting Information, Dynamic Update, Preparing Installation, Installing Windows, and Finalizing Installation. The following sections describe each of these installation phases in greater detail.

Phase 1: Collecting Information

In the first installation phase, the Setup program asks for the preliminary information that it needs to begin the installation. A wizard-like dialog box appears so that it gather the following information:

- ✔ **Setup Type:** You can choose to perform a new installation or an upgrade.

- ✔ **License Agreement:** The official license agreement is displayed. You have to agree to its terms to proceed.

- ✔ **Product Key:** Enter the 25-character product key that's printed on the sticker attached to the CD-ROM disc case. If Setup says that you entered an invalid product key, double-check it carefully. You probably just typed the key incorrectly.

- ✔ **Setup Options:** You can click Advanced Options to change the file locations used for Setup, but you should stick to the defaults. If you need to use accessibility features, such as the Magnifier, during Setup, click Accessibility Options and enable the features you need. In addition, if you want to change the language setting, click Primary Language and make your selections.

- ✔ **Upgrade to NTFS:** If you want to upgrade a FAT32 system to NTFS, you need to say so now.

Phase 2: Dynamic Update

In the next installation phase, Setup connects to the Microsoft Web site by using your Internet connection and checks to see whether any installation files have been changed. If so, the updated installation files are downloaded at this time. If you don't have a working Internet connection, you have to skip this phase.

Phase 3: Preparing Installation

In this phase, the computer is restarted and booted into a special text-mode Setup program. After the Welcome screen appears, Setup proceeds through these steps:

- ✔ **Partition Setup:** You're asked to choose the partition that you want to use for the installation. You can reconfigure your partitions from this screen by deleting existing partitions or creating new ones. In most cases, you want to install Windows into a single partition that uses all available space on the drive.

- ✔ **Delete Existing Windows Installation:** This page lets you choose whether you want to delete your existing Windows installation or leave it in place. You should choose to delete it unless you want a multiboot installation.

- ✔ **Convert to NTFS:** If you elected to convert an existing FAT32 partition to NTFS, the conversion takes awhile.

  Now is a good time to get a fresh cup of coffee.

- ✔ **Copying Files:** Now Windows copies its installation files to your hard drive. This step also takes awhile.

Phase 4: Installing Windows

Now that the drive has been set up and the installation files copied, Windows Setup reboots your computer back into Windows mode and begins the actual process of installing Windows. You're taken through the following steps:

- ✔ **Installing Devices:** Windows automatically examines each and every device on the computer and installs and configures the appropriate device drivers. This step can take awhile.

- ✔ **Regional and Language Options:** In this step, you're asked to enter information about your region and language.

  If you're in the U.S., you can accept the defaults. Otherwise, you can change the settings appropriately.

- ✔ **Personalize Your Software:** In this step, you can enter your name and your company name. Your name is required, but the company name is optional.

- ✔ **License Modes:** In this step, you choose whether you purchased per-server or per-device/per-user licensing. You can change this setting later, but you can only change the setting once.

  If you're not sure, double-check the invoice that Microsoft shipped along with the software.

- ✔ **Computer Name and Administrator Name:** Enter the computer name and Administrator account password here.

  Be sure to write down the password and keep it in a secure location. You'll be in serious trouble if you forget it.

- ✔ **Date and Time Settings:** If the date and time information is incorrect, you can change it here.

- ✔ **Network Settings:** In most cases, you can select the Typical option in this step to install the network features that are used most often: Client for Microsoft Networks, Network Load Balancing, File and Printer

Sharing for Microsoft Networks, and Internet Protocol (TCP/IP). If you don't want to use these defaults, you can select Custom Settings, and then configure these features yourself.

✔ **Workgroup or Domain:** Next, you're asked whether the computer is part of a workgroup or a domain. Choose the appropriate option and enter the workgroup or domain name.

✔ **Copying Files:** Windows copies files, updates the registry, and ties up any loose ends. This step can take a long time, so you may want to go for a walk.

Phase 5: Finalizing Installation

To complete the installation, Setup saves your settings and reboots the computer one final time. When the computer restarts, press Ctrl+Alt+Delete to bring up the Log On dialog box. Enter the password you created for the Administrator account and click OK, and you're logged on. Now the real fun begins.

Life after Setup

After the Setup program completes its duty, you still have several tasks to complete before your server is ready to use. The following sections describe these post-installation chores.

Logging on

After the Setup program restarts your computer for the last time, you must log on to the server by using the Administrator account:

1. **Press Ctrl+Alt+Delete to open the Log On to Windows dialog box.**

2. **Type the password you created for the Administrator account during setup.**

3. **Click OK to log on.**

   Windows grinds and whirs for a moment while it starts up and then displays the familiar Windows desktop.

Activating Windows

The Microsoft Product Activation feature is designed to prevent you from installing an illegal copy of Windows or other Microsoft software products.

After you install a product, you have 30 days to activate it. If you don't activate the product within 30 days, it stops working. To prevent that from happening, activate the software immediately after installing it.

Fortunately, activating a Windows server operating system is easy to do if you have a working Internet connection. Windows displays a pop-up reminder in the notification area (in the right corner of the taskbar). Just click this bubble to start the Activation Wizard, as shown in Figure 7-3.

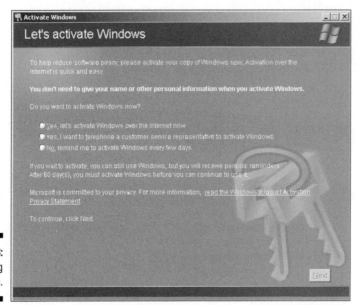

Figure 7-3:
Activating
Windows.

When you activate a Microsoft software product, a unique code is assigned to your system and sent to Microsoft, where the code is stored in a Product Activation database. The code includes information about the configuration of your computer, so Microsoft can tell whether someone tries to install the same copy of the software on a different computer.

The activation code is based on ten hardware characteristics and allows for you to make certain changes to your computer without having to reactivate. The Product Activation feature has a certain amount of built-in tolerance to hardware changes. As a result, you can add another hard drive or more memory to your server without having to reactivate. But, if you change the computer too much, Product Activation thinks you've stolen the software or are trying to install it on a second computer. In that case, you'll have to contact Microsoft and convince them that you've just done a major overhaul of the server computer and should be allowed to reactivate your software. Good luck. For the details about how Product Activation determines when you need to reactivate, see the nearby sidebar "How much change is too much?"

How much change is too much?

Microsoft's Product Activation feature uses an activation code that's based in part on your computer's hardware configuration. In particular, the code includes information about the following ten hardware components of your system:

- ✔ The display adapter
- ✔ The SCSI disk adapter
- ✔ The IDE disk adapter
- ✔ The network adapter's MAC address
- ✔ The amount of RAM
- ✔ The processor type
- ✔ The processor's serial number
- ✔ The hard drive device type
- ✔ The hard drive's volume serial number
- ✔ The CD-ROM, CD-RW, or DVD-ROM drive

To determine whether your computer's hardware has changed, Product Activation uses a voting system that compares the hardware that was present when the product was first installed with the current hardware. For each component that's the same, one vote is tallied — except for the network card's MAC address, which counts for three votes. If you get at least seven votes, you don't have to reactivate the product. However, if you get fewer than seven votes, you have to reactivate.

Suppose that you upgrade the computer's hard drive and add 128MB of memory. Because the network card is the same, it counts for three votes. The SCSI disk adapter, IDE disk adapter, processor type, serial number, and CD-ROM drive score an additional five votes, for a total of nine votes. Because you exceeded seven votes, you don't have to reactivate.

However, suppose also that you then replace the network interface card. Now you don't get the three votes for the network card, so you have only six votes and will need to reactivate the product. (You may be able to thwart this process by making sure that the new hard drive uses the same volume serial number as the old drive.)

You can activate your software in two ways:

- ✔ The easiest way is automatically over the Internet.
- ✔ If you don't have a working Internet connection, you can do it over the phone. However, you'll probably be put on hold for a while until a customer service representative can answer. Then you have to read a 50-digit number over the phone and write down the long confirmation number that you're given to type into the Activation dialog box. Product Activation over the Internet is a lot easier.

If your company has a volume licensing agreement with Microsoft, you don't have to bother with Product Activation; it doesn't apply to products purchased under a volume licensing agreement.

Downloading service packs

Service packs are maintenance updates to an operating system that contain minor enhancements and bug fixes. Most of the fixes in a service pack address security problems that have been discovered since the operating system was first released. The usual way to get service packs is by downloading them from the operating system vendor's Web site.

Depending on the operating system version you installed, you may or may not need to apply a service pack immediately after installing the operating system. The Windows Server 2003 Setup program automatically checks for updates before it installs the operating system, so you shouldn't normally have to install a service pack after running Setup. However, you may need to do so with other operating systems.

Unfortunately, applying service packs is something you have to do throughout the life of the server. Microsoft and other operating system vendors periodically release new service packs to correct problems as they arise.

Testing the installation

After Setup finishes, check to make sure that your server is up and running. Here are some simple checks you can perform to make sure that your server has been properly installed:

- ✔ Check the Event Viewer to see whether it contains any error messages related to installation or startup. Depending on the Windows server version you're using, you can open the Event Viewer by choosing Start➪ Administrative Tools➪Event Viewer or Start➪Program Files➪ Administrative Tools➪Event Viewer. (Non-Windows server operating systems have similar features that allow you to view event logs.)

- ✔ Check your TCP/IP settings by running the command `ipconfig /all` from a command prompt. This command tells you whether TCP/IP is running and shows you the host name, IP address, and other useful TCP/IP information.

- ✔ To make sure that you can reach the server over the network, open a command prompt at a client computer and attempt to ping the server by entering the command `ping hostname` where *hostname* is the name displayed by the `ipconfig` command for the server.

Configuring Server Roles

After you install your server operating system and verify that the installation was successful, your next step is to configure the various services you want the server to provide. You'll find information about configuring services for specific network operating systems in later chapters throughout this book. For now, I want to show you the Configure Your Server Wizard, which is built into Windows Server 2003. This wizard starts automatically the first time you log on to Windows Server 2003. You can get back into this wizard at any time by choosing Start➪All Programs➪Administrative Tools➪Configure Your Server.

After displaying some preliminary configuration information, the wizard lets you set up a default Typical configuration for a first server or a custom configuration that lets you choose which services you want to enable. I suggest that you choose Custom configuration even if this is the first server on your network. That way, you can see which services are being set up and how they will be configured.

Figure 7-4 shows the Server Role page of the Configure Your Server Wizard. This page lets you configure the various roles your server will play. You can use the wizard to configure one of these roles at a time by choosing one of the roles from the list and clicking Next. This action takes you through one or more pages that ask for configuration information for the server role you selected. You eventually come back to this page, where you can configure other server roles.

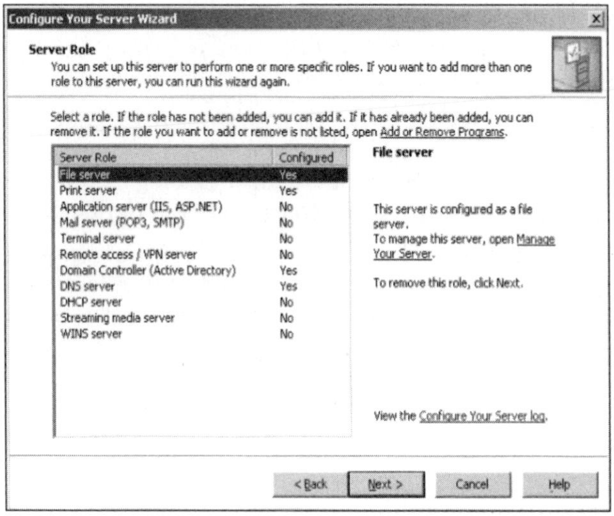

Figure 7-4: You can use this page to configure the roles your server will play.

The following list describes the server roles you can configure:

- **File Server:** This role allows you to create shared folders that can be accessed by network users. You can set up disk quotas to limit the amount of storage available to each user, and you can set up an indexing service that helps users quickly find their files.

- **Print Server:** This role allows you to share printers connected to the server with network users.

✔ **Application Server:** This is a fancy name for Internet Information Services, Microsoft's Web server. If you want the server to host Web sites, you need to configure the application server role.

✔ **Mail Server:** This role provides basic e-mail features based on the standard Internet mail protocols (POP3 and SMTP).

✔ **Terminal Server:** This role lets other users run applications on the server computer as though they're working at the server.

✔ **Remote Access/VPN Server:** This role enables dialup connections and virtual private network connections, which work like dialup connections but operate over the Internet rather than over a private phone line.

✔ **Domain Controller:** This role enables Active Directory and designates the server as a domain controller so that it can manage user accounts, logon activity, and access privileges.

✔ **DNS Server:** This role configures the computer as a DNS server for the network so that it can resolve Internet names. For smaller networks, you'll probably use your ISP's DNS server. You probably need your own DNS server only for large networks.

✔ **DHCP Server:** A DHCP server assigns IP addresses to computers automatically so that you don't have to manually configure an IP address for each computer. On many networks, the router that provides the network's connection to the Internet doubles as a DHCP server. Unless your network is really large, you probably don't need two DHCP servers.

✔ **Streaming Media Server:** If you plan on using digital media (such as audio or video) over your network, you should set up the Streaming Media Server role. One common use of streaming media is for online conferencing using programs, such as Microsoft NetMeeting.

✔ **WINS Server:** This role allows the server to translate NetBIOS names to IP addresses. All Windows networks should have at least one WINS server. However, you need two or more only for very large networks.

Chapter 8

Configuring Windows XP and Vista Clients

....

In This Chapter

▶ Configuring network connections for Windows clients

▶ Setting the computer name, description, and workgroup

▶ Joining a domain

▶ Setting logon options

....

*B*efore your network setup is complete, you must configure the network's client computers. In particular, you have to configure each client's network interface card so that it works properly, and you have to install the right protocols so that the clients can communicate with other computers on the network.

Fortunately, the task of configuring client computers for the network is child's play in Windows. For starters, Windows automatically recognizes your network interface card when you start up your computer. All that remains is to make sure that Windows properly installed the network protocols and client software.

With each version of Windows, Microsoft has simplified the process of configuring client network support. In this chapter, I describe the steps for configuring networking for Windows XP and Vista.

Configuring Network Connections

Windows automatically detects the presence of a network adapter; normally, you don't have to install device drivers manually for the adapter. When Windows detects a network adapter, it automatically creates a network connection and configures it to support basic networking protocols. However, you may need to change the configuration of a network connection manually. The procedures for Windows XP and Vista are described in the following sections.

Configuring Windows XP network connections

The following steps show how to configure your network connection on a Windows XP system:

1. **Choose Start➪Control Panel to open the Control Panel.**

   The Control Panel appears.

2. **Double-click the Network Connections icon.**

   The Network Connections folder appears, as shown in Figure 8-1.

3. **Right-click the connection that you want to configure and then choose Properties from the menu that appears.**

   You can also select the network connection and click Change Settings of This Connection in the task pane.

   Either way, the Properties dialog box for the network connection appears, as shown in Figure 8-2.

4. **To configure the network adapter card settings, click Configure.**

   This action summons the Properties dialog box for the network adapter, as shown in Figure 8-3. This dialog box has five tabs that let you configure the NIC:

   • *General:* This tab shows basic information about the NIC, such as the device type and status. For example, the device shown in Figure 8-3 is a D-Link DFE-530TX+ PCI Adapter. (It's installed in slot 3 of the computer's PCI bus.)

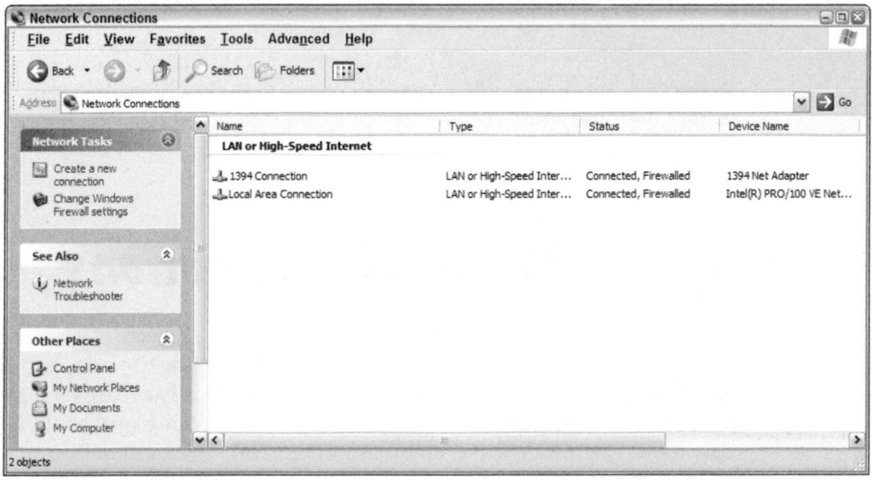

Figure 8-1:
The
Network
Connections
folder.

Name	Type	Status	Device Name
LAN or High-Speed Internet			
1394 Connection	LAN or High-Speed Inter…	Connected, Firewalled	1394 Net Adapter
Local Area Connection	LAN or High-Speed Inter…	Connected, Firewalled	Intel(R) PRO/100 VE Net…

Network Connections

File Edit View Favorites Tools Advanced Help

Back ·   ·   Search   Folders

Address Network Connections   Go

Network Tasks
  Create a new connection
  Change Windows Firewall settings

See Also
  Network Troubleshooter

Other Places
  Control Panel
  My Network Places
  My Documents
  My Computer

2 objects

If you're having trouble with the adapter, you can click the Troubleshoot button to open the Windows XP Hardware Troubleshooter. You can also disable the device if it's preventing other components of the computer from working properly.

- *Advanced:* This tab lets you set a variety of device-specific parameters that affect the operation of the NIC. For example, some cards allow you to set the speed parameter (typically at 10 Mbps or 100 Mbps) or the number of buffers the card should use.

Consult the manual that came with the card before you play around with any of those settings.

- *Driver:* This tab displays information about the device driver that's bound to the NIC and lets you update the driver to a newer version, roll back the driver to a previously working version, or uninstall the driver.

- *Resources:* With this tab, you can use manual settings to limit the system resources used by the card — including the memory range, I/O range, IRQ, and DMA channels.

In the old days, before Plug and Play cards, you had to configure these settings whenever you installed a card, and it was easy to create resource conflicts. Windows configures these settings automatically so that you should rarely need to fiddle with them.

- *Power Management:* This tab lets you set power-management options. You can specify that the network card be shut down whenever the computer goes into sleep mode — and that the computer wake up periodically to refresh its network state.

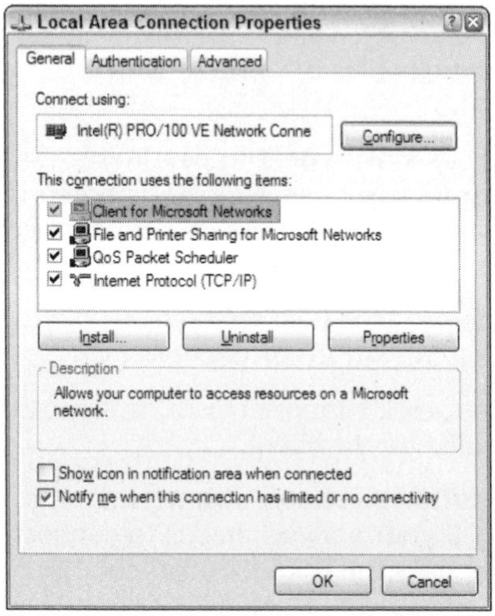

Figure 8-2:
The Properties dialog box for a network connection.

Figure 8-3:
The
Properties
dialog box
for a
network
adapter.

When you click OK to dismiss the network adapter's Properties dialog box, the network connection's Properties dialog box closes. Select the Change Settings for This Connection option again to continue the procedure.

5. **Make sure that the network items your client requires are listed in the network connection Properties dialog box.**

The following list describes the items you commonly see listed here. Note that not all networks need all these items:

- *Client for Microsoft Networks:* This item is required if you want to access a Microsoft Windows network. It should always be present.

- *File and Printer Sharing for Microsoft Networks:* This item allows your computer to share its files or printers with other computers on the network.

  This option is usually used with peer-to-peer networks, but you can use it even if your network has dedicated servers. However, if you don't plan to share files or printers on the client computer, you should disable this item.

- *Internet Protocol (TCP/IP):* This item enables the client computer to communicate by using the TCP/IP protocol.

  If all servers on the network support TCP/IP, this protocol should be the only one installed on the client.

- *NWLink IPX/SPX/NetBIOS Compatible Transport Protocol:* This protocol is required only if your network needs to connect to an older NetWare network that uses the IPX/SPX protocol.

In most modern networks, you should enable TCP/IP only and leave this item disabled.

6. **If a protocol that you need isn't listed, click the Install button to add the needed protocol.**

A dialog box appears, asking whether you want to add a network client, protocol, or service. Click Protocol and then click Add. A list of available protocols appears. Select the one you want to add and then click OK. (You may be asked to insert a disk or the Windows CD.)

7. **Make sure that the network client that you want to use appears in the list of network resources.**

For a Windows-based network, make sure that Client for Microsoft Networks is listed. For a NetWare network, make sure that Client Service for NetWare appears. If your network uses both types of servers, you can choose both clients.

If you have NetWare servers, use the NetWare client software that comes with NetWare rather than the client supplied by Microsoft with Windows.

8. **If the client that you need isn't listed, click the Install button to add the client that you need, click Client, and then click Add. Then choose the client that you want to add and click OK.**

The client you selected is added to the network connection's Properties dialog box.

9. **To remove a network item that you don't need (such as File and Printer Sharing for Microsoft Networks), select the item and click the Uninstall button.**

For security reasons, make it a point to remove any clients, protocols, or services that you don't need.

10. **To configure TCP/IP settings, click Internet Protocol (TCP/IP) and then click Properties to display the TCP/IP Properties dialog box. Adjust the settings and then click OK.**

The TCP/IP Properties dialog box, as shown in Figure 8-4, lets you choose from these options:

- *Obtain an IP Address Automatically:* Choose this option if your network has a DHCP server that assigns IP addresses automatically. Choosing this option drastically simplifies the administering of TCP/IP on your network. (See Chapter 6 for more information about DHCP.)

- *Use the Following IP Address:* If your computer must have a specific IP address, choose this option and then type the computer's IP address, subnet mask, and default gateway address. (For more information about these settings, see Chapter 6.)

- *Obtain DNS Server Address Automatically:* The DHCP server can also provide the address of the Domain Name System (DNS) server that the computer should use. Choose this option if your network has a DHCP server. (See Chapter 6 for more information about DNS.)

- *Use the Following DNS Server Addresses:* Choose this option if a DNS server isn't available. Then type the IP address of the primary and secondary DNS servers.

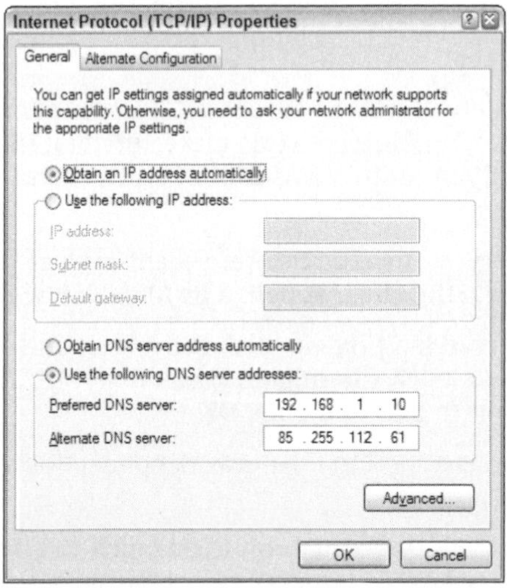

Figure 8-4:
Configuring
TCP/IP.

Configuring Windows Vista network connections

The procedure for configuring a network connection on Windows Vista is similar to the procedure for Windows XP, except that Microsoft decided to bury the configuration dialog boxes a little deeper in the bowels of Windows.

To find the settings you need, follow these steps:

1. **Choose Start⇨Control Panel to open the Control Panel.**

   The Control Panel appears.

2. **Choose View Network Status and Tasks under the Network and Internet heading.**

   This step opens the Network and Sharing Center, as shown in Figure 8-5.

3. **Click Manage Network Connections.**

   The Network Connections folder appears, as shown in Figure 8-6.

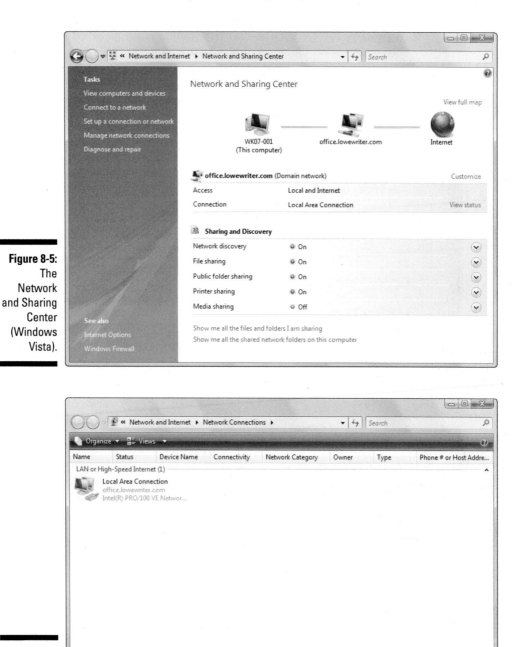

Figure 8-5:
The
Network
and Sharing
Center
(Windows
Vista).

Figure 8-6:
The
Network
Connections
folder.

4. **Right-click the connection that you want to configure and then choose Properties from the menu that appears.**

   The Properties dialog box for the network connection appears, as shown in Figure 8-7. If you compare this dialog box with the dialog box that was shown earlier, in Figure 8-2, you see that they're the same.

5. **Click Configure to configure the network connection.**

   From this point, the steps for configuring the network connection are the same as they are for Windows XP. As a result, you can continue beginning with Step 4 in the previous section, "Configuring Windows XP network connections."

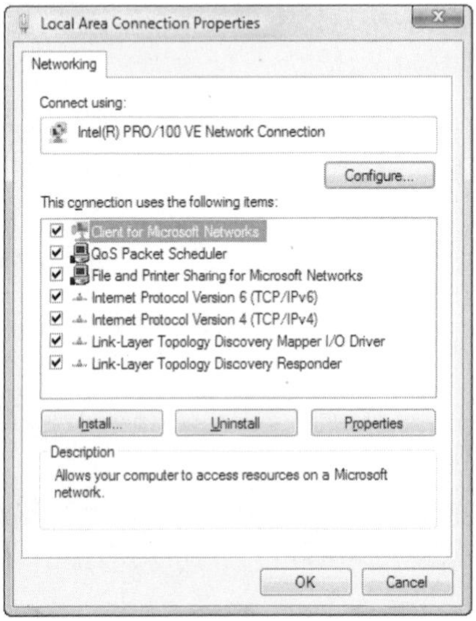

Figure 8-7: The Properties dialog box for a network connection (Windows Vista).

Configuring Client Computer Identification

Every client computer must identify itself to participate in the network. The computer identification consists of the computer's name, an optional description, and the name of either the workgroup or the domain to which the computer belongs.

The computer name must follow the rules for NetBIOS names; it may be 1 to 15 characters long and may contain letters, numbers, or hyphens but no spaces or periods. For small networks, it's common to make the computer name the same as the username. For larger networks, you may want to develop a naming scheme that identifies the computer's location. For example, a name such as C-305-1 may be assigned to the first computer in Room 305 of Building C. Or MKTG010 may be a computer in the Marketing department.

If the computer will join a domain, you need to have access to an Administrator account on the domain unless the administrator has already created a computer account on the domain. Note that only Windows 2000, Windows XP, and Windows Server (NT, 2000, and 2003) computers can join a domain. (Windows 98 or 95 users can access the domain's resources by logging on to the domain as users, but domain computer accounts for Windows 9*x* clients aren't required.)

When you install Windows on the client system, the Setup program asks for the computer name and workstation or domain information. You can change this information later, if you want. The procedure varies depending on whether you're using Windows XP or Windows Vista.

Configuring Windows XP computer identification

To change the computer identification in Windows XP, follow these steps:

1. **Open the Control Panel and double-click the System icon to open the System Properties dialog box.**

2. **Click the Computer Name tab.**

   The computer identification information is displayed.

3. **Click the Change button.**

   This step displays the Computer Name Changes dialog box, as shown in Figure 8-8.

4. **Type the new computer name and then specify the workgroup or domain information.**

   To join a domain, select the Domain radio button and type the domain name into the appropriate text box. To join a workgroup, select the Workgroup radio button and type the workgroup name in the corresponding text box.

5. **Click OK.**

6. **If you're prompted, enter the username and password for an Administrator account.**

   You're asked to provide this information only if a computer account has not already been created for the client computer.

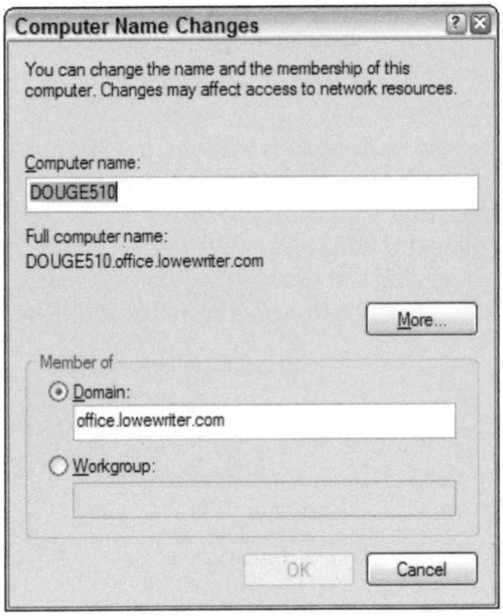

Figure 8-8:
The
Computer
Name
Changes
dialog box
(Windows
XP).

7. **When a dialog box appears, informing you that you need to restart the computer, click OK. Then restart the computer.**

You're done!

Configuring Windows Vista computer identification

To change the computer identification in Windows Vista, follow these steps:

1. **Choose the Start button, and then right-click Computer and choose Properties.**

   This step displays the System information window, as shown in Figure 8-9. Notice the section that lists computer name, domain, and workgroup settings.

2. **Click the Change Settings link.**

   If a dialog box appears and asks for your permission to continue, click Continue. The System Properties dialog box then appears, as shown in Figure 8-10.

3. **Click the Change button.**

   This step displays the Computer Name/Domain Changes dialog box, as shown in Figure 8-11.

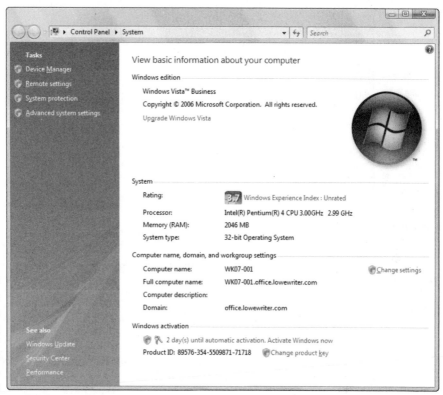

Figure 8-9:
The System
Information
window
(Windows
Vista).

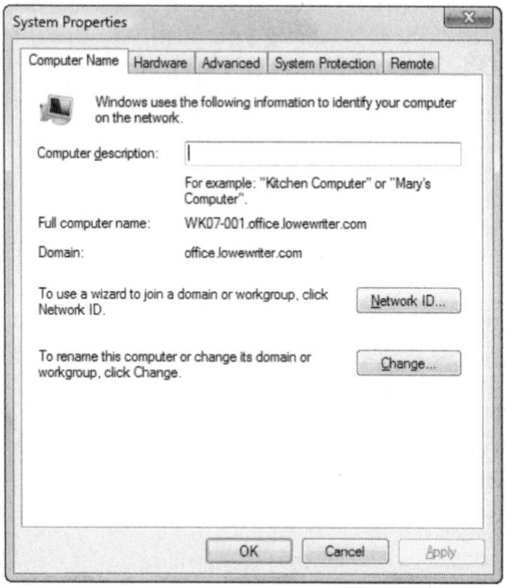

Figure 8-10:
The System
Properties
dialog box
(Windows
Vista).

Figure 8-11:
The
Computer
Name/
Domain
Changes
dialog box
(Windows
Vista).

4. **Enter the computer name and the workgroup or domain name.**

   If you want to join a domain, choose the Domain option button and type the domain name. To join a workgroup, choose the Workgroup option and type the workgroup name.

5. **Click OK.**

6. **Enter the username and password for an Administrator account when prompted.**

   You're asked to provide this information only if a computer account has not already been created for the client computer.

7. **When a dialog box appears, informing you that you need to restart the computer, click OK. Then restart the computer.**

   The computer is then added to the domain or workgroup.

Configuring Network Logon

Every user who wants to access a domain-based network must log on to the domain by using a valid user account. The user account is created on the domain controller — not on the client computer.

Network logon isn't required to access workgroup resources. Instead, workgroup resources can be password-protected to restrict access.

When you start a Windows computer that has been configured to join a domain, as described in the section "Configuring Client Computer Identification," earlier in this chapter, the Log On to Windows dialog box is displayed. The user can use this dialog box to log on to a domain by entering a domain username and password and then selecting the domain that she wants to log on to (from the Log On To drop-down list).

You can create local user accounts in Windows that allow users to access resources on the local computer. To log on to the local computer, the user selects This Computer from the Log On To drop-down list and enters the username and password for a local user account. When a user logs on by using a local account, he isn't connected to a network domain. To log on to a domain, the user must select the domain from the Log On To drop-down list.

If the computer isn't part of a domain, Windows can display a friendly logon screen that displays an icon for each of the computer's local users. The user can log on simply by clicking the appropriate icon and entering a password. (This feature isn't available for computers that have joined a domain.)

Note that if the user logs on by using a local computer account rather than a domain account, she can still access domain resources. A Connect To dialog box appears whenever the user attempts to access a domain resource. Then the user can enter a domain username and password to connect to the domain.

Chapter 9

Wireless Networking

In This Chapter

▶ Looking at wireless network standards

▶ Reviewing some basic radio terms

▶ Considering infrastructure and ad hoc networks

▶ Working with a wireless access point

▶ Configuring Windows for wireless networking

With wireless networking, you don't need cables to connect your computers. Instead, wireless networks use radio waves to send and receive network signals. As a result, a computer can connect to a wireless network at any location in your home or office.

Wireless networks are especially useful for notebook computers. After all, the main benefit of a notebook computer is that you can *move* it.

This chapter introduces the ins and outs of using a wireless network.

Diving into Wireless Networking

A *wireless network* is a network that uses radio signals rather than direct cable connections to exchange information.

A computer with a wireless network connection is like a cellphone. Just as you don't have to be connected to a phone line to use a cellphone, you don't have to be connected to a network cable to use a wireless networked computer.

The following list summarizes some key concepts and terms that you need to understand to set up and use a basic wireless network:

✔ A wireless network is often referred to as a *WLAN,* for *wireless local-area network.*

Some people prefer to switch the acronym around to *local-area wireless network,* or *LAWN.*

The term *Wi-Fi* is often used to describe wireless networks, although it technically refers to just one form of wireless networks: the 802.11b standard. See the section "Eight-Oh-Two-Dot-Eleven Something? (Or, Understanding Wireless Standards)," later in this chapter, for more information.

✔ A wireless network has a name, known as an *SSID.* SSID stands for *service set identifier.* (Wouldn't that make a great *Jeopardy!* question? I'll take obscure four-letter acronyms for $400, please!)

All the computers that belong to a single wireless network must have the same SSID.

✔ Wireless networks can transmit over any of several channels.

For computers to talk to each other, they must be configured to transmit on the same channel.

✔ The simplest type of wireless network consists of two or more computers with wireless network adapters.

This type of network is an *ad hoc mode network.*

✔ A more complex type of network is an *infrastructure mode network.* All this really means is that a group of wireless computers can be connected to not only each other but also an existing cabled network via a device called a *wireless access point,* or *WAP.* (I tell you more about ad hoc and infrastructure networks later in this chapter.)

A Little High School Electronics

I was a real nerd in high school: I took three years of electronics. The electronics class at my school was right next door to the auto shop. Of course, all the cool kids took auto shop, and only nerds like me took electronics. We hung in there, though, and found out all about capacitors and diodes while the cool kids were learning how to raise their cars and install 2-gigawatt stereo systems.

It turns out that a little of that high school electronics information proves useful when it comes to wireless networking — not much, but a little. You'll understand wireless networking much better if you know the meanings of some basic radio terms.

Waves and frequencies

For starters, *radio* consists of electromagnetic waves that are sent through the atmosphere. You can't see or hear them, but radio receivers can pick them up and convert them into sounds, images, or — in the case of wireless networks — data.

Radio waves are cyclical waves of electromagnetic energy that repeat at a particular rate, or *frequency*. Figure 9-1 shows two frequencies of radio waves: The first is one cycle per second; the second is two cycles per second. (Real radio doesn't operate at a frequency that low, but I figured one and two cycles per second is easier to draw than 680,000 cycles per second or 2.4 million cycles per second.)

The measure of a frequency is *cycles per second,* which indicates how many complete cycles the wave makes in one second. (Duh.) In honor of Heinrich Hertz, who did not invent catsup but rather was the first person to success-fully send and receive radio waves (it happened in the 1880s), *cycles per second* is usually referred to as *hertz,* abbreviated Hz. Thus, 1 Hz is one cycle per second. Incidentally, when the prefix *K* (for kilo, or 1,000), *M* (for mega, 1 million), or *G* (for giga, 1 billion) is added to the front of Hz, the *H* is still capitalized. Thus, 2.4 MHz (not 2.4 Mhz) is correct.

The beauty of radio frequencies is that transmitters can be tuned to broad-cast radio waves at a precise frequency. Likewise, receivers can be tuned to receive radio waves at a precise frequency and ignore waves at other frequencies. That's why you can tune the radio in your car to listen to dozens of different radio stations: Each station broadcasts at its own frequency.

Wavelength and antennas

A term related to frequency is *wavelength*. Radio waves travel at the speed of light. The term *wavelength* refers to how far the radio signal travels with each cycle. For example, because the speed of light is roughly 300 million meters per second, the wavelength of a 1 Hz radio wave is about 300 million meters. The wavelength of a 2 Hz signal is about 150 million meters.

As you can see, the wavelength decreases as the frequency increases. The wavelength of a typical AM radio station broadcasting at 580 KHz is about 500 meters. For a TV station broadcasting at 100 MHz, it's about 3 meters. For a wireless network broadcasting at 2.4 GHz, the wavelength is about 12 centimeters.

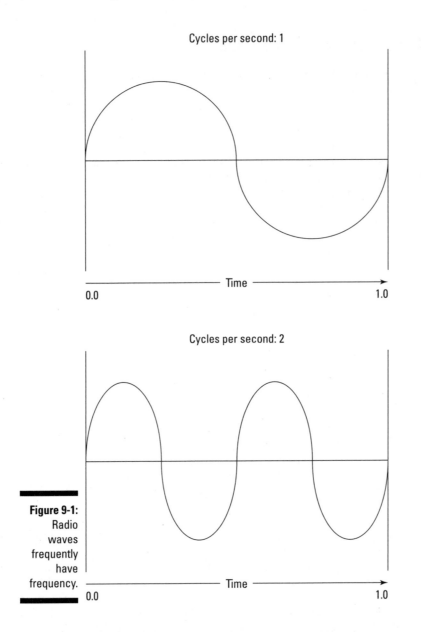

Cycles per second: 1

Time

0.0   1.0

Cycles per second: 2

Figure 9-1:
Radio
waves
frequently
have
frequency.

Time

0.0   1.0

It turns out that the shorter the wavelength, the smaller the antenna needs to be in order to adequately receive the signal. As a result, higher-frequency transmissions need smaller antennas. You may have noticed that AM radio stations usually have huge antennas mounted on top of tall towers, but cellphone transmitters are much smaller and their towers aren't nearly as tall. That's because cellphones operate on a higher frequency than AM radio stations do. So who decides what type of radio gets to use specific frequencies? That's where spectrums and the FCC come in.

Spectrums and the FCC

The term *spectrum* refers to a continuous range of frequencies on which radio can operate. In the United States, the Federal Communications Commission (FCC) regulates not only how much of Janet Jackson can be shown at the Super Bowl but also how various portions of the radio spectrum can be used. Essentially, the FCC has divided the radio spectrum into dozens of small ranges called *bands* and restricted certain uses to certain bands. For example, AM radio operates in the band from 535 KHz to 1,700 KHz.

Table 9-1 lists some of the most popular bands. Note that some of these bands are wide — for example, UHF television begins at 470 MHz and ends at 806 MHz, but other bands are restricted to a specific frequency. The difference between the lowest and highest frequency within a band is the *bandwidth*.

Table 9-1	Popular Bands of the Radio Spectrum
Band	*What It's Used For*
535 KHz–1,700 KHz	AM radio
5.9 MHz–26.1 MHz	Short wave radio
26.96 MHz–27.41 MHz	Citizens Band (CB) radio
54 MHz–88 MHz	Television (VHF channels 2 through 6)
88 MHz–108 MHz	FM radio
174 MHz–220 MHz	Television (VHF channels 7 through 13)
470 MHz–806 MHz	Television (UHF channels)
806 MHz–890 MHz	Cellular networks
900 MHz	Cordless phones
1850 MHz–1990 MHz	PCS Cellular
2.4 GHz–2.4835 GHz	Cordless phones and wireless networks (802.11b and 802.11g)
4 GHz–5 GHz	Large-dish satellite TV
5 GHz	Wireless networks (802.11a)
11.7 GHz–12.7 GHz	Small-disk satellite TV

And now, a word from the irony department

I was an English literature major in college, so I like to use literary devices, such as irony. Of course, irony doesn't come up much in computer books. So, when it does, I like to jump on it like a hog out of the water.

Here's my juicy bit of irony for today: The first Ethernet system was a wireless network. Ethernet traces its roots back to a network developed at the University of Hawaii in 1970: the *Alohanet.* This network transmitted its data by using small radios. If two computers tried to broadcast data at the same time, the computers detected the collision and tried again after a short, random delay. This technique was the inspiration for the basic technique of Ethernet, now called *carrier sense multiple access with collision detection* (CSMA/CD). The wireless Alohanet network inspired Robert Metcalfe to develop his cabled network, *Ethernet,* as his doctoral thesis at Harvard in 1973.

For the next 20 years or so, Ethernet was pretty much a cable-only network. It wasn't until the mid-1990s that Ethernet finally returned to its wireless roots.

Two of the bands in the spectrum are allocated for use by wireless networks: 2.4 GHz and 5 GHz. Note that these bands aren't devoted exclusively to wireless networks. In particular, the 2.4 GHz band shares its space with cordless phones. As a result, cordless phones can sometimes interfere with wireless networks.

Eight-Oh-Two-Dot-Eleventy Something? (Or, Understanding Wireless Standards)

The most popular standards for wireless networks are the IEEE 802.11 standards. These essential wireless Ethernet standards use many of the same networking techniques that the cabled Ethernet standards (in other words, 802.3) use. Most notably, 802.11 networks use the same CSMA/CD technique as cabled Ethernet to recover from network collisions.

The 802.11 standards address the bottom two layers of the IEEE seven-layer model: the Physical layer and the Media Access Control (MAC) layer. Note that TCP/IP protocols apply to higher layers of the model. As a result, TCP/IP runs just fine on 802.11 networks.

The original 802.11 standard was adopted in 1997. Two additions to the standard, 802.11a and 802.11b, were adopted in 1999. The latest and greatest version is 802.11g.

Table 9-2 summarizes the basic characteristics of the three variants of 802.11.

Table 9-2		802.11 Variations	
Standard	*Speeds*	*Frequency*	*Typical Range (Indoors)*
802.11a	Up to 54 Mbps	5 GHz	150 feet
802.11b	Up to 11 Mbps	2.4 GHz	300 feet
802.11g	Up to 54 Mbps	2.4 GHz	300 feet

Most wireless networks are now based on the 802.11b standard. Although 802.11a is faster than 802.11b, it's considerably more expensive and has less range. In addition, 802.11a and 802.11b aren't compatible with each other because 802.11a transmits at 5 GHz and 802.11b transmits at 2.4 GHz. As a result, 802.11a and 802.11b devices can't receive each other's signals.

The new standard, 802.11g, solves this problem by enabling high-speed connections at 2.4 GHz. As a result, 802.11g devices are compatible with existing 802.11b networks.

802.11b networks operate on the same radio frequency as many cordless phones: 2.4 GHz. If you set up an 802.11b network in your home and you also have a 2.4 GHz cordless phone, the network and phone may occasionally interfere with each other. The only way to completely avoid the interference is to switch to a 900 MHz phone or use more-expensive 802.11a network components, which transmit at 5 GHz rather than at 2.4 GHz.

Home on the Range

The maximum range of an 802.11b wireless device indoors is about 300 feet. This range can have an interesting effect when you get a bunch of wireless computers together — such that some of them are in range of each other but others are not. Suppose that Wally, Ward, and the Beaver all have wireless notebooks. Wally's computer is 200 feet away from Ward's computer, and Ward's computer is 200 feet away from Beaver's in the opposite direction (see Figure 9-2). In this case, Ward can access both Wally's computer and Beaver's computer, but Wally can access only Ward's computer, and Beaver can access only Ward's computer. In other words, Wally and Beaver can't access each other's computers because they're outside the 300-feet range limit. (This is starting to sound suspiciously like an algebra problem. Now suppose that Wally starts walking toward Ward at 2 miles per hour and Beaver starts running toward Ward at 4 miles per hour. . . .)

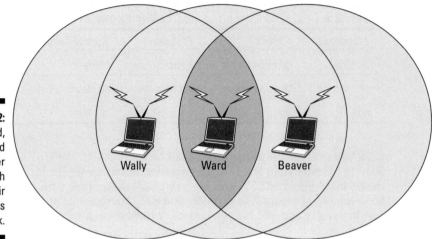

Figure 9-2:
Ward,
Wally, and
Beaver
playing with
their
wireless
network.

Although the normal range for 802.11b is 300 feet, the useful range may be less in actual practice:

✔ Obstacles, such as solid walls, bad weather, cordless phones, microwave ovens, and backyard nuclear reactors can all conspire to reduce the effective range of a wireless adapter. If you're having trouble connecting to the network, sometimes just adjusting the antenna helps.

✔ Wireless networks tend to slow down when the distance increases. The 802.11b network devices claim to operate at 11 Mbps, but they usually achieve that speed only at ranges of 100 feet or less. At 300 feet, they often slow down to 1 Mbps.

✔ At the edge of the wireless device's range, you're more likely to suddenly lose your connection because of bad weather.

Wireless Network Adapters

Each computer that will connect to your wireless network needs a wireless network adapter. The *wireless network adapter* is similar to the network interface card (NIC) that's used for a standard Ethernet connection. However, rather than have a cable connector on the back, a wireless network adapter has an antenna.

You can get several basic types of wireless network adapters, depending on your needs and the type of computer you will use it with:

- ✔ A wireless PCI card is a wireless network adapter that you install into an available slot inside a desktop computer.

  To install this type of card, you need to take your computer apart, so use this type of card only if you have the expertise and the nerves to dig into your computer's guts.

- ✔ A wireless USB adapter is a separate box that plugs into a USB port on your computer. Because the USB adapter is a separate device, it takes up extra desk space. However, you can install it without taking apart your computer.

- ✔ A wireless PC card is designed to slide into the PC card slot found in most notebook computers.

  This card is the type to get if you want to network your notebook.

You can purchase a combination 802.11b/g PCI adapter for under $50. USB versions cost about $10 more.

At first, you may think that wireless network adapters are prohibitively expensive. After all, you can buy a regular Ethernet adapter for as little as $20. However, when you consider that you don't have to purchase and install cable to use a wireless adapter, the price of wireless networking becomes more palatable. And, if you shop around, you can sometimes find wireless adapters for as little as $19.95.

Wireless Access Points

Unlike cabled networks, wireless networks don't need a hub or switch. If all you want to do is network a group of wireless computers, you just purchase a wireless adapter for each computer, put them all within 300 feet of each other, and *voilà!* — instant network.

What if you already have an existing cabled network? For example, you may work at an office with 15 computers all cabled up nicely, and you just want to add a couple of wireless notebook computers to the network. Or, suppose that you have two computers in your den connected to each other with network cable but you want to link up a computer in your bedroom without pulling cable through the attic.

That's where a *wireless access point,* or *WAP,* comes in. A WAP performs two functions:

- ✔ **The WAP acts as a central connection point for all your computers that have wireless network adapters.**

  In effect, the WAP performs essentially the same function as a hub or switch performs for a wired network.

- ✔ **The WAP links your wireless network to your existing wired network so that your wired computer and your wireless computers get along like one big, happy family.** (Sounds like the makings of a Dr. Seuss story. "Now the wireless sneeches had hubs without wires. But the twisted-pair sneeches had cables to thires. . . .")

Wireless access points are sometimes just called access points, or APs. An *access point* is a box that has an antenna (or, often, a pair of antennae) and an RJ-45 Ethernet port. You just plug the access point into a network cable and then plug the other end of the cable into a hub or switch, and your wireless network should be able to connect to your cabled network.

Figure 9-3 shows how an access point acts as a central connection point for wireless computers and how it bridges your wireless network to your wired network.

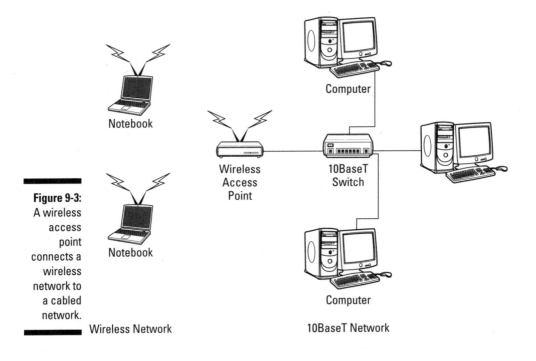

Figure 9-3:
A wireless access point connects a wireless network to a cabled network.

Infrastructure mode

When you set up a wireless network with an access point, you're creating an *infrastructure mode* network. It's called *infrastructure mode* because the access point provides a permanent infrastructure for the network. The access points are installed at fixed physical locations, so the network has relatively stable boundaries. Whenever a mobile computer wanders into the range of one of the access points, it has come into the sphere of the network and can connect.

An access point and all the wireless computers that are connected to it are referred to as a *Basic Service Set,* or *BSS.* Each BSS is identified by a *Service Set Identifier,* or *SSID.* When you configure an access point, you specify the SSID that you want to use. The SSID is often a generic name such as *wireless,* or it can be a name that you create. Some access points use the MAC address of the WAP as the SSID.

Multifunction WAPs

Wireless access points often include other built-in features. For example, some access points double as Ethernet hubs or switches. In that case, the access point will have more than one RJ-45 port. In addition, some access points include broadband cable or DSL firewall routers that enable you to connect to the Internet:

- ✔ An 802.11b wireless access point that lets me connect a notebook computer and a computer located on the other side of the house because I didn't want to run cable through the attic.

- ✔ A 4-port 10/100 MHz switch to which I can connect up to four computers by using twisted-pair cable.

- ✔ A DSL/cable router that I connect to my cable modem. This enables all the computers on the network (cabled and wireless) to access the Internet.

A multifunction access point that's designed to serve as an Internet gateway for home networks sometimes is a *residential gateway.*

Roaming

You can use two or more wireless access points to create a large wireless network in which computer users can roam from area to area and still be connected to the wireless network. As the user moves out of the range of one access point, another access point automatically picks up the user and takes over without interrupting the user's network service.

To set up two or more access points for roaming, you must carefully place the WAPs so that all areas of the office or building that are being networked are in range of at least one of the WAPs. Then just make sure that all the computers and the access points use the same SSID and channel.

Two or more access points joined for the purposes of roaming, along with all the wireless computers connected to any of the access points, form an *Extended Service Set,* or *ESS.* The access points in the ESS are usually connected to a wired network.

One current limitation of roaming is that each access point in an ESS must be on the same TCP/IP subnet. That way, a computer that roams from one access point to another within the ESS retains the same IP address. If the access points had a different subnet, a roaming computer would have to change IP addresses when it moved from one access point to another.

Wireless bridging

Another use for wireless access points is to bridge separate subnets that can't easily be connected by cable. For example, two office buildings may be only about 50 feet apart. To run cable from one building to the other, you'd have to bury conduit — a potentially expensive job. Because the buildings are so close, though, you can probably connect them with a pair of wireless access points that function as a *wireless bridge* between the two networks. Connect one of the access points to the first network and the other access point to the second network. Then configure both access points to use the same SSID and channel.

Ad hoc networks

A wireless access point isn't necessary to set up a wireless network. Anytime two or more wireless devices come within range of each other, they can link up to form an *ad hoc network.* For example, if you and a few of your friends all have notebook computers with 802.11b/g wireless network adapters, you can meet anywhere and form an ad hoc network.

All the computers within range of each other in an ad hoc network are called an *Independent Basic Service Set,* or *IBSS.*

Configuring a Wireless Access Point

The physical setup for a wireless access point is pretty simple: You take it out of the box, put it on a shelf or on top of a bookcase near a network jack and a power outlet, plug in the power cable, and plug in the network cable.

The software configuration for an access point is a little more involved but still not complicated. It's usually done by using a Web interface. To get to the configuration page for the access point, you need to know the access point's IP address. Then you just type that address into the address bar of a browser from any computer on the network.

Multifunction access points usually provide DHCP and NAT services for the networks and double as the network's gateway router. As a result, they typically have a private IP address that's at the beginning of one of the Internet's private IP address ranges, such as 192.168.0.1 or 10.0.0.1. Consult the documentation that came with the access point to find out more.

If you use a multifunction access point that is both your wireless access point and your Internet router and you can't remember the IP address, run the IPCONFIG command at a command prompt from any computer on the network. The default gateway IP address should be the IP address of the access point.

Basic configuration options

Figure 9-4 shows the main configuration screen for a typical wireless access point router. I called up this configuration page by entering 192.168.1.1 in the address bar of a Web browser and then supplying the logon password when I was prompted.

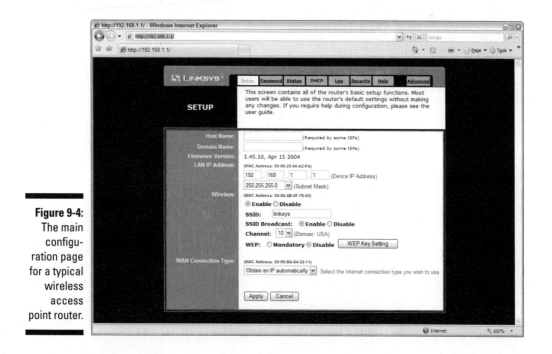

Figure 9-4: The main configuration page for a typical wireless access point router.

This configuration page offers the following configuration options that are related to the wireless access point functions of the device. Although these options are specific to this particular device, most access points have similar configuration options:

✔ **Enable/Disable:** Enables or disables the device's wireless access point functions.

✔ **SSID:** The Service Set Identifier used to identify the network. Most access points have well-known defaults.

You can talk yourself into thinking that your network is more secure by changing the SSID from the default to something more obscure, but in reality that protects you only from first-grade hackers. By the time most hackers get into the second grade, they know that even the most obscure SSID is easy to get around. I recommend that you leave the SSID at the default and apply better security measures, as described in Chapter 10.

✔ **Allow SSID Broadcast to Associate?** Disables the access point's periodic broadcast of the SSID. Normally, the access point regularly broadcasts its SSID so that wireless devices that come within range can detect the network and join in.

For a more secure network, you can disable this function. Then a wireless client must already know the network's SSID to join the network.

✔ **Channel:** Lets you select one of 11 channels on which to broadcast. All the access points and computers in the wireless network should use the same channel.

If you find that your network frequently loses connections, try switching to another channel. You may be experiencing interference from a cordless phone or other wireless device operating on the same channel.

Switching channels is also a friendly way for neighbors with wireless networks to stay out of each other's way. For example, if you share a building with another tenant who also has a wireless network, you can agree to use separate channels so that your wireless networks don't interfere with each other. Keep in mind that this agreement doesn't give you any real measure of security because your neighbor could secretly switch back to your channel and listen in on your network. You still need to secure your network as described in Chapter 10.

✔ **WEP — Mandatory or Disable:** Lets you use a security protocol called *wired equivalent privacy.*

DHCP configuration

You can configure most multifunction access points to operate as a DHCP server. For small networks, it's common for the access point to also be the DHCP server for the entire network. In that case, you need to configure the access point's DHCP server. Figure 9-5 shows the DHCP configuration page for the Linksys WAP router. To enable DHCP, select the Enable option and then specify the other configuration options to use for the DHCP server.

Larger networks that have more-demanding DHCP requirements are likely to have a separate DHCP server running on another computer. In that case, you can defer to the existing server by disabling the DHCP server in the access point.

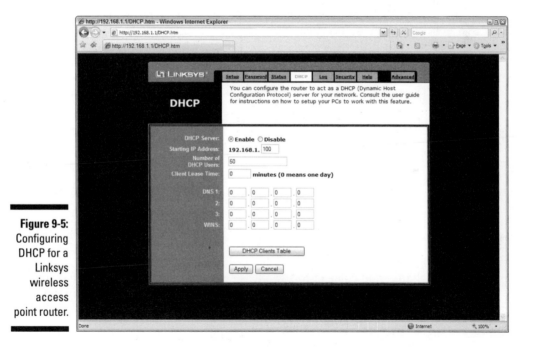

Figure 9-5:
Configuring
DHCP for a
Linksys
wireless
access
point router.

Configuring Windows for Wireless Networking

The first step in configuring Windows XP for wireless networking is to install the appropriate device driver for your wireless network adapter. To do that, you need the installation CD that came with the adapter. Follow the instructions that came with the adapter to install the drivers.

Windows XP has some nice built-in features for working with wireless networks. Follow these steps to access the features:

1. **Open the Network Connections folder.**

   Choose Start➪Control Panel and then double-click the Network Connections icon.

2. **Right-click the wireless network connection and then choose Properties to open the Properties dialog box.**

3. **Click the Wireless Networks tab.**

   The wireless networking options are displayed, as shown in Figure 9-6.

Figure 9-6:
Configuring
wireless
networking
in Windows
XP.

Each time you connect to a wireless network, Windows XP adds that network to this dialog box. Then you can juggle the order of the networks in the Preferred Networks section to indicate which network you prefer to join if you find yourself within range of two or more networks at the same time. You can use the Move Up and Move Down buttons next to the Preferred Networks list to change your preferences.

To add a network that you haven't yet joined, click the Add button. This action opens the dialog box shown in Figure 9-7. Here, you can type the SSID value for the network that you want to add. You can also specify other information, such as whether to use data encryption, how to authenticate yourself, and whether the network is an ad hoc rather than an infrastructure network.

When your computer comes within range of a wireless network, a pop-up balloon appears on the taskbar, indicating that a network is available. If one of your preferred networks is within range, clicking the balloon automatically connects you to that network. If Windows XP doesn't recognize any of the networks, clicking the balloon displays the Wireless Network Connection dialog box. With this dialog box, you can choose the network that you want to join (if more than one network is listed) and then click Connect to join the selected network.

After you join a wireless network, a network status icon appears in the notification area of the taskbar. You can quickly see the network status by hovering the mouse cursor over this icon; a balloon appears to indicate the state of the connection. For more detailed information, you can click the status icon to display the Wireless Network Connection Status dialog box, as shown in Figure 9-8.

Figure 9-7:
Adding a
wireless
network in
Windows
XP.

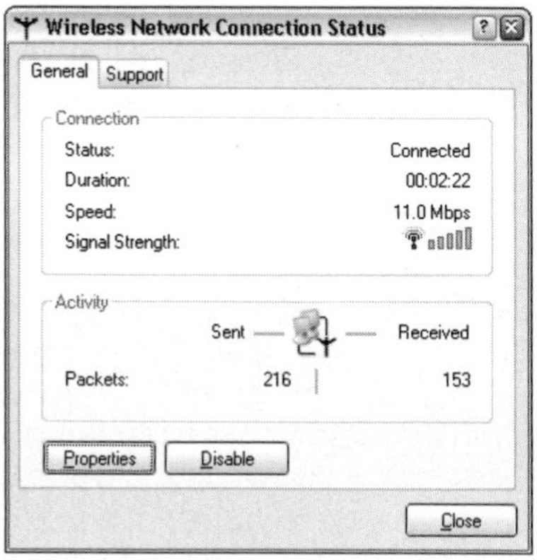

Figure 9-8:
The
Wireless
Network
Connection
Status
dialog box.

This dialog box provides the following items of information:

- ✔ **Status:** Indicates whether you're connected.
- ✔ **Duration:** Indicates how long you've been connected.
- ✔ **Speed:** Indicates the current network speed.

    Ideally, this option should say 11 Mbps for an 802.11b network, or 54 Mbps for an 802.11a or 802.11g network. However, if the network connection is not of the highest quality, the speed may drop to a lower value.

- ✔ **Signal Strength:** Displays a graphical representation of the quality of the signal.
- ✔ **Packets Sent & Received:** Indicates how many packets of data you sent and received over the network.

You can click the Properties button to open the Connection Properties dialog box for the wireless connection.

Part III
Getting Connected

The 5th Wave   By Rich Tennant

"Frankly, the idea of an entirely wireless future scares me to death."

In this part . . .

After you build your network, the chapters in this part show you how to connect it to the outside world. You'll learn how to connect your network to the Internet, set up and manage an e-mail server, set up a corporate intranet, use your network as a telephone system, and connect to your network from home. Whew! You'll be more connected than a Hollywood talent agent.

Chapter 10

Connecting Your Network to the Internet

In This Chapter

▶ Looking at DSL and cable

▶ Examining T1 and T3 connections

▶ Using a router

▶ Securing your connection with a firewall

▶ Using the firewall that comes with Windows

So you decided to connect your network to the Internet. All you have to do is run to the local computer discount store, buy a cable modem, and plug it in, right? Wrong. Unfortunately, connecting to the Internet involves more than just installing a modem. For starters, you have to make sure that a modem is the right way to connect — other methods are faster but more expensive. Then you have to select and configure the software you use to access the Internet. Finally, you have to lie awake at night worrying whether hackers are breaking into your network via its Internet connection.

Connecting to the Internet

Connecting to the Internet isn't free. For starters, you have to purchase the computer equipment necessary to make the connection. Then you have to obtain a connection from an *Internet Service Provider,* or *ISP.* The ISP charges you a monthly fee that depends on the speed and capacity of the connection.

The following sections describe the most commonly used methods of connecting network users to the Internet.

Connecting with cable or DSL

For small and home offices, the two most popular methods of connecting to the Internet are cable and DSL. Cable and DSL connections are often called *broadband connections,* for technical reasons you don't really want to know.

Cable Internet access works over the same cable that brings 40 billion TV channels into your home, whereas DSL is a digital phone service that works over a standard phone line. Both offer three major advantages over normal dialup connections:

✔ **Cable and DSL are much faster than dialup connections.**

A cable connection can be anywhere from 10 to 200 times faster than a dialup connection, depending on the service you get. And the speed of a DSL line is comparable to cable. (Although DSL is a dedicated connection, cable connections are shared among several subscribers. The speed of a cable connection may slow down when several subscribers use the connection simultaneously.)

✔ **With cable and DSL, you're always connected to the Internet.**

You don't have to connect and disconnect each time you want to go online. No more waiting for the modem to dial your service provider and listening to the annoying modem shriek as it attempts to establish a connection.

✔ **Cable and DSL don't tie up a phone line while you're online.**

With cable, your Internet connection works over TV cables rather than over phone cables. With DSL, the phone company installs a separate phone line for the DSL service, so your regular phone line isn't affected.

Unfortunately, there's no such thing as a free lunch, and the high-speed, always-on connections offered by cable and DSL don't come without a price. For starters, you can expect to pay a higher monthly access fee for cable or DSL. In most areas of the United States, cable runs about $50 per month for residential users; business users can expect to pay more, especially if more than one user will be connected to the Internet via the cable.

The cost for DSL service depends on the access speed you choose. In some areas, residential users can get a relatively slow DSL connection for as little as $30 per month. For higher access speeds or for business users, DSL can cost substantially more.

Cable and DSL access aren't available everywhere. If you live in an area where cable or DSL isn't available, you can still get high-speed Internet access by using a satellite hookup. With satellite access, you still need a modem and a phone line to send data from your computer to the Internet. The satellite is used only to receive data from the Internet. Still, a satellite setup like this is much faster than a modem-only connection.

Connecting with high-speed private lines: T1 and T3

If your network is large and high-speed Internet access is a high priority, contact your local phone company (or companies) about installing a dedicated high-speed digital line. These lines can cost you plenty (on the order of hundreds of dollars per month), so they're best suited for large networks in which 20 or more users are accessing the Internet simultaneously.

A T1 line has a connection speed of up to 1.544 Mbps. A T3 line is faster yet: It transmits data at an amazing 44.184 Mbps. Of course, T3 lines are also considerably more expensive than T1 lines.

If you don't have enough users to justify the expense of an entire T1 or T3 line, you can lease just a portion of the line. With a *fractional T1 line,* you can get connections with speeds of 128 Kbps to 768 Kbps, and with a *fractional T3 line,* you can choose speeds ranging from 4.6 Mbps to 32 Mbps.

Setting up a T1 or T3 connection to the Internet is stuff best left to professionals. Getting this type of connection to work is far more complicated than setting up a basic LAN.

You may be wondering whether T1 or T3 lines are really any faster than cable or DSL connections. After all, T1 runs at 1.544 Mbps and T3 runs at 44.184 Mbps, and cable and DSL claim to run at comparable speeds. But there are many differences that justify the substantial extra cost of a T1 or T3 line. In particular, a T1 or T3 line is a dedicated line — not shared by any other users. T1 and T3 are higher-quality connections, so you actually get the 1.544 or 44.184 connection speeds. In contrast, both cable and DSL connections usually run at substantially less than their advertised maximum speeds because of poor-quality connections.

Sharing an Internet connection

After you choose a method to connect to the Internet, you can turn your attention to setting up the connection so that more than one user on your network can share it. The best way to do that is by using a separate device called a *router.* An inexpensive router for a small network can be had for under $100. Routers suitable for larger networks will, naturally, cost a bit more.

Because all communications between your network and the Internet must go through the router, the router is a natural place to provide the security measures necessary to keep your network safe from the many perils of the Internet. As a result, a router used for Internet connections often doubles as a firewall, as described in the section "Using a firewall," later in this chapter.

Securing Your Connection with a Firewall

If your network is connected to the Internet, a whole host of security issues bubble to the surface. You probably connected your network to the Internet so that your network's users could get out to the Internet. Unfortunately, however, your Internet connection is a two-way street. It not only enables your network's users to step outside the bounds of your network to access the Internet, but it also enables others to step in and access your network.

And step in they will. The world is filled with hackers who are looking for networks like yours to break into. They may do it just for the fun of it, or they may do it to steal your customers' credit card numbers or to coerce your mail server into sending thousands of spam messages on behalf of the bad guys. Whatever their motive, rest assured that your network will be broken into if you leave it unprotected.

Using a firewall

A *firewall* is a security-conscious router that sits between the Internet and your network with a single-minded task: preventing *them* from getting to *us*. The firewall acts as a security guard between the Internet and your LAN. All network traffic into and out of the LAN must pass through the firewall, which prevents unauthorized access to the network.

Some type of firewall is a must-have if your network has a connection to the Internet, whether that connection is broadband (cable modem or DSL), T1, or some other high-speed connection. Without it, sooner or later a hacker will discover your unprotected network and tell his friends about it, and within a few hours your network will be toast.

You can set up a firewall in two basic ways:

- ✔ **Firewall appliance:** The easiest way. It's basically a self-contained router with built-in firewall features.

  Most firewall appliances include Web-based interfaces that enable you to connect to the firewall from any computer on your network by using a browser. You can then customize the firewall settings to suit your needs.

- ✔ **Server computer:** Can be set up to function as a firewall computer.

  The server can run just about any network operating system, but most dedicated firewall systems run Linux.

Whether you use a firewall appliance or a firewall computer, the firewall must be located between your network and the Internet, as shown in Figure 10-1. Here, one end of the firewall is connected to a network hub, which is, in turn, connected to the other computers on the network. The other end of the firewall is connected to the Internet. As a result, all traffic from the LAN to the Internet (and vice versa) must travel through the firewall.

The term *perimeter* is sometimes used to describe the location of a firewall on your network. In short, a firewall is like a perimeter fence that completely surrounds your property and forces all visitors to enter through the front gate.

In large networks, it's sometimes hard to figure out exactly where the perimeter is located. If your network has two or more WAN connections, make sure that every one of those connections connects to a firewall and not directly to the network. You can do this by providing a separate firewall for each WAN connection or by using a firewall with more than one WAN port.

Some firewall routers can also enforce virus protection for your network. For more information about virus protection, see Chapter 23.

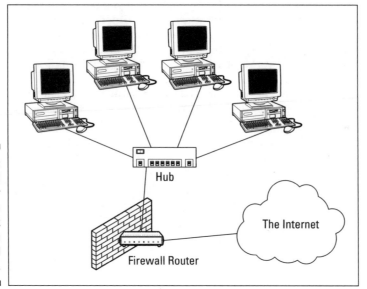

Figure 10-1:
A firewall
router
creates a
secure link
between a
network and
the Internet.

Hub

The Internet

Firewall Router

The built-in Windows firewall

Both Windows XP and Vista include a built-in firewall that provides basic packet-filtering firewall protection. In most cases, you're better off using a dedicated firewall router because these devices provide better security features than the built-in Windows firewall does. Still, the built-in firewall is suitable for home networks or very small office networks.

Here are the steps that activate the built-in firewall in Windows XP or Vista:

1. **Choose Start⇨Control Panel.**

   The Control Panel appears.

2. **Click the Windows Firewall icon.**

   This step opens the Windows Firewall dialog box. Figure 10-2 shows the Windows Vista version.

3. **Select the On (Recommended) option.**

   This option enables the firewall.

4. **Click OK.**

   That's all there is to it.

Note that the firewall that's included with Windows Vista has additional options you can configure. However, I recommend against fiddling with those options unless you've taken an upper-division college course in computer security.

Do *not* enable the Windows Internet firewall if you're using a separate firewall router to protect your network. Because the other computers on the network are connected directly to the router and not to your computer, the firewall doesn't protect the rest of the network. Additionally, as an unwanted side effect, the rest of the network will lose the capability of accessing your computer.

Beginning with Windows XP Service Pack 2, the firewall is turned on by default. If your computer is already behind a firewall, disable the Windows firewall that's enabled by Service Pack 2.

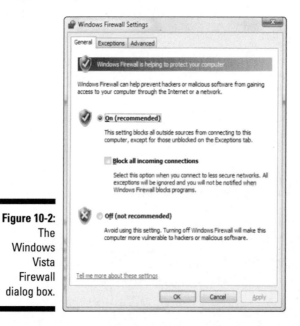

Figure 10-2:
The
Windows
Vista
Firewall
dialog box.

Chapter 11

Running a Mail Server

In This Chapter

▶ Working with the Exchange Server consoles

▶ Managing mailboxes

▶ Granting mailbox access

*O*ne of the most important ways in which network users connect is through e-mail. As a result, a mail server is a vital component of all but the smallest networks.

For Windows networks, the most common mail server is Exchange, properly known as *Microsoft Exchange Server 2003* in its current incarnation. Although there are alternative e-mail servers, Exchange is the most commonly used.

In this chapter, you discover how to perform the most commonly requested maintenance chores in Exchange Server, such as how to create a new mailbox, grant a user access to an additional mailbox, and deal with mailbox size limits.

This chapter doesn't delve into the intricacies of installing and setting up Exchange. That subject is best left to the pros. After an Exchange server is set up, basic maintenance of it (adding and deleting users and configuring Outlook, for example) is relatively easy.

Using the Exchange System Manager Console

Most management tasks for Exchange Server are performed from one of two management consoles. To manage an individual user's e-mail requirements, you use Active Directory Users and Computers, as described in detail in Chapter 16. I discuss several of the Exchange-specific features of this console later in this chapter.

To manage Exchange Server itself, you work with the Exchange System Manager console, as shown in Figure 11-1. You can use this console to perform such chores as monitoring the status of the server, setting system mailbox size limits, and creating public folders.

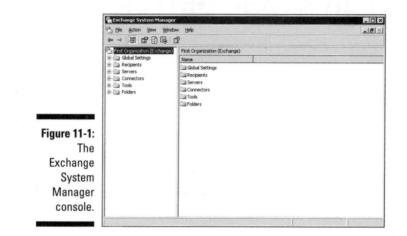

Figure 11-1: The Exchange System Manager console.

Managing Mailboxes

When you create a new user by using the Add User Wizard from the Server Management console, an Exchange mailbox is created automatically for the new user. As a result, you don't usually have to create Exchange mailboxes separately. On occasion, though, you may need to modify some aspect of a user's Exchange configuration.

Several tabs in the user account Properties dialog box are useful for managing mailboxes. To summon this dialog box, choose Start⇨All Programs⇨ Administrative Tools⇨Active Directory Users and Computers. Then drill down to the user account you need to modify and double-click it to bring up the Properties dialog box. The following sections describe the Exchange features that are available from the various tabs of this dialog box.

The Exchange General tab

The Exchange General tab, as shown in Figure 11-2, lets you set these options:

- **Alias:** The default name is the user's name, but you can change it if you want.

- **Delivery Restrictions:** Set a message size limit for incoming and outgoing messages. You can also specify whom the user can receive messages from.

✔ **Delivery Options:** Create a forwarding address and grant permission to other users to send on behalf of this account.

✔ **Storage Limits:** Set the storage limits for the user's mailbox. You can have a warning message sent whenever the mailbox reaches one size limit and then prevent the user from sending or receiving mail after the mailbox reaches a second size limit.

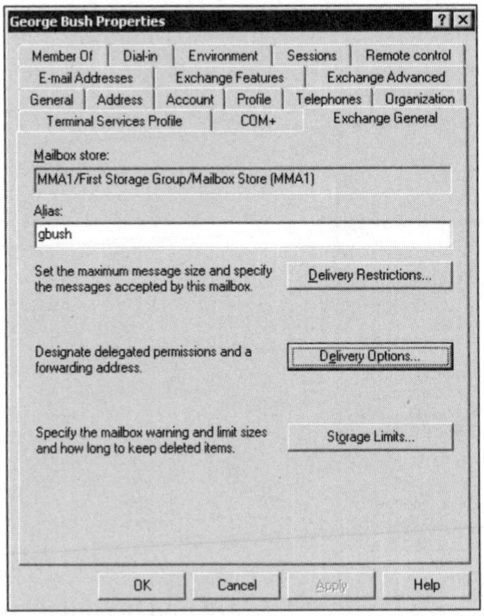

Figure 11-2:
The
Exchange
General tab.

The E-mail Addresses tab

The E-mail Addresses tab of the User Properties dialog box, as shown in Figure 11-3, displays the e-mail addresses associated with a user account. If an e-mail address has been assigned incorrectly, you can use this dialog box to change it. Just select the incorrect e-mail address, click the Edit button, and enter the correct e-mail address. You can also add or remove an e-mail address from this dialog box.

The Exchange Features tab

Figure 11-4 shows the Exchange Features tab of the user Properties dialog box, which lets you configure optional Exchange features for the user.

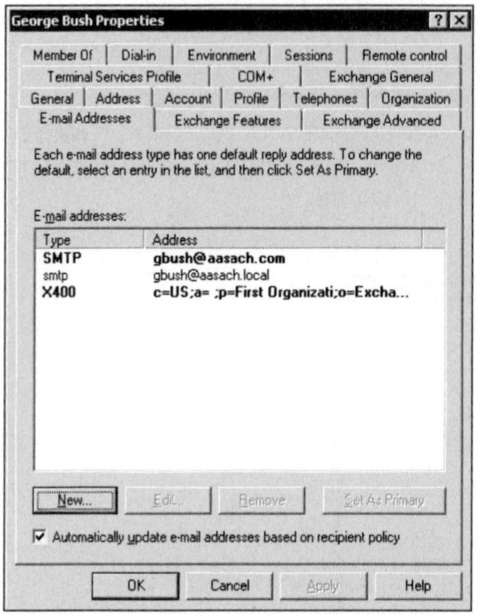

Figure 11-3:
The E-mail
Addresses
tab.

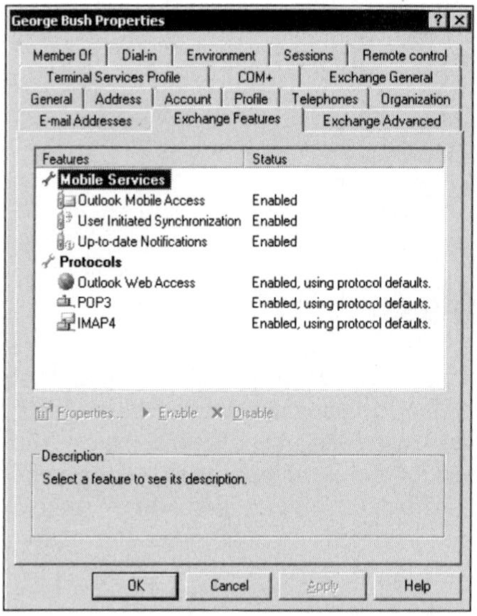

Figure 11-4:
The
Exchange
Features
tab.

The following list describes these features:

- **Outlook Mobile Access:** The user can access Exchange data from a mobile device, such as a cellphone or PDA.

- **User Initiated Synchronization:** The user can start a synchronization operation, to update the mobile device's data from the data on the Exchange server.

✓ **Up-to-Date Notifications:** Enable automatic synchronizations.

✓ **Outlook Web Access:** The user can access her Exchange mailbox from a Web browser rather than from an Outlook client. With this feature enabled, the user can read e-mail from any computer that has an Internet connection.

✓ **POP3:** Enable Internet e-mail by using the POP3 protocol.

✓ **IMAP4:** Enable Internet e-mail by using the IMAP4 protocol.

The Exchange Advanced tab

On the Exchange Advanced tab, as shown in Figure 11-5, you can configure various advanced features of Exchange.

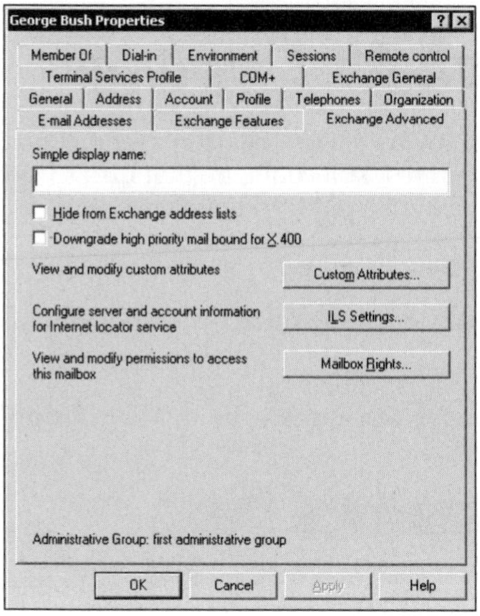

Figure 11-5:
The
Exchange
Advanced
tab.

The following list describes these features:

✓ **Simple Display Name:** Specify a display name used by computers that can't display the full display name. You probably don't have to mess with this feature unless your computers can't display ASCII characters.

✓ **Hide from Exchange Address Lists:** Check this option to prevent a user from appearing in address lists. This option is useful for mailboxes that you don't want to be widely known.

✓ **Downgrade High Priority Mail Bound for X.400:** This option is compatible with the original X.400 standard, which was first released in 1984. If you exchange mail with old-style X.400 systems, you may need to use this option.

✓ **Custom Attributes:** This button leads to a dialog box that lets you track up to 15 different custom attributes for a user. You can safely ignore this option.

✓ **ILS Settings:** If you have an Internet Locator Service server installed, you can click this button to configure it. ILS lets online users find each other. It's used by applications, such as NetMeeting.

✓ **Mailbox Rights:** The most frequently used feature on the Exchange Advanced tab, it lets you grant access to this user's mailbox to other users. For more information, see the section "Viewing Another Mailbox," later in this chapter.

Configuring Outlook for Exchange

When you create an Active Directory user, the user is automatically set up with a mailbox. However, you must still configure that user's Outlook client software to connect to the user's account. Follow these steps:

1. **Start Outlook on the user's computer.**

   An Outlook icon is usually near the top of the Start menu.

2. **Choose Tools⇨E-mail Accounts.**

   The E-mail Accounts dialog box appears, as shown in Figure 11-6.

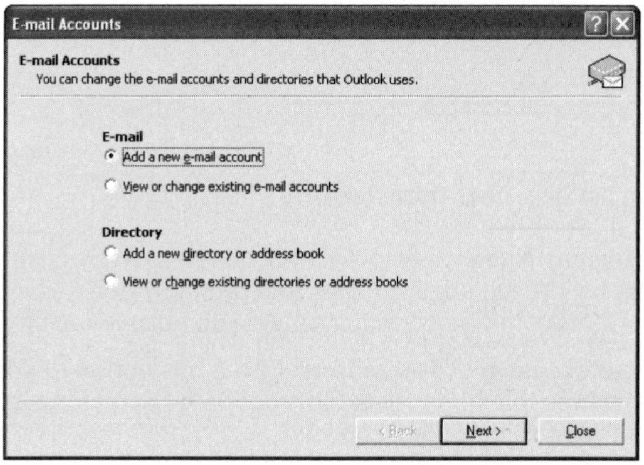

Figure 11-6: The first page of the E-mail Accounts dialog box.

3. **Select the Add a New E-mail Account option and then click Next.**

   The dialog box, as shown in Figure 11-7, appears. This dialog box lists the various types of e-mail accounts that you can create for Outlook.

4. **Select the Microsoft Exchange Server option and then click Next.**

   The dialog box, as shown in Figure 11-8, appears.

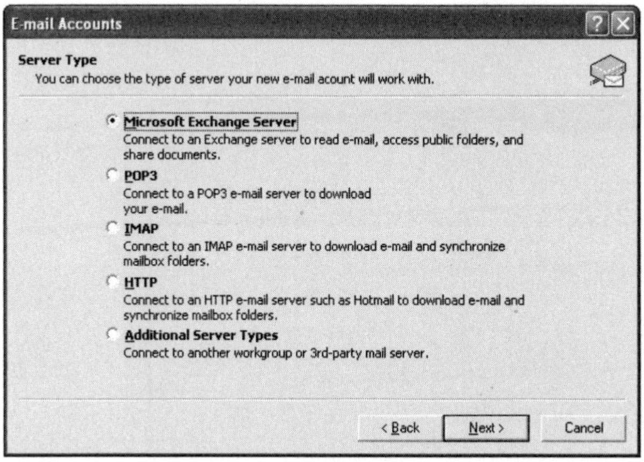

Figure 11-7: Outlook can handle many different types of e-mail accounts.

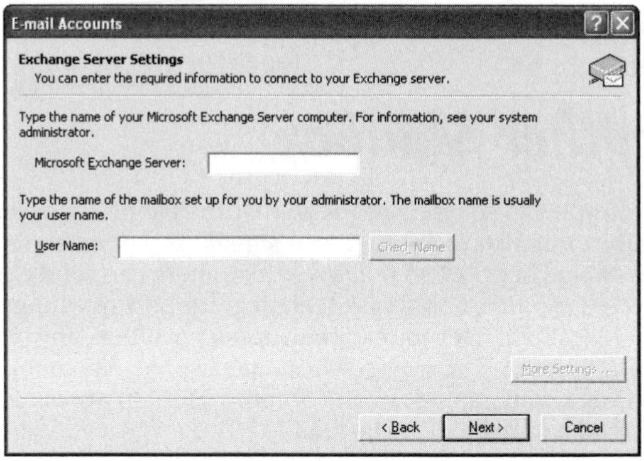

Figure 11-8: You must identify the Exchange server and provide a username.

5. **Enter the name of the Exchange server and the username in the appropriate text boxes, and then click Next.**

   You see this message:

   ```
   The E-Mail account you have just added will not
   start until you choose Exit from the File menu
   and then restart Microsoft Outlook.
   ```

6. Click OK.

The message dialog box disappears, and the last page of the E-Mail Accounts Wizard appears, as shown in Figure 11-9.

7. Click the Finish button.

The wizard is dismissed.

8. Choose File⇨Exit to close Outlook and then restart Outlook.

The mailbox should now be configured.

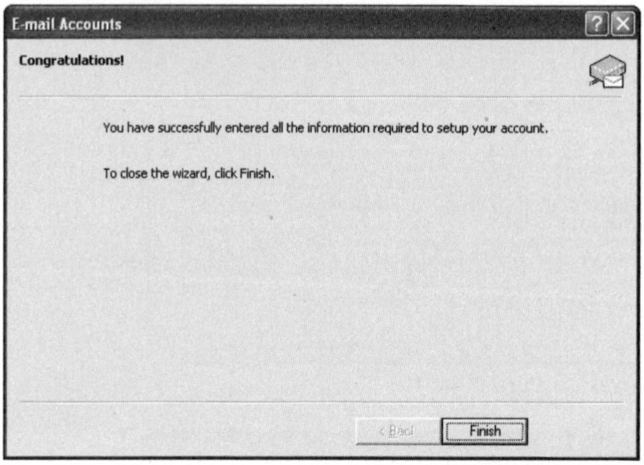

Figure 11-9: Don Pardo, tell them what they've done.

Viewing Another Mailbox

Sometimes you want to set up Outlook so that the user has access to not just his main mailbox but also to another user's mailbox. For example, you may create a user named Support so that your customers can send e-mail to Support@YourCompany.com to ask technical support questions. If you don't set up at least one user to read the Support mailbox, any mail sent to Support@YourCompany.com languishes unanswered. Assuming that that's not what you want, you can set up one or more users to access the Support mailbox and read and respond to its mail.

First, you must configure the Support user account's mailbox so that it grants access rights to the user you want to have access to the account. Follow these steps:

1. On the server, choose Start⇨Active Directory Users and Computers, and then find and double-click the e-mail account that you want to access from another user's copy of Outlook.

The Properties dialog box appears.

2. **Click the Exchange Advanced tab and then click the Mailbox Rights button.**

   The Permissions for Support dialog box appears and displays the Mailbox Rights tab, as shown in Figure 11-10.

3. **Click the Add button.**

   This step brings up the Select Users, Computers, or Groups dialog box.

4. **Type the name of the user you want to grant access to and then click OK.**

   You return to the Permissions for Support dialog box. The user you added is selected in the list of users with access to the mailbox.

5. **Select the Allow check box for the Full Mailbox Access option to grant the user full access to the mailbox and then click OK.**

   The Mailbox Rights dialog box is dismissed.

6. **Click OK.**

   The user Properties dialog box is dismissed.

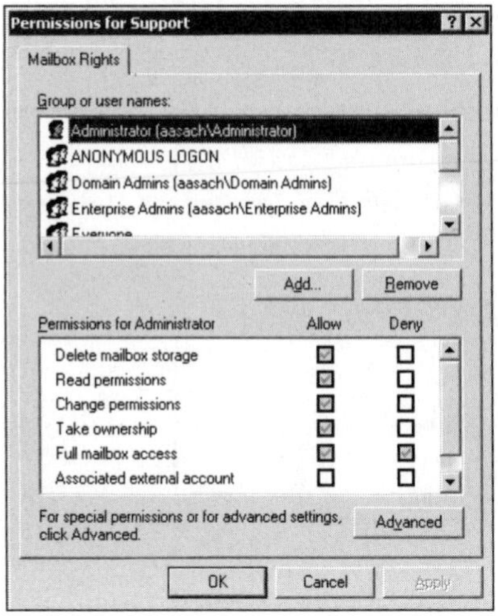

Figure 11-10:
The Mailbox
Rights tab.

After you grant access to the account, you can configure the user's copy of Outlook to read the Support account. Follow these steps:

1. **On the user's computer, start Outlook and choose Tools⇨ E-mail Accounts.**

   The E-mail Accounts dialog box (refer to Figure 11-6) is displayed.

2. **Select the View or Change Existing E-Mail Accounts option and then click Next.**

   The dialog box, as shown in Figure 11-11, is displayed. This dialog box lists the e-mail accounts that have been configured for the Outlook client.

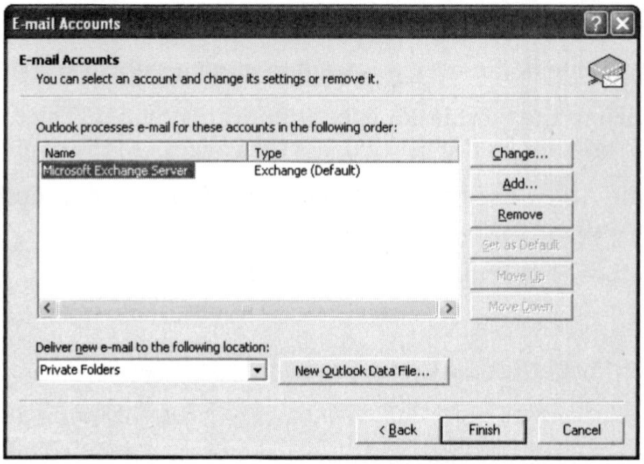

Figure 11-11:
The e-mail accounts configured for an Outlook client.

3. **Select the Microsoft Exchange Server account and then click the Change button.**

   The Exchange Server Settings dialog box appears, as shown in Figure 11-12.

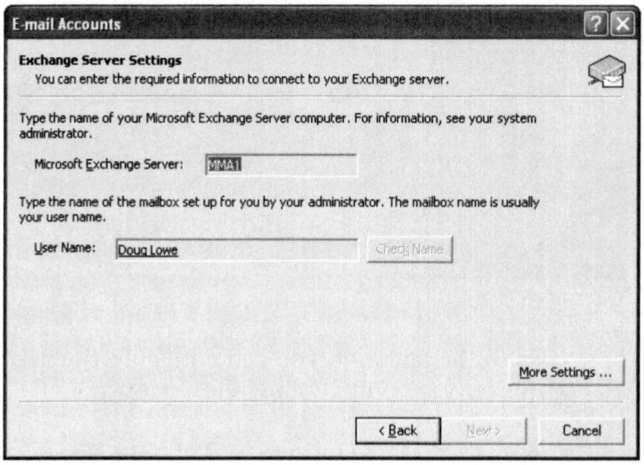

Figure 11-12:
The Exchange Server Settings dialog box.

4. **Click the More Settings button and then click the Advanced tab.**

   The Advanced tab of the Microsoft Exchange Server dialog box appears, as shown in Figure 11-13.

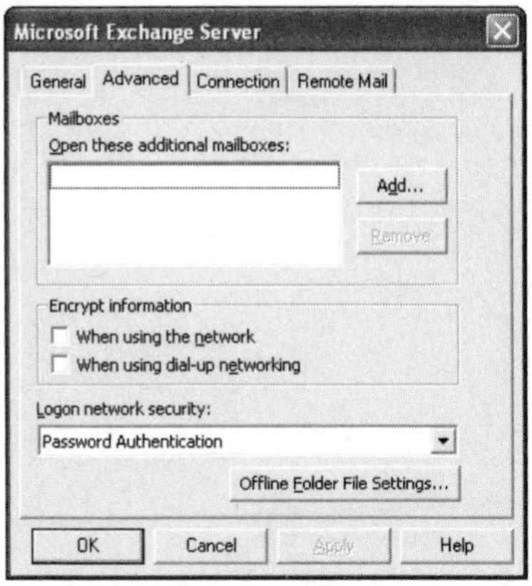

Figure 11-13:
The
Advanced
tab of the
Microsoft
Exchange
Server
dialog box.

> **Microsoft Exchange Server**
>
> General | Advanced | Connection | Remote Mail
>
> **Mailboxes**
> Open these additional mailboxes:
>
> [   ]   Add...
>   Remove
>
> **Encrypt information**
> ☐ When using the network
> ☐ When using dial-up networking
>
> Logon network security:
> [Password Authentication ▼]
>
> Offline Folder File Settings...
>
> OK   Cancel   Apply   Help

5. **Click the Add button.**

   A dialog box prompts you for the name of the mailbox you want to add.

6. **Type the name of the mailbox you want to add and then click OK.**

   The mailbox is added to the list box in the Microsoft Exchange Server dialog box.

7. **Click OK.**

   You return to the Exchange Settings dialog box.

8. **Click Next and then click Finish.**

   You're done! You can now view the Support mailbox.

To view the mailbox, choose View⇨Folder List to open the Folder List window in Outlook. Then double-click the Support mailbox in the list to open it.

Chapter 12

Creating an Intranet

· ·

In This Chapter

▶ Getting acquainted with intranets

▶ Finding good uses for intranets

▶ How to set up a simple intranet

▶ How to manage IIS

· ·

*N*o, I'm not mispronouncing the word *Internet.* The term *intranet* has gained popularity in recent years. It's similar to the Internet, but with a twist: Rather than connect your computer to millions of other computers around the world, an intranet connects your computer to other computers in your company or organization. How is an intranet different from your ordinary, run-of-the-mill network? Read on, and I'll explain.

What Is an Intranet?

Everyone knows that the Internet, and especially the World Wide Web, has become a phenomenon. Millions of computer users worldwide surf the Web, and many join the bandwagon every day.

Recently, ingenious network managers at large companies figured out that although the Web is interesting for distributing public information to the world, the Web is even better for distributing private information within a company. Thus, the idea of intranets was born. An *intranet* is a network that is built by using the same tools and protocols that are used by the global Internet but applied instead to an organization's internal network.

 Think of an intranet as a small, private version of the World Wide Web. Anyone who connects to your local-area network (LAN) can access your intranet. The intranet is accessed by using a Web browser, such as Internet Explorer or Firefox. However, users don't need an Internet connection because the information on the intranet is stored on the company's server computers rather than on a computer that must be accessed from the Internet.

The intranet is analogous to a closed-circuit television system, which can be viewed only by people within the organization that owns the system. In contrast, the Internet is more like cable television in that anyone who's willing to pay $20 or so per month can watch.

Here are two interesting but contradictory points of view about the significance of intranets:

- ✔ Some computer industry pundits say that intranets are more popular than the Internet. For example, many companies that sell Web development tools make more money selling software used for intranets than for the Internet.

- ✔ On the other hand, other industry pundits think that the intranet phenomenon is merely a fad that some other promising new technology, such as pet rocks or hula hoops, will replace in a few years. Only time will tell.

What Do You Use an Intranet For?

Intranets can distribute just about any type of information within a company. Intranets use two basic types of applications:

- ✔ **Publishing application:** Information is posted in the form of pages that you can view from any computer with access to the intranet. This type of intranet application is commonly used for company newsletters, policy manuals, and price lists, for example.

  Publishing applications are simple to set up. In fact, you may be able to set up one yourself without a lot of outside help from highly paid computer consultants.

- ✔ **Transaction application:** Information is gathered from users of the intranet who file online expense reports, report problems to the help desk, or enroll in employee benefit programs, for example.

  Expect to spend big bucks on computer consulting to get an intranet transaction application set up.

Here's the key difference between these two types of intranet applications:

- ✔ **In a publishing application, information flows in one direction.** It flows from the intranet to the user. The user requests some information, and the intranet system delivers it.

- ✔ **In a transaction application, information flows in both directions.** Not only does the user request information from the intranet system, but the intranet system itself also requests information from the user.

What You Need to Set Up an Intranet

To properly set up an intranet, you need the right tools. Here's a list of requirements:

- ✓ **A network:** An intranet doesn't require its own cabling; it can operate on your existing network.

- ✓ **A server computer that's dedicated to the intranet:** Make sure that this computer has plenty of RAM (at least 2GB) and gigabytes of disk space (at least 100GB). Of course, the more users your network has and the more information you intend to place on the server, the more RAM and disk storage you need.

- ✓ **Windows Server 2003 or a Linux operating system:** Web server software requires one or the other.

- ✓ **Web server software for the server computer:** You need to install a Web server, such as IIS (for Windows servers) or Apache (for Linux or Windows servers).

A Webless intranet

The correct way to set up a proper intranet is to set up a Windows-based server running IIS or a Linux-based server running Apache or some other Web server. However, you can create a rudimentary intranet without going to the trouble of setting up an actual Web server. Here's how:

1. **Set up a share on a file server that will hold the HTML files that make up your intranet.**

2. **Create an HTML file for the home page of your intranet and save the file in the location you create in Step 1.**

    I recommend that you name it `index.html`.

3. **Create any other HTML files that your intranet needs.**

    The `index.html` file should include links to these pages.

4. **Point your Web browser to the `index.html` file at the shared network location.**

    For example, if the server is named `iserver` and the share is named `intranet`, enter this information into your browser's address box: **\\iserver\intranet\index.html**. *Voilà!* — you have an instant intranet without the fuss of a Web server.

This rudimentary intranet works without a Web server because a Web browser can display HTML files directly, without the need for a Web server. However, without a Web server, your intranet is limited in what it can do. In particular, all its pages must be *static* (their content is fixed). For *dynamic* content, which users interact with, you need to set up a Web server.

✔ **Programs to help you create Web pages:** If you're the type who dreams in binary, you can create Web pages by typing HTML codes directly into text files. In that case, the only program you need is Notepad. Alternatively, you can use a program designed specifically for creating web pages, such as Microsoft FrontPage, or perhaps something fancier, such as Adobe Dreamweaver. If you're going to develop transaction-based applications, you need additional tools.

How to Set Up an IIS Web Server

Microsoft's Web server for Windows server operating systems is *Internet Information Services,* or *IIS.* IIS is included with Windows Server 2003 but isn't enabled by default. So, you need to configure it before you can use it to create an intranet. Here are the steps:

1. **Choose Start⇨All Programs⇨Administrative Tools⇨Configure Your Server Wizard.**

   This step launches the Configure Your Server Wizard, which displays a friendly greeting screen.

2. **Click Next.**

   The Configure Your Server Wizard displays a screen full of helpful tips, which you should read.

   The only tip you need to pay attention to for this procedure is the one that advises you to have your Windows Server 2003 Setup CD handy. If you don't have it nearby, go get it before you continue.

3. **Click Next.**

   The Configure Your Server Wizard grinds and whirs for a moment and then displays the page shown in Figure 12-1.

4. **Select the Application Server (IIS, ASP.NET) option and then click Next.**

   The Configure Your Server Wizard displays the options for installing IIS, as shown in Figure 12-2.

5. **Select both the FrontPage Server Extensions option and the Enable ASP.NET option.**

   There's no real reason not to enable both these options, so I recommend that you select them both, even if you're not sure that you need them:

   • *FrontPage Server Extensions:* Makes it easier to work with FrontPage to create Web pages for your intranet.

   • *Enable ASP.NET:* Enables the ASP.NET programming platform, which lets you create sophisticated, Web-based programs for your intranet.

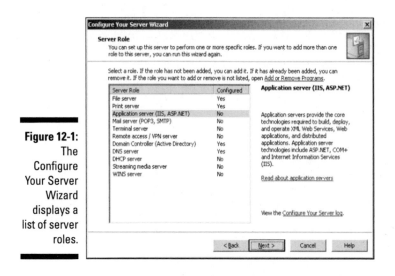

Figure 12-1:
The
Configure
Your Server
Wizard
displays a
list of server
roles.

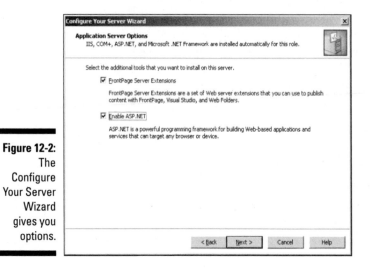

Figure 12-2:
The
Configure
Your Server
Wizard
gives you
options.

6. Click Next.

The wizard displays a summary page that indicates the options you selected, as shown in Figure 12-3.

7. Click Next.

The wizard installs IIS and ASP.NET. This process may take a few minutes, so be patient.

If you're prompted to insert the Windows Server 2003 Setup CD, do so cheerfully.

After the installation is finished, the page shown in Figure 12-4 is displayed.

8. **Click Finish.**

You're done!

How to Create a Simple Intranet Page

After you configure IIS, it's ready to start serving up Web pages for your intranet. All you have to do is create Web pages and save them in the correct location. For the default Web site created by IIS, this location is `c:\inetpub\webroot`.

To get you started, follow these steps to create a simple home page that displays the text *Welcome to my Intranet!*

1. **On the server, choose Start⇨All Programs⇨Accessories⇨Notepad.**

   Notepad, the handy-dandy free text editor, appears.

2. **Type these three lines in the Notepad window:**

   ```
   <h1>
   Welcome to my Intranet!
   </h1>
   ```

3. **Choose File⇨Save, navigate to `c:\inetpub\webroot`, and save the file as `index.htm`.**

   Be sure to save the file as `index.htm`, not `index.html`.

4. **Close Notepad.**

5. **Open a Web browser on a client computer that's connected to the network.**

6. **Enter the server name in the address bar and press Enter.**

   Your intranet comes to life, as shown in Figure 12-5.

Granted, this intranet doesn't do much. You're on your own now to create more interesting Web pages for your intranet. Just save the pages in `c:\inetpub\webroot`.

Figure 12-5:
Behold your intranet!

Managing IIS

You can manage IIS by using the IIS Manager, as shown in Figure 12-6. To start this tool, choose Start⇨All Programs⇨Administrative Tools⇨Internet Information Services (IIS) Manager.

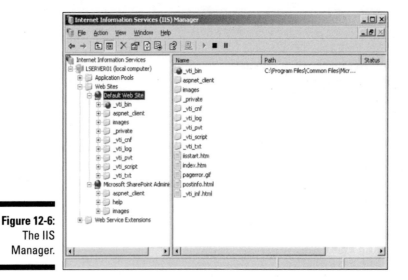

Figure 12-6:
The IIS
Manager.

The pane on the left side of the IIS Manager lists all the Web sites managed by the server. The Default Web Site folder is the Web site that's displayed when the user uses a Web browser to browse to the server.

You can right-click a Web site in the IIS Manager and choose Properties to display the Web site's Properties page, as shown in Figure 12-7.

A lot of information is presented in the nine tabs of this dialog box. The most important items are described in this list:

- ✔ **IP Address:** In most cases, this field is set to All Unassigned, which means that this Web site will be associated with all IP addresses for the server that aren't specifically assigned to other Web sites.

- ✔ **Home Directory:** This tab tells you where on the server's hard drive the HTML and other files for the Web site are located. For the default Web site, the standard location is c:\inetpub\webroot. If you want to store the files somewhere else, change the Local Path field on this tab.

✔ **Documents:** This tab contains a list of filenames that are used when the user navigates to the Web site but doesn't provide a filename. For example, when you enter just the server name without a filename, IIS searches the Web site's home directory for one of the files listed on this tab. The default is to look for the following files, in this order:

```
default.htm
default.asp
index.htm
iisstart.htm
Default.aspx
```

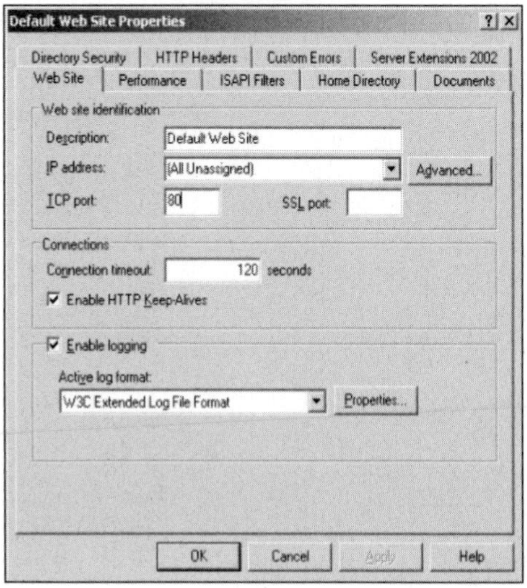

Figure 12-7:
The
Properties
dialog box
for the
default
Web site.

Chapter 13

Is It a Phone or a Computer? (Or, Understanding VoIP and Convergence)

. . . .

In This Chapter

▶ How VoIP works

▶ Advantages of VoIP

▶ Disadvantages of VoIP

▶ Some popular VoIP providers

. . . .

*O*ne of the newest trends in networking is the convergence of two distinct but similar types of networks: computer networks and telephone networks. Both types of networks can be either cabled or wireless, and both can carry voice and data. In other words, the distinction between computer networks and telephone networks is getting blurry.

This chapter gives you a brief introduction to *VoIP,* a technology that lets you send voice data over your computer network. In other words, VoIP attempts to make your phone cables obsolete by having the computer network handle voice traffic.

 This chapter isn't a complete guide to VoIP. For that, check out *VoIP For Dummies,* written by Timothy V. Kelly and published by Wiley.

Understanding VoIP

VoIP, which stands for *Voice Over IP (Internet Protocol),* works much the same as a regular telephone. However, rather than connect to the public telephone network, your phones connect directly to the Internet. The main benefit is reduced cost, especially if you make a lot of long distance phone calls. Most VoIP services charge a single flat monthly rate, usually in the neighborhood of $25–$35.

When you use a normal phone to make a long distance call, your voice is transmitted (usually in digital form) over the *public switched telephone network,* or *PSTN.* Along the way, you're charged by-the-minute fees by your long distance service provider.

When you use VoIP, your voice is still converted into digital form. However, rather than be sent over private networks owned by telephone companies, it is sent over the Internet. Because the Internet uses the IP protocol, the digital data that represents your voice must be converted into packets that can be sent reliably over IP — hence the name Voice Over IP, or VoIP.

Carrying telephone conversations over the Internet isn't new. In fact, the technology has been around for many years. Only recently has the technology become inexpensive enough to catch on for residential service. That's why you may not have heard of VoIP until now.

There are two basic approaches to setting up VoIP:

- ✔ **Software-only VoIP systems:** These run on your computer and enable you to talk free with anyone else anywhere in the world provided they're using the same software you are.

  The best-known software-only VoIP system is Skype (www.skype.com). The advantage of Skype is that it's free. Software-only VoIP has two major drawbacks:

  - You can only use it from your computer. You can't just pick up a phone, dial a number, and make a call via Skype.

  - The other person must use Skype. You can't just call anyone.

    A fee-based system, *SkypeOut,* lets you call regular phone numbers from Skype for about $0.02 per minute (way cheap).

  Skype is great if you do most of your long distance calling to geeks who don't mind sitting at the computer for "phone" calls.

- ✔ **VoIP services, such as Vonage and AT&T CallVantage:** These services don't require a computer. They use an *Analog Telephone Adapter (ATA)* that connects a normal telephone to the Internet. The adapter lets you use VoIP pretty much as though it were a regular telephone. You just pick up the phone and dial a number. The fact that the call is routed over the Internet rather than over the public phone network is, for the most part, transparent.

Advantages of VoIP

VoIP service has several compelling advantages over traditional telephone service. Here are a few:

- **Long distance calls over VoIP are cheaper than they are over traditional phone service.** With VoIP, you typically pay a fixed monthly rate of $25–$35 for unlimited calls — long distance or not. If your phone bill now runs more than $35 per month, you may want to consider VoIP.

- **You can take your ATA device with you on the road and use it anywhere that you can plug into the Internet.** For example, you can go on vacation and take your ATA with you. Then you can plug into the Internet and receive or make calls by using your home phone number. (Of course, you don't *have* to take your ATA with you. After all, avoiding calls from your in-laws may be the reason you're going on vacation in the first place.)

- **Because calls are carried over the Internet and not over the public switched telephone network, your phone isn't tied to a specific area code.** In fact, VoIP lets you choose any area code you want. For example, if your small company is located in Fresno, you can get a VoIP service with a 415 area code so that your customers will think you're in San Francisco.

  An enterprising small business in Fresno can set up two VoIP lines with a 415 area code and a 212 area code. Your customers will think that you have offices in San Francisco and New York, even though both numbers ring phones in sunny Fresno.

- **Choosing a local area code saves on phone charges.** Suppose that your office is in Fresno, but nearly all your clients are in San Francisco. Setting up a 415 VoIP number lets your clients dial your number as a local call. Choosing an area code other than your real area code isn't always just for looks.

- **VoIP services have more features in the standard package.** Features, such as *call waiting, call forwarding, caller ID, 3-way calling,* and *voice mail,* usually don't cost extra with VoIP.

- **Modern VoIP audio quality is as good as traditional phone service.** Sometimes, it's *better.*

- **VoIP services have additional features that you can use if you connect a computer to the ATA device.** For example, some services can send your voice-mail messages to an e-mail account as attachments. Then you can use Microsoft Outlook or another mail program to listen to your voice mail.

Disadvantages of VoIP

You have to consider a few disadvantages before you switch your phone service over to VoIP. Here are the most important ones:

- ✔ **You must have a reliable broadband Internet connection.** If your Internet connection goes down, so will your VoIP connection.

- ✔ **The ATA requires electrical power to work.** As a result, you can't use your VoIP phone during a power outage unless you connect it to an Uninterruptible Power Supply (UPS). In contrast, traditional telephones draw their power directly from the phone lines. That's why traditional phones continue to work even during power outages.

- ✔ **VoIP isn't really mobile in the same sense as a cellphone.** You probably need a cellphone, too.

- ✔ **Calls to the 911 emergency system are problematic with VoIP services.** The basic problem is that the 911 system is designed to contact *local* emergency dispatchers. Because VoIP services aren't tied to a particular location, you must notify your VoIP provider of your location for 911 to work. If you take your VoIP ATA with you on a trip and then forget to notify your provider of your new location before dialing 911, you're connected to emergency services in your hometown, not in your present location.

Popular VoIP Providers

If you're thinking of switching to VoIP, investigate these services:

- ✔ **Vonage:** One of the oldest and most popular VoIP providers. A residential customer can get unlimited access for $24.95 per month. Or, you can get a 500-minute plan for $14.95 per month. See www.vonage.com.

- ✔ **AT&T CallVantage:** The basic plan for residential customers, with unlimited long distance, costs $29.95 per month. See www.usa.att.com/callvantage.

- ✔ **Cablevision Optimum Voice:** The Cablevision Optimum Voice plan costs $34.95 per month. See www.optimumvoice.com.

- ✔ **Verizon VoiceWing:** The basic unlimited service plan is $29.95 per month. Like Vonage, Verizon offers a 500-minute plan for $14.95 per month. See www.voicewing.com.

Chapter 14

Connecting from Home

. . . .

In This Chapter

▶ Accessing your e-mail with Outlook Web Access

▶ Using a virtual private network

. . . .

A typical computer user takes work home to work on in the evening or over the weekend and bring back to the office the following weekday. This arrangement can work okay, except that exchanging information between your home computer and your office computer isn't easy.

One way to exchange files is to mark them for offline access, as described in Chapter 3. However, this approach has its drawbacks. What if someone goes to the office on Saturday and modifies the same file you're working on at home? What if you get home and discover that the file you need is on a folder you didn't mark for offline access?

What about e-mail? Offline access doesn't give you access to your company e-mail account, so you can't check whether you have mail in your Inbox or send mail from your company e-mail account.

This chapter introduces two features that can alleviate these problems. The first is Internet-based access to your e-mail via Outlook Web Access (OWA) in Microsoft Exchange. The second is the *virtual private network* (VPN), which lets you connect to your network from home as though you were at work so that you can safely access all your network resources as though you were locally connected to the network.

Using Outlook Web Access

Most people who connect to their office networks from home really just need their e-mail. If the only reason for accessing the office network is to get e-mail, Outlook Web Access is a simple, easy tool.

Outlook Web Access (OWA) is a Microsoft Exchange Server feature that can access your company e-mail from any computer that has an Internet connection. The remote computer just needs a Web browser and an Internet connection; no VPN or other special configuration is required.

The best part is that you don't have to do anything special to enable OWA; it's enabled by default when you install Microsoft Exchange 2003. Although you can configure plenty of options to improve its use, OWA is functional right out of the box.

To access OWA from any Web browser, just browse to the address that's designated for your organization's OWA. The default address is the DNS name of your mail server, followed by `/exchange`. For example, for the mail server `smtp.lowewriter.com`, the OWA address is `smtp.lowewriter.com/exchange`.

The connection must use the secure version of the normal HTTP Web protocol. You must type **https://** before the OWA address. The complete address will be something like `https://smtp.lowewriter.com/exchange`.

When you browse to your OWA address, you're prompted to enter a name and password. Use your regular network logon name and password. OWA will appear in the browser window, as in Figure 14-1.

Figure 14-1: OWA looks a lot like Outlook.

If you're familiar with Outlook, you'll have no trouble using OWA. Almost all Outlook's features are available, including your Inbox, calendar, contacts, tasks, reminders, and even public folders. You can even set up an Out of Office reply.

One difference between OWA and Outlook is that there's no menu bar across the top. However, most of the functions that are available from the menu bar are available elsewhere in OWA. If you can't find a feature, look in the Options page, which you can reach by clicking Options at the bottom left of the window. Figure 14-2 shows the Options page. As you can see, this page lets you create an Out of Office reply, set your signature, and change a variety of other options.

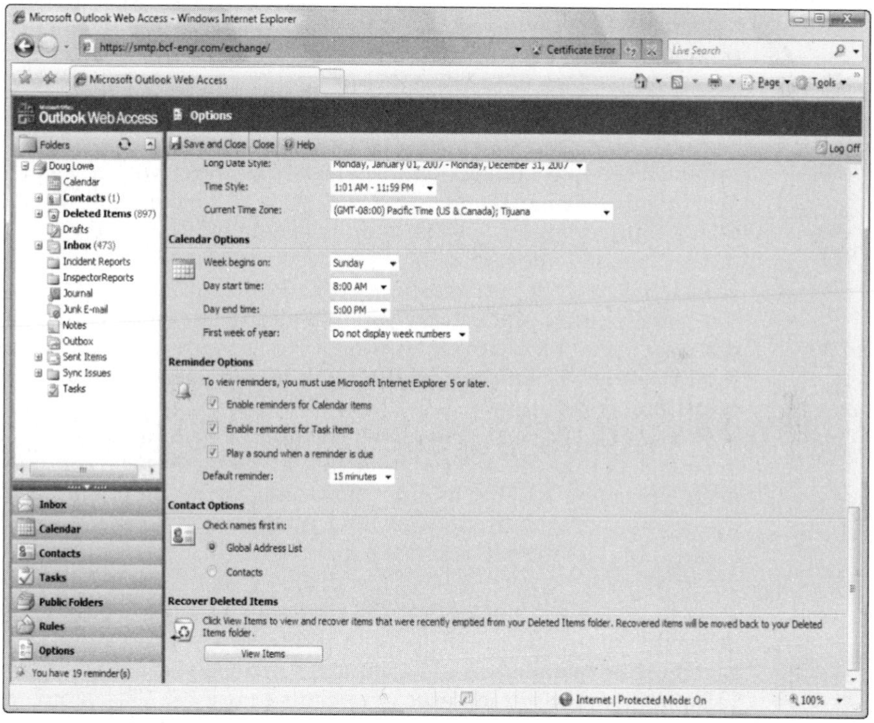

Figure 14-2: Setting OWA options.

Using a Virtual Private Network

The term *virtual private network,* or *VPN,* refers to several different types of secure forms of Internet communication. In this chapter, a VPN is a secure channel between a remote computer and a local network. This type of VPN enables you to log on to your company network from your home computer. Then you can access any resource on your company network as though you were using a computer that's physically connected to the company network. In other words, the VPN extends the reach of the company network to include your home computer.

The security mechanism that makes this magic work is the Internet protocol known as IPSec. The details of how IPSec works are way beyond the scope of this humble little book. Suffice it to say that IPSec encrypts all the Internet traffic related to the VPN. This encryption effectively creates a secret tunnel between the office network and your home computer. Thus, the VPN connection is secure.

Although the VPN connection itself is secure, the *computer* that the VPN connects to may not be. Using a VPN with your home computer is analogous to taking your computer to work and plugging it in to the network. If your computer is already infected with a virus, you run the very real risk of letting that virus loose on your corporate network. As a result, you must be certain that the same security precautions you use with your company network are in use with any computer that you let connect to the network via a VPN. You must therefore ensure that the computer has, at minimum, adequate antivirus protection in place.

In most networks, the VPN is implemented by the firewall router that connects the network to the Internet. Thus, if you plan on providing VPN capability for your network users, you should make sure that the router you use to connect to the Internet has VPN support built in.

The office network side of the VPN is provided by the firewall router. The other side of the VPN — the remote computers — is provided by software that must be installed on the computers themselves. Send a copy of this software home with each user who wants to use the VPN, along with detailed instructions on how to install and configure it. Either that, or you'll have to visit each person's home to install and configure the software yourself. (I wrote instructions for installing VPN software for a user who has a vacation home in Monterey, California. Unfortunately, the instructions were clear enough that he was able to install the VPN software himself, so I didn't have to make a house call. Next time, I'm writing the instructions in Latin.)

After a remote user has used a VPN to connect to your network, the user can access any of the network's shared resources. For example, the user can map network drives and access shared network folders and can also use network printers. And, she can use Outlook to access her e-mail.

Part IV
Network Management For Dummies

The 5th Wave   By Rich Tennant

"Ironically, he went out there looking for a 'hot spot.'"

In this part . . .

You discover that there's more to networking than installing the hardware and software. After you get your network up and running, you have to keep it up and running. That's called *network management*.

The chapters in this part show you how to set up your network's security system, improve your network's performance, and protect your network from disaster. At times, things may get a bit technical, but no one said that life is easy.

Chapter 15

Welcome to Network Management

In This Chapter

▶ Exploring the many jobs of the network administrator

▶ Documenting the network

▶ Dusting, vacuuming, and mopping

▶ Managing network users

▶ Choosing the right tools

▶ Getting certified

Help wanted. Network administrator to help small business get control of a network run amok. Must have sound organizational and management skills. Only moderate computer experience required. Part-time only.

Does this sound like an ad that your company should run? Every network needs a network administrator, whether the network has 2 computers or 2,000. Of course, managing a 2,000-computer network is a full-time job, whereas managing a 2-computer network isn't. At least, it shouldn't be.

This chapter introduces you to the boring job of network administration. Oops — you're probably reading this chapter because you've been elected to be the network manager, so I'd better rephrase that:

This chapter introduces you to the wonderful, exciting world of network management! Oh, boy! This is going to be fun!

What a Network Administrator Does

A network administrator "administers" a network: Installing, configuring, expanding, protecting, upgrading, tuning, and repairing the network.

A network administrator takes care of the network hardware (such as cables, hubs, switches, routers, servers, and clients) and the network software (such as network operating systems, e-mail servers, backup software, database servers, and application software). Most important, the administrator takes care of network users by answering their questions, listening to their troubles, and solving their problems.

On a big network, these responsibilities constitute a full-time job. Large networks tend to be volatile: Users come and go, equipment fails, software chokes, and life in general seems to be one crisis after another.

Smaller networks are much more stable. After you get your network up and running, you probably won't have to spend much time managing its hardware and software. An occasional problem may pop up, but with only a few computers on the network, problems should be few and far between.

Regardless of the network's size, the administrator attends to common chores:

- **Get involved in every decision to purchase new computers, printers, or other equipment.**

- **Put on the pocket protector whenever a new computer is added to the network.** The network administrator's job includes considering changes in the cabling configuration, assigning a computer name to the new computer, integrating the new user into the security system, and granting user rights.

- **Whenever a software vendor releases a new version of its software, read about the new version and decide whether its new features warrant an upgrade.** In most cases, the hardest part of upgrading to new software is determining the _migration path_ — that is, upgrading your entire network to the new version while disrupting the network and its users as little as possible. This statement is especially true if the software in question happens to be your network operating system because any change to the network operating system can potentially impact the entire network.

  Between upgrades, software vendors periodically release patches and service packs that fix minor problems. For more information, see Chapter 23.

- **Perform routine chores, such as backing up the servers, archiving old data, and freeing up server disk space.** Much of the task of network administration involves making sure that things keep working, by finding and correcting problems before users notice that something is wrong. In this sense, network administration can be a thankless job.

- **Gather, organize, and track the entire network's software inventory.** You never know when something will go haywire on the ancient Windows 95 computer that Joe in Marketing uses, and you have to reinstall that old copy of Lotus Approach. Do you have any idea where the installation disks are?

Picking a Part-Time Administrator and Providing the Right Resources

The larger the network, the more technical support it needs. Small networks — with just one or two dozen computers — can manage with just a part-time network administrator. Ideally, this person should be a closet computer geek: someone who has a secret interest in computers but doesn't like to admit it; someone who will take home books to read over the weekend; and someone who enjoys solving computer problems just for the sake of solving them.

The job of managing a network requires some computer skills, but it isn't entirely a technical job. Much of the work is routine housework. Basically, the network administrator does the electronic equivalent of dusting, vacuuming, and mopping the network periodically, to keep it from becoming a mess.

Here are some resources the network administrator needs:

- ✔ **Allow enough time for network administration.** For a small network (no more than 20 or so computers), an hour or two each week is enough time to do the job. More time is needed upfront while the network administrator settles into the job and discovers the ins and outs of the network. After an initial settling-in period, network administration for a small-office network doesn't take more than an hour or two per week. (Larger networks take more time.)

- ✔ **Give the position some teeth.** You need to make sure that everyone knows who the network administrator is and that he has the authority to make decisions about the network, such as which access rights each user has, which files can and can't be stored on the server, and how often backups are done.

- ✔ **Provide backup.** The network administrator needs an *understudy* — someone who knows almost as much about the network, is eager to make a mark, and smiles when the worst network jobs are "delegated."

- ✔ **Supply a job title and a job description.** The network manager should have some sort of official title, such as Network Boss, Network Czar, Vice President in Charge of Network Operations, or Dr. Net. A badge, a personalized pocket protector, or a set of Spock ears helps, too.

Here are some suggestions for picking a part-time network administrator. Make sure that the person you choose

- ✔ **Is organized:** Conduct a surprise office inspection and place the person with the neatest desk in charge of the network.

    Don't warn anyone in advance, or else everyone may mess up their desks intentionally the night before the inspection.

✔ **Is assertive and willing to irritate people to get the job done:** A good network administrator should ensure that backups are working *before* a disk fails and that everyone is following good antivirus practices *before* a virus wipes out the entire network.

✔ **Knows how to install the software:** Usually, the person who installs the network is also the network administrator. This is appropriate because no one understands the network better than the person who designs and installs it.

Documenting the Network

One of the network administrator's main jobs is to keep the network documentation up-to-date. I suggest that you keep all important information about your network in a three-ring binder. Give this binder a clever name, such as The Network Binder. Here are some items it should include:

✔ **An up-to-date diagram of the network:** This diagram can be a detailed floor plan showing the location of each computer or a more abstract and Picasso-like depiction. Anytime you change the network layout, update the diagram. Include a detailed description of the change, the date that the change was made, and the reason for the change.

Microsoft sells the *Visio* program, which is specially designed for creating network diagrams. I highly recommend it.

✔ **A detailed inventory of your computer equipment:** Table 15-1 provides a sample checklist you can use to keep track of your computer equipment.

✔ **A System Information printout for each computer:** Choose Start⇨ All Programs⇨Accessories⇨System Tools⇨System Information.

✔ **A detailed list of network shares and standard drive assignments:** Don't just list the name of each network share; provide a brief description of each share's purpose as well.

✔ **Any other information that you think may be useful:** Give details about how you must configure a particular application program to work with the network and copies of every network component's original invoice — just in case something breaks and you need to seek warranty service.

✔ **Backup schedules:** Include a schedule of when each server is backed up as well as an explanation of the tape rotation schedule.

Never put passwords in the binder!

Table 15-1	Computer Equipment Checklist
Computer location:	
User:	
Manufacturer:	
Model number:	
Serial number:	
Date purchased:	
CPU type and speed:	
Memory:	
Hard drive size:	
Video type:	
Printer type:	
Other equipment:	
Operating system version:	
Application software and version:	
Network card type:	
MAC address:	

Even if you keep track of the information in your network binder by using a spreadsheet or database program, keep a *printed* copy of the information on hand.

If your network is large, you may want to invest in a *network-discovery* program, such as NetworkView Software's NetworkView (www.networkview.com). This program can gather the network documentation automatically: It scans the network carefully for every computer, printer, router, and other device it can find and then builds a database of information. The program then automatically draws a pretty diagram and chugs out helpful reports.

Performing Routine Chores

Much of the network manager's job is routine stuff — the equivalent of vacuuming, dusting, and mopping, or changing your car's oil and rotating the tires.

These tasks are boring, but they have to be done:

- ✔ **Create backups:** The network manager must ensure that the network is properly backed up. If something goes wrong and the network isn't backed up, guess who gets the blame? On the other hand, if disaster strikes yet you're able to recover everything from yesterday's backup with only a small amount of work lost, who gets the pat on the back, the fat bonus, and the vacation in the Bahamas? Chapter 21 describes the options for network backups. Read it *soon.*

- ✔ **Provide security:** Another major task for a network administrator is sheltering the network from the evils of the outside world. These evils come in many forms, including hackers trying to break into your network and virus programs arriving through e-mail. Chapter 22 describes this task in more detail.

- ✔ **Cleanup:** Users think that the network server is like the attic: They want to throw files up there and leave them forever. No matter how much disk storage your network has, your users will fill it up sooner than you think, so the network manager gets the fun job of cleaning up the attic once in a while. The best advice I can offer is to continually complain about how messy it is up there and warn your users that spring cleaning is on the to-do list.

Managing Network Users

Managing network technology is the easiest part of network management. Computer technology can be confusing at first, but computers aren't as confusing as people. The real challenge of managing a network is managing the network's users.

The difference between managing technology and managing users is obvious: You can figure out computers, but who can ever really figure out people? The people who use the network are much less predictable than the network itself. Here are some tips for dealing with users:

- ✔ **Make user training a key part of the network manager's job.** Make sure that everyone who uses the network understands how it works and how to use it. If the network users don't understand how the network works, they may unintentionally do all kinds of weird things to it.

- ✔ **Treat network users respectfully.** If users don't understand how to use the network, it's not their fault. Explain it to them. Offer a class. Buy each one a copy of this book, and tell them to read it during the lunch hour. Hold their hands. Just don't treat them like idiots.

- ✔ **Create a network cheat sheet.** It should contain everything users need to know about using the network — on one page. Everyone needs a copy.

- ✔ **Be as responsive as possible.** If you don't quickly fix a network user's problem, he may try to fix it. You don't want that to happen.

The better you understand the psychology of network users, the more prepared you are for the strangeness they often serve up. Toward that end, I recommend that you read the *Diagnostic and Statistical Manual of Mental Disorders* (also known as *DSM-IV*) from cover to cover.

Acquiring Software Tools for Network Administrators

Network managers need certain tools to get their jobs done. Managers of big, complicated, expensive networks need big, complicated, expensive tools. Managers of small networks need small tools.

Some of the tools that a manager needs are hardware tools, such as screw-drivers, cable crimpers, and hammers. The tools I'm talking about, however, are software tools. I mention a couple of them earlier in this chapter: Visio (to help you draw network diagrams) and a network-discovery tool to help you map your network. Here are a few others:

- **Built-in TCP/IP commands:** Many of the software tools that you need in order to manage a network come with the network itself. As the network manager, you should read through the manuals that come with your net-work software to see which management tools are available. For example, Windows includes a `net diag` command that you can use to make sure that all the computers on a network can communicate with each other. (You can run `net diag` from an MS-DOS prompt.) For TCP/IP networks, you can use the TCP/IP diagnostic commands that are summarized in Table 15-2.

- **System Information:** This program, which comes with Windows, is a useful utility for network managers.

- **Hotfix Checker:** This handy tool from Microsoft scans your computers to see which patches need to be applied. You can download the Hotfix Checker for free from the Microsoft Web site. Just go to `www.microsoft.com` and search for **hfnetchk.exe**.

- **Baseline Security Analyzer:** If you prefer GUI-based tools, check out this program, which you can download for free from the Microsoft Web site. To find it, go to `www.microsoft.com` and search for **Microsoft Baseline Security Analyzer**.

- **A third-party utility:** Get one of those 100-in-1 utility programs, such as Symantec's Norton Utilities. It has invaluable utilities for repairing dam-aged hard drives, rearranging the directory structure of your hard drive, and gathering information about your computer and its equipment.

Never use a hard-drive repair program that isn't designed to work with the operating system or version that your computer uses or the file system you installed. Anytime you upgrade to a newer version of your operating system, also upgrade your hard-drive repair program to a version that supports the new operating system version.

✔ **Protocol analyzer:** A *protocol analyzer* (or *packet sniffer*) can monitor and log the individual packets that travel along your network. You can configure the protocol analyzer to filter specific types of packets, watch for specific types of problems, and provide statistical analysis of the captured packets.

Most network administrators agree that *Sniffer,* by Sniffer Technologies (www.sniffer.com) is the best protocol analyzer available. However, it's also one of the most expensive. If you prefer a free alternative, check out *Ethereal,* which you can download for free from www.ethereal.com.

✔ **Network Monitor:** Windows 2000 and Windows XP — as well as Windows 2000 Server and Windows Server 2003 — include this program; it provides basic protocol analysis and can often help solve pesky network problems.

Table 15-2	TCP/IP Diagnostic Commands
Command	*What It Displays*
arp	Address resolution information used by the Address Resolution Protocol (ARP)
hostname	Your computer's host name
ipconfig	Current TCP/IP settings
nbtstat	The status of NetBIOS over TCP/IP connections
netstat	Statistics for TCP/IP
nslookup	DNS information
ping	Verification that a specified computer can be reached
route	The PC's routing tables
tracert	The route from your computer to a specified host

Building a Library

Scotty delivered one of his best lines in the original *Star Trek* series when he refused to take shore leave so that he could get caught up on his technical journals. "Don't you ever relax?" asked Kirk. "I am relaxing!" Scotty replied.

To be a good network administrator, you need to read computer books — lots of them. And you need to enjoy doing it. If you're the type who takes computer books with you to the beach, you'll make a great network administrator.

Read books on a variety of topics. I don't recommend specific titles, but I do recommend that you get a good, comprehensive book on each of these topics:

- Network cabling and hardware
- Ethernet
- Windows 2000 Server
- Windows Server 2003
- Windows XP Professional
- Windows Vista
- Exchange
- Linux
- TCP/IP
- DNS and BIND
- SendMail
- Exchange Server
- Security and hacking
- Wireless networking

In addition to reading books, you may also want to subscribe to some magazines to keep up with what's happening in the networking industry. Here are a few you probably should consider, along with their Web addresses:

- *InformationWeek:* www.informationweek.com
- *InfoWorld:* www.infoworld.com
- *Network Computing:* www.networkcomputing.com
- *Network:* www.networkmagazine.com
- *Windows & .NET:* www.winntmag.com
- *2600:* www.2600.com (a great magazine on computer hacking and security)

The Internet is one of the best sources of technical information for network administrators. Stock your browser's Favorites menu with plenty of Web sites that contain useful networking information. Many Web sites have online newsletters you can subscribe to so that you regularly get fresh information by e-mail.

Pursuing Certification

Remember the scene near the end of *The Wizard of Oz* when the Wizard grants the Scarecrow a diploma, the Cowardly Lion a medal, and the Tin Man a testimonial?

Network certifications are kind of like that. I can picture the scene now:

The Wizard: "And as for you, my network-burdened friend, any geek with thick glasses can administer a network. Back where I come from, there are people who do nothing but configure Cisco routers all day long. And they don't have any more brains than you do. But they have one thing you don't have: certification. And so, by the authority vested in me by the Universita Committeeatum E Pluribus Unum, I hereby confer upon you the coveted certification of CND."

You: "CND?"

The Wizard: "Yes, that's, uh, *Certified Network Dummy.*"

You: "The Seven Layers of the OSI Reference Model are equal to the Sum of the Layers on the Opposite Side. Oh, rapture! I feel like a network administrator already!"

Certification doesn't guarantee that you really know how to administer a network. That ability comes from real-world experience — not from exam crams.

However, certification is important in today's competitive job market. So, you may want to pursue certification — not just to improve your skills but also to improve your résumé. Certification is an expensive proposition. Its tests can cost several hundred dollars each, and depending on your technical skills, you may need to buy books to study or enroll in training courses before you take the tests.

You can pursue two basic types of certification: vendor-specific and vendor-neutral. The major networking vendors (such as Microsoft, Novell, and Cisco) provide certification programs for their own equipment and software. CompTIA, a nonprofit industry trade association, provides the best-known vendor-neutral certification.

Chapter 16

Managing User Accounts with Active Directory

In This Chapter

▶ Understanding user accounts

▶ Creating user accounts

▶ Setting account options

▶ Working with groups

▶ Creating a logon script

*E*very user who accesses a network must have a *user account.* User accounts let you control who can access the network and who can't. In addition, user accounts let you specify which network resources each user can use. Without user accounts on your network, all your resources are open to anyone who casually drops by your network.

Basics of Windows User Accounts

User accounts are one of the basic tools for managing a Windows server. As a network administrator, you spend a large percentage of your time dealing with user accounts — creating new ones, deleting expired ones, resetting passwords for forgetful users, granting new access rights, and so on. Before I get into the specific procedures of creating and managing user accounts, this section presents an overview of user accounts and how they work.

Local accounts versus domain accounts

A *local account* is a user account that is stored on a particular computer and applies to only that computer. Typically, each computer on your network has a local account for each person who uses that computer.

In contrast, a *domain account* is a user account that is stored by Active Directory and can be accessed from any computer that's a part of the domain. Domain accounts are centrally managed. This chapter deals primarily with setting up and maintaining domain accounts.

User account properties

Every user account has a number of important *account properties* that specify the characteristics of the account. The three most important account properties are

✔ **Username:** A unique name that identifies the account. The user must enter her username when logging on to the network.

The username is public information. Other network users can (and often, should) find out your username.

✔ **Password:** A secret word needed to access the account.

You can set up Windows to enforce password *policies,* such as

  • The minimum length of the password

  • Whether the password must contain both letters and numerals

  • How frequently the user must change the password

✔ **Group membership:** Indicates the group or groups to which the user account belongs. Group memberships are the key to granting access rights to users so that they can

  • Access network resources, such as file shares or printers

  • Perform network tasks, such as creating new user accounts or backing up the server

Groups are a handy way to send e-mail to multiple users. For example, if all users in your marketing department are members of a group named Marketing, you send them all an e-mail by addressing the mail to the Marketing group.

Many other account properties record information about the user, such as her contact information and whether she's allowed to access the system only at certain times or from certain computers. I describe the most important of these features in later sections of this chapter.

Creating a New User

To create a new domain user account in Windows Server 2003, follow these steps:

1. **Choose Start⇨Administrative Tools⇨Active Directory Users and Computers.**

   This step fires up the Active Directory Users and Computers management console, as shown in Figure 16-1.

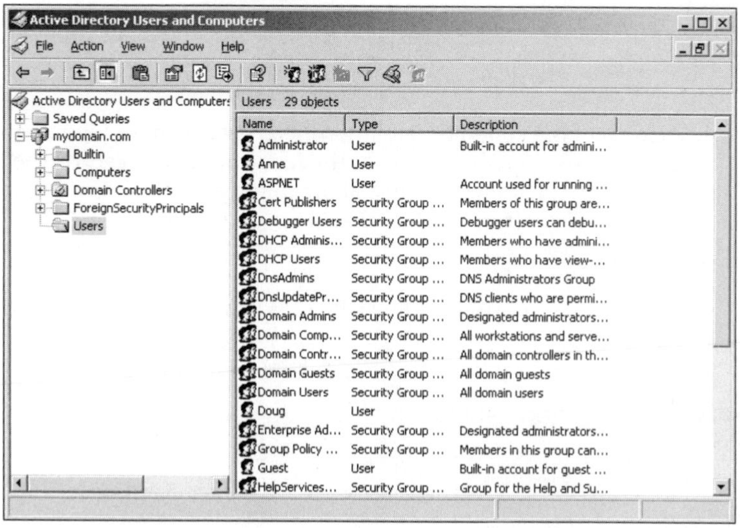

Figure 16-1: The Active Directory Users and Computers management console.

2. **Right-click the domain that you want to add the user to and then choose New⇨User.**

   This step calls the New Object Wizard, as shown in Figure 16-2.

3. **Type the user's first name, middle initial, and last name.**

   As you type the name, the New Object Wizard automatically fills in the Full Name field.

4. **Change the Full Name field if you want it to appear differently than proposed.**

   For example, you may want to reverse the first and last names so that the last name appears first.

5. **Type the user logon name.**

   This name must be unique within the domain.

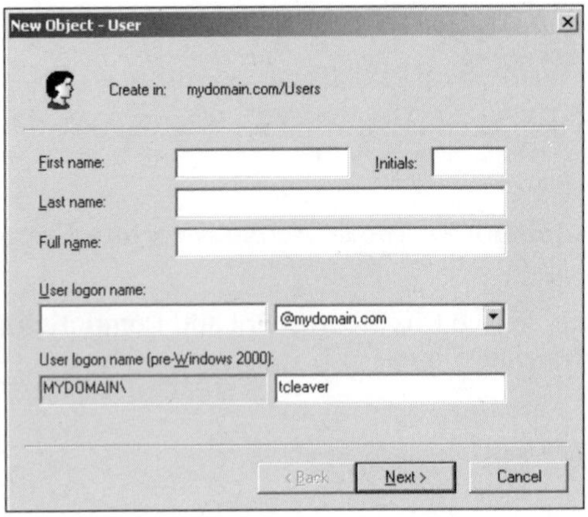

Figure 16-2:
Creating a
new user.

Pick a naming scheme to follow when creating user logon names. For example, use the first letter of the first name followed by the complete last name, the complete first name followed by the first letter of the last name, or any other scheme that suits your fancy.

6. Click Next.

The second page of the New Object Wizard appears, as shown in Figure 16-3.

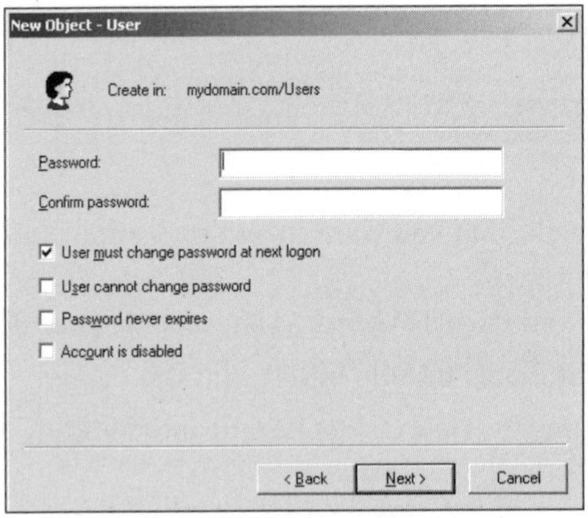

Figure 16-3:
Setting the
user's
password.

7. Type the password twice.

You're asked to type the password twice, so type it correctly. If you don't type it identically in both boxes, you're asked to correct your mistake.

8. **Specify the password options that you want to apply.**

    The following password options are available:

    - User must change password at next logon.

    - User cannot change password.

    - Password never expires.

    - Account is disabled.

    For more information about these options, see the section, "Setting account options," later in this chapter.

9. **Click Next.**

    You're taken to the final page of the New Object Wizard, as shown in Figure 16-4.

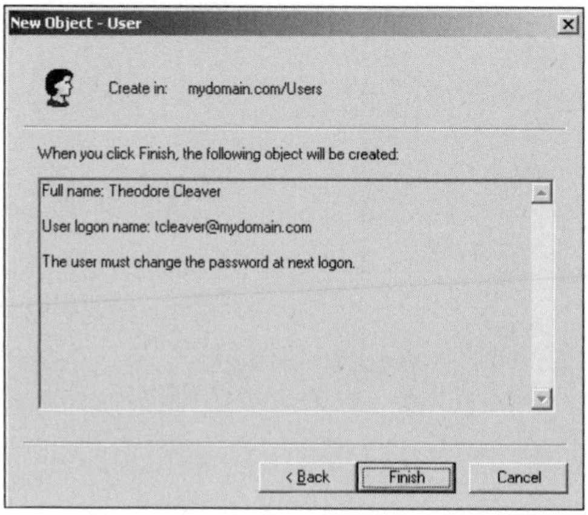

New Object - User

Create in: mydomain.com/Users

When you click Finish, the following object will be created:

Full name: Theodore Cleaver

User logon name: tcleaver@mydomain.com

The user must change the password at next logon.

< Back   Finish   Cancel

Figure 16-4:
Verifying
the user
account
information.

10. **Verify that the information is correct and then click Finish to create the account.**

    If the account information isn't correct, click the Back button and correct the error.

You're done! Now you can customize the user's account settings. You'll probably want to add the user to one or more groups. You may also want to add contact information for the user or set up other account options.

Setting User Properties

After you create a user account, you can set additional properties for the user by right-clicking the new user and choosing Properties. This action brings up the User Properties dialog box, which has about a million tabs that you can use to set various properties for the user. Figure 16-5 shows the General tab, which lists basic information about the user, such as the user's name, office location, and phone number.

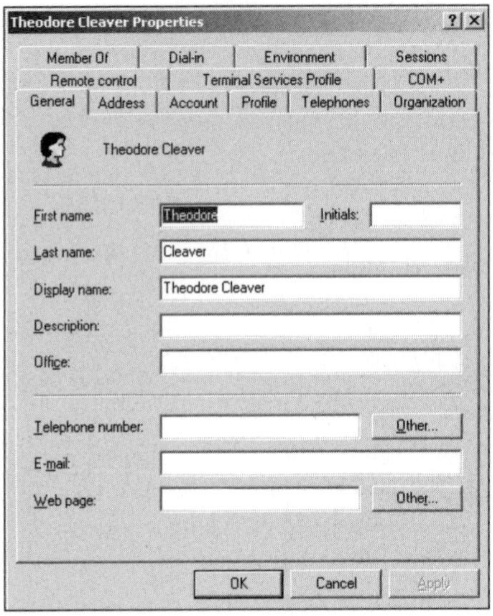

Figure 16-5:
The General
tab.

The following sections describe some of the administrative tasks that you can perform by using the tabs in the User Properties dialog box.

Changing a user's contact information

Several tabs in the User Properties dialog box contain contact information for the user:

- ✔ **Address tab:** Change the user's street address, post office box, city, state, zip code, and so on.
- ✔ **Telephones tab:** Specify the user's phone numbers.
- ✔ **Organization tab:** Record the user's job title and the name of his or her boss.

Setting account options

The Account tab of the User Properties dialog box, as shown in Figure 16-6, features a variety of interesting options that you can set for the user. From this dialog box, you can change the user's logon name. In addition, you can change the password options that you set when you created the account and set an expiration date for the account.

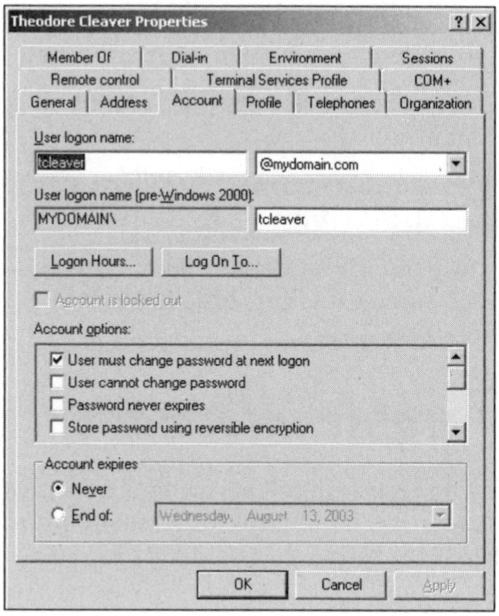

Figure 16-6:
The
Account
tab.

The following account options are in the Account Options list box:

- **User must change password at next logon:** Use this option, which is selected by default, to create a one-time-only password that can get the user started with the network. The first time the user logs on to the network, he is asked to change the password.

- **User cannot change password:** Use this option if you don't want to allow users to change their passwords. (Obviously, you can't use this option and the previous one at the same time.)

- **Password never expires:** Use this option if you want to bypass the password expiration policy for this user so that he never has to change his password.

- **Store password using reversible encryption:** This option stores passwords by using an encryption scheme that hackers can easily break, so avoid it like the plague.

- **Account is disabled:** Use this option to create an account that you don't yet need. As long as the account remains disabled, the user cannot log on.

  See the section, "Disabling and Enabling User Accounts," later in this chapter, to find out how to enable a disabled account.

✔ **Smart card is required for interactive logon:** If the user's computer has a smart card reader to automatically read security cards, check this option to require the user to use it.

✔ **Account is trusted for delegation:** This option indicates that the account is trustworthy and can set up delegations.

This feature is usually reserved for Administrator accounts.

✔ **Account is sensitive and cannot be delegated:** Prevent other users from impersonating this account.

✔ **Use DES encryption types for this account:** Beef up the encryption for applications that require extra security.

✔ **Do not require Kerberos preauthentication:** Select this option if you use a different implementation of the Kerberos protocol.

Setting a user's profile information

The Profile tab, as shown in Figure 16-7, lets you configure the user's profile information. This dialog box lets you configure three bits of information related to the user's profile:

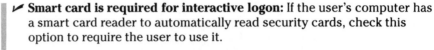

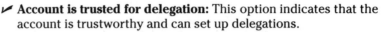

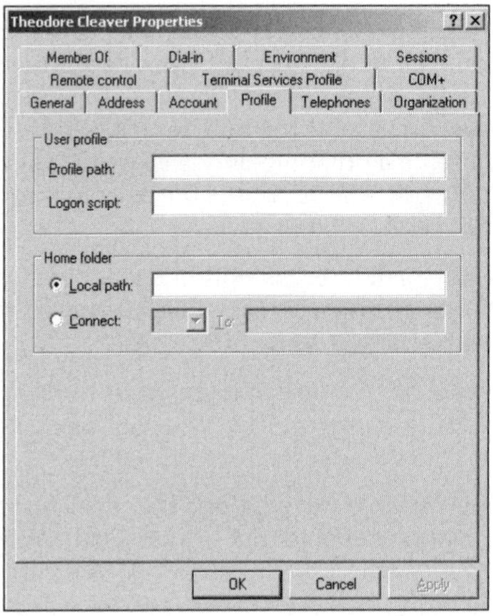

Figure 16-7:
The Profile
tab.

✔ **Profile path:** Specifies the location of the user's roaming profile.

For more information, see Chapter 22.

✔ **Logon script:** The name of the user's logon script. A *logon script* is a batch file that's run whenever the user logs on. The main purpose of the logon script is to map the network shares that the user requires access to.

Logon scripts are a carryover from the early versions of Windows NT Server. In Windows Server 2003, a profile is the preferred way to configure the user's computer when she logs on, including setting up network shares. However, many administrators still like the simplicity of logon scripts. For more information, see the section, "Creating a Logon Script," later in this chapter.

✔ **Home folder:** Where you specify the default storage location for the user. Follow these steps:

1. *Set up a network share on a file server.*

   Typically, this share is named Home.

2. *Assign a drive letter (usually H) that points to this location and specifies the variable %USERNAME%, like this:*

   ```
   \\fileserver01\Home\%USERNAME%
   ```

Windows substitutes the user's actual username to determine the folder where the user's files are stored. For example, if the user's username is `bcleaver`, the user's home folder is `\\fileserver01\Home\ bcleaver`.

The Profile tab lets you *specify the location of* an existing profile for the user, but it doesn't let you set up the profile. For more information about setting up a profile, see Chapter 22.

Resetting User Passwords

By some estimates, the single most time-consuming task of most network administrators is resetting user passwords. It's tempting to think that users are just forgetful idiots, but put yourself in their shoes. Network administrators insist that users set their passwords to something incomprehensible, such as 94kD82leL384K, that they change it a week later to something even less memorable, such as dJUQ63DWd8331, and that they don't write it down. Then they get mad when users forget their passwords.

When a user calls and says that she forgot her password, the least you can do is be cheerful when you reset it for her. She probably spent 15 minutes trying to remember it before giving up and admitting failure.

Here's the procedure to reset the password for a user domain account:

1. **Log on as an administrator.**

   You must have administrator privileges to perform this procedure.

2. **Choose Start⇨Administrative Tools⇨Active Directory Users and Computers.**

   The Active Directory Users and Computers management console appears.

3. **Click Users in the console tree.**

4. **In the Details pane, right-click the user who forgot her password and choose Reset Password.**

5. **Type the new password in both password boxes.**

   You type the password *twice* to ensure you type it correctly.

   If you check the User Must Change Password at Next Logon option, the password that you assign works for only one logon. As soon as the user logs on, she is required to change the password.

6. **Click OK.**

   That's all there is to it! The user's password is now reset.

Disabling and Enabling User Accounts

If you want to temporarily prevent a user from accessing the network, you can disable his account. Then you can enable the account later, when you're ready to restore the user to full access. Follow these steps:

1. **Log on as an administrator.**

   You must have administrator privileges to perform this procedure.

2. **Choose Start⇨Administrative Tools⇨Active Directory Users and Computers.**

   The Active Directory Users and Computers management console appears.

3. **Click Users in the console tree.**

4. **In the Details pane, right-click the user that you want to enable or disable. Then choose either Enable Account or Disable Account to enable or disable the user.**

Deleting a User

Deleting a user account is surprisingly easy. Just follow these steps:

1. **Log on as an administrator.**

   You must have administrator privileges to perform this procedure.

2. **Choose Start⇨Administrative Tools⇨Active Directory Users and Computers.**

   The Active Directory Users and Computers management console appears.

3. **Click Users in the console tree.**

4. **In the details pane, right-click the user that you want to delete and then choose Delete.**

   Windows asks whether you really want to delete the user.

5. **Click Yes.**

   Poof! The user account is deleted.

Working with Groups

A *group* is a special type of account that represents a set of users who have common network access needs. Groups can dramatically simplify the task of assigning network access rights to users. Rather than assign access rights to each user individually, groups let you assign rights to the *group*. Those rights extend to any *user* that you add to the group.

Creating a group

To create a group, follow these steps:

1. **Log on as an administrator.**

   You must have administrator privileges to perform this procedure.

2. **Choose Start⇨Administrative Tools⇨Active Directory Users and Computers.**

   The Active Directory Users and Computers management console appears.

3. **Right-click the domain to which you want to add the group and then choose New⇨Group.**

   The New Object – Group dialog box appears, as shown in Figure 16-8.

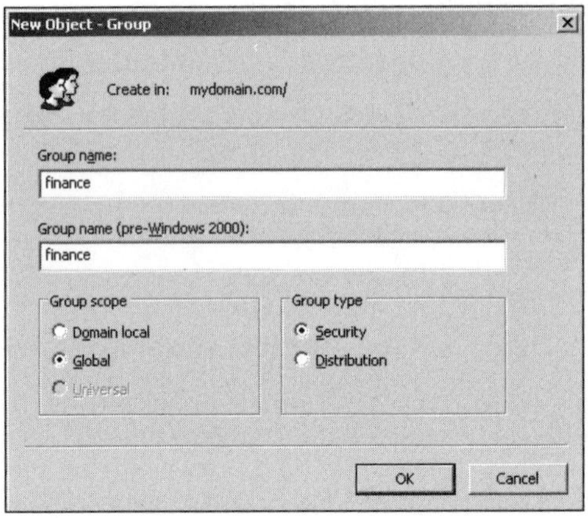

Figure 16-8:
Creating a
new group.

4. **Type the name for the new group.**

   Enter the name in both text boxes.

5. **Click OK.**

   The group is created.

Adding a member to a group

Groups are collections of objects, called *members*. The members of a group can be user accounts or other groups. When you create a group, it has no members. As a result, the group isn't useful until you add a *member*. Follow these steps to add a member to a group:

1. **Log on as an administrator.**

   You must have administrator privileges to perform this procedure.

2. **Choose Start⇨Administrative Tools⇨Active Directory Users and Computers.**

   The Active Directory Users and Computers management console appears.

3. **Open the folder that contains the group to which you want to add members and then double-click the group.**

   The Group Properties dialog box appears.

4. **Click the Members tab.**

The members of the group are displayed, as shown in Figure 16-9.

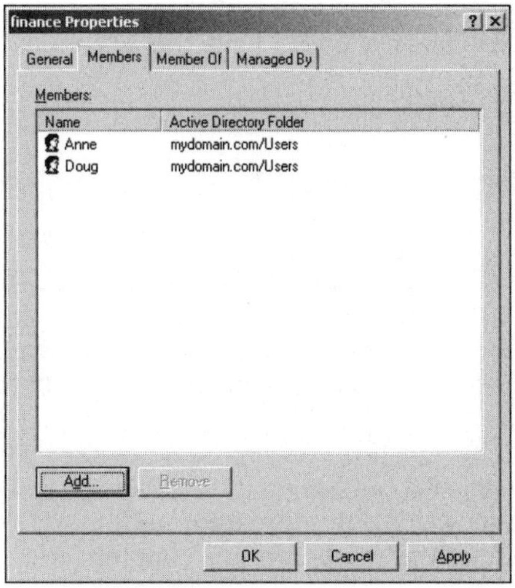

Figure 16-9:
Adding
members to
a group.

5. **Type the name of a user or group that you want to add to this group, and then click Add.**

6. **Repeat Step 5 for each user or group that you want to add.**

7. **Click OK.**

The Group Properties dialog box also has a Member Of tab, which lists each group that the current group is a member of.

Adding members to a group is only half the process of making a group useful. The other half is adding access rights to the group so that the members of the group can *do* something, as shown in Chapter 22.

Creating a Logon Script

A *logon script* is a batch file that's run automatically whenever a user logs on. The most common reason for using a logon script is to map the network shares that the user needs access to. For example, a simple logon script maps three network shares:

```
echo off
net use m: \\/server1\shares\admin
net use n: \\server1\shares\mktg
net use o: \\server2\archives
```

Here, two shares on `server1` are mapped to drives M and N, and a share on `server2` is mapped to drive O.

If you want, you can use the special variable `%username%` to get the user's username. This strategy is useful if you created a folder for each user and you want to map a drive to each user's folder, as in this example:

```
net use u: \\server1\users\%username%
```

For example, if a user logs on with the username `dlowe`, drive U is mapped to `\\server1\users\dlowe`.

Scripts should be saved in the Scripts folder, which is buried deep in the bowels of the SYSVOL folder — typically, `c:\Windows\SYSVOL\Sysvol\`*domainname*`\Scripts`, where *domainname* is your domain name. Because you often need to access this folder, I suggest creating a shortcut to it on your desktop.

After you create a logon script, you can assign it to a user by using the Profile tab of the User Properties dialog box. For more information, see the section, "Setting a user's profile information," earlier in this chapter.

Chapter 17

Managing Network Storage

● ●

In This Chapter

▶ Understanding network storage

▶ Setting permissions

▶ Sharing folders

▶ Configuring and managing a file server

● ●

*O*ne key purpose of most computer networks is to provide shared access to disk storage. In this chapter, you find out about several ways that a network can provide shared disk storage. Then you discover how to configure Windows Server 2003 to operate as a file server.

Understanding Network Storage

Many network servers exist solely for the purpose of making disk space available to network users. As networks grow to support more users and as users require more disk space, network administrators are continually finding ways to add more storage to their networks. The following sections describe some key concepts for providing network storage.

File servers

A *file server* is simply a network server whose primary role is to share its disk drives. It's the most common way to provide shared network storage.

A file server can be anything from a simple desktop computer that has been pressed into service as a file server to an expensive ($25,000 or more) server with redundant components so that the server can continue to run when a component fails. A file server can even consist of advanced disk subsystems with racks of disk drives that can be replaced without shutting down the server.

One of the most common advanced disk subsystems for file servers is RAID, or Redundant Array of Inexpensive Disks. A *RAID* system, which is a type of disk storage that hardly ever fails, works by lumping together several disk drives and treating them as though they're a single humongous drive. RAID uses some fancy techniques devised by computer nerds at Berkeley. These techniques ensure that if one of the disk drives in the RAID system fails, no data is lost. The disk drive that failed can be removed and repaired, and the data that was on it can be reconstructed from the other drives.

Most of this chapter is devoted to showing you how to configure Windows Server 2003 to run as a file server.

Storage appliances

A *storage appliance* is a device specifically designed for providing shared network storage. Also known as *NAS,* or *Network Attached Storage,* it's a self-contained file server that's preconfigured and ready to run. All you have to do to set it up is take it out of the box, plug it in, and turn it on. Storage appliances are easy to set up and configure, easy to maintain, and less expensive than traditional file servers.

A typical entry-level storage appliance is the Dell 725N. This self-contained file server is built into a small rack-mount chassis. It supports up to four hard drives with a total capacity of up to one terabyte (or 1,000GB). The 475N has a dual-processor motherboard that can hold up to 3GB of memory and two built-in 10/100/1000 Mbps network ports. An LCD display on the front panel displays the device's IP address.

The Dell 725N runs a special version of Windows Server 2003: Windows Storage Server 2003. This version of Windows, designed specifically for NAS devices, allows you to configure the network storage from any computer on the network by using a Web browser.

Note that some storage appliances use customized versions of Linux rather than Windows Storage Server. Also, in some systems, the operating system resides on a separate hard drive that's isolated from the shared disks so users are prevented from inadvertently damaging the operating system.

Understanding Permissions

One key concept for managing network storage is permissions. *Permissions* allow users to access shared resources on a network. Simply sharing a disk doesn't guarantee that a given user can access the data it contains. Windows makes this decision based on the permissions that have been assigned to various groups for the resource and group memberships of the user. If the user belongs to a group that has been granted permission to access the resource, the access is allowed. If not, access is denied.

In theory, the permissions concept sounds simple. In practice, however, it can get quite complicated. This list explains some of the nuances of how access control and permissions work:

- Every object — that is, every file and folder — on an NTFS volume has a set of permissions called the *Access Control List,* or *ACL,* associated with it.

- The ACL identifies the users and groups that can access the object and specifies which level of access each user or group has. For example, a folder's ACL may specify that one group of users can read files in the folder while another group can read and write files in the folder and a third group is denied access to the folder.

- Container objects — files and volumes — allow their ACLs to be inherited by the objects they contain. As a result, if you specify permissions for a folder, those permissions extend to the files and child folders that appear within it.

- Table 17-1 describes the six types of permissions that can be applied to files and folders on an NTFS volume.

- The six file and folder permissions are composed of various combinations of *special permissions* that grant more-detailed access to files or folders. Table 17-2 lists the special permissions that apply to each of the six file and folder permissions.

- You should assign permissions to groups rather than to individual users. Then, if a particular user needs access to a particular resource, add that user to a group that has permission to use the resource.

Table 17-1	File and Folder Permissions
Permission	*Description*
Full control	Grants unrestricted access to the file or folder.
Modify	Grants the right to read the file or folder, delete the file or folder, change the contents of the file or folder, or change the attributes of the file or folder. Allows you to create new files or subfolders within the folder.
Read & Execute	Grants the right to read or execute the file and grants the right to list the contents of the folder or to read or execute any of the files in the folder.
List Folder Contents	Applies only to folders and grants the right to list the contents of the folder.
Write	Grants the right to change the contents of a file or its attributes. Grants the right to create new files and sub-folders within the folder.
Read	Grants the right to read the contents of a file or folder.

Table 17-2			Special Permissions			
Special Permission	*Full Control*	*Modify*	*Read & Execute*	*List Folder Contents*	*Read*	*Write*
Traverse Folder/Execute File	✔	✔	✔	✔		
List Folder/Read Data	✔	✔	✔	✔	✔	
Read Extended Attributes	✔	✔	✔	✔	✔	
Create Files/Write Data	✔	✔				✔
Create Folders/Append Data	✔	✔				✔
Write Attributes	✔	✔				✔
Write Extended Attributes	✔	✔				✔
Delete Subfolders and Files	✔					
Delete	✔	✔				
Read Permissions	✔	✔	✔	✔	✔	✔
Change Permissions	✔					
Take Ownership	✔					
Synchronize	✔	✔	✔	✔	✔	✔

Understanding Shares

A *share* is simply a folder that is made available to other users using the network. Each share has the following elements:

> ✔ **Share name:** The name by which the share is known over the network. To make the names compatible on older computers, stick to eight-character share names whenever possible.

➤ **Path:** The path to the folder on the local computer that's being shared, such as `C:\Accounting`.

➤ **Description:** A one-line description of the share.

➤ **Permissions:** A list of users or groups that have been granted access to the share.

When you install Windows and configure various server roles, special shared resources are created to support those roles. Don't disturb these special shares unless you know what you're doing. Table 17-3 lists some of the more common special shares.

Table 17-3	Special Shares
Share Name	*Description*
`drive$`	The root directory of a drive
`ADMIN$`	Used for remote administration of a computer and points to the operating system folder (usually, `C:\Windows`)
`IPC$`	Used by named pipes, a programming feature that lets processes communicate with one another
`NETLOGON`	Required for domain controllers to function
`SYSVOL`	A required domain controller share
`PRINT$`	Used for remote administration of printers
`FAX$`	Used by fax clients

Some special shares end with a dollar sign ($). These *hidden shares* aren't visible to users. However, you can still access them by typing the complete share name (including the dollar sign) when the share is needed. For example, the special share `C$` is created to allow you to connect to the root directory of the C: drive from a network client. You wouldn't want your users to see this share, would you? (Of course, shares such as `C$` are also protected by privileges so that if an ordinary user finds out that `C$` is the root directory of the server's C: drive, he still can't access it.)

Configuring the File Server Role

A handy wizard in Windows Server 2003 automatically configures the computer as a file server. Follow these steps to use this wizard:

1. **Log on as an administrator.**

   You need administrator rights to make the changes called for by this wizard.

2. **Choose Start⇨Administrative Tools⇨Manage Your Server.**

   The Manage Your Server page appears, as shown in Figure 17-1. It shows the various roles you configured for the server. If the File Server role already appears, you can skip the rest of this procedure — you already configured the computer to be a file server.

3. **Select the Add or Remove a Role option.**

   A message suggests that you take some preliminary steps, such as connecting network cables and installing modems. Read this list, just to make sure that you completed them all already.

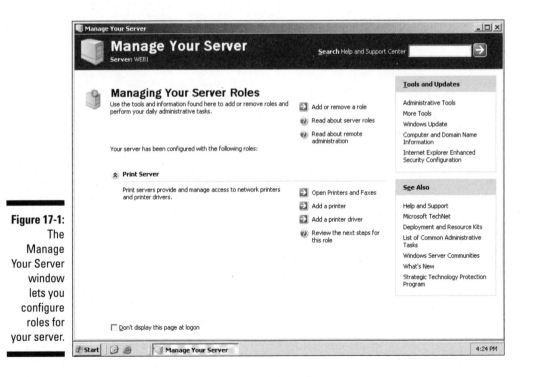

Figure 17-1:
The
Manage
Your Server
window
lets you
configure
roles for
your server.

4. Click Next until you see the Server Role page.

The Server Role page, as shown in Figure 17-2, lists the various roles you can configure for the server.

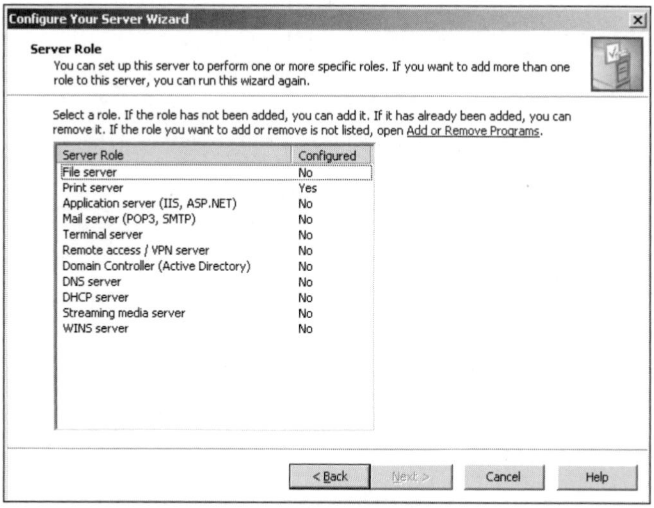

Configure Your Server Wizard

Server Role

You can set up this server to perform one or more specific roles. If you want to add more than one role to this server, you can run this wizard again.

Select a role. If the role has not been added, you can add it. If it has already been added, you can remove it. If the role you want to add or remove is not listed, open Add or Remove Programs.

Server Role	Configured
File server	No
Print server	Yes
Application server (IIS, ASP.NET)	No
Mail server (POP3, SMTP)	No
Terminal server	No
Remote access / VPN server	No
Domain Controller (Active Directory)	No
DNS server	No
DHCP server	No
Streaming media server	No
WINS server	No

< Back   Next >   Cancel   Help

Figure 17-2:
The Server Role page.

5. Select File Server and then click Next.

The File Server Disk Quotas page appears, as shown in Figure 17-3. This page lets you

- *Set up disk quotas to track and limit the amount of disk space used by each user.*

  The default setting is to limit each user to a paltry 5MB of disk space. Microsoft recommends that you set a low limit and then change it for users who need more space.

- *Specify the consequences to occur when a user exceeds the quota.*

  By default, no consequences are specified, so the quota is just a tracking device. If you want, you can tell Windows to refuse to let the user have more space than the quota specifies, or you can specify that an event be logged to let you know that a user has exceeded the quota.

6. Specify the disk quota settings you want to use and then click Next.

The Indexing Service page appears. It lets you indicate whether you want to activate the Windows Indexing Service for the file server. Few users take advantage of the Indexing Service, but if you need it, it's available here.

In most cases, activating the Indexing Service is a bad idea because it can dramatically slow down the performance of the server.

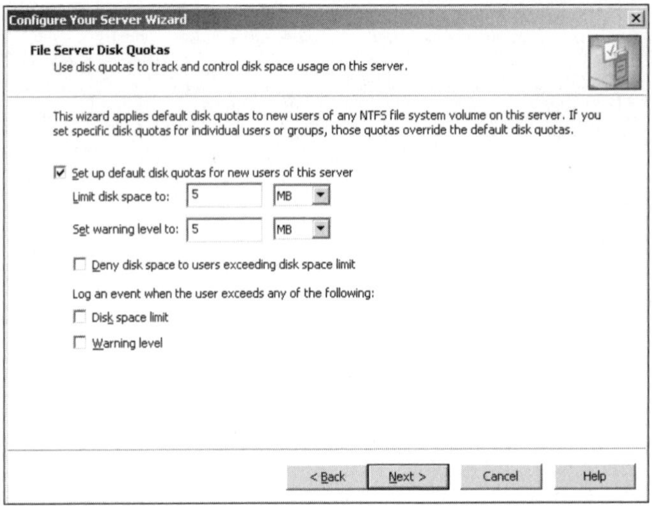

Configure Your Server Wizard

File Server Disk Quotas
Use disk quotas to track and control disk space usage on this server.

This wizard applies default disk quotas to new users of any NTFS file system volume on this server. If you set specific disk quotas for individual users or groups, those quotas override the default disk quotas.

☑ Set up default disk quotas for new users of this server

Limit disk space to: [5] [MB ▼]

Set warning level to: [5] [MB ▼]

☐ Deny disk space to users exceeding disk space limit

Log an event when the user exceeds any of the following:

☐ Disk space limit

☐ Warning level

[< Back] [Next >] [Cancel] [Help]

Figure 17-3: The File Server Disk Quotas page.

---

7. **Select the Yes check box if you want to use the Indexing Service or leave No selected to disable Indexing, and then click Next.**

   A summary page appears, listing the options you selected.

8. **Click Next.**

   The computer grinds and whirs for a moment as it configures the file server. In a moment, the Share a Folder Wizard appears so that you can set up the initial file shares for the server.

9. **Use the Share a Folder Wizard to share one or more folders.**

   For the complete procedure for using this wizard, see the section "Sharing a folder from the File Server Manager," later in this chapter.

   After you're finished with the Share a Folder Wizard, you see the dialog box, as shown in Figure 17-4.

10. **Click Finish.**

    You return to the Manage Your Server page, which now lists the File Server role as active.

That's it. You've configured the computer to be a file server.

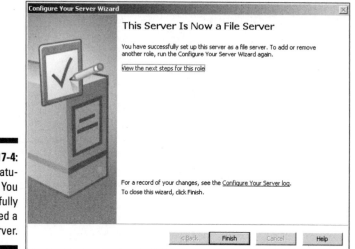

Managing Your File Server

Windows Server 2003 has a handy File Server Manager console, as shown in Figure 17-5. From this console, you can easily create new shares, set up the permissions for a share, or delete a share. To summon the File Server Manager, choose Start⇨Administrative Tools⇨Manage Your Server and then choose Manage File Server.

The following sections describe some of the more common procedures that you use when managing your file server.

Sharing a folder from the File Server Manager

To be useful, a file server should offer one or more *shares* — folders designated as publicly accessible on the network. You can see a list of the current shares available from a file server by opening the File Server Manager and clicking Shares in the console tree. The File Server Manager displays the share name, description, and network path for each share you already created.

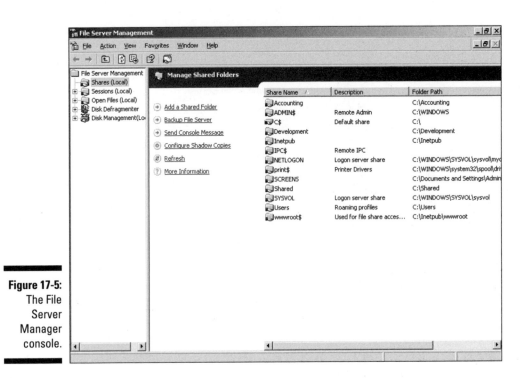

Figure 17-5:
The File
Server
Manager
console.

To create additional shares, use the Share a Folder Wizard, as described in this procedure:

1. **Select Shares from the console tree and then choose Action⇨ New Share.**

   The Share a Folder Wizard appears, as shown in Figure 17-6.

Figure 17-6:
The Share
a Folder
Wizard
comes
to life.

2. Click Next.

The wizard asks you which folder you want to share, as shown in Figure 17-7.

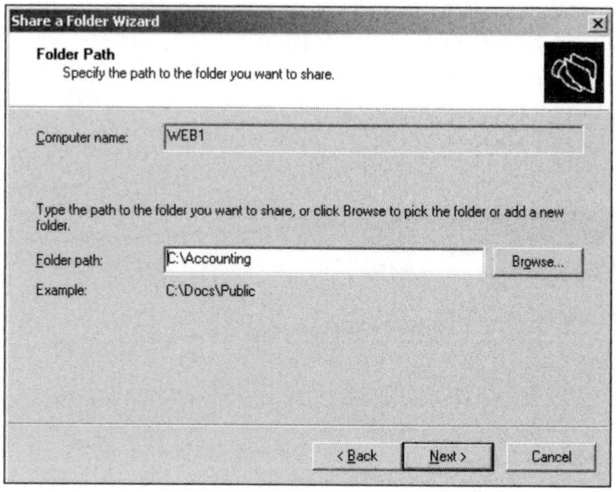

Figure 17-7:
Specify the
folder you
want to
share.

3. Type the path of the folder that you want to share over the network and then click Next.

If you aren't sure of the path, click the Browse button. This action displays a dialog box that lets you search the server's hard drive for a folder to share. You can also create a new folder from this dialog box if the folder you want to share doesn't yet exist. After you select or create the folder to share, click OK to return to the wizard.

The dialog box, as shown in Figure 17-8, appears.

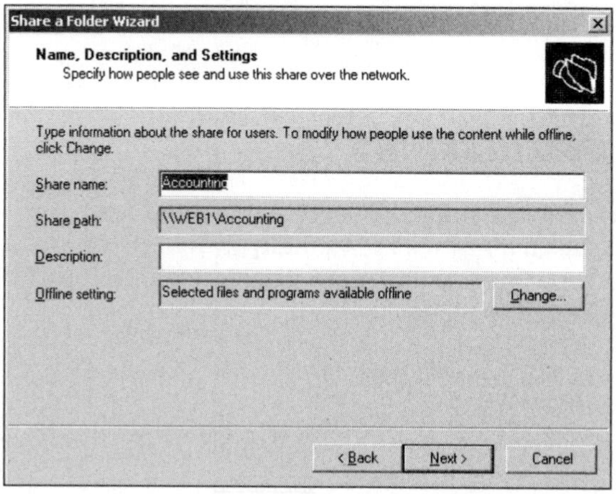

Figure 17-8:
Assigning a
share name.

4. **In the Share Name box, type the name that you want to use for the share, and type a description of the share in the Description box.**

   The default name is the name of the folder being shared. If the folder name is long, you can use a more succinct name here.

   The description is strictly optional but can sometimes help users determine the intended contents of the folder.

5. **Click Next.**

   The dialog box, as shown in Figure 17-9, appears.

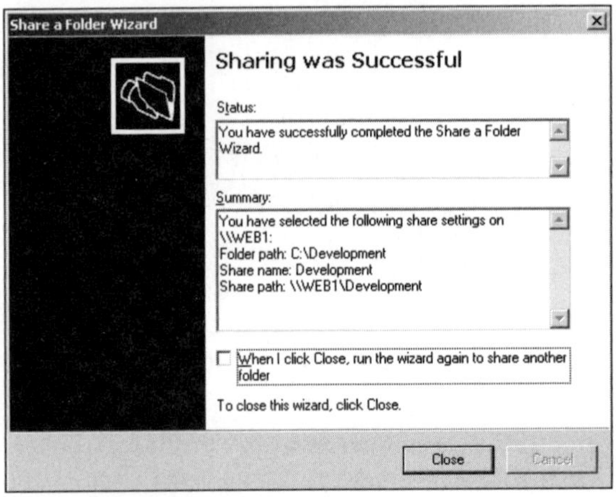

Figure 17-9: The share was created successfully!

6. **If you want to create another share, select the When I Click Close, Run the Wizard Again check box, click Finish, and return to Step 3; otherwise, click Finish to dismiss the wizard.**

   If you click Finish, you return to the File Server Management console. The share or shares you created now appear in the list.

Granting permissions

When you first create a file share, all users are granted read-only access to the share. If you want to allow users to modify files in the share or allow them to create new files, you need to add more permissions. Follow these steps to do it from the File Server Manager:

1. **Click Shares in the console tree.**

   A list of all the server's shares appears.

2. **Right-click the share you want to set permissions for, choose Properties, and then click the Share Permissions tab.**

   The dialog box, as shown in Figure 17-10, appears. This dialog box lists all the users and groups to whom you granted permission for the folder. When you select a user or group from the list, the check boxes at the bottom of the list change to indicate which specific permissions you assigned to each user or group.

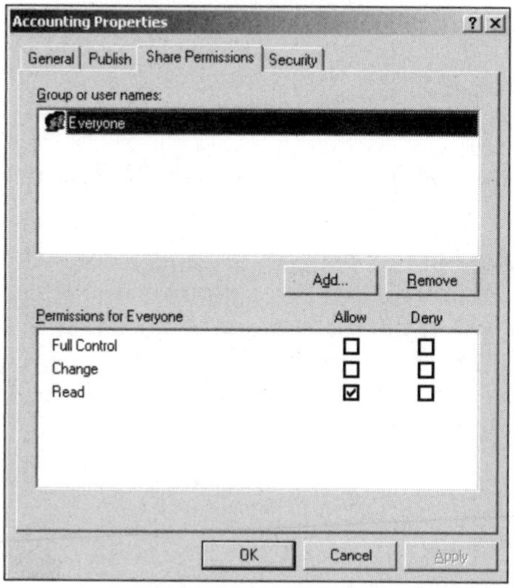

Figure 17-10: The Share Permissions tab.

Accounting Properties	?	×

General | Publish | Share Permissions | Security |

Group or user names:

Everyone

Add...   Remove

Permissions for Everyone	Allow	Deny
Full Control	☐	☐
Change	☐	☐
Read	☑	☐

OK   Cancel   Apply

3. **Click Add.**

   The Select Users, Computers, or Groups dialog box appears. You can use it to indicate which users or groups should be allowed to access the share.

4. **Type the name of the user or group to whom you want to grant permission and then click OK.**

   You return to the Share Permissions tab, with the new user or group added.

5. **Select the appropriate Allow or Deny check boxes to specify which permissions to allow for the user or group.**

   Repeat Steps 3–5 for any other permissions you want to add.

6. **When you're done, click OK.**

Here are a few other thoughts to ponder when you add permissions:

- ✔ If you want to grant full access to everyone for this folder, don't bother adding another permission. Instead, select the Everyone group, and then select the Allow check box for each permission type.

- ✔ You can remove a permission by selecting it and then clicking Remove.

- ✔ If you'd rather not fuss with the File Server Manager, you can set the permissions from My Computer:

  1. Right-click the shared folder.

  2. Choose Sharing and Security.

  3. Click the Permissions button.

  You can then follow the first set of steps in this section, starting at Step 3.

- ✔ The permissions assigned in this procedure apply to only the share itself. The underlying folder can also have permissions assigned to it. If that's the case, whichever of the restrictions is more restrictive always applies. For example, if the share permissions grant a user Full Control but the folder permission grants the user only Read access, the user will have read-only access to the folder.

Chapter 18

Network Performance Anxiety

In This Chapter

▶ Understanding performance problems

▶ Looking at bottlenecks

▶ Developing a procedure for solving performance problems

▶ Monitoring performance

▶ Implementing other tips for speeding up your network

*T*he term *network performance* refers to how efficiently the network responds to users' needs. Obviously, any access to resources that involves the network is slower than similar access that doesn't involve the network. For example, opening a Word document that resides on a network file server takes longer than opening a similar document that resides on the user's local hard drive. However, it shouldn't take *much* longer. If it does, you have a network performance problem.

This chapter is a general introduction to the practice of tuning your network so that it performs as well as possible. Keep in mind that many specific bits of network tuning advice are scattered throughout this book. In this chapter, you can find some specific techniques for analyzing your network's performance, taking corrective action when a performance problem develops, and charting your progress.

Why Administrators Hate Performance Problems

Network performance problems are among the most difficult network problems to track down and solve. If a user simply can't access the network, it usually doesn't take long to figure out why: The cable is unplugged, a network card is malfunctioning, or the user doesn't have permission to access the resource, for example. After you do a little investigating, the problem usually reveals itself, and you fix it and move on to the next problem.

Unfortunately, performance problems are messier. Here are just a few reasons that network administrators hate performance problems:

- ✓ **Performance problems are difficult to quantify.** Exactly how much slower is the network now than it was a week ago, a month ago, or even a year ago? Sometimes the network just *feels* slow, but you can't quite define exactly how slow it really is.

- ✓ **Performance problems usually develop gradually.** Sometimes a network slows down suddenly and drastically. More often, though, the network gradually gets slower, a little bit at a time, until one day its users notice that the network is slow.

- ✓ **Performance problems often go unreported.** Users gripe about the problem to each other around the water cooler, but they don't formally contact you to let you know that the network seems 10 percent slower than usual. As long as they can still access the network, they just assume that the problem is temporary or that they're imagining a problem.

- ✓ **Many performance problems are intermittent.** Sometimes a user calls you and complains that a certain network operation has become slower than molasses, and by the time you get to that person's desk, the operation performs in a snap. Sometimes you can find a pattern to the intermittent behavior, such as it's slower in the morning than in the afternoon or it's slow only while backups are running or while the printer is working. At other times, you can't find a pattern: Sometimes the operation is slow, and sometimes it isn't.

- ✓ **Performance tuning isn't an exact science.** Improving performance sometimes involves educated guesswork. Will upgrading all users from 100 Mbps to 1 Gbps improve performance? Probably. Will segmenting the network improve performance? Maybe. Will adding another 4GB of RAM to the server improve performance? Hopefully.

- ✓ **The solution to a performance problem is sometimes a hard sell.** If a user can't access the network because of a malfunctioning component, the purchase of a replacement is usually undeniably justified. However, if the network is slow and you think that you can fix it by upgrading the entire network to gigabit Ethernet, you may have trouble selling management on the upgrade.

What Exactly Is a Bottleneck?

The term *bottleneck* doesn't refer in any way to the physique of the typical computer geek. Rather, computer geeks coined the phrase when they discovered that the tapered shape of a bottle of Jolt cola limited the rate at which they could consume the beverage. "Hey," a computer geek said one day, "the gently tapered narrowness of this bottle's neck imposes a distinct limiting effect upon the rate at which I can consume the tasty caffeine-laden beverage contained within. This observation draws to mind a hitherto undiscovered yet obvious analogy to the limiting effect that a single slow component of a computer system can have upon the performance of the system as a whole."

"Fascinating," replied all the other computer geeks, who were fortunate enough to be present at that historic moment.

The term stuck and is used to this day to draw attention to the simple fact that a computer system is only as fast as its slowest component. It's the computer equivalent of the old truism that a chain is only as strong as its weakest link.

For a simple demonstration of this concept, consider what happens when you print a word-processing document on a slow printer. Your word-processing program reads the data from disk and sends it to the printer. Then you sit and wait while the printer prints the document.

Would buying a faster CPU or adding more memory make the document print faster? No. The CPU is already much faster than the printer, and your computer already has more than enough memory to print the document. The printer itself is the bottleneck, so the only way to print the document faster is to replace the slow printer with a faster one.

Here are some other, random thoughts about bottlenecks:

- ✔ **A computer system always has a bottleneck.** Suppose that you decide that the bottleneck on your file server is a slow SATA hard drive, so you replace it with the fastest SCSI drive money can buy. Now the hard drive is no longer the bottleneck: The drive can process information faster than the controller card to which the disk is connected. You didn't really eliminate the bottleneck — you just moved it from the hard drive to the disk controller. No matter what you do, the computer will always have a component that limits the overall performance of the system.

- ✔ **One way to limit the effect of a bottleneck is to avoid waiting for the bottleneck.** For example, print spooling lets you avoid waiting for a slow printer. Although spooling doesn't speed up the printer, it frees you to do other work while the printer chugs along. Similarly, disk caching lets you avoid waiting for a slow hard drive.

One reason that computer geeks switched from Jolt cola to Snapple is that Snapple bottles have wider necks.

The Five Most Common Network Bottlenecks

Direct from the home office in sunny Fresno, California, here are the ten — oops, five — most common network bottlenecks, in no particular order.

The hardware inside your servers

Your servers should be powerful computers capable of handling all the work your network will throw at them. Don't cut corners by using a bottom-of-the-line computer that you bought at a discount computer store.

The following list describes the four most important components of your server hardware:

- ✔ **Processor:** Your server should have a powerful processor. Any processor that's available in an $800 computer from a low-cost general appliance store is generally not a processor that you want to see in your file server. In other words, avoid processors designed for consumer-grade home computers.

- ✔ **Memory:** You can't have too much memory. Memory is cheap, so don't skimp. Don't even think about running a server with fewer than 2GB of RAM.

- ✔ **Disk:** Don't mess around with inexpensive IDE hard drives. To have a respectable system, you should have nothing but SCSI drives.

- ✔ **Network card:** A $9.95 network card may be fine for your home network, but don't use one in a file server that supports 100 users and expect to be happy with the server's performance. Remember that the server computer uses the network more often than any clients do. Equip your servers with good network cards.

The server's configuration options

All network operating systems have options that you can configure. Some of these options can make the difference between a pokey network and a zippy network. Unfortunately, no hard-and-fast rules exist for setting these options. Otherwise, you wouldn't have options.

The following important tuning options are available for most servers:

- ✔ **Virtual memory options:** *Virtual memory* refers to disk paging files that the server uses when it doesn't have enough real memory to do its work. Few servers ever have enough real memory, so virtual memory is always an important server feature. You can specify the size and location of the virtual memory paging files.

    For the best performance, provide at least 1½ times the amount of real memory. For example, if you have 4GB of real memory, allocate at least 6GB of virtual memory. If necessary, you can increase this size later.

- ✔ **Disk striping:** Use the disk defragmenter to optimize the data storage on your server's disks.

    If the server has more than one hard drive, you can increase performance by creating *striped volumes,* which allow disk I/O operations to run concurrently on each of the drives in the stripe set.

- ✔ **Network protocols:** Make sure that your network protocols are configured correctly and remove any protocols that aren't necessary.

- ✔ **Free disk space on the server:** Servers like to have plenty of breathing room on their disks.

    If the amount of free disk space on your server drops precipitously low, the server chokes up and slows to a crawl. Make sure that your server has plenty of space — a few gigabytes of unused disk space provides a healthy buffer.

Servers that do too much

One common source of network performance problems is a server overloaded with too many duties. Just because a modern network operating system comes equipped with dozens of different types of services doesn't mean that you should enable and use them all on a single server. If a single server is bogged down because of too much work, add a second server to relieve the first server of some of its chores. Remember the old saying: "Many hands make light work."

For example, if your network needs more disk space, consider adding a second file server rather than adding another drive to the server that already has four nearly full drives. Better yet, purchase a file server appliance dedicated to the task of serving files.

As a side benefit, your network will be easier to administer and more reliable if you place separate functions on separate servers. For example, if a single server doubles as a file server and a mail server, you lose both services if you have to take down the server to perform an upgrade or repair a failed component. However, if you have separate file and mail server computers, only one of the services is interrupted if you have to take down one of the servers.

The network infrastructure

The infrastructure consists of the cables and any switches, hubs, routers, and other components that sit between your clients and your servers.

The following network infrastructure items can slow down your network:

- ✔ **Hubs:** Because switches are inexpensive now, you can affordably solve many performance problems by replacing old, outdated hubs with switches. Using switches rather than hubs reduces the overall load on your network.

- ✔ **Segment sizes:** Keep the number of computers and other devices on each network segment to a reasonable number. About 20 devices is usually the right number. (Note that if you replace your hubs with switches, you instantly cut the size of each segment because each port on a switch constitutes a separate segment.)

- ✔ **The network's speed:** If you have an older network, you may discover that many — if not all — of your users are still working at 10 Mbps. Upgrading to 100 Mbps speeds up the network dramatically. Upgrading to 1 Gbps speeds it up even more.

- ✔ **The backbone speed:** If your network uses a backbone to connect segments, consider upgrading the backbone to 1 Gbps.

The hardest part about improving the performance of a network is determining where the bottlenecks are. With sophisticated test equipment and years of experience, network gurus can make good educated guesses. Without the equipment and experience, you can still make good uneducated guesses.

Malfunctioning components

Sometimes a malfunctioning network card or other component slows down the network. For example, a switch may malfunction intermittently, occasionally letting packets through but dropping enough of them to slow down the network. After you identify the faulty component, replacing it restores the network to its original speed.

Tune Your Network the Compulsive Way

You can tune your network in one of two ways. The first is to think about it a bit, take a guess at an approach that may improve performance, try that approach, and see whether the network seems to run faster. This strategy is the way most people go about tuning the network.

You can also try the compulsive way, which is suitable for people who organize their sock drawers by color and their food cupboards alphabetically by food group. The compulsive approach to tuning a network goes something like this:

1. **Establish a method for objectively testing the performance of some aspect of the network.**

   In this method, you create a *benchmark*. The result of your benchmark is a *baseline*.

2. **Change one variable of your network configuration and rerun the test.**

   For example, you may think that increasing the size of the disk cache can improve performance. Change the cache size, restart the server, and run the benchmark test. Note whether performance improves, stays the same, or becomes worse.

3. **Repeat Step 2 for each variable that you want to test.**

Here are some salient points to keep in mind if you decide to tune your network the compulsive way:

- ✔ **If possible, test each variable separately.** In other words, before proceeding, reverse the changes you made to other network variables.

- ✔ **Write down the results of each test** so that you have an accurate record of the effect that each change makes on your network's performance.

- ✔ **Be sure to change only one aspect of the network each time you run the benchmark.** If you make several changes, you don't know which one caused the change. One change may improve performance, but the other change may worsen performance so that the changes cancel each other out — kind of like offsetting penalties in a football game.

- ✔ **If possible, conduct the baseline test during normal working hours, when the network is undergoing its normal workload.**

- ✔ **To establish the network's baseline performance, run the benchmark test two or three times to make sure that the results are repeatable.**

Monitor Network Performance

One way to monitor network performance is to use a stopwatch to see how long it takes to complete common network tasks, such as opening documents or printing reports. If you choose to monitor your network by using the stopwatch technique, you may want to get a clipboard, baseball cap, and gray sweat suit, to complete the ensemble.

A more high-tech approach to monitoring network performance is to use a monitor program that automatically gathers network statistics for you. After you set up the monitor, it plugs away, silently spying on your network and recording in performance logs the activity it sees. You can then review those performance logs to see how your network is doing.

For large networks, you can purchase sophisticated monitoring programs that run on their own, dedicated servers. For small- and medium-size networks, you can probably use the built-in monitoring facilities that come with the network operating system. For example, Figure 18-1 shows the Performance Monitor tool that comes with Windows Server 2003. Other operating systems come with similar tools.

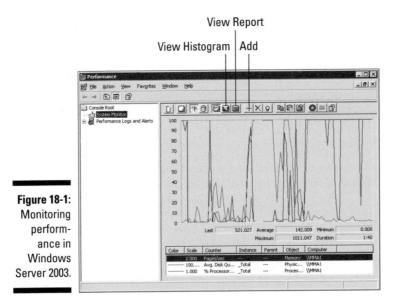

Figure 18-1: Monitoring performance in Windows Server 2003.

The Windows Performance Monitor lets you keep track of several different aspects of system performance at a time. You track each performance aspect by setting up a *counter.* You can choose from dozens of different counters. Table 18-1 describes some of the most commonly used counters. Note that each counter refers to a server object, such as physical disk, memory, or processor.

Table 18-1	Commonly Used Performance Counters	
Object	*Counter*	*What It Indicates*
Physical Disk	% Free Space	The percentage of free space on the server's physical disks. The free space should measure at least 15 percent.
Physical Disk	Average Queue Length	How many disk operations are waiting while the disk is busy servicing other disk operations. The number of operations should be two or fewer.
Memory	Pages/Second	The number of pages retrieved from the virtual memory page files per second. A typical threshold is about 2,500 pages per second.
Processor	% Processor Time	The percentage of the processor's time that it is doing work rather than sitting idle. The amount of time should be 85 percent or less.

To add a counter, follow these steps:

1. **In the Performance Monitor, click the Add button to display the Add Counters dialog box, as shown in Figure 18-2.**

   The Add button is the one with the Plus sign, as shown in Figure 18-1.

2. **Select from the Performance Object drop-down list the object that you want to track, choose the counter that you want to add from the list, and click Add.**

   You can add more than one counter from this dialog box.

3. **When you finish adding counters, click Close to dismiss the Add Counters dialog box.**

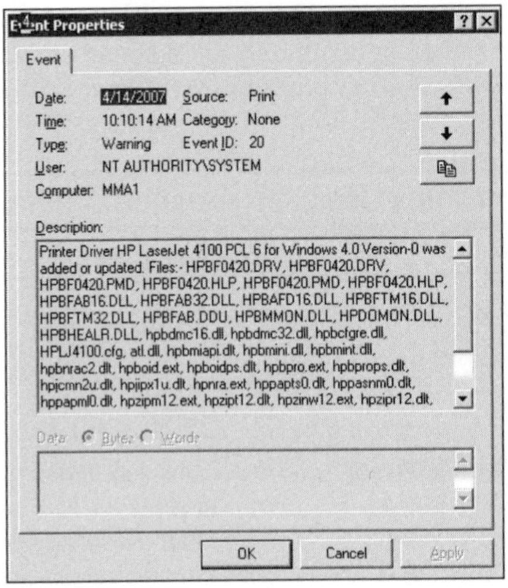

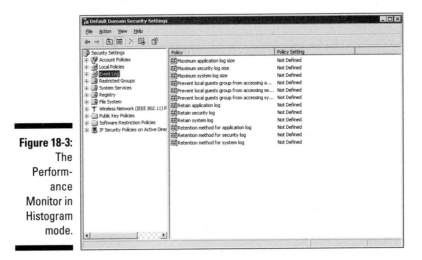

Figure 18-2:
Adding
performance
counters.

You can switch the display to a histogram, as shown in Figure 18-3, by clicking the View Histogram button. This action displays your performance counters as bar graphs, which can sometimes make it easier to spot which
counter is causing the most activity.

Figure 18-3:
The
Perform-
ance
Monitor in
Histogram
mode.

You can also switch the display to Report mode by clicking the View Report
button, as shown in Figure 18-4. Here, the performance data is displayed in
numeric form.

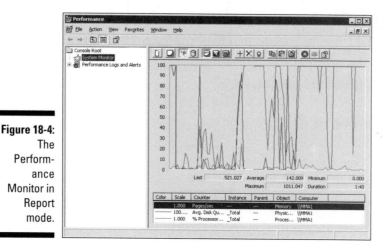

Figure 18-4:
The
Perform-
ance
Monitor in
Report
mode.

The act of gathering performance data slows down your server, so don't leave performance logging on all the time. Use it only occasionally to gather baseline data or when you're experiencing a performance problem.

Creating Performance Logs

Rather than stare at the Performance console for hours on end and wait for a performance glitch to occur, you can use the Performance console to set up logs that can track performance data over time. When the network is running well, you can collect log data to act as a baseline so that you know when performance has slipped. When the network isn't acting well, you can collect log data to help isolate the problem.

The Performance console can create two types of logs:

- ✔ **Counter logs** simply accumulate performance-counter data that you can display in summarized form later.

- ✔ **Trace logs** measure the performance of certain types of memory and resource events.

To set up a counter log, follow these steps:

1. **Right-click Counter Logs in the console tree and choose New Log Settings.**

    This action brings up a dialog box that asks for the name of the counter log.

2. **Type a name for your log and then click OK.**

   A dialog box similar to the one shown in Figure 18-5 appears.

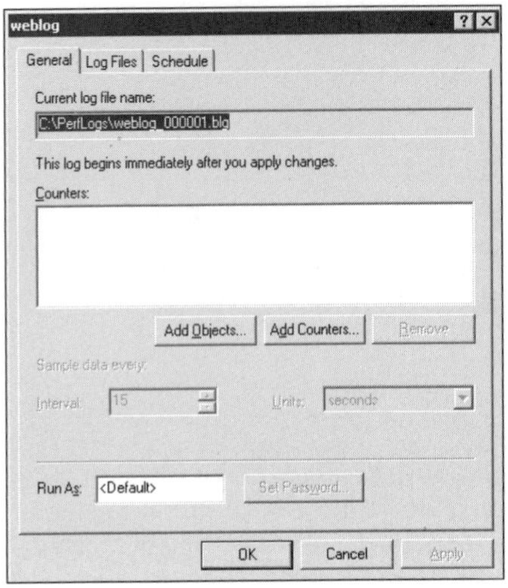

Figure 18-5:
Setting up
a perform-
ance log.

3. **Click Add Counters to add a counter to the log.**

   This action brings up the Add Counters dialog box, which was shown back in Figure 18-2.

4. **Select the object that you want from the Performance Object drop-down list, choose the counter you want to add from the list, and click Add.**

   The counter is added to the Counters list.

5. **Repeat Step 4 for each counter that you want to track.**

   You can track as many counters as you want.

6. **Click Close.**

   The Add Counters dialog box closes.

7. **If you want to schedule the log to run automatically, click the Schedule tab and set up the schedule.**

   Use this tab to specify automatic start and stop times so that the log runs automatically.

8. **Click OK.**

   You return to the Performance Monitor.

If you didn't schedule the monitor to start and stop automatically, you can start the log manually by selecting the log and then clicking the Start button on the toolbar. When you want to stop the log, select the log and click the Stop button.

To display the data accumulated by a performance log, click the System Monitor in the console tree and then click the View Log Data button on the toolbar. This action brings up the System Monitor Properties dialog box with the Source tab selected, as shown in Figure 18-6. You can then select the log file that you want to display and click OK. If the log file doesn't appear in the list, click the Add button, select the file, and click OK.

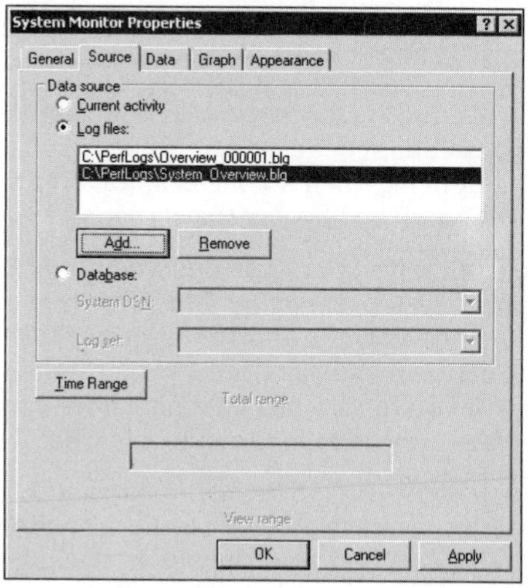

Figure 18-6:
Choosing
a log to
display.

System Monitor Properties

General | Source | Data | Graph | Appearance |

Data source
- Current activity
- Log files:

C:\PerfLogs\Overview_000001.blg
C:\PerfLogs\System_Overview.blg

[Add...]   [Remove]

- Database:
System DSN:
Log set:

[Time Range]   Total range

View range

[OK]   [Cancel]   [Apply]

Here are a few more considerations for performance monitoring:

- ✔ You can use the Performance Monitor to view real-time data or to view data that you save in a log file. Although real-time data gives you an idea about what's happening with the network at a particular moment, the more useful information comes from the logs.

- ✔ You can schedule logging to occur at certain times of the day and for certain intervals. For example, you may schedule the log to gather data every 15 seconds from 9 to 9:30 every morning and then again from 3 to 3:30 every afternoon.

- ✔ Even if you don't have a performance problem now, you should set up performance logging and let it run for a few weeks to gather some baseline data. If you develop a problem later on, the baseline data will prove invaluable as you research the problem.

TIP
- ✔ The act of gathering performance data slows down your server, so don't leave performance logging on all the time. Use it only occasionally to gather baseline data or when you're experiencing a performance problem.

More Performance Tips

Here are a few last-minute performance tips that barely made it into this chapter:

- ✔ You can often find the source of a slow network by staring at the network hubs or switches for a few minutes. These devices have colorful arrays of green and red lights. The green lights flash whenever data is transmitted; the red lights flash when a collision occurs. An occasional red flash is normal, but if one or more of the red lights is flashing repeatedly, the computer connected to that port may have a faulty network card or cable.

- ✔ Check for scheduled tasks, such as backups, batched database updates, or report jobs. If at all possible, schedule these tasks to run after normal business hours, such as at night when no one is in the office. These jobs tend to slow down the network by hogging the server's hard drives.

- ✔ Sometimes, faulty application programs can degrade performance. For example, some programs develop a *memory leak:* They use memory but forget to release the memory after they finish. Programs with memory leaks can slowly eat up all the memory on a server until the server runs out and grinds to a halt. If you think a program may have a memory leak, contact the manufacturer of the program to see whether a fix is available.

- ✔ A common source of performance problems on client computers is *spyware,* those annoying programs that you almost can't help but pick up when you surf the Internet. Spyware can slow a system to a crawl. Fortunately, you can remove it with a variety of free or inexpensive spyware removal tools. For more information, use Google or another search engine to search for **spyware removal.**

Chapter 19

Solving Network Problems

· ·

In This Chapter

▶ Checking the obvious things

▶ Fixing computers that have expired

▶ Pinpointing the cause of trouble

▶ Restarting client and server computers

▶ Reviewing network event logs

▶ Keeping a record of network woes

· ·

*F*ace it: Networks are prone to breaking.

They have too many parts. Cables. Connectors. Cards. Switches. Routers. All these parts must be held together in a delicate balance; the network equilibrium is all too easy to disturb. Even the best-designed computer networks sometimes act as though they're held together by baling wire, chewing gum, and duct tape.

To make matters worse, networks breed suspicion. After your computer is attached to a network, users begin to blame the network every time something goes wrong, regardless of whether the problem has anything to do with the network. You can't get columns to line up in a Word document? Must be the network. Your spreadsheet doesn't add up? The @@#$% network is acting up again. The stock market is down? Arghhh!!!!!!

The worst thing about network failures is that sometimes they can shut down an entire company. It's not so bad if just one user can't access a particular shared folder on a file server. If a critical server goes down, however, your network users may be locked out of their files, their applications, their e-mail, and everything else they need to conduct business as usual. When that happens, they beat down your doors and don't stop until you get the network back up and running.

In this chapter, I describe some of the most likely causes of network trouble and suggest some basic troubleshooting techniques that you can employ when your network goes on the fritz.

When Bad Things Happen to Good Computers

The following basic troubleshooting steps specify what you should examine at the first sign of network trouble. In many (if not most) of the cases, one of the following steps can get your network back up and running:

1. **Make sure that your computer and all devices attached to it are plugged in.**

   Computer geeks love it when a user calls for help and they get to tell that person that the computer isn't plugged in or that the power strip it's plugged into is turned off. They write it down in their geek logs so that they can tell their geek friends about it later. They may even want to take your picture so that they can show it to their geek friends. (Most "accidents" involving computer geeks are a direct result of this kind of behavior. Try to be tactful when you ask a user whether he's sure that the computer is turned on.)

2. **Make sure that your computer is properly connected to the network.**

3. **Note any error messages that appear on the screen.**

4. **Check the free disk space on your computer and on the server.**

   When a computer runs out of disk space or comes close to it, strange things can happen. Sometimes you get a clear error message indicating such a situation, but not always. Sometimes the computer just grinds to a halt; operations that used to take a few seconds now take a few minutes.

5. **Do a little experimenting to find out whether the problem is indeed a network problem or just a problem with the computer itself.**

   See the section, "Time to Experiment," later in this chapter, for some simple things that you can do to isolate a network problem.

6. **Try restarting the computer.**

   An amazing number of computer problems are cleared up by simply restarting the computer. Of course, in many cases the problem recurs, so you have to eventually isolate the cause and fix the problem. Some problems are only intermittent, and a simple reboot is all that's needed.

7. **Try restarting the network server.**

   See the section, "How to Restart a Network Server," later in this chapter.

How to Fix Dead Computers

If a computer seems dead, here are some items to check:

- ✔ **The plug:** Is the computer plugged in?

- ✔ **The surge protector:** If the computer is plugged into a surge protector or a power strip, make sure that the surge protector or power strip is plugged in and turned on. If the surge protector or power strip has a light, it should be glowing.

- ✔ **The On–Off switch:** Make sure that the computer's On–Off switch is turned on. This advice sounds too basic to even include here, but some computers are set up so that the computer's power switch is always left in the On position and the computer is turned on or off by means of the switch on the surge protector or power strip. Many computer users are surprised to find out that their computers have On/Off switches on the backs of the cases.

  To complicate matters, newer computers have a Sleep feature, in which they appear to be turned off but are really just sleeping. All you have to do to wake this type of computer is jiggle the mouse a little. (I used to have an uncle like that.) You can easily assume that the computer is turned off, press the power button, wonder why nothing happened, and then press the power button and hold it down, hoping that something will happen. If you hold down the power button long enough, the computer will turn itself off. Then, when you turn the computer back on, you see a message saying that the computer wasn't shut down properly. Arghhh! The moral of the story is to jiggle the mouse if the computer seems to have nodded off.

- ✔ **The fan:** If you think that the computer isn't plugged in but it looks like it is, listen for the fan. If the fan is running, the computer is getting power and the problem is more serious than an unplugged power cord. (If the fan isn't running but the computer is plugged in and the power is on, the fan may be out to lunch.)

- ✔ **The electrical outlet:** If the computer is plugged in, turned on, and still not running, plug a lamp into the outlet to make sure that power is getting to the outlet. You may need to reset a tripped circuit breaker or replace a bad surge protector. Or, you may need to call the power company. (If you live in California, don't bother. It probably won't do any good.)

  Surge protectors have a limited life span. After a few years of use, many surge protectors continue to provide electrical power for your computer, but the components that protect your computer from power surges no longer work. If you're using a surge protector that is more than two or three years old, replace it with a new one.

- ✓ **The monitor:** The monitor has a separate power cord and switch. Make sure that the monitor is plugged in and turned on. (The monitor has *two* cables that must be plugged in. One runs from the back of the monitor to the back of the computer; the other is a power cord that comes from the back of the monitor and must be plugged into an electrical outlet.)

- ✓ **Cables:** Your keyboard, monitor, mouse, and printer are all connected to the back of your computer by cables. Make sure that these cables are all plugged in securely.

  Make sure that the other ends of the monitor and printer cables are plugged in properly, too.

- ✓ **Monitor adjustment:** Some monitors have knobs that you can use to adjust the contrast and brightness of the monitor's display. If the computer is running but the screen is dark, try adjusting these knobs. They may have been turned down all the way.

- ✓ **Internal components:** If you're reasonably competent and daring, try turning off the computer, unplugging it, opening the case, and carefully removing and then reseating components, such as memory and video cards. These components often come unseated from their sockets. Removing and reinstalling them can often revive a dead computer.

Ways to Check a Network Connection

The cables that connect client computers to the rest of the network are finicky beasts. They can break at a moment's notice. By *break,* I don't necessarily mean to physically break in two. Although some broken cables look like someone took pruning shears to the cable, most cable problems aren't visible to the naked eye.

You can quickly tell whether the cable connection to the network is good by looking at the back of your computer. Look for a small light located near the spot where the cable plugs in; if this light is glowing steadily, the cable is good. If the light is dark or it's flashing intermittently, you have a cable problem (or a problem with the network card or the hub or switch that the other end of the cable is plugged into).

If the light isn't glowing steadily, try removing the cable from your computer and reinserting it. This action may cure the weak connection.

- ✓ Hopefully, your network is wired so that each computer is connected to the network with a short (six feet or so) patch cable. One end of the patch cable plugs into the computer, and the other end plugs into a cable connector mounted on the wall. Try quickly disconnecting and reconnecting the patch cable. If that doesn't do the trick, try to find a spare patch cable that you can use.

✔ Switches are prone to having cable problems, too — especially switches that are wired in a "professional manner" involving a rat's nest of patch cables. Be careful whenever you enter the lair of the rat's nest. If you need to replace a patch cable, be very careful when you disconnect the suspected bad cable and reconnect the good cable in its place.

A Bunch of Error Messages Just Flew By!

Are error messages displayed when your computer boots? If so, they can provide invaluable clues to determine the source of the problem.

If you see error messages when you start up your computer, keep these points in mind:

✔ Don't panic if you see a lot of error messages. Sometimes a simple problem that's easy to correct can cause a plethora of error messages when you start your computer. The messages may look as though your computer is falling to pieces, but the fix may be very simple.

✔ If the messages fly by so fast that you can't see them, press your computer's Pause key. Your computer comes to a screeching halt, giving you a chance to catch up on your error-message reading. After you read enough of them, press the Pause key again to get things moving. (On computers that don't have a Pause key, press Ctrl+Num Lock or Ctrl+S to do the same thing.)

✔ If you missed the error messages the first time, restart the computer and watch them again.

✔ Better yet, press F8 when you see the message `Starting Windows`. This action displays a menu from which you can select from several startup options, including one that processes each line of your `CONFIG.SYS` file separately so that you can see the messages displayed by each command before proceeding to the next command.

Double-Check Your Network Settings

I swear that little green men sneak into offices at night, turn on computers, and mess up TCP/IP configuration settings just for kicks. These little green men are affectionately known as *networchons*.

Remarkably, network configuration settings sometimes get inadvertently changed so that a computer, which enjoyed the network for months or even years, one day can't access the network. One of the first things you do, after making sure that the computers are turned on and that the cables aren't broken, is a basic review of the computer's network settings. Check these items:

- ✓ **TCP/IP settings:** At a command prompt, run `ipconfig` to make sure that TCP/IP is up and running on the computer and that the IP addresses, subnet masks, and default gateway settings look right.

- ✓ **Protocols:** Call up the network connection's Properties dialog box and make sure that the necessary protocols are installed correctly.

- ✓ **Computer name:** Open the System Properties dialog box (double-click the System icon in the Control Panel), and check the Computer Name tab. Make sure that the computer name is unique and that the domain or workgroup name is spelled properly.

- ✓ **Permissions:** Double-check the user account to make sure that the user has permission to access the resources she needs.

Time to Experiment

If you can't find an obvious explanation for your troubles (the computer is unplugged, for example), experiment to narrow the possibilities. Design your experiments to answer one basic question: Is it a network problem or a local computer problem?

Here are some ways you can narrow the cause of the problem:

- ✓ **Try performing the same operation on someone else's computer.** If no one on the network can access a network drive or printer, something is probably wrong with the network. On the other hand, if the error occurs on only one computer, the problem is likely on that computer. The wayward computer may not be communicating reliably with the network or configured properly for the network, or the problem may have nothing to do with the network.

- ✓ **If you can perform the operation on another computer without problems, try using your own username to log on to the network on another computer.** Then see whether you can perform the operation without error. If you can, the problem is probably on your computer. If you can't, the problem may be with the way your user account is configured.

- ✓ **If you can't log on at another computer, try waiting for a bit.** Your account may be temporarily locked out. This problem can happen for a variety of reasons — the most common of which is trying to log on with the wrong password several times in a row. If you're still locked out an hour later, call the network administrator and offer a doughnut.

Who's on First

When you troubleshoot a networking problem, it's often useful to find out who is logged on to a network server. For example, if a user cannot access a file on the server, you can check to see whether he is logged on. If so, you know that the user's account is valid, although he may not have permission to access the particular file or folder he wants. On the other hand, if the user isn't logged on, the problem may lie in the account itself or in the way the user is attempting to connect to the server.

Another useful technique is to find out who's logged on if you need to restart the server. For more information about restarting a server, see the section, "How to Restart a Network Server," later in this chapter.

To find out who is logged on to a Windows Server 2003 server, follow these steps:

1. **Open the Computer Management window by choosing Start➪Administrative Tools➪Computer Management.**

2. **Open System Tools in the tree list, open Shared Folders, and select Sessions.**

   A list of users who are logged on appears.

   You can select Open Files to find out which files are being used by network users.

How to Restart a Client Computer

Sometimes trouble gets a computer so tied up in knots that the only thing you can do is reboot. In some cases, the computer just starts acting weird. Strange characters appear on the screen, or Windows goes haywire and doesn't let you close programs. Sometimes the computer gets so confused that it can't even move. It just sits there, like a deer staring at oncoming headlights. It doesn't move, no matter how hard you press the Esc key or the Enter key. You can move the mouse all over your desktop, or you can even throw it across the room, but the mouse pointer on the screen stays perfectly still.

When a computer starts acting strangely, you need to reboot. If you must reboot, do so as cleanly as possible. I know that this procedure may seem elementary, but the technique for safely restarting a client computer is worth repeating, even if it's basic:

1. **Save your work if you can.**

   Use the File➪Save command, if you can, to save any documents or files that you were editing when things started to go haywire. If you can't use the menus, try clicking the Save button on the toolbar. If that doesn't work, try pressing Ctrl+S — the standard keyboard shortcut for the Save command.

2. **Close any running programs if you can.**

   Choose the File⇨Exit command or click the Close button in the upper-right corner of the program window. Or press Alt+F4.

3. **Shut down the computer.**

   For Windows XP, choose Start⇨Turn Off Computer. For Windows Vista, click the Start button, click the right-arrow that appears next to the padlock icon, and choose Shut Down.

   The Shut Down Windows dialog box appears.

4. **Select the Restart option and then click OK.**

   Your computer restarts itself.

If restarting your computer doesn't seem to fix the problem, you may need to turn your computer off all the way and then turn it on again. To do so, follow Steps 1–3 in the previous steps. Choose the Shut Down option rather than the Restart option, and then click OK. Depending on your computer, Windows either turns off your computer or displays a message stating that you can now safely turn off your computer. If Windows doesn't turn off the computer for you, flip the On–Off switch to turn off your computer. Wait a minute or so and then turn the computer back on.

Most newer computers don't immediately shut themselves off when you press the power button. Instead, you must hold down the power button for a few seconds to turn off the power. This precaution is designed to prevent you from accidentally powering down your computer.

Here are a few techniques to try if you have trouble restarting your computer:

  ✔ If your computer refuses to respond to the Start⇨Shut Down command, try pressing Ctrl+Alt+Delete — the "three-finger salute." It's appropriate to say "Queueue" while you do it.

  When you press Ctrl+Alt+Delete, Windows 9*x* and later versions attempt to display a dialog box from which you can close any running programs or shut down your computer entirely. Unfortunately, sometimes Windows 9*x* becomes so confused that it can't display the Restart dialog box, in which case pressing Ctrl+Alt+Delete may restart your computer.

  ✔ If Ctrl+Alt+Delete doesn't do anything, you reached the last resort. The only thing left to do is press the Reset button on your computer.

Pressing the Reset button is a drastic action that you should take only after your computer becomes completely unresponsive. Any work you haven't saved to disk is lost. (Sniff.) (If your computer doesn't have a Reset button, turn off the computer, wait a few moments, and then turn on the computer again.)

✔ If at all possible, save your work before restarting your computer. Any work you haven't saved is lost. Unfortunately, if your computer is totally tied up in knots, you probably can't save your work. In that case, you have no choice other than to push your computer off the digital cliff.

How to Restart Network Services

Once in a while, the network operating system (NOS) service which supports the task that's causing you trouble inexplicably stops or gets stuck. If users can't access a server, it may be because one of the key network services has stopped or is stuck.

You can review the status of services by using the Services tool, as shown in Figure 19-1. To display it, choose Services from the Administrative Tools menu. Review this list to make sure that all key services are running. If a key service is paused or stopped, restart it.

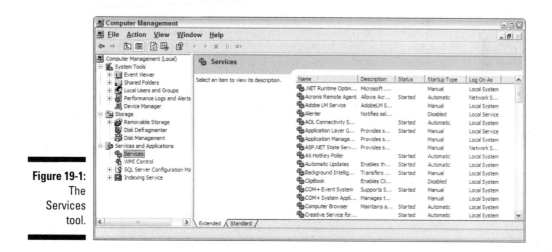

Figure 19-1:
The
Services
tool.

Which service qualifies as a *key* service depends on which roles you defined for the server. Table 19-1 lists a few key services that are common to most Windows network operating systems. However, many servers require other services.

Table 19-1	Key Windows Services
Service	*What It Does*
Computer Browser	Maintains a list of computers on the network that can be accessed. If this service is disabled, the computer cannot use browsing services, such as My Network Places.
DHCP Client	Enables the computer to obtain its IP address from a DHCP server. If this service is disabled, the computer's IP address isn't configured properly.
DNS Client	Allows the computer to access a DNS server to resolve DNS names. If this service is disabled, the computer cannot handle DNS names, including Internet addresses and Active Directory names.
Server	Provides basic file and printer sharing services for the server. If this service is stopped, clients cannot connect to the server to access files or printers.
Workstation	Enables the computer to establish client connections with other servers. If this service is disabled, the computer cannot connect to other servers.

Key services usually stop for a reason, so simply restarting a stopped service probably won't solve your network's problem — at least, not for long. Review the system log to look for any error messages that may explain why the service stopped in the first place.

If you're using Windows 2000 Server or Windows Server 2003, you can double-click a service to display a dialog box that describes the service. This information can come in handy if you're not certain what a particular service does.

How to Restart a Network Server

Sometimes, the only way to flush out a network problem is to restart the network server that's experiencing trouble.

Restarting a network server is an action you should take only as a last resort. Network operating systems are designed to run for months or even years at a time without rebooting. Restarting a server invariably results in a temporary shutdown of the network. If you must restart a server, try to do it during off hours.

Before you restart a server, check to see whether a specific service that's required has been paused or stopped. You may be able to just restart the individual service rather than the entire server. For more information, see the section, "How to Restart Network Services," earlier in this chapter.

Here's the basic procedure for restarting a network server for Windows Server 2003:

1. **Make sure that everyone is logged off the server.**

   The easiest way to do that is to restart the server after normal business hours, when everyone has gone home for the day. Then you can just shut down the server and let the shutdown process forcibly log off any remaining users.

   To find out who's logged on, refer to the section, "Who's on First," earlier in this chapter.

2. **After you're sure that all users have logged off, shut down the network server.**

   Behave like a good citizen if possible — decently and in order. For Windows servers, choose the Start➪Shut Down command.

   Windows Server 2003 doesn't let you shut down the server without providing a reason for the shutdown. When you press Ctrl+Alt+Delete, a dialog box appears, as shown in Figure 19-2. In this dialog box, you can choose from the drop-down list one of several predetermined reasons for planned or unplanned shutdowns. You can also provide additional details about the shutdown. This dialog box doesn't let you shut down until you select a reason and type at least one character in the Comment text box. The information you supply is entered into the server's system log, which you can review by using the Event Viewer.

3. **Reboot the server computer, or turn it off and then on again.**

   Watch the server start up, to make sure that no error messages appear.

4. **Tell everyone to log back on and make sure that everyone can now access the network.**

Remember this advice when you consider restarting the network server:

✔ Restarting the network server is more drastic than restarting a client computer. Make sure that everyone saves their work and logs off the network before you do it! You can cause major problems if you blindly turn off the server computer while users are logged on.

✔ Obviously, restarting a network server is a major inconvenience to every network user. Offer treats.

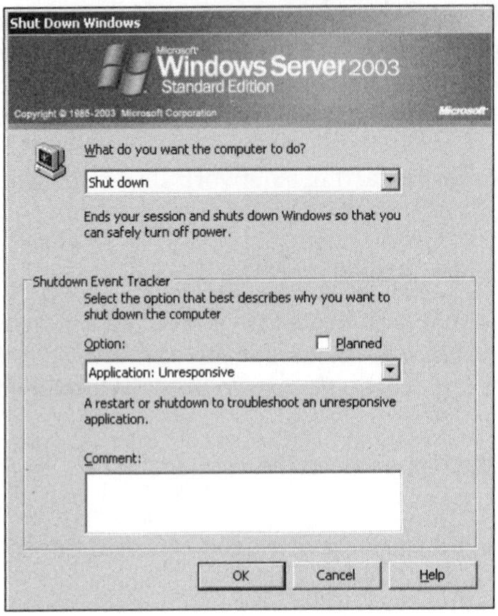

Figure 19-2:
Tracking
shutdowns
in Windows
Server 2003.

Look at Event Logs

One of the most useful troubleshooting techniques for diagnosing network problems is to review the network operating system's built-in event logs. These logs contain information about interesting and potentially troublesome events that occur during the daily operation of your network. Ordinarily, these logs run in the background and quietly gather information about network events. When something goes wrong, you can check the logs to see whether the problem generated a noteworthy event. In many cases, the event logs contain an entry that pinpoints the exact cause of the problem and suggests a solution.

To display the event logs in a Windows server, use the Event Viewer, available from the Administrative Tools menu. For example, Figure 19-3 shows the Event Viewer from a Windows Server 2003 system. The tree listing on the left side of the Event Viewer lists five categories of events that are tracked:

- Application events
- Security events
- System events
- Directory Service events
- File Replication Service events

Select one of these options to see the log that you want to view. For details about a particular event, double-click the event; this action displays a dialog box that lists detailed information about the event.

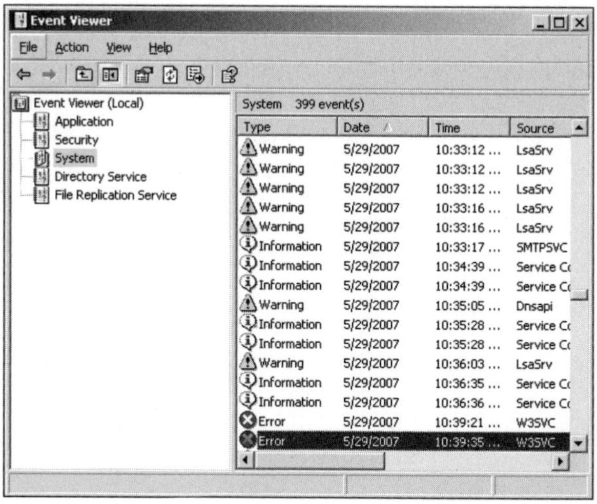

Figure 19-3:
Event logs
keep
track of
interesting
and
potentially
troublesome
events.

Document Your Trials and Tribulations

For a large network, consider investing in problem-management software that tracks each problem through the entire process of troubleshooting, from initial report to final resolution. For small- and medium-size networks, compiling preprinted forms in a three-ring binder is probably sufficient. Or, record your log in a Word document or Excel spreadsheet.

Regardless of how you track your network problems, the tracking log should include this information:

- ✔ The real name and the network username of the person reporting the problem.

- ✔ The date the problem was first reported.

- ✔ An indication of the severity of the problem. Is it merely an inconvenience, or is a user unable to complete her work because of the problem? Does a workaround exist?

- ✔ The name of the person assigned to resolve the problem.

- ✔ A description of the problem.

- ✔ A list of the software involved, including version numbers.

- ✔ A description of the steps taken to solve the problem.

- ✔ A description of any intermediate steps that were taken to try to solve the problem, along with an indication of whether those steps were "undone" when they didn't help solve the problem.

- ✔ The date the problem was finally resolved.

Chapter 20

How to Stay on Top of Your Network and Keep Its Users Off Your Back

In This Chapter

▶ Training your users

▶ Organizing a library

▶ Finding sources for help

▶ Coming up with great excuses

A network manager has a rotten deal. Users come to you whenever anything goes wrong, regardless of whether the problem has anything to do with the network. They knock on your door if they can't log on, if they lost a file, or if they can't remember how to use the microwave.

This chapter shows a few basic rules to simplify your life as a network manager.

Train Your Users

After you first get your network up and running, invite all the network users to Network Obedience School so that you can teach them how to behave on the network. Show them the basics of accessing the network, make sure that they understand how to share files, and explain the rules to them.

A great way to prepare your users for this session is to ask them to read the first three chapters of this book. I wrote those chapters with the network user in mind, so they explain the basic facts of network life. If your users read those chapters first, they're in a much better position to ask good questions during obedience school.

Here are more ways to make the training process painless for you and your users:

- ✔ **Write a summary of what your users need to know about the network — on one page, if possible.** Include everyone's user IDs, the names of the servers, network drive assignments and printers, and the procedure for logging on to the network. Everyone needs a copy of this Network Cheat Sheet.

- ✔ **Emphasize the etiquette of network life.** Make sure that everyone understands that not all free space on the network drive is personal space — it's shared, and it should be used sparingly. Explain the importance of treating other people's files with respect. Ask users to check with their fellow users before sending a three-hour print job to the printer.

- ✔ **Don't bluff your way through your role as network manager.** If you're not a computer genius, don't pretend to be one just because you know a little more than everyone else. Tell users that everyone is in this together and that you will do your best to try to solve any network problems that may come up.

Organize a Library

As the network manager, every network user expects you to be an expert at every computer program he uses. That task is manageable when you have only two network users and they only use Microsoft Word. But if you have a gaggle of users who use a bevy of programs, being an expert in all them is next to impossible.

The only solution is a well-stocked computer library that has all the information you may need to solve problems that come up. When a user bugs you with a new bug, you can say with confidence, "I'll get back to you on that one."

Your library should include these items:

- ✔ **A copy of your network binder:** All the information you need about the configuration of your network should be in this binder. (Don't put the original copy of the network binder in the library. Keep the original under lock and key in your office. And keep an extra copy off-site in a safe place.)

- ✔ **A copy of the manuals for every program used on the network:** Most users ignore the manuals, so they don't mind if you "borrow" them for the library. If a user won't part with a manual, at least make a note of the manual's location so that you know where to find it.

✔ **A copy of the *Windows Resource Kit* for every version of Windows in use on your network:** You can get the *Windows Resource Kit* at any bookstore that has a well-stocked section of computer books.

✔ **A copy of the network software manual or manuals.**

✔ **At least 20 copies of this book:** (Hey, I have bills to pay.) Seriously, your library should contain books appropriate to your level of expertise. Of course, *For Dummies* books are available on just about every major computer subject. Devoting an entire shelf to these yellow-and-black books isn't a bad idea.

Keep Up with the Computer Industry

The computer business changes fast, and your users probably expect you to be abreast of all the latest trends and developments. They ask, "What do you think about the new version of SkyWriter? Should we upgrade or stick with Version 23?"

"We need an Intranet Web site. What's the best Web page editor for under $200?"

"My kid wants video-editing software. Which is better, VideoPro or MovieNow?"

The only way to give halfway intelligent answers to questions like these is to read about the industry. Visit your local newsstand and pick out a few computer magazines that appeal to you. Here are some more tips for keeping up:

✔ **Subscribe to at least one general-interest computer magazine and one magazine specifically written for network users.** That way, you can keep abreast of general trends and the specific stuff that applies just to networks.

✔ **Subscribe to e-mail newsletters that cover the systems you use.**

✔ **Look for magazines that have a mix of good how-to articles and reviews of new products.**

✔ **Don't overlook the value of the advertisements in many of the larger computer magazines.** Some people (I'm one of 'em) subscribe to certain magazines to read the ads as much as to read the articles.

✔ **Most computer magazines are quite technical.** Look for magazines written to your current level of expertise. You may discover that you outgrow one magazine and are ready to replace it with one that's more technical.

Remember That the Guru Needs a Guru

No matter how much you know about computers, plenty of people know more than you do. This rule seems to apply at every rung of the ladder of computer experience. I'm sure that a top rung exists somewhere, occupied by the world's best computer guru. I'm not sitting on that rung, and neither are you. (Not even Bill Gates is sitting on that rung. Bill Gates got where he is by hiring people on higher rungs.)

As the local computer guru, one of your most valuable assets can be a friend who's a notch or two above you. That way, when you run into a real stumper, you have a friend you can call for advice. Here are some tips for handling your own guru:

- ✔ **In dealing with your own guru, don't forget the Computer Geek's Golden Rule: "Do unto your guru as you would have your own users do unto you."** Don't pester your guru with simple stuff that you just haven't spent the time to think through. If you *have* thought it through and can't come up with a solution, however, give your guru a call. Most computer experts welcome the opportunity to tackle an unusual computer problem. It's a genetic defect.

- ✔ **If you don't already know someone who knows more about computers than you do, consider joining your local PC users' group.** The group may have a subgroup that specializes in your networking software — or may be devoted entirely to local folks who use the same networking software that you use. Odds are, that you'll make a friend or two at a users' group meeting.

    You can probably convince your boss to pay your fees to join the group.

- ✔ **If you can't find a real-life guru, try to find an online guru.** Check out the various computing newsgroups on the Internet. Subscribe to online newsletters that are automatically delivered to you by e-mail.

Spew Helpful Bluffs and Excuses

As a network administrator, sometimes you just can't solve a problem immediately. You can do two things in this situation.

The first solution is to explain that the problem is particularly difficult and that you'll have a solution as soon as possible.

The second solution is to look the user in the eye and try a *phony* explanation:

- ✔ It was the *version* of your software. ("Oh, they fixed that with version 39.")
- ✔ It was those cheap, imported memory chips.
- ✔ It was those Democrats. Or Republicans. Or hanging chads. Whatever.
- ✔ The problem was caused by stray static electricity. Those types of problems are difficult to track down. Users who don't properly discharge themselves before using their computers can cause all kinds of problems.
- ✔ You need more memory.
- ✔ You need a bigger disk.
- ✔ You need a dual-core processor to do that.
- ✔ Jar-Jar Binks did it.
- ✔ You can't do that in Windows Vista.
- ✔ You can *only* do that in Windows Vista.
- ✔ You're not using Windows Vista, are you?
- ✔ It could be a virus.
- ✔ Or sunspots.
- ✔ All work and no beer makes Homer something, something, something. . . .

Part V
Protecting Your Network

NETWORK ADMIN

"We found where the security breach in the WLAN was originating. It was coming in through another rogue robot-vac. This is the third one this month. Must have gotten away from its owner, like all the rest."

In this part . . .

One of the major annoyances of running a network is keeping the network safe. The world is full of crazy people who get their kicks from trying to bring innocent networks like yours to their knees.

The chapters in this part describe the most important things you can do as a network administrator to keep your network safe. You'll learn about backing up critical data, protecting your network from viruses and other threats, and hardening your Internet connection to keep intruders at bay.

Chapter 21

Backing Up Your Data

In This Chapter

▶ Understanding the need for backups

▶ Working with tape drives and other backup media

▶ Understanding the different types of backups

▶ Mastering tape rotation and other details

*I*f you're the hapless network manager, the safety of the data on your network is your responsibility. In fact, it's your primary responsibility. You get paid to lie awake at night worrying about your data. Will it be there tomorrow? If it's not, can *you* get it back? And — most importantly — if you can't get it back, will *you* be there tomorrow?

This chapter covers the ins and outs of being a good, responsible, trust-worthy network manager. They don't give out merit badges for this stuff, but they should.

Backing Up Your Data

Having data backed up is the cornerstone of any disaster recovery plan. Without backups, a simple hard drive failure can set your company back days or even weeks while it tries to reconstruct lost data. In fact, without backups, your company's very existence is in jeopardy.

The main goal of backups is simple: Keep a spare copy of your network's critical data so that, no matter what happens, you never lose more than one day's work. The stock market may crash, hanging chads may factor into another presidential election, and George Lucas may decide to make a pre-prequel. However, you never lose more than one day's work if you stay on top of your backups.

The way to do this, naturally, is to make sure that data is backed up on a daily basis. In many networks, it's feasible to back up all the network hard drives every night. However, even if full nightly backups aren't possible, you can still use techniques that can ensure that every file on the network has a backup copy that's no more than one day old.

All about Tapes and Tape Drives

If you plan on backing up the data on your network server's hard drives, you need something to back up the data to. You can copy the data onto CDs, but a 500GB hard drive would need more than 750 CDs to do a full backup. That's a few more disks than most people want to keep in the closet. You could use DVDs, but you'll need about a dozen of them, and it will take an hour or so to fill each one. So you'll have to devote a Saturday to creating your backup.

Because of the limitations of CDs and DVDs, most network administrators back up network data to tape. Depending on the make and model of the tape drive, you can copy as much as 800GB of data onto a single tape.

One of the benefits of tape backup is that you can run it unattended. In fact, you can schedule tape backup to run automatically during off hours, when no one is using the network. In order for unattended backups to work, you must ensure that you have enough tape capacity to back up your entire network server's hard drive without having to manually switch tapes. If your network server has only 100GB of data, you can easily back it up onto a single tape. However, if you have 1,000GB of data, invest in a tape drive that features a magazine changer that can hold several tapes and automatically cycle them in and out of the drive. That way, you can run your backups unattended.

Here are some additional thoughts concerning tape backups:

- ✔ A popular style of tape backup for small servers is *Travan drives*. Travan drives come in a variety of models with tape capacities ranging from 20GB to 40GB. You can purchase a 20GB drive for under $200.

- ✔ For larger networks, you can get tape backup units that offer higher capacity and faster backup speed than Travan drives but for more money, of course. DAT (digital audio tape) units can back up as much as 80GB on a single tape, and DLT (digital linear tape) drives can store up to 200GB on one tape. DAT and DLT drives can cost $1,000 or more, depending on the capacity.

- ✔ If you're really up the backup creek with hundreds of gigabytes to back up, you can get robotic tape backup units that automatically fetch and load tape cartridges from a library, so you can do complete backups without having to load tapes manually. Naturally, these units aren't cheap: The small ones, which have a library of about eight tapes and a total backup capacity of over 5,000GB, start at about $4,000.

Backup Software

All versions of Windows come with a built-in backup program. In addition, most tape drives come with backup programs that are often faster or more flexible than the standard Windows backup.

You can also purchase sophisticated backup programs that are specially designed for networks that have multiple servers with data that must be backed up. For a basic Windows file server, you can use the backup program that comes with Windows Server. Server versions of Windows come with a decent backup program that can run scheduled, unattended tape backups.

Backup programs do more than just copy data from your hard drive to tape. Backup programs use special compression techniques to squeeze your data so that you can cram more data onto fewer tapes. Compression factors of 2:1 are common, so you can usually squeeze 100GB of data onto a tape that would hold only 50GB of data without compression. (Tape drive manufacturers tend to state the capacity of their drives by using compressed data, assuming a 2:1 compression ratio. So a 200GB tape has an uncompressed capacity of 100GB.)

Whether you achieve a compression factor of 2:1 depends on the nature of the data you're backing up:

✔ If your network is used primarily by Office applications and is filled with Word and Excel documents, you'll probably get better than 2:1 compression.

✔ If your network data consists primarily of graphic image files, you probably won't get much compression. Most graphic image file formats are compressed already, so they can't be compressed much more by the backup software's compression methods.

Backup programs also help you keep track of which data has been backed up and which hasn't. They also offer options, such as incremental or differential backups that can streamline the backup process, as I describe in the next section.

If your network has more than one server, invest in good backup software. The most popular is Yosemite Backup, made by Yosemite Technology. See www.yosemitetech.com. Besides being able to handle multiple servers, one of the main advantages of backup software (such as Yosemite Backup) is that it can properly back up Microsoft Exchange server data.

Types of Backups

You can perform five different types of backups. Many backup schemes rely on full backups daily, but for some networks, it's more practical to use a scheme that relies on two or more of these backup types.

The differences among the fives types of backup involve a little technical detail known as the *archive bit*. The archive bit indicates whether a file has been modified since the last time it was backed up. The archive bit is a little flag that's stored along with the filename, creation date, and other directory information. Any time that a program modifies a file, the archive bit is set to the On position. That way, backup programs know that the file has been modified and needs to be backed up.

The differences among the various types of backup center around whether they use the archive bit to determine which files to back up, and whether they flip the archive bit to the Off position after they back up a file. Table 21-1 summarizes these differences, and they're explained in the following sections.

Backup programs allow you to select any combination of drives and folders to back up. As a result, you can customize the file selection for a backup operation to suit your needs. For example, you can set up one backup plan that backs up all a server's shared folders and drives plus its mail server stores but leaves out folders that rarely change, such as the operating system folders or installed program folders. You can then back up those folders on a less regular basis. The drives and folders that you select for a backup operation are collectively called the *backup selection*.

Table 21-1	How Backup Types Use the Archive Bit	
Backup Type	*Selects Files Based on Archive Bit?*	*Resets Archive Bits after Backing Up?*
Normal	No	Yes
Copy	No	No
Daily	No*	No
Incremental	Yes	Yes
Differential	Yes	No

Selects files based on the Last Modified date.

The archive bit would've made a good Abbott and Costello routine. ("All right, I wanna know who modified the archive bit." "What." "Who?" "No, what." "Wait a minute . . . just tell me what's the name of the guy who modified the archive bit!" "Right.")

Normal backups

A *normal backup*, also called a *full backup,* is the most basic type of backup. In a normal backup, all files in the backup selection are backed up — regardless of whether the archive bit has been set. In other words, the files are backed up even if they haven't been modified since the last time they were backed up. When each file is backed up, its archive bit is reset, so backups that select files based on the archive bit setting won't back up the files.

When a normal backup finishes, none of the files in the backup selection will have their archive bits set. As a result, if you immediately follow a normal backup with an incremental backup or a differential backup, no files will be selected for backup by the incremental or differential backup because no files will have their archive bits set.

The easiest backup scheme is to simply schedule a normal backup every night. That way, all your data is backed up on a daily basis. So if the need arises, you can restore files from a single tape or set of tapes. Restoring files is more complicated when other types of backups are involved.

Do normal backups nightly if you have the tape capacity to do them unattended — that is, without having to swap tapes. If you can't do an unattended normal backup because the amount of data to be backed up is greater than the capacity of your tape drive or drives, you'll have to use other types of backups in combination with normal backups.

If you can't get a normal backup on a single tape and you can't afford a second tape drive or a tape changer, take a hard look at the data that's being included in the backup selection. I recently worked on a network that was having trouble backing up onto a single tape. When I examined the data that was being backed up, I discovered a large amount of static data that was essentially an online archive of old projects. This data was necessary because network users needed it for research purposes, but the data was read-only. Even though the data never changed, it was being backed up to tape every night, and the backups required two tapes. After we removed this data from the cycle of nightly backups, the backups were able to squeeze onto a single tape again.

If you remove static data from the nightly backup, make sure that you have a secure backup of the static data, either on tape, CD-RW, or some other media.

Copy backups

A *copy backup* is similar to a normal backup, except that the archive bit isn't reset when each file is copied. As a result, copy backups don't disrupt the cycle of normal and incremental or differential backups.

Copy backups are usually not incorporated into regular, scheduled backups. Instead, you use a copy backup when you want to do an occasional one-shot backup. For example, if you're about to perform an operating system upgrade, you should back up the server before proceeding. If you do a full backup, the archive bits are reset, and your regular backups are disrupted. However, if you do a copy backup, the archive bits of any modified files remain unchanged. As a result, your regular normal and incremental or differential backups are unaffected.

If you don't incorporate incremental or differential backups into your backup routine, the difference between a copy backup and a normal backup is moot.

Daily backups

A *daily backup* backs up just those files that have been changed the same day that the backup is performed. A daily backup examines the modification date stored with each file's directory entry to determine whether a file should be backed up. Daily backups don't reset the archive bit.

I'm not a big fan of this option because of the small possibility that some files may slip through the cracks. Someone may be working late one night and modify a file after the evening's backups have completed, but before midnight. Those files won't be included in the following night's backups. Incremental or differential backups, which rely on the archive bit rather than the modification date, are more reliable.

Incremental backups

An *incremental backup* backs up only those files that you've modified since the last time you did a backup. Incremental backups are a lot faster than full backups because your network users probably modify only a small portion of the files on the server in any given day. As a result, if a full backup takes three tapes, you can probably fit an entire week's worth of incremental backups on a single tape.

When an incremental backup copies each file, it resets the file's archive bit. That way, the file will be backed up again before your next normal backup only when a user modifies the file again.

Here are some thoughts about using incremental backups:

✔ The easiest way to use incremental backups is to do

- A *normal* backup every Monday.

 If your full backup takes more than 12 hours, you may want to do it on Friday so that it can run over the weekend.

- An *incremental* backup on each other normal business day (for example, Tuesday, Wednesday, Thursday, and Friday).

✔ When you use incremental backups, the complete backup consists of the full backup tapes and all the incremental backup tapes that you've made since you did the full backup.

 If the hard drive crashes and you have to restore the data onto a new drive, you first restore Monday's normal backup and then you restore each of the subsequent incremental backups.

✔ Incremental backups complicate the task of restoring individual files because the most recent copy of the file may be on the full backup tape or on any of the incremental backups.

 Backup programs keep track of the location of the most recent version of each file in order to simplify the process.

✔ When you use incremental backups, you can choose whether you want to

- *Store* each incremental backup on its own tape.

- *Append* each backup to the end of an existing tape.

 Often, you can use a single tape for a week of incremental backups.

Differential backups

A *differential backup* is similar to an incremental backup except that it doesn't reset the archive bit when files are backed up. As a result, each differential backup represents the difference between the last normal backup and the current state of the hard drive.

To do a full restore from a differential backup, you first restore the last normal backup and then you restore the most recent differential backup.

For example, suppose that you do a normal backup on Monday and differential backups on Tuesday, Wednesday, and Thursday, and your hard drive crashes Friday morning. Friday afternoon, you install a new hard drive. Then, to restore the data, you first restore the normal backup from Monday. Then, you restore the differential backup from Thursday. The Tuesday and Wednesday differential backups aren't needed.

The differences between incremental and differential backups are that

- ✔ **Incremental** backups result in smaller and faster backups.

- ✔ **Differential** backups are easier to restore.

    If your users often ask you to restore *individual files,* consider differential backups.

Local versus Network Backups

When you back up network data, you have two basic approaches to running the backup software: You can perform a *local backup* in which the backup software runs on the file server itself and backs up data to a tape drive that's installed in the server, or you can perform a *network backup* in which you use one network computer to back up data from another network computer. In a network backup, the data has to travel over the network to get to the computer that's running the backup.

If you run the backups from the file server, you'll tie up the server while the backup is running. Your users will complain that their access to the server has slowed to a snail's pace. On the other hand, if you run the backup over the network from a client computer or a dedicated backup server, you'll flood the network with gigabytes of data being backed up. Your users will then complain that the entire network has slowed to a snail's pace.

Network performance is one of the main reasons you should try to run your backups during off hours, when other users aren't accessing the network. Another reason to do this is so that you can perform a more thorough backup. If you run your backup while other users are accessing files, the backup program is likely to skip over any files that are being accessed by users at the time the backup runs. As a result, your backup won't include those files. Ironically, the files most likely to get left out of the backup are often the files that need backing up the most because they're the files that are being used and modified.

Here are some extra thoughts on client and server backups:

- ✔ You may think that backing up directly from the server would be more efficient than backing up from a client because data doesn't have to travel over the network. Actually, this assumption doesn't always hold because the network may well be faster than the tape drive. The network probably won't slow down backups unless you back up during the busiest time of the day, when hordes of network users are storming the network gates.

✔ To improve network backup speed and to minimize the effect that network backups have on the rest of the network, consider using a 1,000 Mbps switch rather than a normal 100 Mbps switch to connect the servers and the backup client. That way, network traffic between the server and the backup client won't bog down the rest of the network.

✔ Any files that are open while the backups are running won't get backed up. That's usually not a problem because backups are run at off hours when people have gone home for the day. However, if someone leaves his or her computer on with a Word document open, that Word document won't be backed up. One way to solve this problem is to set up the server so that it automatically logs everyone off the network before the backups begin.

✔ Some backup programs have special features that enable them to back up open files. For example, the Windows Server 2003 backup does this by creating a snapshot of the volume when it begins, thus making temporary copies of any files that are modified during the backup. The backup backs up the temporary copies rather than the versions being modified. When the backup finishes, the temporary copies are deleted.

How Many Sets of Backups Should You Keep?

Don't try to cut costs by purchasing one backup tape and reusing it every day. What happens if you accidentally delete an important file on Tuesday and don't discover your mistake until Thursday? Because the file didn't exist on Wednesday, it won't be on Wednesday's backup tape. If you have only one tape that's reused every day, you're outta luck.

The safest scheme is to use a new backup tape every day and keep all your old tapes in a vault. Pretty soon, though, your tape vault can start looking like the warehouse where they stored the Ark of the Covenant at the end of *Raiders of the Lost Ark.*

As a compromise between these two extremes, most users purchase several tapes and rotate them. That way, you always have several backup tapes to fall back on, just in case the file you need isn't on the most recent backup tape. This technique is *tape rotation,* and several variations are commonly used:

✔ The simplest approach is to purchase three tapes and label them A, B, and C. You use the tapes on a daily basis in sequence: A the first day, B the second day, C the third day; then A the fourth day, B the fifth day, C the sixth day, and so on. On any given day, you have three *generations* of backups: today's, yesterday's, and the day-before-yesterday's. Computer geeks like to call these the *grandfather, father,* and *son* tapes.

✔ Another simple approach is to purchase five tapes and use one each day of the workweek.

✔ A variation of this scheme is to buy eight tapes. Take four of them and write *Tuesday* on one label, *Wednesday* on the second, *Thursday* on the third, and *Friday* on the fourth label. On the other four tapes, write *Monday 1, Monday 2, Monday 3,* and *Monday 4.* Now, tack up a calendar on the wall near the computer and number all the Mondays in the year: 1, 2, 3, 4, 1, 2, 3, 4, and so on.

On Tuesday through Friday, you use the appropriate daily backup tape. When you do a full backup on Monday, you consult the calendar to decide which Monday tape to use. With this scheme, you always have four weeks' worth of Monday backup tapes, plus individual backup tapes for the rest of the week.

✔ If bookkeeping data lives on the network, make a backup copy of all your files (or at least all your accounting files) immediately before closing the books each month; then retain those backups for each month of the year. Does that mean you should purchase 12 additional tapes? Not necessarily. If you back up just your accounting files, you can probably fit all 12 months on a single tape. Just make sure that you back up with the "append to tape" option rather than the "erase tape" option so that the previous contents of the tape aren't destroyed. Also, treat this accounting backup as completely separate from your normal daily backup routine.

You should also keep at least one recent full backup at another location. That way, if your office should fall victim to an errant Scud missile or a rogue asteroid, you can re-create your data from the backup copy that you stored off-site.

A Word about Tape Reliability

From experience, I've found that although tape drives are very reliable, they do run amok once in a while. Problem is, they don't always tell you when they're not working. A tape drive — especially the less expensive Travan drives — can spin along for hours, pretending to back up your data, when in reality, your data isn't being written reliably to the tape. In other words, a tape drive can trick you into thinking that your backups are working just fine, but when disaster strikes and you need your backup tapes, you may just discover that the tapes are worthless.

Don't panic! You have a simple way to assure yourself that your tape drive is working. Just activate the "compare after backup" feature of your backup software. Then, as soon as your backup program finishes backing up your data, it rewinds the tape, reads each backed-up file, and compares it with the original version on the hard drive. If all files compare, you know your backups are trustworthy.

Here are some additional thoughts about the reliability of tapes:

- The "compare after backup" feature doubles the time required to do a backup, but that doesn't matter if your entire backup fits on one tape. You can just run the backup after hours. Whether the backup and repair operation takes one hour or ten doesn't matter, as long as it's finished by the time the network users arrive at work the next morning.

- If your backups require more than one tape, you may not want to run the "compare after backup" feature every day. However, be sure to run it periodically to check that your tape drive is working.

- If your backup program reports errors, throw away the tape and use a new tape.

- Actually, you should ignore that last comment about waiting for your backup program to report errors. You should discard tapes *before* your backup program reports errors. Most experts recommend that you should use a tape only about 20 times before discarding it. If you use the same tape every day, replace it monthly. If you have tapes for each day of the week, replace them twice a year. If you have more tapes than that, figure out a cycle that replaces tapes after about 20 uses.

About Cleaning the Heads

An important aspect of backup reliability is proper maintenance of your tape drives. Every time you back up to tape, little bits and specks of the tape rub off onto the read and write heads inside the tape drive. Eventually, the heads become too dirty to reliably read or write data.

To counteract this problem, clean the tape heads regularly. The easiest way to clean them is to use a special tape-cleaning cartridge. To clean the heads with a tape-cleaning cartridge, insert the cartridge into the tape drive. The drive automatically recognizes that you've inserted a cleaning cartridge and performs a special routine that wipes the special cleaning tape back and forth over the heads to clean them. When the cleaning routine is done, the tape's ejected. The whole thing takes about 30 seconds.

Because the maintenance requirements of each drive differ, you should check the drive's user's manual to find out how and how often to clean the drive. As a general rule, clean the drives once a week.

The most annoying aspect of tape drive cleaning is that the cleaning cartridges have a limited lifespan. Unfortunately, if you insert a used-up cleaning cartridge, the drive accepts it and pretends to clean the drive. For this reason, keep track of the number of times you've used the cleaning cartridge and replace it when you've exceeded the number of uses recommended by the manufacturer.

Backup Security

Backups create an often-overlooked security exposure for your network. No matter how carefully you set up user accounts and enforce password policies, if any user (including a guest) can perform a backup of the system, that user may make an unauthorized backup. In addition, your backup tapes themselves are vulnerable to theft. As a result, you should make sure that your backup policies and procedures are secure by taking the following measures:

- ✔ Set up a user account for the user who does backups. Because this user account has backup permission for the entire server, guard its password carefully. Anyone who knows the username and password of the backup account can log on and bypass any security restrictions that you place on that user's normal user ID.

- ✔ You can counter potential security problems by restricting the backup user ID to a certain client and a certain time of the day. If you're really clever (and paranoid), you can probably set up the backup user's account so that the only program it can run is the backup program.

- ✔ Use encryption to protect the contents of your backup tapes.

- ✔ Secure the backup tapes in a safe location, such as, um, *a safe*.

Chapter 22

Securing Your Network

In This Chapter

▶ Assessing the risk for security

▶ Determining your basic security philosophy

▶ Physically securing your network equipment

▶ User account security

▶ Other network security techniques

*B*efore you had a network, computer security was easy. You simply locked your door when you left work for the day. You could rest easy, secure in the knowledge that the bad guys would have to break down the door to get to your computer.

The network changes all that. Now, anyone with access to any computer on the network can break into the network and steal *your* files. Not only do you have to lock your door, but you have to make sure that other people lock their doors, too.

Fortunately, network operating systems have built-in provisions for network security. This situation makes it difficult for someone to steal your files, even if they do break down the door. All modern network operating systems have security features that are more than adequate for all but the most paranoid users.

When I say *more* than adequate, I mean it. Most networks have security features that would make even Maxwell Smart happy. Using all these security features is kind of like Smart insisting that the Chief lower the "Cone of Silence." The Cone of Silence worked so well that Max and the Chief couldn't hear each other! Don't make your system so secure that even the good guys can't get their work done.

If any of the computers on your network are connected to the Internet, you must harden your network against intrusion via the Internet. For more information, see Chapter 23. Also, if your network supports wireless devices, you have wireless security issues. For information about security for wireless networks, see Chapter 9.

Do You Need Security?

Most small networks are in small businesses or departments where everyone knows and trusts everyone else. Folks don't lock up their desks when they take a coffee break, and although everyone knows where the petty cash box is, money never disappears.

Network security isn't necessary in an idyllic setting like this one, is it? You bet it is. Here's why any network should be set up with at least some concern for security:

- ✔ Even in the friendliest office environment, some information is and should be confidential. If this information is stored on the network, you want to store it in a directory that's available only to authorized users.

- ✔ Not all security breaches are malicious. A network user may be routinely scanning through his or her files and come across a filename that isn't familiar. The user may then call up the file, only to discover that it contains confidential personnel information, juicy office gossip, or your résumé. Curiosity, rather than malice, is often the source of security breaches.

- ✔ Sure, everyone at the office is trustworthy now. However, what if someone becomes disgruntled, a screw pops loose, and he or she decides to trash the network files before jumping out the window? What if someone decides to print a few $1,000 checks before packing off to Tahiti?

- ✔ Sometimes the mere opportunity for fraud or theft can be too much for some people to resist. Give people free access to the payroll files, and they may decide to vote themselves a raise when no one is looking.

- ✔ If you think that your network doesn't contain any data that's worth stealing, think again. For example, your personnel records probably contain more than enough information for an identity thief: names, addresses, phone numbers, social security numbers, and so on. Also, your customer files may contain your customers' credit card numbers.

- ✔ Hackers who break into your network may be looking to plant a *Trojan horse* program on your server, which enables them to use your server for their own purposes. For example, someone may use your server to send thousands of unsolicited spam e-mail messages. The spam won't be traced back to the hackers; it'll be traced back to you.

- ✔ Not everyone on the network knows enough about how Windows and the network work to be trusted with full access to your network's data and systems. A careless mouse click can wipe out a directory of network files. One of the best reasons for activating your network's security features is to protect the network from mistakes made by users who don't know what they're doing.

Two Approaches to Security

When you're planning how to implement security on your network, first consider which of two basic approaches to security you'll take:

- ✔ An **open-door type** of security, in which you grant everyone access to everything by default and then place restrictions just on those resources to which you want to limit access.

- ✔ A **closed-door type** of security, in which you begin by denying access to everything and then grant specific users access to the specific resources that they need.

In most cases, the open-door policy is easier to implement. Typically, only a small portion of the data on a network really needs security, such as confidential employee records, or secrets, such as the Coke recipe. The rest of the information on a network can be safely made available to everyone who can access the network.

If you choose the closed-door approach, you set up each user so that he or she has access to nothing. Then, you grant each user access only to those specific files or folders that he or she needs.

The closed-door approach results in tighter security but can lead to the Cone of Silence Syndrome: Like Max and the Chief who can't hear each other talk while they're under the Cone of Silence, your network users will constantly complain that they can't access the information that they need. As a result, you'll find yourself often adjusting users' access rights. Choose the closed-door approach only if your network contains a lot of sensitive information, and only if you're willing to invest time administrating your network's security policy.

You can think of the open-door approach as an *entitlement model,* in which the basic assumption is that users are entitled to network access. In contrast, the closed-door policy is a *permissions model,* in which the basic assumption is that users aren't entitled to anything but must get permissions for every network resource that they access.

Physical Security: Locking Your Doors

The first level of security in any computer network is *physical security.* I'm amazed when I walk into the reception area of an accounting firm and see an unattended computer sitting on the receptionist's desk. Often, the receptionist has logged on to the system and then walked away from the desk, leaving the computer unattended.

Physical security is important for workstations but vital for servers. Any good hacker can quickly defeat all but the most paranoid security measures if they can gain physical access to a server. To protect the server, follow these guidelines:

- ✔ Lock the computer room.
- ✔ Give the key only to people you trust.
- ✔ Keep track of who has the keys.
- ✔ Mount the servers on cases or racks that have locks.
- ✔ Disable the floppy drive on the server.

  A common hacking technique is to boot the server from a floppy, thus bypassing the security features of the network operating system.

- ✔ Keep a trained guard dog in the computer room and feed it only enough to keep it hungry and mad. (Just kidding.)

There's a big difference between a *locked door* and *a door with a lock*. Locks are worthless if you don't use them.

Client computers should be physically secure:

- ✔ Instruct users to not leave their computers unattended while they're logged on.
- ✔ In high-traffic areas (such as the receptionist's desk), users should secure their computers with the keylock, if the computer has one.
- ✔ Users should lock their office doors when they leave.

Here are some other threats to physical security that you may not have considered:

- ✔ The nightly cleaning crew probably has complete access to your facility. How do you know that the person who vacuums your office every night doesn't really work for your chief competitor or doesn't consider computer hacking to be a sideline hobby? You don't, so consider the cleaning crew to be a threat.
- ✔ What about your trash? Paper shredders aren't just for Enron accountants. Your trash can contain all sorts of useful information: sales reports, security logs, printed copies of the company's security policy, even handwritten passwords. For the best security, every piece of paper that leaves your building via the trash bin should first go through a shredder.
- ✔ Where do you store your backup tapes? Don't just stack them up next to the server. Not only does that make them easy to steal, it also defeats one of the main purposes of backing up your data in the first place:

securing your server from physical threats, such as fires. If a fire burns down your computer room and the backup tapes are sitting unprotected next to the server, your company may go out of business and you'll certainly be out of a job. Store the backup tapes securely in a fireproof safe and keep a copy off-site, too.

✔ I've seen some networks in which the servers are in a locked computer room, but the hubs or switches are in an unsecured closet. Remember that every unused port on a hub or a switch represents an open door to your network. The hubs and switches should be secured just like the servers.

Securing User Accounts

Next to physical security, the careful use of user accounts is the most important type of security for your network. Properly configured user accounts can prevent unauthorized users from accessing the network, even if they gain physical access to the network. The following sections describe some of the steps that you can take to strengthen your network's use of user accounts.

Obfuscating your usernames

Huh? When it comes to security, *obfuscation* simply means picking obscure usernames. For example, most network administrators assign usernames based on some combination of the user's first and last name, such as BarnyM or baMiller. However, a hacker can easily guess such a user ID if he or she knows the name of at least one employee. After the hacker knows a username, he or she can focus on breaking the password.

You can slow down a hacker by using names that are more obscure. Here are some suggestions on how to do that:

✔ Add a random three-digit number to the end of the name. For example: BarnyM320 or baMiller977.

✔ Throw a number or two into the middle of the name. For example: Bar6nyM or ba9Miller2.

✔ Make sure that usernames are different from e-mail addresses. For example, if a user's e-mail address is `baMiller@Mydomain.com`, do *not* use baMiller as the user's account name. Use a more obscure name.

WARNING!

Do *not* rely on obfuscation to keep people out of your network! Security by obfuscation doesn't work. A resourceful hacker can discover the most obscure names. Obfuscation can *slow* intruders, not stop them. If you slow intruders down, you're more likely to discover them before they crack your network.

Using passwords wisely

One of the most important aspects of network security is the use of passwords.

Usernames aren't usually considered *secret.* Even if you use obscure names, even casual hackers will eventually figure them out.

Passwords, on the other hand, are top secret. Your network password is the one thing that keeps an impostor from logging on to the network by using your username and therefore receiving the same access rights that you ordinarily have. *Guard your password with your life.*

Here are some tips for creating good passwords:

- ✔ Don't use obvious passwords, such as your last name, your kid's name, or your dog's name.

- ✔ Don't pick passwords based on your hobbies. A friend of mine is a boater, and his password is the name of his boat. Anyone who knows him can quickly guess his password. Five lashes for naming your password after your boat.

- ✔ Store your password in your head — not on paper.

  Especially bad: Writing your password down on a sticky note and sticking it on your computer's monitor.

- ✔ Most network operating systems enable you to set an expiration time for passwords. For example, you can specify that passwords expire after 30 days. When a user's password expires, the user must change it. Your users may consider this process a hassle, but it helps to limit the risk of someone swiping a password and then trying to break into your computer system later.

- ✔ You can configure user accounts so that when they change passwords, they can't reuse a *recent* password. For example, you can specify that the new password can't be identical to any of the user's past three passwords.

- ✔ You can also configure security policies so that passwords must include a mixture of uppercase letters, lowercase letters, numerals, and special symbols. Thus, passwords like DIMWIT or DUFUS are out. Passwords like 87dIM@wit or duF39&US are in.

- ✔ Some administrators of small networks opt against passwords altogether because they feel that security isn't an issue on their network. Or short of that, they choose obvious passwords, assign every user the same password, or print the passwords on giant posters and hang them throughout the building. Ignoring basic password security is rarely a good idea, even in small networks. You should consider not using passwords only if your network is very small (say, two or three computers), if you don't keep sensitive data on a file server, or if the main reason for the network is to share access to a printer rather than sharing files.

(Even if you don't use passwords, imposing basic security precautions, like limiting access that certain users have to certain network directories, is still possible. Just remember that if passwords aren't used, nothing prevents a user from signing on by using someone else's username.)

Generating passwords for dummies

How do you come up with passwords that no one can guess but that you can remember? Most security experts say that the best passwords don't correspond to any words in the English language but consist of a random sequence of letters, numbers, and special characters. Yet, how in the heck are you supposed to memorize a password like `Dks4%DJ2`? Especially when you have to change it three weeks later to something like `3pQ&X(d8`.

Here's a compromise solution that enables you to create passwords that consist of two four-letter words back to back. Take your favorite book (if it's this one, you need to get a life) and turn to any page at random. Find the first four- or five-letter words on the page. Suppose that word is `When`. Then repeat the process to find another four- or five-letter word; say you pick the word `Most` the second time. Now combine the words to make your password: `WhenMost`. I think you'll agree that `WhenMost` is easier to remember than `3PQ&X(D8` and is probably just about as hard to guess. I probably wouldn't want the folks at the Los Alamos Nuclear Laboratory using this scheme, but it's good enough for most of us.

Here are additional thoughts on concocting passwords from your favorite book:

- ✔ If the words end up being the same, pick another word. And pick different words if the combination seems too commonplace, such as `WestWind` or `FootBall`.

- ✔ For an interesting variation, insert a couple of numerals or special characters between the words. You end up with passwords like `into#cat`, `ball3%and`, or `tree47wing`. If you want, use the page number of the second word as a separator. For example, if the words are *know* and *click* and the second word comes from page 435, use `know435click`.

- ✔ To further confuse your friends and enemies, use medieval passwords by picking words from Chaucer's *Canterbury Tales*. Chaucer is a great source for passwords because he lived before the days of word processors with spell-checkers. He wrote *seyd* instead of *said, gret* instead of *great, welk* instead of *walked, litel* instead of *little*. And he used lots of seven-letter and eight-letter words suitable for passwords, such as *glotenye* (gluttony), *benygne* (benign), and *opynyoun* (opinion). And he got A's in English.

- ✔ If you use any of these password schemes and someone breaks into your network, don't blame me. You're the one who's too lazy to memorize `D#Sc$h4@bb3xaz5`.

✔ If you do decide to go with passwords, such as KdI22UR3xdkL, you can find random password generators on the Internet. Just go to a search engine, such as Google (www.google.com), and search for Password Generator. You'll find Web pages that generate random passwords based on criteria that you specify, such as how long the password should be, whether it should include letters, numbers, punctuation, uppercase and lowercase letters, and so on.

Secure the Administrator account

It stands to reason that at least one network user must have the authority to use the network without any of the restrictions imposed on other users. This user is the *administrator*. The administrator is responsible for setting up the network's security system. To do that, the administrator must be exempt from all security restrictions.

Many networks automatically create an administrator user account when you install the network software. The username and password for this initial administrator are published in the network's documentation and are the same for all networks that use the same network operating system. One of the first things that you must do after getting your network up and running is to change the password for this standard administrator account. Otherwise, your elaborate security precautions are a complete waste of time. Anyone who knows the default administrator username and password can access your system with full administrator rights and privileges, thus bypassing the security restrictions that you so carefully set up.

Don't forget the password for the administrator account! If a network user forgets his or her password, you can log on as the supervisor and change that user's password. If you forget the administrator's password, though, you're stuck.

Managing User Security

User accounts are the backbone of network security administration. Through the use of user accounts, you can determine who can access your network as well as what network resources each user can and can't access. You can restrict access to the network to just specific computers or to certain hours of the day. In addition, you can lock out users who no longer need to access your network. The following sections describe the basics of setting up user security for your network.

User accounts

Every user who accesses a network must have a *user account*. User accounts allow the network administrator to determine who can access the network and what network resources each user can access. In addition, the user account can be customized to provide many convenience features for users, such as a personalized Start menu or a display of recently used documents.

Every user account is associated with a *username* (sometimes called a *user ID*), which the user must enter when logging on to the network. Each account also has other information associated with it. In particular:

- ✔ **The user's password:** This also includes the password policy, such as how often the user has to change his or her password, how complicated the password must be, and so on.

- ✔ **The user's contact information:** This includes full name, phone number, e-mail address, mailing address, and other related information.

- ✔ **Account restrictions:** This includes restrictions that allow the user to log on only during certain times of the day. This feature can restrict your users to normal working hours so that they can't sneak in at 2 a.m. to do unauthorized work. This feature also discourages your users from working overtime because they can't access the network after hours, so use it judiciously. You can also specify that the user can log on only at certain computers.

- ✔ **Account status:** You can temporarily disable a user account so the user can't log on.

- ✔ **Home directory:** This specifies a shared network folder where the user can store documents.

- ✔ **Dial-in permissions:** These authorize the user to access the network remotely via a dialup connection.

- ✔ **Group memberships:** These grant the user certain rights based on groups to which they belong.

  For more information, see the section, "Group therapy," later in this chapter.

Built-in accounts

Most network operating systems come preconfigured with two built-in accounts, named Administrator and Guest. In addition, some server services, such as Web or database servers, create their own user accounts under which to run. The following sections describe the characteristics of these accounts.

- **The Administrator account:** The Administrator account is the King of the Network. This user account isn't subject to any of the account restrictions to which mere mortal accounts must succumb. If you log on as the administrator, you can do anything. For this reason, avoid using the Administrator account for routine tasks. Log in as the Administrator only when you really need to.

  Because the Administrator account has unlimited access to your network, it's imperative that you secure it immediately after you install the server. When the NOS Setup program asks for a password for the Administrator account, start with a good random mix of uppercase and lowercase letters, numbers, and symbols. Don't pick some easy-to-remember password to get started, thinking you'll change it to something more cryptic later. You'll forget, and in the meantime, someone will break in and reformat the server's C: drive or steal your customer's credit card numbers.

- **The Guest account:** Another commonly created default account is the *Guest account.* This account is set up with a blank password and — if any — access rights. The Guest account is designed to allow anyone to step up to a computer and log on, but after they do, it then prevents them from doing anything. Sounds like a waste of time to me. I suggest you disable the Guest account.

- **Service accounts:** Some network users aren't actual people. I don't mean that some of your users are subhuman. Rather, some users are actually software processes that require access to secure resources, and therefore, require user accounts. These user accounts are usually created automatically for you when you install or configure server software.

  For example, when you install Microsoft's Web server (IIS), an Internet user account called IUSR is created. The complete name for this account is `IUSR_<servername>`. So if the server is named WEB1, the account is named `IUSR_WEB1`. IIS uses this account to allow anonymous Internet users to access the files of your Web site.

  Don't mess with these accounts unless you know what you're doing. For example, if you delete or rename the IUSR account, you must reconfigure IIS to use the changed account. If you don't, IIS will deny access to anyone trying to reach your site. (Assuming that you *do* know what you're doing, renaming these accounts can increase your network's security. However, don't start playing with these accounts until you've researched the ramifications.)

User rights

User accounts and passwords are the front line of defense in the game of network security. After a user accesses the network by typing a valid user ID and password, the second line of security defense — *rights* — comes into play.

In the harsh realities of network life, all users are created equal, but some users are more equal than others. The Preamble to the Declaration of Network Independence contains the statement "We hold these truths to be self-evident, that *some* users are endowed by the network administrator with certain inalienable rights. . . ."

The rights that you can assign to network users depend on which network operating system you use. These are some of the possible user rights for *Windows servers:*

- ✔ **Log on locally:** The user can log on to the server computer directly from the server's keyboard.

- ✔ **Change system time:** The user can change the time and date registered by the server.

- ✔ **Shut down the system:** The user can perform an orderly shutdown of the server.

- ✔ **Back up files and directories:** The user can perform a backup of files and directories on the server.

- ✔ **Restore files and directories:** The user can restore backed-up files.

- ✔ **Take ownership of files and other objects:** The user can take over files and other network resources that belong to other users.

NetWare has a similar set of user rights.

Permissions (who gets what)

User rights control what a user can do on a network-wide basis. *Permissions* enable you to fine-tune your network security by controlling access to specific network resources, such as files or printers, for individual users or groups. For example, you can set up permissions to allow users into the accounting department to access files in the server's \ACCTG directory. Permissions can also enable some users to read certain files but not modify or delete them.

Each network operating system manages permissions in a different way. Whatever the details, the effect is that you can give permission to each user to access certain files, folders, or drives in certain ways. For example, you might grant a user full access to some files but grant read-only access to other files.

Any permissions you specify for a folder apply automatically to any of that folder's subfolders, unless you explicitly specify different permissions for the subfolder.

You can use Windows permissions only for files or folders that are created on drives formatted as NTFS volumes. If you insist on using FAT or FAT32 for your Windows shared drives, you can't protect individual files or folders on the drives. This is one of the main reasons for using NTFS for your Windows servers.

Group therapy

A *group account* is an account that doesn't represent an individual user. Instead, it represents a group of users who use the network in a similar way. Instead of granting access rights to each of these users individually, you can grant the rights to the group and then assign individual users to the group. When you assign a user to a group, that user inherits the rights specified for the group.

For example, suppose that you create a group named Accounting for the accounting staff and then allow members of the Accounting group access to the network's accounting files and applications. Then, instead of granting each accounting user access to those files and applications, you simply make each accounting user a member of the Accounting group.

Here are a few additional details about groups:

✔ Groups are one of the keys to network management nirvana. As much as possible, avoid managing network users individually. Instead, clump them into groups and manage the groups. When all 50 users in the accounting department need access to a new file share, would you rather update 50 user accounts or just 1 group account?

✔ A user can belong to more than one group. Then, the user inherits the rights of each group. For example, you can have groups set up for Accounting, Sales, Marketing, and Finance. A user who needs to access both Accounting and Finance information can be made a member of both groups. Likewise, a user who needs access to both Sales and Marketing information can be made a member of both the Sales and Marketing groups.

✔ You can grant or revoke specific rights to individual users to override the group settings. For example, you may grant a few extra permissions for the manager of the accounting department. You may also impose a few extra restrictions on certain users.

User profiles

User profiles are a Windows feature that keeps track of an individual user's preferences for his or her Windows configuration. For a non-networked computer, profiles enable two or more users to use the same computer, each with his or her own desktop settings, such as wallpaper, colors, Start menu options, and so on.

The real benefit of user profiles becomes apparent when profiles are used on a network. A user's profile can be stored on a server computer and accessed whenever that user logs on to the network from any Windows computer on the network.

The following are some of the elements of Windows that are governed by settings in the user profile:

✔ Desktop settings from the Display Properties dialog box, including wallpaper, screen savers, and color schemes.

✔ Start menu programs and Windows toolbar options.

✔ Favorites, which provide easy access to the files and folders that the user accesses often.

✔ Network settings, including drive mappings, network printers, and recently visited network locations.

✔ Application settings, such as option settings for Microsoft Word.

✔ The My Documents folder.

Logon scripts

A *logon script* is a batch file that runs automatically whenever a user logs on. Logon scripts can perform several important logon tasks for you, such as mapping network drives, starting applications, synchronizing the client computer's time-of-day clock, and so on. Logon scripts reside on the server. Each user account can specify whether to use a logon script and which script to use.

This sample logon script maps a few network drives and synchronizes the time:

```
net use m: \\MYSERVER\Acct
net use n: \\MYSERVER\Admin
net use o: \\MYSERVER\Dev
net time \\MYSERVER /set /yes
```

Logon scripts are a little out of vogue because most of what a logon script does can be done via user profiles. Still, many administrators prefer the simplicity of logon scripts, so they're still used even on Windows Server 2003 systems.

Securing Your Users

Security techniques, such as physical security, user account security, server security, and locking down your servers are child's play compared to the most difficult job of network security: securing your network's users. All the best-laid security plans will go for naught if your users write their passwords on sticky notes and post them on their computers.

The key to securing your network users is to create a written network security policy and to stick to it. Have a meeting with everyone to go over the security policy to make sure that everyone understands the rules. Also, make sure to have consequences when violations occur.

Here are some suggestions for some basic security rules that can be incorporated into your security policy:

- ✔ Never write down your password or give it to someone else.

- ✔ Accounts shouldn't be shared. Never use someone else's account to access a resource that you can't access under your own account. If you need access to some network resource that isn't available to you, formally request access under your own account.

- ✔ Likewise, never give your account information to a co-worker so that he or she can access a needed resource. Your co-worker should instead formally request access under his or her own account.

- ✔ Don't install any software or hardware on your computer without first obtaining permission. This especially includes wireless access devices or modems.

- ✔ Don't enable file and printer sharing on workstations without first getting permission.

- ✔ Never attempt to disable or bypass the network's security features.

Chapter 23

Hardening Your Network

In This Chapter

▶ Understanding what firewalls do

▶ Examining the different types of firewalls

▶ Looking at virus protection

▶ Patching your computers

*I*f your network is connected to the Internet, a whole host of security issues bubble to the surface. You probably connected your network to the Internet so that your network's users could get out to the Internet. Unfortunately, however, your Internet connection is a two-way street. Not only does it enable your network's users to step outside the bounds of your network to access the Internet, but it also enables others to step in and access your network.

And step in they will. The world is filled with hackers who are looking for networks like yours to break into. They may do it just for the fun of it, or they may do it to steal your customer's credit card numbers or to coerce your mail server into sending thousands of spam messages on their behalf. Whatever their motive, rest assured that your network will be broken into if you leave it unprotected.

This chapter presents an overview of three basic techniques for securing your network's Internet connection: controlling access via a firewall, detecting viruses with antivirus software, and fixing security flaws with software patches.

Firewalls

A *firewall* is a security-conscious router that sits between the Internet and your network with a single-minded task: preventing *them* from getting to *us*. The firewall acts as a security guard between the Internet and your LAN. All network traffic into and out of the LAN must pass through the firewall, which prevents unauthorized access to the network.

Some type of firewall is a must-have if your network has a connection to the Internet, whether that connection is broadband (cable modem or DSL), T1, or some other high-speed connection. Without it, sooner or later a hacker will discover your unprotected network and tell his friends about it. Within a few hours your network will be toast.

You can set up a firewall using two basic ways. The easiest way is to purchase a *firewall appliance,* which is basically a self-contained router with built-in firewall features. Most firewall appliances include a Web-based interface that enables you to connect to the firewall from any computer on your network using a browser. You can then customize the firewall settings to suit your needs.

Alternatively, you can set up a server computer to function as a firewall computer. The server can run just about any network operating system, but most dedicated firewall systems run Linux.

Whether you use a firewall appliance or a firewall computer, the firewall must be located between your network and the Internet, as shown in Figure 23-1. Here, one end of the firewall is connected to a network hub, which is, in turn, connected to the other computers on the network. The other end of the firewall is connected to the Internet. As a result, all traffic from the LAN to the Internet and vice versa must travel through the firewall.

Figure 23-1:
A firewall router creates a secure link between a network and the Internet.

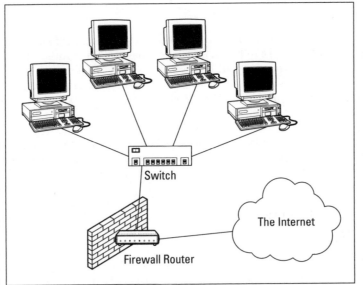

The term *perimeter* is sometimes used to describe the location of a firewall on your network. In short, a firewall is like a perimeter fence that completely surrounds your property and forces all visitors to enter through the front gate.

In large networks — especially campus-wide or even metropolitan networks — it's sometimes hard to figure out exactly where the perimeter is located. If your network has two or more WAN connections, make sure that every one of those connections connects to a firewall and not directly to the network. You can do this by providing a separate firewall for each WAN connection or by using a firewall with more than one WAN port.

The Many Types of Firewalls

Firewalls employ four basic techniques to keep unwelcome visitors out of your network. The following sections describe these basic firewall techniques.

Packet filtering

A *packet-filtering* firewall examines each packet that crosses the firewall and tests the packet according to a set of rules that you set up. If the packet passes the test, it's allowed to pass. If the packet doesn't pass, it's rejected.

Packet filters are the least expensive type of firewall. As a result, packet-filtering firewalls are very common. However, packet filtering has a number of flaws that knowledgeable hackers can exploit. As a result, packet filtering by itself doesn't make for a fully effective firewall.

Packet filters work by inspecting the source and destination IP and port addresses contained in each TCP/IP packet. *TCP/IP ports* are numbers that are assigned to specific services that help to identify for which service each packet is intended. For example, the port number for the HTTP protocol is 80. As a result, any incoming packets headed for an HTTP server will specify port 80 as the destination port.

Port numbers are often specified with a colon following an IP address. For example, the HTTP service on a server whose IP address is 192.168.10.133 would be 192.168.10.133:80.

Literally thousands of established ports are in use. Table 23-1 lists a few of the most popular ports.

Table 23-1	Some Well-Known TCP/IP Ports
Port	**Description**
20	File Transfer Protocol (FTP)
21	File Transfer Protocol (FTP)
22	Secure Shell Protocol (SSH)
23	Telnet
25	Simple Mail Transfer Protocol (SMTP)
53	Domain Name Server (DNS)
80	World Wide Web (HTTP)
110	Post Office Protocol (POP3)
119	Network News Transfer Protocol (NNTP)
137	NetBIOS Name Service
138	NetBIOS Datagram Service
139	NetBIOS Session Service
143	Internet Message Access Protocol (IMAP)
161	Simple Network Management Protocol (SNMP)
194	Internet Relay Chat (IRC)
389	Lightweight Directory Access Protocol (LDAP)
396	NetWare over IP
443	HTTP over TLS/SSL (HTTPS)

The rules that you set up for the packet filter either permit or deny packets that specify certain IP addresses or ports. For example, you may permit packets that are intended for your mail server or your Web server and deny all other packets. Or, you may set up a rule that specifically denies packets that are heading for the ports used by NetBIOS. This rule keeps Internet hackers from trying to access NetBIOS server resources, such as files or printers.

One of the biggest weaknesses of packet filtering is that it pretty much trusts that the packets themselves are telling the truth when they say who they're from and who they're going to. Hackers exploit this weakness by using a hacking technique called *IP spoofing*, in which they insert fake IP addresses in packets that they send to your network.

Another weakness of packet filtering is that it examines each packet in isolation, without considering what packets have gone through the firewall before and what packets may follow. In other words, packet filtering is *stateless*. Rest assured that hackers have figured out how to exploit the stateless nature of packet filtering to get through firewalls.

In spite of these weaknesses, packet filter firewalls have several advantages that explain why they're commonly used:

- ✔ **Packet filters are very efficient.** They hold up each inbound and outbound packet for only a few milliseconds while they look inside the packet to determine the destination and source ports and addresses. After these addresses and ports have been determined, the packet filter quickly applies its rules and either sends the packet along or rejects it. In contrast, other firewall techniques have a more noticeable performance overhead.

- ✔ **Packet filters are almost completely transparent to users.** The only time a user will be aware that a packet filter firewall is being used is when the firewall rejects packets. Other firewall techniques require that clients and/or servers be specially configured to work with the firewall.

- ✔ **Packet filters are inexpensive.** Most routers include built-in packet filtering.

Stateful packet inspection (SPI)

Stateful packet inspection, also known as *SPI,* is a step up in intelligence from simple packet filtering. A firewall with SPI looks at packets in groups rather than individually. It keeps track of which packets have passed through the firewall and can detect patterns that indicate unauthorized access. In some cases, the firewall may hold on to packets as they arrive until the firewall has gathered enough information to make a decision about whether the packets should be authorized or rejected.

Stateful packet inspection was once found only on expensive, enterprise-level routers. Now, however, SPI firewalls are affordable enough for small- or medium-sized networks to use.

Circuit-level gateway

A *circuit-level gateway* manages connections between clients and servers based on TCP/IP addresses and port numbers. After the connection is established, the gateway doesn't interfere with packets flowing between the systems.

For example, you could use a Telnet circuit-level gateway to allow Telnet connections (port 23) to a particular server and prohibit other types of connections to that server. After the connection is established, the circuit-level gateway allows packets to flow freely over the connection. As a result, the circuit-level gateway can't prevent a Telnet user from running specific programs or using specific commands.

Application gateway

An *application gateway* is a firewall system that is more intelligent than a packet-filtering, stateful packet inspection, or circuit-level gateway firewall. Packet filters treat all TCP/IP packets the same. In contrast, application gateways know the details about the applications that generate the packets that pass through the firewall. For example, a Web application gateway is aware of the details of HTTP packets. As a result, it can examine more than just the source and destination addresses and ports to determine whether the packets should be allowed to pass through the firewall.

In addition, application gateways work as proxy servers. Simply put, a *proxy server* is a server that sits between a client computer and a real server. The proxy server intercepts packets that are intended for the real server and processes them. The proxy server can examine the packet and decide to pass it on to the real server, or it can reject the packet. Or the proxy server may be able to respond to the packet itself, without involving the real server at all.

For example, Web proxies often store copies of commonly used Web pages in a local cache. When a user requests a Web page from a remote Web server, the proxy server intercepts the request and checks to see whether it already has a copy of the page in its cache. If so, the Web proxy returns the page directly to the user. If not, the proxy passes the request on to the real server.

Application gateways are aware of the details of how various types of TCP/IP servers handle sequences of TCP/IP packets, so they can make more intelligent decisions about whether an incoming packet is legitimate or is part of an attack. As a result, application gateways are more secure than simple packet-filtering firewalls, which can deal with only one packet at a time.

The improved security of application gateways, however, comes at a price. Application gateways are more expensive than packet filters, both in terms of their purchase price and in the cost of configuring and maintaining them. In addition, application gateways slow the network performance down because they do more detailed checking of packets before allowing them to pass.

The Built-In Firewall in Windows XP and Windows Vista

Both Windows XP and Windows Vista come with a built-in packet-filtering firewall. If you don't have a separate firewall router, you can use this built-in firewall to provide a basic level of protection. Here are the steps to activate this feature in Windows XP or Vista:

1. **Choose Start➪Control Panel.**

   The Control Panel appears.

2. **Click the Windows Firewall link.**

   This brings up the dialog box, as shown in Figure 23-2.

3. **Select the On (Recommended) option.**

   This option enables the firewall.

4. **Click OK.**

   That's all there is to it.

Do *not* enable the Windows Firewall if you're using a separate firewall router to protect your network. Because the other computers on the network are connected directly to the router and not to your computer, the firewall won't protect the rest of the network. Additionally, as an unwanted side effect, the rest of the network will lose the ability to access your computer.

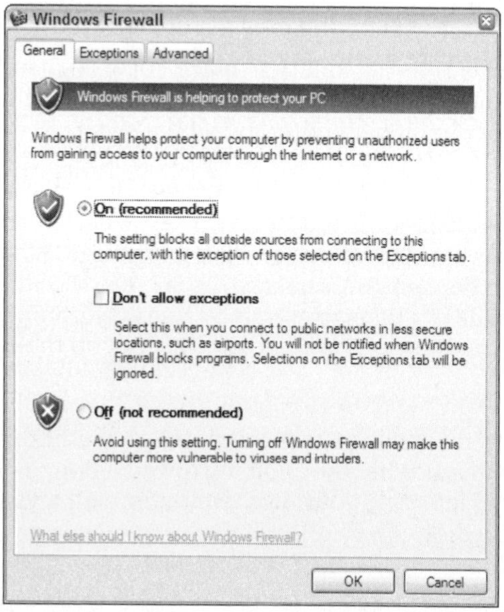

Figure 23-2:
The Windows Firewall dialog box.

With Windows XP Service Pack 2, the firewall is turned on by default. If your computer is already behind a firewall, disable the Windows Firewall that's enabled by Service Pack 2.

Windows Vista includes an advanced version of the Windows Firewall that has additional configuration options. Unless you're well versed in security techniques, you'll want to leave these advanced options configured with their default settings.

Virus Protection

Viruses are one of the most misunderstood computer phenomena around these days. What is a virus? How does it work? How does it spread from computer to computer? I'm glad you asked.

What is a virus?

Make no mistake — viruses are real. Now that most people are connected to the Internet, viruses have really taken off. Every computer user is susceptible to attacks by computer viruses, and using a network increases your vulnerability because it exposes all network users to the risk of being infected by a virus that lands on any one network user's computer.

Viruses don't just spontaneously appear out of nowhere. *Viruses* are computer programs that are created by malicious programmers who've lost a few screws and should be locked up.

What makes a virus a virus is its capability to make copies of itself that can be spread to other computers. These copies, in turn, make still more copies that spread to still more computers, and so on, ad nauseam.

Then, the virus waits patiently until something triggers it — perhaps when you type a particular command or press a certain key, when a certain date arrives, or when the virus creator sends the virus a message. What the virus does when it strikes also depends on what the virus creator wants the virus to do. Some viruses harmlessly display a "gotcha" message. Some send e-mail to everyone it finds in your address book. Some wipe out all the data on your hard drive. Ouch.

A few years back, viruses moved from one computer to another by latching themselves onto floppy disks. Whenever you borrowed a floppy disk from a buddy, you ran the risk of infecting your own computer with a virus that may have stowed away on the disk.

Nowadays, virus programmers have discovered that e-mail is a much more efficient method to spread their viruses. Typically, a virus masquerades as a useful or interesting e-mail attachment, such as instructions on how to make $1,000,000 in your spare time, pictures of naked celebrities, or a Valentine's Day greeting from your long-lost sweetheart. When a curious but unsuspecting user double-clicks the attachment, the virus springs to life, copying itself onto the user's computer and, in some cases, sending copies of itself to all the names in the user's address book.

After the virus has worked its way onto a networked computer, the virus can then figure out how to spread itself to other computers on the network.

Here are some more tidbits about protecting your network from virus attacks:

- The term *virus* is often used to refer not only to true virus programs (which can replicate themselves) but also to any other type of program that's designed to harm your computer. These programs include so-called *Trojan horse* programs that usually look like games but are, in reality, hard drive formatters.

- A *worm* is similar to a virus, but it doesn't actually infect other files. Instead, it just copies itself onto other computers on a network. After a worm has copied itself onto your computer, there's no telling what it may do there. For example, a worm may scan your hard drive for interesting information, such as passwords or credit card numbers, and then e-mail them to the worm's author.

- Computer virus experts have identified several thousand "strains" of viruses. Many of them have colorful names, such as the I Love You virus, the Stoned virus, and the Michelangelo virus.

- Antivirus programs can recognize known viruses and remove them from your system, and they can spot the telltale signs of unknown viruses. Unfortunately, the idiots who write viruses aren't idiots (in the intellectual sense), so they're constantly developing new techniques to evade detection by antivirus programs. New viruses are frequently discovered, and antivirus programs are periodically updated to detect and remove them.

Antivirus programs

The best way to protect your network from virus infection is to use an antivirus program. These programs have a catalog of several thousand known viruses that they can detect and remove. In addition, they can spot the types of changes that viruses typically make to your computer's files, thus decreasing the likelihood that some previously unknown virus will go undetected.

It'd be nice if Windows came with built-in antivirus software, but alas, it does not. So you have to purchase a program on your own. The three best-known antivirus programs for Windows are Norton AntiVirus by Symantec, McAfee's VirusScan, and Trend Micro's OfficeScan.

The people who make antivirus programs have their fingers on the pulse of the virus world and often release updates to their software to combat the latest viruses. Because virus writers are constantly developing new viruses, your antivirus software is next to worthless unless you keep it up-to-date by downloading the latest updates.

The following are several approaches to deploying antivirus protection on your network:

- ✔ You can install antivirus software on each network user's computer. This technique would be the most effective if you could count on all your users to keep their antivirus software up-to-date. Because that's an unlikely proposition, you may want to adopt a more reliable approach to virus protection.

- ✔ Managed antivirus services place antivirus client software on each client computer in your network. Then, an antivirus server automatically updates the clients on a regular basis to make sure that they're kept up-to-date.

- ✔ Server-based antivirus software protects your network servers from viruses. For example, you can install antivirus software on your mail server to scan all incoming mail for viruses and remove them before your network users ever see them.

- ✔ Some firewall appliances include antivirus enforcement checks that don't allow your users to access the Internet unless their antivirus software is up-to-date. This type of firewall provides the best antivirus protection available.

Safe computing

Besides using an antivirus program, you can take a few additional precautions to ensure virus-free computing. If you haven't talked to your kids about these safe-computing practices, you had better do so soon.

- ✔ Regularly back up your data. If a virus hits you and your antivirus software can't repair the damage, you may need the backup to recover your data. Make sure that you restore from a backup that was created before you were infected by the virus!

- ✔ If you buy software from a store and discover that the seal has been broken on the disk package, take the software back. Don't try to install it on your computer. You don't hear about tainted software as often as you hear about tainted beef, but if you buy software that's been opened, it may well be laced with a virus infection.

✔ Use your antivirus software to scan your disk for virus infection after your computer has been to a repair shop or worked on by a consultant. These guys don't intend harm, but they occasionally spread viruses accidentally, simply because they work on so many strange computers.

✔ Don't open e-mail attachments from people you don't know or attachments you weren't expecting.

✔ Use your antivirus software to scan any floppy disk or CD-ROM that doesn't belong to you before you access any of its files.

Patching Things Up

One of the annoyances that every network manager faces is applying software patches to keep the operating system and other software up to date. A software *patch* is a minor update that fixes the small glitches that crop up from time to time, such as minor security or performance issues. These glitches aren't significant enough to merit a new version of the software, but they're important enough to require fixing. Most of the patches correct security flaws that computer hackers have uncovered in their relentless attempts to prove that they are smarter than the security programmers at Microsoft or Novell.

Periodically, all the recently released patches are combined into a *service pack*. Although the most diligent network administrators apply all patches when they're released, many administrators just wait for the service packs:

✔ For all versions of Windows, you can use the Windows Update Web site to apply patches to keep your operating system and other Microsoft software up-to-date. Windows Update scans your computer's software and creates a list of software patches and other components that you can download and install. You can either

- Find Windows Update in the Start menu.
- Fire up Internet Explorer and go to `windowsupdate.microsoft.com`.

You can configure Windows Update to automatically notify you of updates so you don't have to remember to check for new patches.

✔ Novell periodically posts patches and updates to NetWare on its product-support Web site (`support.novell.com`).

You can subscribe to a service that automatically sends you e-mail to let you know of new patches and updates.

Keeping a large network patched can be one of the major challenges of network administration. If you have more than a few dozen computers on your network, consider investing in server-based software that's designed to simplify the process. For example, PatchLink (www.patchlink.com) is a server-based program that collects software patches from a variety of manufacturers and lets you create distributions that are automatically pushed out to client computers. With software like PatchLink, you don't have to rely on end users to download and install patches, and you don't have to visit each computer individually to install patches.

Part VI
Beyond Windows

The 5th Wave   By Rich Tennant

"Oh look, this must be one of those PCs that are assembled by prison inmates. It came bundled with a homemade shank in the mousepad."

In this part . . .

Although Bill Gates might be reluctant to admit it, Windows isn't the only operating system now used on personal computers. The two chapters in this part introduce you to the basics of networking with the two most popular alternatives to Windows: Linux and Macintosh.

Chapter 24

Networking with Linux

. . . .

In This Chapter

▶ Finding out about Linux and how it differs from Windows

▶ Choosing which version of Linux to use for your server

▶ Installing Linux as well as configuring network settings and user accounts

▶ Using Samba to create a file server

. . . .

L *inux,* the free operating system based on Unix, is becoming more and more popular as an alternative to expensive server operating systems, such as Windows Server 2003 and NetWare. In fact, by some estimates, more computers are now running the Linux operating system than they're running the Macintosh operating system. You can use Linux as a Web server for the Internet or for an intranet, and you can use it as a firewall or a file-and-print server on your local area network.

Linux was created in 1991 by Linus Torvalds, who was at the time an under-graduate student at the University of Helsinki in Finland. Linus thought it'd be fun to create his own operating system based on Unix for his brand-new PC. In the nearly ten years since Linux was first conceived, Linux has become a full-featured operating system that is fast and reliable.

This chapter shows the basics of setting up a Linux server on your network and using it as a file server, as a Web server for the Internet or an intranet, as an e-mail server, and as a router and firewall to help connect your network to the Internet.

 Linux is a complicated operating system. Understanding how to use it can be a daunting task, especially if your only prior computer experience is with Windows. Wiley Publishing, Inc., has *For Dummies* books that make Linux less painful. Check out *Linux For Dummies,* 8th Edition, by Dee-Ann LeBlanc and *Linux For Dummies Quick Reference,* 3rd Edition, by Phil Hughes and Viktorie Navratilova.

Comparing Linux with Windows

If your only computer experience is with Windows, you're in for a steep learning curve when you first get into Linux. There are many fundamental differences between the Linux operating system and Windows. Here are some of the more important differences:

- ✔ **Linux is a multiuser operating system.** Therefore, more than one user can log on and use a Linux computer at the same time:

  - Two or more users can log on to a Linux computer from the same keyboard and monitor by using virtual consoles, which let you switch from one user session to another with a special key combination.

  - Users can log on to the Linux computer from a terminal window running on another computer on the network.

Most versions of Windows are single-user systems. Only one user at a time can log on to a Windows computer and run commands. (Windows 2003 can be configured as a multiuser system with terminal services.)

- ✔ **Linux doesn't have a built-in graphical user interface (GUI) as Windows does.** Instead, the GUI in Linux is provided by an optional component called *X Window System.* You can run Linux without X Window, in which case you interact with Linux by typing commands. If you prefer to use a GUI, you must install and run X Window.

X Window is split into two parts:

  - A server component *(X server)* manages multiple windows and provides graphics services for application programs.

  - A user interface component *(window manager)* provides user interface features, such as menus, buttons, toolbars, and a taskbar.

Several window managers are available, each with a different look and feel. With Windows, you're stuck with the user interface that Microsoft designed. With Linux, you can use the user interface of your choosing.

- ✔ **Linux can't run Windows programs.** Therefore, you can't run Microsoft Office on a Linux system; instead, you must find a similar program that's written specifically for Linux. Many Linux distributions come with an office suite called *StarOffice,* which provides word processing, spreadsheet, presentation, graphics, database, e-mail, calendar, and scheduling software. Thousands of other programs are available for Linux.

Windows emulator programs — the best-known is Wine — can run some Windows programs on Linux. But the emulators run only some Windows programs, and they run them slower than they would run on a Windows system.

- ✔ **Linux doesn't do Plug and Play the way Windows does.** Major Linux distributions come with configuration programs that can automatically detect and configure the most common hardware components, but Linux doesn't have built-in support for Plug-and-Play hardware devices. You're more likely to run into a hardware-configuration problem with Linux than with Windows.

✔ **Linux uses a different system for accessing disk drives and files than Windows does.** For an explanation of how the Linux file system works, see the "I can't see my C drive!" sidebar that's coming up in this chapter.

✔ **Linux runs better on older hardware than the current incarnations of Windows do.** Linux is an ideal operating system for an older Pentium computer with at least 32MB of RAM and 2GB of hard-drive space.

If you're fond of antiques, Linux can run well on even a 486 computer with as little as 4MB of RAM and a few hundred MB of disk space.

I can't see my C drive!

Well, no, but that's normal. Linux and Windows have completely different ways of referring to your computer's disk drives and partitions. The differences can take some getting used to for experienced Windows users.

Windows uses a separate letter for each drive and partition on your system. For example, if you have a single drive formatted into three partitions, Windows identifies the partitions as drives C, D, and E. Each of these drives has its own `root` directory, which can in turn contain additional directories used to organize your files. As far as Windows is concerned, drives C, D, and E are completely separate drives, even though the drives are actually just partitions on a single drive.

Linux doesn't use drive letters. Instead, Linux combines all the drives and partitions into a single directory hierarchy. In Linux, one of the partitions is designated as the `root partition`. The `root` is roughly analogous to the C drive on a Windows system. Then, the other partitions can be *mounted* on the `root` partition and treated as if they were directories on the `root` partition. For example, you might designate the first partition as the `root` partition and then mount the second partition as `/user` and the

third partition as `/var`. Then any files stored in the `/user` directory would actually be stored in the second partition, and files stored in the `/var` directory would be stored in the third partition.

The directory where a drive mounts is the drive's *mount point.*

Notice that Linux uses regular forward-slash characters (`/`) to separate directory names rather than the backward-slash characters (`\`) used by Windows. Typing backslashes instead of regular slashes is one of the most common mistakes made by new Linux users.

While we're on the subject, Linux uses a different convention for naming files, too. In Windows, filenames end in a three-letter extension that's separated from the rest of the filename by a period. The extension is used to indicate the file type. For example, files that end in `.exe` are program files, but files that end in `.doc` are word-processing documents.

Linux doesn't use filename extensions, but periods are often used in Linux filenames to separate different parts of the name — and the last part often indicates the file type. For example, `ldap.conf` and `pine.conf` are both configuration files.

Choosing a Linux Distribution

Because the *kernel* (that is, the core operating functions) of the Linux operating system is free, several companies have created their own *distributions* of Linux, which include the Linux operating system along with a bundle of packages to go along with it, such as administration tools, Web servers, and other useful utilities, as well as printed documentation. These distributions are inexpensive — ranging from $25–$100 — and are well worth the small cost.

The following are some of the more popular Linux distributions:

- ✔ **Fedora** is one of the popular Linux distributions. At one time, Fedora was an inexpensive distribution offered by Red Hat. But Red Hat recently changed its distribution strategy by announcing that its inexpensive distribution would become a community project known as Fedora so that it could focus on its more expensive Enterprise editions. You can't purchase Fedora, but you can download it free from `http://fedora.redhat.com`. You can also obtain it by buying a book that includes the Fedora distribution on DVD or CD-ROM.

 All the examples in this book are based on Fedora Core 3.

- ✔ **Linux-Mandriva** is another popular Linux distribution, one that's often recommended as the easiest for first-time Linux users to install. Go to `www.mandriva.com` for more information.

- ✔ **SuSE** (pronounced "Soo-zuh," like the famous composer of marches) is a popular Linux distribution that comes on six CD-ROMs and includes more than 1,500 Linux application programs and utilities, including everything you need to set up a network, Web, e-mail, or electronic commerce server. You can find more information at `www.suse.com`.

- ✔ **Slackware,** one of the oldest Linux distributions, is still popular — especially among Linux old-timers. A full installation of Slackware gives you all the tools you need to set up a network or Internet server. See `www.slackware.com` for more information.

All distributions of Linux include the same core components — the Linux kernel, an X server, popular windows managers (such as GNOME and KDE), compilers, and Internet programs (such as Apache and Sendmail). However, not all Linux distributions are created equal. The manufacturer of each distribution creates its own installation and configuration programs to install and configure Linux.

The installation program is what makes or breaks a Linux distribution. All the distributions I list in this section have easy-to-use installation programs that automatically detect the hardware present on your computer and configure Linux to work with that hardware, eliminating most (if not all) manual configuration chores. The installation programs also let you select the Linux packages you want to install and let you set up one or more user accounts besides the `root` account.

Installing Linux

All the Linux distributions I describe in the section, "Choosing a Linux Distribution," earlier in this chapter, include an installation program that simplifies the task of installing Linux on your computer. The installation program asks you a series of questions about your hardware, what components of Linux you want to install, and how you want to configure certain features. Then it copies the appropriate files to your hard drive and configures your Linux system.

If the thought of installing Linux gives you hives, you can buy computers with Linux preinstalled, just as you can buy computers with Windows already installed.

Before you begin to install Linux, I recommend several planning steps:

✔ Make a list of all the *hardware components* on your computer and how they're *configured*.

Be as specific as you can: Write down each component's manufacturer and model number, as well as configuration information, such as the component's IRQ and I/O address, if appropriate.

✔ Decide how you want to *partition* your hard drive for Linux.

Although Windows is usually installed into a single disk partition, Linux installations typically require at least *three* hard-drive partitions:

- **A boot partition:** This should be small — 16MB is recommended. The boot partition contains the operating system kernel and is required to start Linux properly on some computers.

- **A swap partition:** This should be about twice the size of your computer's RAM. For example, if the computer has 64MB of RAM, allocate a 128MB swap partition. Linux uses this partition as an extension of your computer's RAM.

- **A `root` partition:** This, in most cases, uses up the remaining free space on the disk. The `root` partition contains all the files and data used by your Linux system.

You can also create additional partitions if you wish. The installation program includes a disk-partitioning feature that lets you set up your disk partitions and indicate the mount point for each partition. (For more information about disk partitions, see the sidebar, "I can't see my C drive!," earlier in this chapter.)

Linux is happy to share your hard drive with another operating system, such as Windows. However, you may have to repartition your disk to install Linux without erasing your existing operating system. If you need to repartition your hard drive, I recommend you pick up a copy of PowerQuest's PartitionMagic (www.powerquest.com) or a similar partitioning program, which will allow you to juggle your partitions without losing your existing operating system.

✔ Decide which *optional Linux packages* to install along with the Linux kernel:

- If you have enough drive space, install all the packages that come with your distribution. That way, if you decide you need to use a package, you won't have to figure out how to install the package outside of the installation program.

- If you're tight on space, make sure that you at least install the basic *network* and *Internet server* packages, including Apache, Sendmail, FTP, and Samba.

✔ Set the password for the root account.

✔ In most distributions, you choose whether to create at least one *user account*.

Create at least one user account during installation so you can log on to Linux as a *user* (not with the root account). As a user, you can experiment with Linux commands without accidentally deleting or corrupting a needed system file.

On Again, Off Again

Any user who accesses a Linux system, whether locally or over a network, must be authenticated by a valid user account on the system. The following sections lay out the whys, hows, and wherefores of logging on and logging off a Linux system — and how to shut down the system.

Logging on and logging off is the same thing as (respectively) logging in and logging out. Nobody has decided which term should dominate, so lots of people still argue about whether they're logging in or . . . .

Logging on (or is that in?)

When Linux boots up, it displays a series of startup messages while it starts the various services that comprise a working Linux system. Assuming you selected X server when you installed Linux, you're eventually greeted by the screen, as shown in Figure 24-1. To log on to Linux, enter your user ID on this screen, press Enter, type your password, and press Enter again.

As a part of the installation process, the Setup Agent created a user account for you. Use this user account rather than the root user account whenever possible. Use the root account only when you're making major changes to the system's configuration. When you're doing routine work, log on as an ordinary user to avoid accidentally corrupting your system.

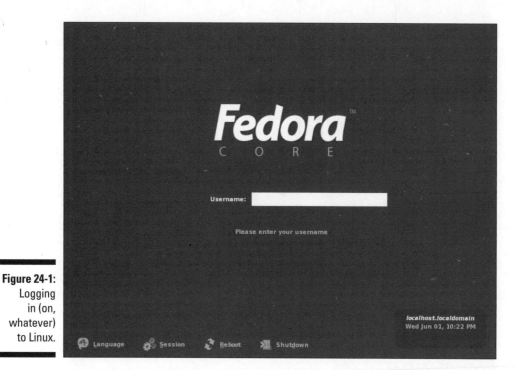

Figure 24-1:
Logging
in (on,
whatever)
to Linux.

When you log, ah, *in,* Linux grinds its gears for a moment and then displays the GNOME desktop, which I describe later in this chapter.

If you didn't install X server, you see a text-mode login prompt that resembles this:

```
Fedora Core release 3 (Heidelberg)
Kernel 2.6.9-1 on an i686

LSERVER login:
```

The `login` prompt displays the Linux version (Fedora Core release 3), the kernel version it's based on (2.6.9-1), the CPU architecture (i686), and the server's hostname (LSERVER). To log in, type your user ID, press Enter, type the password, and press Enter again.

When you've successfully logged in, you're greeted by a semifriendly prompt similar to this:

```
Last login: Sun Jul 20 20:00:56 on :0
[doug@LSERVER doug]$
```

The prompt character in the standard Linux shell is a dollar sign ($) rather than a greater-than sign (>) as it is in MS-DOS or Windows. Also, notice that prompt indicates your username and server (doug@LSERVER) as well as the name of the current directory (doug).

Logging off

After you log on, you probably want to know how to log off. If you logged on to GNOME, you can log off by clicking the main menu and choosing the Log Out command. A dialog box asks whether you're sure you want to log out. Click OK.

In a command shell, you can log out in three ways:

- ✔ Enter the logout command.
- ✔ Enter the exit command.
- ✔ Press Ctrl+D.

Shutting down

Like any operating system, you shouldn't turn off the power to a Linux server without shutting down the system. There are three ways to shut down Linux:

- ✔ Press Ctrl+Alt+Delete.
- ✔ From GNOME, click the main menu and choose Log Out. When the confirmation dialog box appears, select Shut Down or Restart, and then click OK.
- ✔ From a command shell, enter the halt command.

Using GNOME

Although you can do all your Linux configuration chores from the command line, Fedora includes a number of GNOME-based configuration tools for many configuration tasks. Although you can do most of your Linux configuration from GNOME, you do need to use a command line once in a while.

Figure 24-2 shows a typical GNOME desktop with the Text Editor application open. As you can see, the GNOME desktop looks a lot like Microsoft Windows. In fact, many of the basic skills for working with Windows — such as moving or resizing windows, minimizing or maximizing windows, and using drag and drop to move items between windows — work almost exactly the same in GNOME. So you should feel right at home.

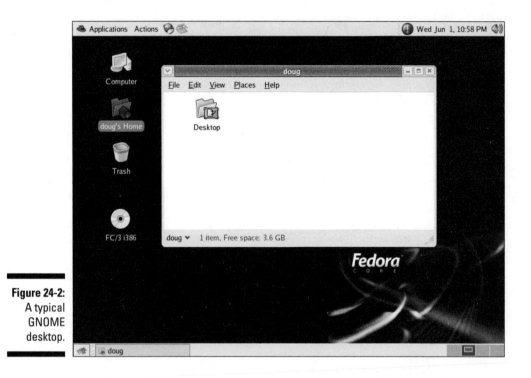

Figure 24-2:
A typical
GNOME
desktop.

The following list describes some key features of the GNOME desktop:

✔ On the **desktop** itself, you'll find several icons that let you access common features. The Home icon lets you access your home directory. The Computer icon is similar to the Windows My Computer icon. And the Trash icon is similar to the Recycle Bin in Windows.

✔ The **panel** at the top of the desktop area includes several menus and icons. The Applications menu lists applications you can run, and the Actions menu lists actions you can perform.

✔ The **down arrow** at the top-left corner of each window reveals a menu of things that you can do with the window. Try the Roll Up command; it reduces a window to its title bar but leaves the window on the desktop. To restore the window, click the down arrow and choose Unroll. This menu also lets you move the window to a different workspace.

✔ **Workspaces,** you ask? A *workspace* is like a separate desktop where you can keep windows open to reduce the clutter on your screen. The panel beneath the desktop area contains a tool — the Workspace Switcher — which lets you switch active workspaces by clicking one of the rectangles in the grid.

Getting to a Command Shell

There are two basic ways to get to a *command shell* (the program that provides the command line) when you need to run Linux commands directly:

✔ Press Ctrl+Alt+F*x* (that is, one of the function keys) to switch to one of the virtual consoles. Then you can log on and run commands to your heart's content. When you're done, press Ctrl+Alt+F7 to return to GNOME.

✔ Open a command shell directly in GNOME by choosing Main Menu➪ System Tools➪Terminal. This opens a command shell in a window on the GNOME desktop, as shown in Figure 24-3. Because this shell runs within the user account GNOME is logged in as, you don't have to log on. You just start typing commands. When you're done, type **Exit** to close the window.

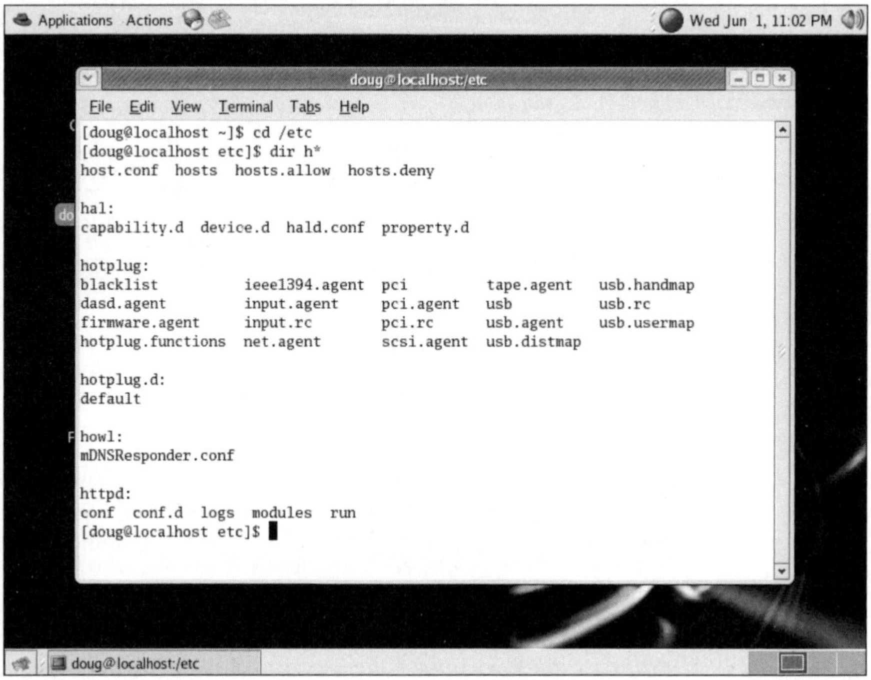

```
Applications  Actions                              Wed Jun 1, 11:02 PM

                    doug@localhost:/etc                      _ □ ✖

   File  Edit  View  Terminal  Tabs  Help

[doug@localhost ~]$ cd /etc
[doug@localhost etc]$ dir h*
host.conf  hosts  hosts.allow  hosts.deny

hal:
capability.d  device.d  hald.conf  property.d

hotplug:
blacklist          ieee1394.agent  pci          tape.agent   usb.handmap
dasd.agent         input.agent     pci.agent    usb          usb.rc
firmware.agent     input.rc        pci.rc       usb.agent    usb.usermap
hotplug.functions  net.agent       scsi.agent   usb.distmap

hotplug.d:
default

howl:
mDNSResponder.conf

httpd:
conf  conf.d  logs  modules  run
[doug@localhost etc]$

  doug@localhost:/etc
```

Figure 24-3: Using a Terminal window to run Linux commands.

Managing User Accounts

One of the most common network administration tasks is adding a user account. The Setup program may create a single user account for you when you first install Linux. But you'll probably need to create more Linux user accounts.

Each Linux user account has the following information associated with it:

- ✔ **Username:** The name the user types to log on to the Linux system.
- ✔ **Full name:** The user's full name.
- ✔ **Home directory:** The directory in which the user will be placed when he or she logs in. In Fedora Linux, the default home directory is /home/username. For example, if the username is blowe, the home directory is /home/blowe.
- ✔ **Shell:** The program used to process Linux commands. Several shell programs are available. In most distributions, the default shell is /bin/bash.
- ✔ **Group:** You can create group accounts, which make it easy to apply identical access rights to groups of users.
- ✔ **User ID:** The internal identifier for the user.

You can add a new user by using the useradd command. For example, to create a user account named slowe and use default values for the other account information, open a Terminal window (or switch to a virtual console) and type this command:

```
# useradd slowe
```

The useradd command has many optional parameters you can use to set account information, such as the user's home directory and shell.

Fortunately, most Linux distributions come with special programs that simplify routine system-management tasks. Fedora is no exception. It comes with a program called User Manager, as shown in Figure 24-4. To start this program, choose Applications⇨System Settings⇨User and Groups.

To create a user account with User Manager, click the Add User button. This brings up a dialog box that asks for the username, password, and other information. Fill out this dialog box and then click OK.

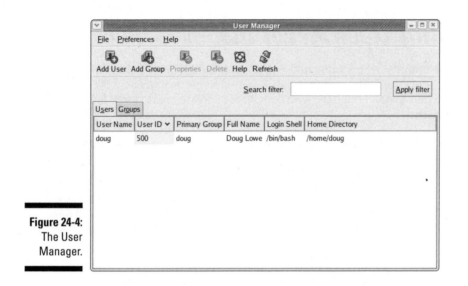

Figure 24-4:
The User
Manager.

The User Manager also lets you create groups. You can simplify the task of administering users by applying access rights to groups rather than individual users. Then, when a user needs access to a resource, you can add the user to the group that has the needed access.

To create a group, click the Add Group button. A dialog box appears, asking for the name of the new group. Type the name you want and then click OK.

To add a user to a group, click the Groups tab in the User Manager. Then, double-click the name of the group you want to add users to. This brings up the Group Properties dialog box. Click the Group Users tab and then check off the users you want to belong to the group.

Network Configuration

In many cases, configuring a Linux server for networking is a snap. When you install Linux, the installation program automatically detects your network adapters and installs the appropriate drivers. Then you're prompted for basic network-configuration information, such as the computer's IP address, hostname, and so on.

However, you may need to manually change your network settings after installation. Or you may need to configure advanced networking features that aren't configured during installation. In the following sections, you get a look at the basic procedures for configuring Linux networking services.

Using the Network Configuration Program

Before you can use a network interface to access a network, you have to con-figure the interface's basic TCP/IP options, such as its IP address, hostname, DNS servers, and so on. In this section, I show you how to do that by using Fedora's Network Configuration program. You can access this program by choosing Main Menu⇨System Settings⇨Network.

Most other Linux distributions have similar programs.

The Network Configuration program lets you configure the basic TCP/IP settings for a network interface by pointing and clicking your way through tabbed windows. You can call up this program by choosing Main Menu⇨ System Settings⇨Network. Figure 24-5 shows the Network Configuration program in action.

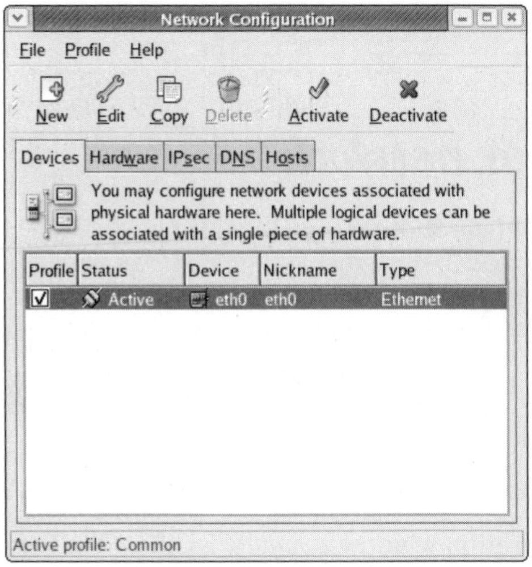

Figure 24-5:
The Network Configuration program.

Notice that the main window of the Network Configuration lists all the network interfaces installed in your computer. You can select any of the interfaces and click Edit to bring up a window similar to the one shown in Figure 24-6. This window lets you set the configuration options for the network interface, such as its IP address and other TCP/IP-configuration information.

Restarting your network

Whenever you make a configuration change to your network, you must restart the Linux networking services before the change can take effect. If you find that requirement annoying, just be thankful that you don't have to restart the entire computer. Simply restarting the network services is sufficient.

You can restart the network services from a GNOME desktop. Follow these steps:

1. **Choose Main Menu⇨System Settings⇨Server Settings⇨Services.**

   The Service Configuration window appears, as shown in Figure 24-7.

2. **Select the Network service.**

   You'll have to scroll down the list of services to find it.

3. **Click the Restart button.**

   The service is stopped and then started again. When it's finished, a small dialog box displaying the message Network Restart Successful is displayed.

4. **Click OK.**

   You're returned to the Service Configuration program.

5. **Close the Service Configuration program.**

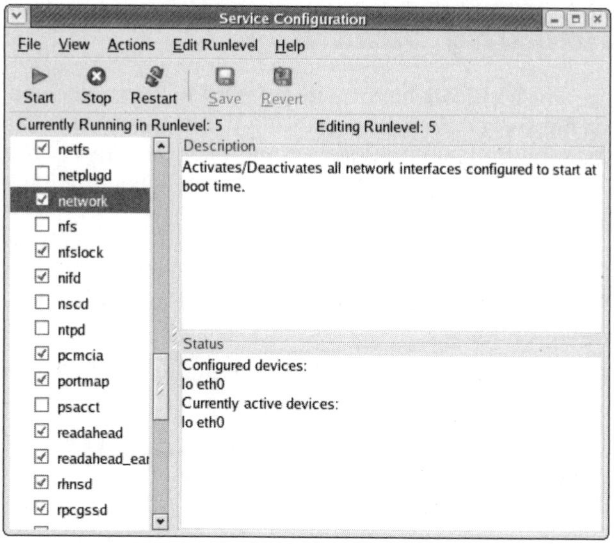

Figure 24-7:
The Service
Config-
uration
window.

If you prefer working in a command shell, you can restart the network by entering the command `service network restart`. Doing so results in a display like this:

```
Shutting down interface eth0:                          [  OK
                    ]
Shutting down loopback interface:                      [  OK
                    ]
Setting network parameters:                            [  OK
                    ]
Bringing up loopback interface:                        [  OK
                    ]
Bringing up interface eth0:                            [  OK
                    ]
```

Doing the Samba Dance

Until now, you probably thought of Samba as an intricate Brazilian dance with fun rhythms. But in the Linux world, *Samba* refers to a file- and printer-sharing program that allows Linux to mimic a Windows file and print server so Windows computers can use shared Linux directories and printers. If you want to use Linux as a file or print server in a Windows network, you have to know how to dance the Samba.

Understanding Samba

Because Linux and Windows have such different file systems, you can't create a Linux file server simply by granting Windows users access to Linux directories. Windows client computers couldn't access files in the Linux directories. There are just too many differences between the file systems — these, for example:

- Linux filenames are case-sensitive; Windows filenames aren't. For example, in Windows, `File1.txt` and `file1.txt` are the same file. In Linux, they're different files.

- Linux filenames can contain periods. In Windows, only one period is allowed — and it separates the filename from the file extension.

- Windows has file attributes, such as Read-only and Archive. Linux doesn't have these.

More fundamentally, Windows networking uses a protocol called *SMB,* which stands for *Server Message Block,* to manage the exchange of file data between file servers and clients.

Linux doesn't have SMB support built in. That's why Samba is required.

Samba is a program that mimics the behavior of a Windows-based file server by implementing the SMB protocol. When you run Samba on a Linux server, Windows computers on your network see the Linux server as if it were a Windows server.

Like a Windows server, Samba works by creating and designating certain directories as shares. A *share* is simply a directory that's made available to other users via the network. Each share has the following elements:

- **Share name:** The name by which the share is known over the network. Share names should be eight characters whenever possible.

- **Path:** The path to the directory on the Linux computer that's being shared, such as `\Users\Doug`.

- **Description:** A one-line description of the share.

- **Access:** A list of users or groups that have been granted access to the share.

Samba includes a client program that lets a Linux computer access Windows files servers.

Why did Samba's developers choose to call their program *Samba?* Simply because the protocol that Windows file and print servers use to communicate with one another is called *SMB,* which stands for *Server Message Block.* Add a couple of vowels to *SMB* and you get *Samba.*

Installing Samba

If you didn't install Samba when you installed Linux, you have to install it now. The easiest way to do that is to use Fedora's GNOME-based package management tool to install Samba. Just insert the Fedora distribution CD in the CD drive and then click Yes when you're asked whether you want to run the `autorun` program. Then, when the Package Management window appears, select the Windows File Server group, which installs the Samba packages for you.

One sure way to render a Samba installation *absolutely useless* is to enable the default Linux firewall settings on the computer that runs Samba. The Linux firewall is designed to prevent users from accessing network services, such as Samba. It's designed to be used between the Internet and your local network, not between Samba and your local network. Although it's possible to configure the firewall to allow access to Samba only to your internal network, a much better option is to run the firewall on a separate computer. That way the firewall computer can concentrate on being a firewall, and the file-server computer can concentrate on serving up files.

Starting and stopping Samba

Before you can use Samba, you must start its two daemons, `smbd` and `nmbd`. Both can be started at once by starting the `smb` service. From a command shell, use this command:

```
service smb start
```

Whenever you make a configuration change, such as adding a new share or a creating a new Samba user, you should stop and restart the service with these commands:

```
service smb restart
```

If you prefer, you can stop and start the service with separate commands:

```
service smb stop
service smb start
```

If you're not sure that Samba is running, enter this command:

```
service smb status
```

You'll get a message indicating whether the smbd and nmbd daemons are running.

To configure Samba to start automatically when you start Linux, use this command:

```
chkconfig -level 35 smb on
```

To make sure the chkconfig command worked right, enter this command:

```
chkconfig -list smb
```

You should see output similar to the following:

```
Smb          0:off  1:off  2:off  3:on   4:off  5:on   6:off
```

Services can be independently configured to start automatically for each of the six *boot levels* of Linux. *Boot level 3* is normal operation without an X server; *level 5* is normal operation with an X server. Thus, setting smb to start for levels 3 and 5 makes smb available whether or not you're using a graphical user interface.

You can also start and stop Samba with the Service Configuration tool, as shown in Figure 24-6. Scroll down the list of services until you find the smb service. You can use the three buttons in the toolbar at the top of the window to start, stop, or restart a service.

Using the Samba Server Configuration tool

Fedora includes a handy GNOME-based configuration tool that simplifies the task of configuring Samba. To start it, choose Main Menu⇨System Settings⇨Server Settings⇨Samba Server. When you do, the Samba Server Configuration window appears, as shown in Figure 24-8. This tool lets you configure basic server settings and manage shares.

To make your Samba server visible on the network, choose Preferences⇨ Server Settings. This brings up a dialog box that lets you set the workgroup name (which must match the workgroup or domain name you want the Samba server to belong to) and a description for the server, as well as some basic security settings that control how users can access the Samba server.

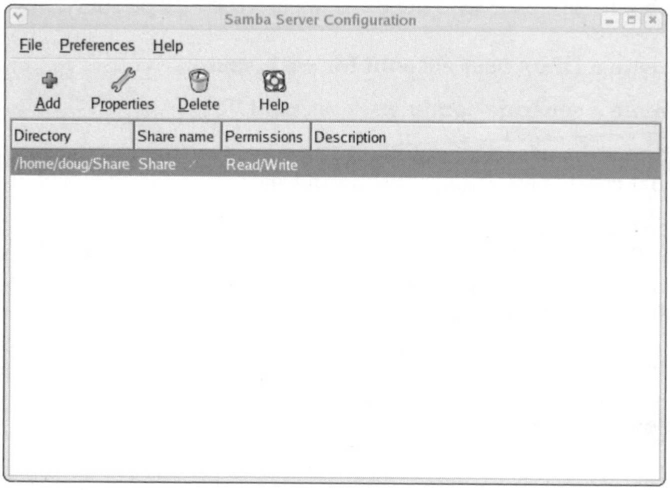

Directory	Share name	Permissions	Description
/home/doug/Share	Share	Read/Write	

Samba Server Configuration

File   Preferences   Help

Add   Properties   Delete   Help

Figure 24-8:
Using the
Samba
Server
Configura-
tion tool.

You can set four basic types of security for your Samba server:

✔ **Domain:** Configures the Samba server to use a Windows domain controller to verify the user. If you specify this option, you must

• Provide the domain controller's name in the Authentication Server field.

• Set Encrypted Passwords to Yes (if you use Domain mode).

✔ **Server:** Configures Samba to use another Samba server to authenticate users.

If you have more than one Samba server, this feature lets you set up user accounts on just one of the servers. Then, in the Authentication Server field, specify the name of the Samba server that should perform the authentication.

✔ **Share:** Authorizes users separately for each share they attempt to access.

✔ **User:** Requires that users provide a valid username and password when they first connect to a Samba server. That authentication then grants them access to all shares on the server, subject to the restrictions of the account they're authorized under.

User mode is the default.

For each network user who needs to access the Samba server, you must

1. **Create a Linux user account for each user.**

2. **Create a separate Samba user account.**

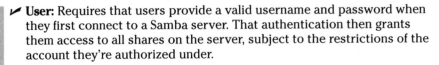

The Samba user account maps to an existing Linux user account, so you must create the Linux user account first.

To create a Samba user account, choose Preferences⟹Samba Users from the Samba Server Configuration window. This brings up the Samba Users dialog box, as shown in Figure 24-9. You can use this dialog box to add, edit, or delete users.

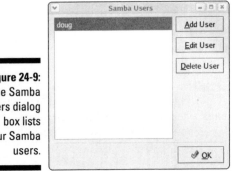

Figure 24-9:
The Samba
Users dialog
box lists
your Samba
users.

To be useful, a file server should offer one or more *shares* — directories that have been designated as publicly accessible via the network. Again, you use the Samba Server Configuration program to manage your shares. To add a share, click the Add button in the Samba Server Configuration program's toolbar. This brings up the Create Samba Share dialog box, as shown in Figure 24-10. You can then

✔ Enter the path for the directory you want to share.

✔ Enter a description for the share.

✔ Select whether to allow either read-only or read-write access.

✔ Click the Access tab if you want to set limits on access (for example, to specific users).

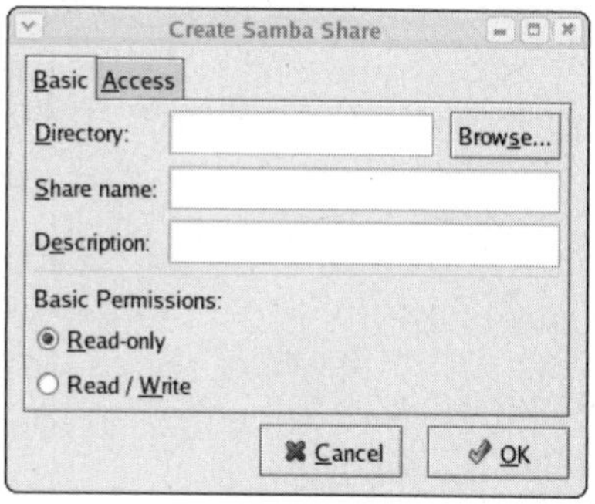

Figure 24-10:
The Create
Samba
Share dialog
box.

Create Samba Share
Basic / Access
Directory: _____ Browse...
Share name: _____
Description: _____
Basic Permissions:
⦿ Read-only
○ Read / Write
✗ Cancel   ✓ OK

When you create a new share using the Samba Configuration program, the share should be immediately visible to network users. If not, try restarting the Samba server, as I describe in the section, "Starting and stopping Samba," in this chapter.

Chapter 25

Macintosh Networking

In This Chapter

▶ Hooking up a Macintosh network

▶ Using a Macintosh network

▶ Mixing Macs and PCs

This book dwells on networking Windows-based computers, as if Microsoft were the only game in town. (Hah! They wish.) To be politically correct, I should at least acknowledge the existence of a different breed of computer: the Apple Macintosh.

This chapter presents what you need to know to hook up a Macintosh network, use a Macintosh network, and mix Macintoshes and Windows PCs on the same network. This chapter isn't a comprehensive tome on Macintoshes, but it's enough to start.

What You Need to Know to Hook Up a Macintosh Network

The following sections present some key things you should know about networking Macintosh computers before you start plugging in cables.

AppleTalk and Open Transport

Every Macintosh ever built, even an original 1984 model, includes networking support. Of course, newer Macintosh computers have better built-in networking features than older Macintosh computers. The newest Macs include built-in 10/100 Mbps Ethernet adapters and sophisticated networking support built in to the operating system — similar to the networking features that come with Windows XP. The beauty of Macintosh networking is that the network card is built in, so you don't have to worry about installing and configuring the network.

Macintosh computers use a set of networking protocols collectively known as *AppleTalk*. Because AppleTalk is built in to every Mac, it's become an inarguable networking standard among Macintosh users. You don't have to worry about the differences between different network operating systems because all Macintosh networking is based on AppleTalk.

AppleTalk has gone through several major revisions since it was first introduced back in 1984. Originally, AppleTalk supported only small networks that operated only over low-speed connections. In 1989, Apple enhanced AppleTalk to support larger networks and faster connections.

In 1996, with the release of Mac OS System 7.5.3, Apple folded AppleTalk into its current networking scheme: *Open Transport*. The idea behind Open Transport is to bring all the different types of communications software used on Macintoshes under a common umbrella — and make them easy to configure and use. Currently, two types of networking are handled by Open Transport:

- **Open Transport/AppleTalk:** Handles local-area networks (LANs) according to the AppleTalk protocols. Open Transport/AppleTalk is a beefed-up version of AppleTalk that's more efficient and flexible.
- **OpenTransport/TCP:** Handles TCP/IP communications, such as Internet connections.

Open Transport is standard fare on all new Macintosh computers; old Macintosh computers can be upgraded to Open Transport, provided they're powerful enough. (The minimum system requirements for Open Transport are a 68030 processor, 5MB of RAM, and MacOS System 7.5.3.)

AppleTalk enables you to subdivide a network into *zones*. Each zone consists of the network users who regularly share information.

AppleTalk zones are similar to *workgroups* in Windows for Workgroups.

Although basic support for networking is built in to every Macintosh, you still have to purchase cables to connect the computers to one another. You have several types of cables to choose from. You can use AppleTalk with two different cabling schemes that connect to the Macintosh printer port, or you can use AppleTalk with faster Ethernet interface cards.

Mac OS X Server

Apple offers a dedicated network operating system known as Mac OS X Server (the *X* is pronounced "Ten," not "Ex"), which is designed for PowerMac G3 or later computers. Mac OS X Server is based on a Unix operating-system kernel known as Mach. Mac OS X Server can handle many network-server tasks as efficiently as any other network operating system, including Windows 2000, NetWare, and Unix.

Who's winning in the AFP West?

AFP is not a division of the NFL but an abbreviation for AppleTalk Filing Protocol. It's the part of AppleTalk that governs how files are stored and accessed on the network. AFP allows files to be shared with non-Macintosh computers. You can integrate Macintoshes into any network operating system that recognizes AFP. NetWare and all versions of Windows since Windows 95 use AFP to support Macintoshes in their networks.

In case you're interested (and you shouldn't be), AFP is a Presentation-Layer protocol. (See Chapter 29 if you don't have a clue what I'm talking about.)

Mac OS X Server is the server version of the Mac OS X operating system, which is the current operating system version for client Macintosh computers.

The Mac OS X Server includes the following features:

- ✔ **Apache Web server,** which also runs on Windows and Linux systems
- ✔ **NetBoot,** a feature that simplifies the task of managing network client computers
- ✔ **File services using AFP**
- ✔ **WebObjects,** a high-end tool for creating Web sites
- ✔ **QuickTime Streaming Server,** which lets the server broadcast multimedia programs over the network

What You Need to Know to Use a Macintosh Network

The following questions often come up after you install the network cable. Note that the following sections assume that you're working with AppleTalk networking using Mac OS X. The procedures may vary somewhat if you're using Open Transport networking or an earlier version of the Macintosh operating system.

Configuring a Mac for networking

Before you can access the network from your Mac, you must configure your Mac for networking: Activate AppleTalk and assign your network name and password.

Activating AppleTalk

After all the cables are in place, you have to activate AppleTalk. Here's how:

1. **Choose the Chooser desk accessory from the Apple menu.**
2. **Click the Active button.**
3. **Close the Chooser.**

Assigning your name and password

After you activate AppleTalk, you're ready to assign an owner name, a password, and a name for your computer. This process allows other network users to access your Mac. Here's how:

1. **Choose the File Sharing control panel from the Apple menu (Apple⇨ Control Panels⇨File Sharing).**
2. **Type your name in the Owner Name field.**
3. **Type a password in the Owner Password field.**

   Don't forget what the password is.

4. **Type a descriptive name for your computer in the Computer Name field.**

   Other network users will know your computer by this name.

5. **Click the Close button.**

Accessing a network printer

Accessing a network printer with AppleTalk is no different than accessing a printer when you don't have a network. If more than one printer is available on the network, you use the Chooser to select the printer you want to use. Chooser displays all the available network printers — just pick the one you want to use. And keep the following points in mind:

✔ **Be sure to enable Background Printing for the network printer.** If you don't, your Mac is tied up until the printer finishes your job — that can be a long time if someone else sent a 500-page report to the printer just before you. When you enable Background Printing, your printer output is captured to a disk file and then sent to the printer later while you continue with other work.

To enable Background Printing

    1. Choose Apple⇨Chooser desk accessory.

    2. Select the printer you want to use from the Chooser.

    3. Click the Background Printing On button.

✔ **Don't enable Background Printing if a dedicated print server has been set up.** In that case, print data is spooled automatically to the print server's disk so your Mac doesn't have to wait for the printer to become available.

Sharing files with other users

To share files on your Mac with other network users, you set up a shared resource. You can share a disk or just individual folders and restrict access to certain users.

Before you can share files with other users, you must activate the AppleTalk file-sharing feature. Here's how:

    1. Choose the File Sharing control panel from the Apple Menu.

    2. Click the Start button in the File Sharing section of the control panel.

    3. Click the Close button.

To share a file or folder, click the file or folder once. Then open the File menu, choose Get Info, and choose Sharing from the submenu that appears. You can also use the Sharing section of the Info window to restrict access to the file or folder.

Accessing shared files

To access files on another Macintosh, follow this procedure:

    1. Choose the Chooser from the Apple menu.

    2. Click the AppleShare icon from the Chooser window.

3. **Click the name of the computer you want to access. (If your network has zones, you must first click the zone you want to access.)**

4. **Click OK.**

   A logon screen appears.

5. **If you have a user account on the computer, click the Registered User button and enter your username and password. Otherwise, click the Guest button and then click OK.**

   A list of shared folders and disks appears.

6. **Click the folders and disks you want to access.**

   A check box appears next to each item. If you check this box, you connect to the corresponding folder or disk automatically when you start your computer.

7. **Click OK.**

 With Mac OS 8.5 and later, you can also use the Network Browser, found in the Apple menu, to access network drives or folders. Just open the Network Browser from the Apple menu, double-click the server that contains the shared disk or folder, and then double-click the drive or folder you want to use.

What You Need to Know to Network Macintoshes with PCs

Life would be too boring if Macs *really* lived on one side of the tracks and PCs lived on the other. If your organization has a mix of both Macs and PCs, odds are you eventually want to network them together. Fortunately, you have several ways:

- ✔ If your network has an OS X Server, you can use the Windows client software that comes with OS X Server to connect any version of Windows to the server. Doing so enables Windows users to access the files and printers on the Macintosh server.

- ✔ The server versions of Windows include a feature called Services for Macintosh that allows Macintosh computers to access files and printers managed by the Windows servers without installing special client software on the Macintosh computers.

- ✔ If you use NetWare, you must purchase separate NetWare client software for your Macintosh computers. After you install this client software, the Macs can access files and printers managed by your NetWare servers.

The biggest complication that occurs when you mix Macintosh and Windows computers on the same network is that the Mac OS and Windows have slightly different rules for naming files. For example:

- Macintosh filenames are limited to 31 characters, but Windows filenames can be up to 255 characters.
- Although a Macintosh filename can include any characters *other than a colon,* Windows filenames can't include backslashes, greater-than or less-than signs, and a few other oddball characters.

The best way to avoid filename problems is to stick with *short names* (under 31 characters) and limit your filenames to *letters, numbers,* and *common symbols* (such as the hyphen or pound sign). Although you can translate any filenames that violate the rules of the system being used into a form that is acceptable to both Windows and the Macintosh, doing so sometimes leads to cryptic or ambiguous filenames. But hey, network administration is as much an art as a science.

Part VII
The Part of Tens

The 5th Wave
By Rich Tennant

"See? I created a little felon figure that runs around our Web site hiding behind banner ads. On the last page, our logo puts him in a non lethal choke hold and brings him back to the home page."

In this part . . .

*I*f you keep this book in the bathroom, the chapters in this section are the ones that you'll read the most. Each chapter consists of ten (more or less) things that are worth knowing about various aspects of networking. Without further ado, here they are, direct from the home office in sunny Fresno, California.

Chapter 26

More Than Ten Big Network Mistakes

In This Chapter

▶ Saving on cable

▶ Turning off or restarting a server when users are logged on

▶ Deleting important files that live on the server

▶ Copying a file from the server, changing it, and copying it back

▶ Sending something to the printer for a second time

▶ Running out of space on a network server

▶ Blaming the network

*J*ust about the time you figure out how to avoid the most embarrassing computer mistakes (such as using your CD drive's tray as a cup holder), the network lands on your computer. Now you have a whole new list of dumb things you can do, mistakes that can give your average computer geek a belly laugh because they seem so basic to him. Well, that's because he's a computer geek. Nobody had to tell *him* not to fold the floppy disk — he was born with an extra gene that gave him an instinctive knowledge of such things.

Here's a list of some of the most common mistakes made by network novices. Avoid these mistakes and you deprive your local computer geek of the pleasure of a good laugh at your expense.

Skimping on Cable

If your network consists of more than a few computers or has computers located in different rooms, invest in a professional-quality cable installation, complete with wall-mounted jacks, patch panels, and high-quality network switches. It's tempting to cut costs by using cheap switches and by stringing inexpensive cable directly from the hubs to each computer on the network. But in the long run, that approach actually proves to be more expensive than investing in a good cable installation in the first place.

Here are just a few of the reasons it pays to do the cabling right in the
first place:

- A good cable installation lasts much longer than the computers it
services. A good cable installation can last 10 or 15 years, long after
the computers on your network have been placed on display in a computer history museum.

- Installing cable is hard work. No one enjoys going up in the attic, poking
his or her head up through ceiling panels and wiping fiberglass insulation out of his or her hair, or fishing cables through walls. If you're going
to do it, do it right so you don't have to do it again in just a few years.
Build your cable installation to last.

- Your network users may be satisfied with 100 Mbps networking now, but
it won't be long before they demand gigahertz speed. And who knows
how fast the next wave of networking will be? If you cut costs by using
plain Cat5 cable instead of more expensive Cat6 cable, you'll have to
replace it later.

- You might be tempted to skip the modular wall jacks and patch cables
and instead just run the cable down the wall, out through a hole, and
then directly to the computer or hub. That's a bad idea because the connectors are the point at which cables are most likely to fail. If a connector fails, you have to replace the entire cable — all the way up the wall,
through the ceiling, and back to the switch. By wiring in a wall-jack and
using a patch cable, you have to replace only the patch cable when a
connector fails.

For more information about professional touches for installing cable, see
Chapter 5.

Turning Off or Restarting a Server Computer While Users Are Logged On

The fastest way to blow your network users' accounts to kingdom come
is to turn off a server computer while users are logged on. Restarting it by
pressing its reset button can have the same disastrous effect.

If your network is set up with a dedicated file server, you probably won't
be tempted to turn it off or restart it. But if your network is set up as a true
peer-to-peer network, where each of the workstation computers — including
your own — also doubles as a server computer, be careful about the impul-
sive urge to turn off or restart your computer. Someone may be accessing a
file or printer on your computer at that very moment.

Before turning off or restarting a server computer, find out whether anyone is logged on. If so, politely ask him or her to log off.

Also, remember that many server problems don't require a server reboot. Instead, you can often correct the problem just by restarting the particular service that's affected.

Deleting Important Files on the Server

Without a network, you can do anything you want to your computer, and the only person you can hurt is yourself. (Kind of like the old "victimless crime" debate.) Put your computer on a network, though, and you take on a certain amount of responsibility. You must find out how to live like a responsible member of the network society.

Therefore, you can't capriciously delete files from a network server just because you don't need them. They may not be yours. You wouldn't want someone deleting your files, would you?

Be especially careful about files that are required to keep the network running. For example, some versions of Windows use a folder named wgpo0000 to hold e-mail. If you delete this folder, your e-mail is history. Look before you delete.

Copying a File from the Server, Changing It, and Then Copying It Back

Sometimes working on a network file is easier if you first copy the file to your local hard drive. Then you can access it from your application program more efficiently because you don't have to use the network. This is especially true for large database files that have to be sorted to print reports.

You're asking for trouble, though, if you copy the file to your PC's local hard drive, make changes to the file, and then copy the updated version of the file back to the server. Why? Because somebody else may be trying the same thing at the same time. If that happens, the updates made by one of you — whoever copies the file back to the server first — are lost.

Copying a file to a local drive is rarely a good idea.

Sending Something to the Printer Again Just Because It Didn't Print the First Time

What do you do if you send something to the printer and nothing happens?

- **Right answer:** Find out why nothing happened and *fix it*.
- **Wrong answer:** Send it again and see whether it works this time.

Some users keep sending it over and over again, hoping that one of these days, it'll take. The result is rather embarrassing when someone finally clears the paper jam and then watches 30 copies of the same letter print. Or when 30 copies of your document print on a different printer because you had the wrong printer selected.

Assuming That the Server Is Safely Backed Up

Some users make the unfortunate assumption that the network somehow represents an efficient and organized bureaucracy worthy of their trust. Far from the truth. Never assume that the network jocks are doing their jobs backing up the network data every day, even if they are. Check up on them. Conduct a surprise inspection one day: Burst into the computer room wearing white gloves and demand to see the backup tapes. Check the tape rotation to make sure that more than one day's worth of backups is available.

If you're not impressed with your network's backup procedures, take it upon yourself to make sure that you never lose any of your data. Back up your most valued files to a CD-RW drive or a flash drive.

Connecting to the Internet without Considering Security Issues

If you connect a non-networked computer to the Internet and then pick up a virus or get yourself hacked into, only that one computer is affected. But if you connect a networked computer to the Internet, the entire network becomes vulnerable.

Beware: Never connect a networked computer to the Internet without first considering the security issues:

- ✔ How will you protect yourself and the network from viruses?

- ✔ How will you ensure that the sensitive files located on your file server don't suddenly become accessible to the entire world?

- ✔ How can you prevent evil hackers from sneaking into your network, stealing your customer file, and selling your customer's credit-card data on the black market?

For answers to these and other Internet-security questions, see Chapter 9.

Plugging In a Wireless Access Point without Asking

For that matter, plugging any device into your network without first getting permission from the network administrator is a big no-no. But Wireless Access Points (WAPs) are particularly insidious. Many users fall for the marketing line that wireless networking is as easy as plugging in one of these devices to the network. Then, your wireless notebook PC or hand-held device can instantly join the network.

The trouble is, so can anyone else within about one-quarter mile of the wireless access point. Therefore, you must employ extra security measures to make sure hackers can't get into your network via a wireless computer located in the parking lot or across the street.

If you think that's unlikely, think again. Several underground Web sites on the Internet actually display maps of unsecured wireless networks in major cities. For more information about securing a wireless network, see Chapter 9.

Thinking You Can't Work Just Because the Network Is Down

A few years back, I realized that I can't do my job without electricity. Should a power failure occur and I find myself without electricity, I can't even light a candle and work with pencil and paper because the only pencil sharpener I have is electric.

Some people have the same attitude about the network: They figure that if the network goes down, they may as well go home. That's not always the case. Just because your computer is attached to a network doesn't mean that it won't work when the network is down. True — if the wind flies out of the network sails, you can't access any network devices. You can't get files from network drives, and you can't print on network printers. But you can still use your computer for local work — accessing files and programs on your local hard drive and printing on your local printer (if you're lucky enough to have one).

Running Out of Space on a Server

One of the most disastrous mistakes to make on a network server is to let it run out of disk space. When you buy a new server with hundreds of gigabytes of disk space, you might think you'll never run out of space. But it's amazing how quickly an entire network full of users can run through a few hundred gigabytes of disk space.

Unfortunately, bad things begin to happen when you get down to a few gigabytes of free space on a server. Windows begins to perform poorly and may even slow to a crawl. Errors start popping up. And, when you finally run out of space completely, users line up at your door demanding an immediate fix:

✔ The best way to avoid this unhappy situation is to monitor the free disk space on your servers on a daily basis. It's also a good idea to keep track of free disk space on a weekly basis so you can look for project trends. For example, if your file server has 100GB of free space and your users chew up about 5GB of space per week, you know you'll most likely run out of disk space in 20 weeks. With that knowledge in hand, you can formulate a plan.

✔ Adding additional disk storage to your servers isn't always the best solution to the problem of running out of disk space. Before you buy more disks, you should

• Look for old and unnecessary files that can be removed.

• Consider using disk quotas to limit the amount of network disk space your users can consume.

Always Blaming the Network

Some people treat the network kind of like the village idiot who can be blamed whenever anything goes wrong. Networks cause problems of their own, but they aren't the root of all evil:

- ✔ If your monitor displays only capital letters, it's probably because you pressed the Caps Lock key.

  Don't blame the network.

- ✔ If you spill coffee on the keyboard, well, that's your fault.

  Don't blame the network.

- ✔ If your toddler sticks Play-Doh in the floppy drive, kids will be kids.

  Don't blame the network.

Get the point?

Chapter 27

Ten Networking Commandments

In This Chapter

▶ Backing up and cleaning up hard drives

▶ Scheduling downtime for maintenance

▶ Keeping spare parts

▶ Training users

▶ Recording your network configuration

> *"Blessed is the network manager who walks not in the council of the ignorant, nor stands in the way of the oblivious, nor sits in the seat of the greenhorn, but delights in the Law of the Network and meditates on this Law day and night."*

—Networks 1:1

And so it came to pass that these Ten Networking Commandments were passed down from generation to generation, to be worn as frontlets between the computer geeks' eyes (taped on the bridges of their broken glasses) and written upon their doorposts. Obey these commandments, and it shall go well with you, with your children, and with your children's children.

1. Thou Shalt Back Up Thy Hard Drive Religiously

Prayer is a good thing, but when it comes to protecting the data on your network, nothing beats a well-thought-out schedule of backups followed religiously. (If this were an actual network Bible, a footnote here would refer you back to related verses in Chapter 21.)

II. Thou Shalt Protect Thy Network from Infidels

Remember Colonel Flagg from *M*A*S*H,* who hid in trashcans looking for Commies? You don't exactly want to become him, but on the other hand, you don't want to ignore the possibility of getting zapped by a virus or your network being invaded by hackers. Make sure that your Internet connection is properly secured with a firewall and don't allow any Internet access that circumvents your security.

To counter virus threats, use network-aware antivirus software to ensure that every user on your network has up-to-date virus protection. And teach your users so they know how to avoid those virus threats that manage to sneak past your virus protection.

III. Thou Shalt Keepeth Thy Network Drive Pure and Cleanse It of Old Files

Don't wait until your 300GB network drive is down to just one cluster of free space before you think about cleaning it up. Set up a routine schedule for disk housekeeping, where you wade through the files and directories on the network disk to remove old junk.

IV. Thou Shalt Not Tinker with Thine Network Configuration Unless Thou Knowest What Thou Art Doing

Networks are finicky things. After yours is up and running, don't mess with it unless you know what you're doing. It may be tempting to log on to your firewall router to see whether you can tweak some of its settings to squeeze another ounce of performance out of it. But unless you know what you're doing, be careful! (Be especially careful if you think you *do* know what you're doing. It's the people who think they know what they're doing — and think no more about it — who get themselves into trouble!)

V. Thou Shalt Not Covet Thy Neighbor's Network

Network envy is a common malady among network managers. If your network users are humming along fine at 100 Mbps, don't covet your neighbor's 1000 Mbps network. If your network users are happy with Windows XP, resist the urge to upgrade to Vista unless you have a really good reason. And if you run Windows Server 2003 Server, fantasizing about Windows Server 2007 is a venial sin.

You're especially susceptible to network envy if you're a gadget freak. There's always a better switch to be had or some fancy network-protocol gizmo to lust after. Don't give in to these base urges! Resist the devil, and he will flee!

VI. Thou Shalt Schedule Downtime before Working upon Thy Network

As a courtesy, try to give your users plenty of advance notice before you take down the network to work on it. Obviously, you can't predict when random problems strike. But if you know you're going to patch the server on Thursday morning, you earn points if you tell everyone about the inconvenience two days before rather than two minutes before. (You'll earn even more points if you patch the server Saturday morning. Tell your boss you'll take next Thursday morning off to make it up.)

VII. Thou Shalt Keep an Adequate Supply of Spare Parts

There's no reason that your network should be down for two days just because a cable breaks. Always make sure that you have at least a minimal supply of network spare parts on hand. (As luck would have it, Chapter 28 suggests ten things you should keep in your closet.)

VIII. Thou Shalt Not Steal Thy Neighbor's Program without a License

How would you like it if Inspector Clouseau barged into your office, looked over your shoulder as you ran Excel from a network server, and asked, "Do you have a liesaunce?"

"A liesaunce?" you reply, puzzled.

"Yes of course, a liesaunce, that is what I said. The law specifically prohibits the playing of a computer program on a network without a proper liesaunce."

You don't want to get in trouble with Inspector Clouseau, do you? License that application.

IX. Thou Shalt Train Thy Users in the Ways of the Network

Don't blame the users if they don't know how to use the network. It's not their fault. If you're the network administrator, your job is to provide training so the network users know how to use the network.

X. Thou Shalt Write Down Thy Network Configuration upon Tablets of Stone

Network documentation should be written down. If you cross the River Jordan, who else will know diddly-squat about the network if you don't write it down somewhere? Write down everything, put it in an official binder labeled *Network Bible,* and protect the binder as if it were sacred.

Your hope should be that 2,000 years from now, when archeologists are exploring caves in your area, they find your network documentation hidden in a jar and marvel at how meticulously the people of our time recorded their network configurations.

They'll probably draw ridiculous conclusions, such as we offered sacrifices of burnt data packets to a deity named TCP/IP and confessed our transgressions in a ritual known as "logging," but that makes it all the more fun.

Chapter 28

Ten Things You Should Keep in Your Closet

. . . .

In This Chapter

▶ Tools

▶ Duct tape

▶ Patch cables

▶ Cable ties

▶ Twinkies

▶ An extra network card

▶ A few cheap network switches

▶ Complete documentation of the network on tablets of stone

▶ The network manuals and disks

▶ Ten copies of this book

. . . .

*W*hen you first network your office computers, you need to find a closet where you can stash some network goodies. If you can't find a whole closet, shoot for a shelf, a drawer, or at least a sturdy cardboard box.

Here's a list of what stuff to keep on hand.

Duct Tape

Duct tape helped get the crew of Apollo 13 back from their near-disastrous moon voyage. You won't actually use it much to maintain your network, but it serves the symbolic purpose of demonstrating that you realize things sometimes go wrong and you're willing to improvise to get your network up and running.

If you don't like duct tape, a little baling wire and chewing gum serve the same symbolic purpose.

Tools

Make sure that you have at least a basic computer toolkit, the kind you can pick up for $15 from just about any office-supply store. You also should have wire cutters, wire strippers, and cable crimpers that work for your network cable type.

Patch Cables

Keep a good supply of patch cables on hand. You'll use them often, when you move users around from one office to another, when you add computers to your network, or when you need to rearrange things at the patch panels (assuming you wired your network using patch panels).

When you buy patch cables, buy them in a variety of lengths and colors. One good way to quickly make a mess of your patch panels is to use 15' cables when 3' cables will do the job. And having a variety of colors can help you sort out a mass of cables.

Cable Ties

Cable ties — those little plastic zip things that you wrap around a group of cables and pull to tighten — can go a long way toward helping keep your network cables neat and organized. You can buy them in bags of 1,000 at big-box home-improvement stores.

Twinkies

If left sealed in their little individually wrapped packages, Twinkies keep for years. In fact, they'll probably outlast the network itself. You can bequeath 'em to future network geeks, ensuring continued network support for generations to come.

Extra Network Cards

Ideally, you want to use identical network cards in all your computers. But if the boss's computer is down, you'd probably settle for whatever network card the corner network street vendor is selling today. That's why you should always keep at least one spare network card in the closet. You can rest easy knowing that if a network card fails, you have an identical replacement card sitting on the shelf, just waiting to be installed — and you won't have to buy one from someone who also sells imitation Persian rugs.

Obviously, if you have only two computers on your network, justifying spending the money for a spare network adapter card is hard. With larger networks, it's easier to justify.

Cheap Network Switches

It's a good idea to keep a couple of cheap (about $20) four- or eight-port network switches on hand. You don't want to use them for your main network infrastructure. But they come in handy when you need to add a computer or printer somewhere and you don't have an available network jack. For example, suppose one of your users has a short-term need for a second computer, but there's only one network jack in the user's office. Rather than pulling a new cable to the user's office, just plug a cheap switch into the existing jack and then plug both of the computers into the switch.

The Complete Documentation of the Network on Tablets of Stone

I've mentioned several times in this book the importance of documenting your network. Don't spend hours documenting your network and then hide the documentation under a pile of old magazines behind your desk. Put the binder in the closet with the other network supplies so that you and everyone else always know where to find it. And keep backup copies of the Word, Excel, Visio, or other documents that make up the network binder in a fireproof safe or at another site.

Don't you dare chisel passwords into the network documentation, though. Shame on you for even thinking about it!

If you decide to chisel the network documentation onto actual stone tablets, consider using *sandstone*. It's attractive, inexpensive, and easy to update (just rub out the old info and chisel in the new). Keep in mind, however, that sandstone is subject to erosion from spilled Diet Coke. Oh, and make sure that you store it on a reinforced shelf.

The Network Manuals and Disks

In the Land of Oz, a common lament of the Network Scarecrow is "If I only had the manual." True, the manual probably isn't a Pulitzer Prize candidate, but that doesn't mean you should toss it in a landfill, either.

Put the *manuals* and *disks* for all the software you use on your network where they belong — in the closet with all the other network tools and artifacts.

Ten Copies of This Book

Obviously, you want to keep an adequate supply of this book on hand to distribute to all your network users. The more they know, the more they stay off your back.

Sheesh, 10 copies may not be enough — 20 may be closer to what you need.

Chapter 29

Layers of the OSI Model

- -

In This Chapter

▶ The Physical Layer

▶ The Data Link Layer

▶ The Network Layer

▶ The Transport Layer

▶ The Session Layer

▶ The Presentation Layer

▶ The Application Layer

- -

*O*SI sounds like the name of a top-secret government agency you hear about only in Tom Clancy novels. What it really stands for, as far as this book is concerned, is *Open System Interconnection,* as in the Open System Interconnection Reference Model, also known as the OSI Reference Model or OSI Model (depending on how pressed for time you are).

The OSI Model breaks the various aspects of a computer network into seven distinct layers. These layers are kind of like the layers of an onion: Each successive layer envelops the layer beneath it, hiding its details from the levels above. (The OSI Model is also like an onion in that if you start to peel it apart to have a look inside, you're bound to shed a few tears.)

The OSI Model isn't itself a networking standard in the same sense that Ethernet and TCP/IP are. Rather, the *OSI Model* is a framework into which the various networking standards can fit. The OSI Model specifies what aspects of a network's operation can be addressed by various network standards. So, in a sense, the OSI Model is sort of a standard's standard.

The first three layers are sometimes called the *lower layers.* They deal with the mechanics of how information is sent from one computer to another over a network. Layers 4–7 are sometimes called the *upper layers.* They deal with how applications relate to the network through application programming interfaces.

Yes, I know the OSI Model has *seven* layers, not ten. The Part of Tens consists of chapters that present *approximately* ten topics worth knowing about. In this case, seven is close enough.

Layer 1: The Physical Layer

The bottom layer of the OSI Model is the Physical Layer. It addresses the physical characteristics of the network, such as the types of cables used to connect devices, the types of connectors used, how long the cables can be, and so on. For example, the Ethernet standard for 100BaseT cable specifies the electrical characteristics of the twisted-pair cables, the size and shape of the connectors, the maximum length of the cables, and so on.

Another aspect of the Physical Layer is that it specifies the electrical characteristics of the signals used to transmit data over cables from one network node to another. The Physical Layer doesn't define any particular meaning for those signals other than the basic binary values 0 and 1. The higher levels of the OSI model must assign meanings to the bits transmitted at the Physical Layer.

One type of Physical Layer device commonly used in networks is a *repeater*. A repeater is used to regenerate signals when you need to exceed the cable length allowed by the Physical Layer standard or when you need to redistribute a signal from one cable onto two or more cables.

An old-style 10BaseT hub is also a Physical Layer device. Technically, a hub is a *multi-port repeater* because its purpose is to regenerate every signal received on any port on all the hub's other ports. Repeaters and hubs don't examine the contents of the signals that they regenerate. If they did, they'd be working at the Data Link Layer, not at the Physical Layer. Which leads us to . . . .

Layer 2: The Data Link Layer

The *Data Link Layer* is the lowest layer at which meaning is assigned to the bits that are transmitted over the network. Data-link protocols address things, such as the size of each packet of data to be sent, a means of addressing each packet so that it's delivered to the intended recipient, and a way to ensure that two or more nodes don't try to transmit data on the network at the same time.

The Data Link Layer also provides basic error detection and correction to ensure that the data sent is the same as the data received. If an uncorrectable error occurs, the data-link standard must specify how the node is to be informed of the error so it can retransmit the data.

At the Data Link Layer, each device on the network has an address known as the *Media Access Control address,* or *MAC address.* This is the actual hardware address, assigned to the device at the factory.

You can see the MAC address for a computer's network adapter by opening a command window and running the `ipconfig /all` command, as shown in Figure 29-1. In this example, the MAC address (identified as the *physical address* in the output) of the network card is `00-50-BA-84-39-11`.

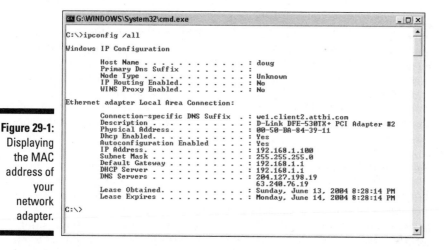

Figure 29-1:
Displaying
the MAC
address of
your
network
adapter.

```
G:\WINDOWS\System32\cmd.exe                                    _□×

C:\>ipconfig /all

Windows IP Configuration

        Host Name . . . . . . . . . . . : doug
        Primary Dns Suffix  . . . . . . :
        Node Type . . . . . . . . . . . : Unknown
        IP Routing Enabled. . . . . . . : No
        WINS Proxy Enabled. . . . . . . : No

Ethernet adapter Local Area Connection:

        Connection-specific DNS Suffix  . : we1.client2.attbi.com
        Description . . . . . . . . . . : D-Link DFE-530TX+ PCI Adapter #2
        Physical Address. . . . . . . . : 00-50-BA-84-39-11
        Dhcp Enabled. . . . . . . . . . : Yes
        Autoconfiguration Enabled . . . : Yes
        IP Address. . . . . . . . . . . : 192.168.1.100
        Subnet Mask . . . . . . . . . . : 255.255.255.0
        Default Gateway . . . . . . . . : 192.168.1.1
        DHCP Server . . . . . . . . . . : 192.168.1.1
        DNS Servers . . . . . . . . . . : 204.127.198.19
                                          63.240.76.19
        Lease Obtained. . . . . . . . . : Sunday, June 13, 2004 8:28:14 PM
        Lease Expires . . . . . . . . . : Monday, June 14, 2004 8:28:14 PM

C:\>
```

One of the most import functions of the Data Link Layer is to provide a way for packets to be sent safely over the physical media without interference from other nodes attempting to send packets at the same time. Ethernet uses a technique called CSMA/CD to accomplish this.

Switches are the most commonly used Data Link Layer devices in most networks. A *switch* is similar to a hub, but instead of regenerating incoming signals of every port, a switch examines the MAC address of every incoming packet to determine which port to send the packet to.

Layer 3: The Network Layer

The *Network Layer* handles the task of routing network messages from one computer to another. The two most popular Layer-3 protocols are IP (which is usually paired with TCP) and IPX (normally paired with SPX for use with Novell and Windows networks).

One important function of the Network Layer is *logical addressing*. As you know, every network device has a physical address called a *MAC address,* which is assigned to the device at the factory. When you buy a network interface card to install in a computer, the MAC address of that card is fixed and can't be changed. But what if you want to use some other addressing scheme to refer to the computers and other devices on your network? This is where the concept of logical addressing comes in; a logical address gives a network device a place where it can be accessed on the network — using an address that you assign.

Logical addresses are created and used by Network Layer protocols, such as IP or IPX. The Network Layer protocol translates logical addresses to MAC addresses. For example, if you use IP as the Network Layer protocol, devices on the network are assigned IP addresses, such as `207.120.67.30`. Because the IP protocol must use a Data Link Layer protocol to actually send packets to devices, IP must know how to translate the IP address of a device into the correct MAC address for the device. You can use the `ipconfig` command to see the IP address of your computer. The IP address shown in that figure is `192.168.1.100`.

Another important function of the Network layer is *routing* — finding an appropriate path through the network. Routing comes into play when a computer on one network needs to send a packet to a computer on another network. In this case, a Network Layer device called a *router* forwards the packet to the destination network. An important feature of routers is that they can be used to connect networks that use different Layer-2 protocols. For example, a router can be used to connect a local-area network that uses Ethernet to a wide-area network that runs on a different set of low-level protocols, such as T1.

Layer 4: The Transport Layer

The Transport Layer is the basic layer at which one network computer communicates with another network computer. The Transport Layer is where you'll find one of the most popular networking protocols: TCP. The main purpose of the Transport Layer is to ensure that packets move over the network reliably and without errors. The Transport Layer does this by establishing connections between network devices, acknowledging the receipt of packets, and resending packets that aren't received or are corrupted when they arrive.

In many cases, the Transport Layer protocol divides large messages into smaller packets that can be sent over the network efficiently. The Transport Layer protocol reassembles the message on the receiving end, making sure that all packets contained in a single transmission are received and no data is lost.

Layer 4a: The Lemon-Pudding Layer

The Lemon-Pudding Layer is squeezed in between the rather dry and taste-less Transport and Session Layers to add flavor and moistness.

Layer 5: The Session Layer

The Session Layer establishes *sessions* (instances of communication and data exchange) between network nodes. A session must be established before data can be transmitted over the network. The Session Layer makes sure that these sessions are properly established and maintained.

Layer 6: The Presentation Layer

The Presentation Layer is responsible for converting the data sent over the network from one type of representation to another. For example, the Presentation Layer can apply sophisticated compression techniques so fewer bytes of data are required to represent the information when it's sent over the network. At the other end of the transmission, the Transport Layer then uncompresses the data.

The Presentation Layer also can scramble the data before it's transmitted and then unscramble it at the other end, using a sophisticated encryption technique that even Sherlock Holmes would have trouble breaking.

Layer 7: The Application Layer

The highest layer of the OSI model, the Application Layer, deals with the tech-niques that application programs use to communicate with the network. The name of this layer is a little confusing because application programs (such as Excel or Word) aren't actually part of the layer. Rather, the Application Layer represents the level at which application programs *interact with the network,* using programming interfaces to request network services. One of the most commonly used application layer protocols is HTTP, which stands for HyperText Transfer Protocol. HTTP is the basis of the World Wide Web.

Index

• Symbols and Numerics •

$ (dollar sign) character in hidden shares, 255
10Base2 cable, 96
10Base5 cable, 96
10BaseT cable, 96
100 Mbps Ethernet, 83
802.11 standards for wireless networks, 174–175
2600 (magazine), 235

• A •

Access databases, 58
accessing
  files, 55, 367–368
  network resources, 29–30
accounts for users
  Administrator account, 320–322
  backups, 312
  contact information, 242
  creating, 239–241
  delegation, 244
  deleting, 247
  disabling, 243, 246
  domain, 238
  enabling, 246
  encryption, 244
  group membership, 238, 247–249
  Guest account, 321–322
  Linux operating system, 351–352
  local, 238
  logon name, 24, 243
  logon script, 245, 249–250
  passwords, 137, 238, 243, 245–246, 318–319
  profile information, 244–245
  properties, 238, 241–245
  security, 137–138, 244, 317–322
  service accounts, 322
  sharing, 326
  smart cards, 244
Active Directory, 136–137
activity indicators (switches), 96
ad hoc mode network, 170, 180
adding
  members to groups, 248–249
  printers, 35–37
administrator
  backup, 229
  resources required, 229
  responsibilities of, 18–19, 227–228, 230–232
  traits to look for, 229
  username, 23
Administrator account, 320–322
Alohanet, 174
Analog Telephone Adapter (ATA), 218–220
AND logical operator, 109
ANSI (American National Standards Institute), 85
ANSI/EIA Standard 568, 85
antennas, 171–172
antivirus programs, 335–336, 382
Apple Mac OS X Server, 139–140
AppleTalk, 363–366
application gateway, 332
Application Layer (OSI Model), 395
application server, 154
archive bit, 304
ARCnet, 82
arp command, 233
ATA (Analog Telephone Adapter), 218–220
AT&T CallVantage VoIP services, 218

• B •

backup programs, 303–304
backups
  archive bit, 304
  backup selection, 304
  CDs, 302
  copy scheme, 304, 306

backups *(continued)*
  daily scheme, 304, 306
  differential scheme, 304, 307–308
  disaster recovery plan, 301–302
  DVDs, 302
  encryption, 312
  full scheme, 305
  hard drive, 28, 381
  incremental scheme, 304, 306–307
  local, 308–309
  mirror, 134
  network, 308–309
  normal scheme, 304, 305
  security, 312
  servers, 376
  tape backups, 302, 309–310
  tape drives, 302, 310–311
  tape rotation, 309–310
  Travan drives, 302, 310
  user accounts, 312
bandwidth, 173
Baseline Security Analyzer, 234
binary numbering system, 107–109
bottlenecks, 266–270
bridges, 103–104
broadband Internet connections, 190
BSS (Basic Service Set), 179
built-in firewalls, 333–334
bus topology, 82
backups

● *C* ●

cable Internet connection, 190
cable ties, 388
cables
  cable ties, 388
  checking, 282–283
  crossover cable, 92–93
  defined, 16
  Ethernet, 81–83
  installing, 87–89
  patch cable, 87, 388
  pin connections for twisted-pair cable,
    90–91
  plenum cable, 86–87
  PVC cable, 86
  shielded twisted-pair (STP) cable, 86
    skimping on, 373–374
    solid cable, 87
    station cable, 87
    stranded cable, 87
    10Base2 cable, 96
    10Base5 cable, 96
    10BaseT cable, 96
    twisted-pair cable, 16, 83–86, 90–91
    unshielded twisted-pair (UTP) cable, 86
carrier sense multiple access with collision
      detection (CSMA/CD), 174
CDs, 302
certifications, 236
Change Permissions permission, 254
checking
    cables, 282–283
    network connection, 282–283
    network settings, 283–284
choosing
    network interface card (NIC), 98–99
    network operating system (NOS), 17
circuit-level gateway, 331–332
class C IP addresses, 113–114
classes of IP addresses
    Class A, 111–113
    Class B, 111–114
    Class C, 111–114
    Class D, 111–112
    Class E, 111–112
client computer identification, 162–166
clients
    defined, 14, 41–42
    DHCP clients, 126–127
    DNS clients, 131–132
closed-door approach to security, 315
command shell (Linux), 350
CompTIA nonprofit industry trade
      association, 236
computer equipment checklist, 231
computer identification, 162–166
computer magazines, 235, 295
computer name, 23
computer tool kit, 89, 388
computers
    dead computer, 281–282
    disk space, 280
    fan, 281
    monitor, 282

On/Off switches, 281
restarting, 280, 285–287
Sleep feature, 281
configuring
  client computer identification, 162–166
  Linux network, 352–354
  Macintosh computer for networking, 366
  network connections, 155–162
  network logon, 166–167
  network protocols, 269, 382
  Outlook for Exchange Server, 200–202
  server roles, 152–154
  WAP (wireless access point), 181–183
configuring server roles
  application server role, 154
  Configure Your Server Wizard, 152–153
  DHCP server role, 154
  DNS server role, 154
  domain controller server role, 154
  file server role, 153, 256–259
  mail server role, 154
  print server role, 153
  remote access/VPN server role, 154
  streaming media server role, 154
  terminal server role, 154
  WINS server role, 154
connecting from home
  Outlook Web Access, 199, 221–223
  virtual private network (VPN), 138, 224
connecting to the Internet
  broadband connections, 190
  cable, 190
  DSL, 190
  Internet Service Provider (ISP), 189
  routers, 191
  shared Internet connection, 191
  T1 dedicated high-speed digital line, 191
  T3 dedicated high-speed digital line, 191
connectors, 91–92
contact information for user account, 242
copy backup scheme, 304, 306
copying files, 375
costs
  file server, 251
  switches, 389
  VoIP (Voice over IP), 219
  Windows Server 2003, 139
counter logs, 275–277
counters, 273–274

Create Files/Write Data permission, 254
Create Folders/Append Data permission, 254
creating
  groups, 247–248
  intranet pages, 212–213
  passwords, 319–320
  user accounts, 239–241
creating a network plan, 63–64
crimp tool, 89
crossover cable, 92–93
CSMA/CD (carrier sense multiple access
    with collision detection), 174

• *D* •

daily backup scheme, 304, 306
daisy-chaining hubs or switches, 96–98
Data Link Layer (OSI Model), 392–393
database servers, 71
databases
  directory databases, 136
  sharing, 58
dead computer, 281–282
dedicated servers, 14–15, 69
delegation for user accounts, 244
Delete permission, 254
Delete Subfolders and Files permission, 254
deleting
  files, 375
  user accounts, 247
Dell 725N storage appliance, 252
DHCP (Dynamic Host Configuration
    Protocol)
  alternative to, 120
  how it works, 120
  IP addresses, 119–120
  options, 120
  reservations, 122–123
  setting up, 120–123
DHCP clients, 126–127
DHCP servers
  configuring DHCP server role, 154
  lease duration, 124
  network server, 120–121
  reservations, 122–123
  scopes, 121–122
  Windows Server 2003 DHCP server,
      124–126, 154
  wireless access point (WAP), 183

diagrams, 72–73
differential backup scheme, 304, 307–308
digital certificates, 138
directories, 26
directory databases, 136
directory services, 135–137
disabling user accounts, 243, 246
disaster recovery plan, 301–302
disk space, 251, 280
disk striping, 269
disks (software disks), 390
distributions of Linux, 344
DNS (Domain Name System), 127–129
DNS clients, 131–132
DNS servers, 130–131, 154
documentation
  back schedule, 230
  computer equipment inventory, 230–231
  network diagram, 230–231
  passwords, 230, 389
  system information, 68–69, 230
  tracking log for network problems, 291–292
  written documentation, 384–385, 389
dollar sign ($) character in hidden
      shares, 255
domain controller server, 154
domain name, 24, 127–130
Domain Name System (DNS), 127–129
domain networks, 24
domain user accounts, 238
domains, 127–129
dotted-decimal notation, 110–111
down (defined), 11
downloading service packs, 152
downtime, 377–378, 383
drive letters, 33
DSL Internet connection, 190
duct tape, 387
DVDs, 302
Dynamic Host Configuration Protocol
      (DHCP)
  alternative to, 120
  how it works, 120
  IP addresses, 119–120
  options, 120
  reservations, 122–123
  setting up, 120–123

• E •

802.11 standards for wireless networks,
      174–175
Electronic Industries Association (EIA), 85
enabling user accounts, 246
encryption
  backups, 312
  user accounts, 244
equipment checklist, 231
error messages, 280, 283
Ethereal program, 234
Ethernet, 81–83, 174
event logs, 290–291
Event Viewer (Windows Server 2003),
      290–291
Exchange Server
  configuring Outlook, 200–202
  E-mail Addresses tab, 197–198
  Exchange Advanced tab, 199–200
  Exchange Features tab, 197–199
  Exchange General tab, 196–197
  Exchange System Manager console,
      195–196
  IMAP4, 199
  mailboxes, 196–197
  Outlook Mobile Access, 198
  Outlook Web Access, 199, 221–223
  POP3, 199
  Up-to-Date Notifications, 199
  User Initiated Synchronization, 198
  viewing another mailbox, 202–205
exclusions, 122

• F •

fan (on computer), 281
Fast Ethernet, 83
FCC (Federal Communications
      Commission), 173
Fedora Linux distribution, 344
File and Printer Sharing feature
  Windows Vista, 44–45
  Windows XP, 42–43
file server
  configuring file server role, 153, 256–259
  cost, 251–252
  defined, 70, 251

managing, 259–262
RAID (Redundant Array of Inexpensive Disks), 251–252
file sharing
  benefits of, 12
  File and Printer Sharing feature (Windows Vista), 44–45
  File and Printer Sharing feature (Windows XP), 42–43
  Macintosh network, 367
  network drive, 26–28
  network operating system (NOS), 134
file system, 134
files
  accessing, 55, 367–368
  copying, 375
  deleting, 375
  offline files, 59–60
  permissions, 253
firewalls
  application gateway, 332
  circuit-level gateway, 331–332
  defined, 192, 327
  packet filters, 329–331
  perimeter, 193, 329
  servers, 192, 328
  stateful packet inspection (SPI), 331
  Windows Vista built-in firewall, 193–194, 333–334
  Windows XP built-in firewall, 193–194, 333–334
fish tape, 89
folders
  home folder, 27
  permissions, 253
  Public folder, 48–50
  shared folders, 26–28, 31–34, 45–48
  shares, 254
FQDN (fully qualified domain name), 129–130
fractional T3 dedicated high-speed digital line, 191
free space, 378, 382
frequency, 171–172
full backup scheme, 305
Full control permission, 253

• G •

generating passwords, 320
Gigabit Ethernet, 83
GNOME desktop (Linux), 348–349
granting permissions, 262–264
group accounts
  adding members, 248–249
  creating, 247–248
  defined, 238, 247
  security, 324–325
Guest account, 321–322

• H •

hackers, 314, 330
hard drive backup, 28, 381
hidden shares, 255
home access to work network
  Outlook Web Access, 199, 221–223
  virtual private network (VPN), 138, 224
home folder, 27
host ID (IP addresses), 110
hostname command, 233
Hotfix Checker program, 234
HTTP (HyperText Transfer Protocol), 395
hubs
  cost of, 94
  daisy-chaining, 96–98
  defined, 10–11, 16
  network performance, 278
  stackable hubs, 98
  versus switches, 95
Hughes, Phil, *Linux For Dummies Quick Reference,* 3rd Edition, 341
HyperText Transfer Protocol (HTTP), 395

• I •

IBM Token Ring, 82
IBSS (Independent Basic Service Set), 180
IIS (Internet Information Services), 154, 210–215
incremental backup scheme, 304, 306–307
InformationWeek (magazine), 235
InfoWorld (magazine), 235

infrastructure, 71–72, 270
infrastructure mode network, 170, 179
installing
  Linux operating system, 345–346
  Microsoft Office, 54
  network cables, 87–89
  network interface card (NIC), 99–100
  network operating system (NOS), 140–149
  Samba, 357
  server operating system, 143–144
  switches, 95
Internet
  connecting to, 189–191
  defined, 11
  security, 376–377
Internet Information Services (IIS),
  154, 210–215
Internet Service Provider (ISP), 189
intranet
  creating pages, 212–213
  defined, 207–208
  Internet Information Services (IIS),
    210–215
  publishing applications, 208
  requirements, 209–210
  setting up, 209–210
  transaction applications, 208
inventory, 65–68
IP addresses
  binary numbering system, 107–109
  classes, 111–114
  defined, 110
  DHCP (Dynamic Host Configuration
    Protocol), 119–123
  dotted-decimal notation, 110–111
  exclusions, 122
  host ID, 110
  logical operations, 109
  multicast address, 111
  network address translation (NAT),
    118–119
  network ID, 110
  private, 118
  public, 118
  scopes, 121–122
  subnet masks, 116–118
  subnets, 115–116
  subnetting, 114–116
IP next generation (IPng), 114

IP spoofing, 330
ipconfig command, 233
IPSec, 224
IPv4, 114
IPv6, 114
ISP (Internet Service Provider), 189

• J •

jacks, 93–94

• K •

Kelly, Timothy V., *VoIP For Dummies,* 217

• L •

LAN (local-area network), 10–11
LAWN (local-area wireless network), 170
LeBlanc, Dee-Ann, *Linux For Dummies,*
    8th Edition, 341
library, 234–235, 294–295
licenses, 384
Linux For Dummies, 8th Edition
    (LeBlanc), 341
Linux For Dummies Quick Reference, 3rd
    Edition (Hughes and Navratilova), 341
Linux operating system
  as alternative to Windows, 15, 71, 342–343
  command shell, 350
  development history, 139, 341
  Fedora distribution, 344
  GNOME desktop, 348–349
  installing, 345–346
  Linux-Mandriva distribution, 344
  logging off, 348
  logging on, 346–348
  network configuration, 352–354
  restarting networking services, 354–355
  Samba, 355–361
  shutting down, 348
  Slackware distribution, 344
  StarOffice program suite, 342
  SuSE distribution, 344
  Unix, 71, 139
  user accounts, 351–352
  X Window System, 342
Linux-Mandriva distribution, 344

List Folder Contents permission, 253
List Folder/Read Data permission, 254
local backup, 308–309, 381
local resources, 21–22
local user accounts, 238
local-area network (LAN), 10–11
local-area wireless network (LAWN), 170
log off, 24–25
log on, 24–25
log out, 24–25
logging off
  Linux operating system log off, 348
  network log off, 39
logging on
  Linux operating system logon, 346–348
  network logon, 24–25
  network operating system (NOS)
     logon, 149
logical addressing, 394
logical operations, 109
login, 24–25
logon name, 24, 243
logon script
  benefits of using, 325–326
  creating, 249–250
  defined, 245
logs
  counter logs, 275–277
  event logs, 290–291
  network performance, 275–277
  trace logs, 275
Lowe, Doug, *Networking All-in-One Desk
     Reference For Dummies,* 2nd Edition, 3
lower layers of the OSI Model, 391

• *M* •

MAC addresses, 104, 393–394
Mac OS X Server, 139–140, 364–365
Macintosh network
  accessing shared files, 367–368
  AppleTalk, 363–366
  configuring a Mac for networking, 366
  file sharing, 367
  Mac OS X Server, 364–365
  Macs and PCs, 368–369
  Open Transport, 364
  printers, 366–367
magazines, 235, 295

mail servers
  configuring, 154
  defined, 71
  Microsoft Exchange Server 2003, 195–205
mainframe computers, 17
malfunctioning components, 270
managing
  file server, 259–262
  users, 232–233
manuals, 390
mapping network drives, 31–34
McAfee's VirusScan, 336
Media Access Control address, 104, 393–394
memory leak, 278
Microsoft Exchange Server 2003
  configuring Outlook, 200–202
  E-mail Addresses tab, 197–198
  Exchange Advanced tab, 199–200
  Exchange Features tab, 197–199
  Exchange General tab, 196–197
  Exchange System Manager console,
     195–196
  IMAP4, 199
  mailboxes, 196
  Outlook Mobile Access, 198
  Outlook Web Access, 199, 221–223
  POP3, 199
  Up-to-Date Notifications, 199
  User Initiated Synchronization, 198
  viewing another mailbox, 202–205
Microsoft Internet Information Services, 154
Microsoft Office
  accessing network files, 55
  installing, 54
  networking features, 53–58
  Office Resource Kit (ORK), 54
  user templates, 56–58
  workgroup templates, 55–58
Microsoft Outlook
  configuring for Exchange Server, 200–202
  Outlook Web Access, 199, 221–223
  viewing another mailbox, 202–205
Microsoft Product Activation feature,
     149–151
Microsoft System Information, 68–69
Microsoft Visio, 72–73
mirror, 134
Modify permission, 253
monitor, 282

monitoring network performance, 272–275
multiboot, 141
multicast address, 111
multitasking, 135

• N •

names
  computer name, 23
  domain name, 24, 127–130
  logon name, 24, 243
  network administrator, 23
  network resources, 23
  networks, 24
  share name, 46–47, 255
  username, 22–23, 25, 238, 317
  workgroup name, 24
Navratilova, Viktorie, *Linux For Dummies Quick Reference,* 3rd Edition, 341
nbtstat command, 233
netstat command, 233
NetWare (Novell), 15, 71, 337
network address translation (NAT), 118–119
network administrator
  backup, 229
  resources required, 229
  responsibilities of, 18–19, 227–228, 230–232
  traits to look for, 229
  username, 23
Network Attached Storage (NAS), 252
network backup, 308–309
network cables
  cable ties, 388
  crossover cable, 92–93
  defined, 16
  Ethernet, 81–83
  installing, 87–89
  patch cable, 87, 388
  pin connections for twisted-pair cable, 90–91
  plenum cable, 86–87
  PVC cable, 86
  shielded twisted-pair (STP) cable, 86
  skimping on, 373–374
  solid cable, 87
  station cable, 87
  stranded cable, 87
  10Base2 cable, 96
  10Base5 cable, 96
  10BaseT cable, 96
  twisted-pair cable, 16, 83–86, 90–91
  unshielded twisted-pair (UTP) cable, 86
network certifications, 236
Network Computing (magazine), 235
network connection
  checking, 282–283
  configuring, 155–162
  troubleshooting, 282–283
  Windows Vista, 160–162
  Windows XP, 156–159
network drives
  defined, 26–28
  drive letters, 33
  mapping, 31–34
network ID (IP addresses), 110
network interface, 10
network interface card (NIC)
  choosing, 98–99
  defined, 16
  extras, 388–389
  installing, 99–100
Network Layer (OSI Model), 393–394
network license, 13
network logon, 166–167
Network (magazine), 235
Network Monitor program, 234
network names. *See* names
network operating system (NOS)
  Apple Mac OS X Server, 139–140
  choosing, 17
  directory services, 135–137
  file-sharing services, 134
  function of, 15–17
  installing, 140–149
  Linux, 15, 71, 139
  logging on, 149
  multiboot, 141
  multitasking, 135
  network support, 133–134
  Novell NetWare, 15, 71
  security services, 137–138
  service packs, 152
  testing the installation, 152
  upgrading, 141
  Windows Server 2003, 15–17, 71, 138–139
  Windows Server 2007, 15, 71

network performance
  bottlenecks, 266–270
  counters, 273–274
  defined, 265
  hubs, 278
  logs, 275–277
  malfunctioning components, 270
  memory leak, 278
  monitoring, 272–275
  scheduled tasks, 278
  servers, 268–270
  spyware, 278
  switches, 278
  troubleshooting, 265–266
  tuning, 271
network plan
  creating, 63–64
  diagrams, 72–73
  examples, 74–79
  infrastructure, 71–72
  inventory, 65–68
  purpose of, 64–65
  system information, 68–69
network protocols, 269, 382
network resources
  accessing, 29–30
  defined, 21–22
  names, 23
network rights, 324
network security. *See* security
network server
  restarting, 280, 285, 288–290
  users, 285
network services, restarting, 287–288
network settings
  checking, 283–284
  troubleshooting, 283–284
network software, 16
network starter kit, 101
network storage
  disk space, 251
  file server, 251–252, 256–262
  permissions, 252–254, 262–264
  shares, 254–255
  storage appliances, 252
network support, 133–134
network topologies, 82

network troubleshooting
  basic steps, 280
  dead computer, 281–282
  documentation, 291–292
  error messages, 280, 283
  event logs, 290–291
  narrowing the cause of the problem, 284
  network connection, 282–283
  network performance, 265–266
  network server, 285, 288–290
  network services, 287–288
  network settings, 283–284
  printing problems, 376
network-discovery program, 231
Networking All-in-One Desk Reference For Dummies, 2nd Edition (Lowe), 3
networks
  benefits of, 12–13
  defined, 10–11
  how they work, 15–17
  logging off, 39
  logging on, 24–25
  names, 24
NetworkView Software's NetworkView, 231
NIC (network interface card)
  choosing, 98–99
  defined, 16
  extras, 388–389
  installing, 99–100
normal backup scheme, 304–305
Norton AntiVirus (Symantec), 336
Norton Utilities (Symantec), 234
NOS (network operating system)
  Apple Mac OS X Server, 139–140
  choosing, 17
  directory services, 135–137
  file-sharing services, 134
  function of, 15–17
  installing, 140–149
  Linux, 15, 71, 139
  logging on, 149
  multiboot, 141
  multitasking, 135
  network support, 133–134
  Novell NetWare, 15, 71
  security services, 137–138
  service packs, 152

NOS *(continued)*
 testing the installation, 152
 upgrading, 141
 Windows Server 2003, 15–17, 71, 138–139
 Windows Server 2007, 15, 71
NOT logical operator, 109
Novell NetWare, 15, 71, 337
nslookup command, 233

• O •

Office (Microsoft)
 accessing network files, 55
 installing, 54
 networking features, 53–58
 Office Resource Kit (ORK), 54
 user templates, 56–58
 workgroup templates, 55–58
OfficeScan (Trend Micro), 336
offline (defined), 11
offline files, 59–60
on the network (defined), 11
100 Mbps Ethernet, 83
online (defined), 11
On/Off switches, 281
Open Transport, 364
open-door approach to security, 315
OR logical operator, 109
OSI Model
 Application Layer, 395
 Data Link Layer, 392–393
 defined, 391
 lower layers, 391
 Network Layer, 393–394
 Physical Layer, 392
 Presentation Layer, 395
 Session Layer, 395
 Transport Layer, 394
 upper layers, 391
Outlook
 configuring for Exchange Server, 200–202
 Outlook Web Access, 199, 221–223
 viewing another mailbox, 202–205

• P •

packet filters, 329–331
packet sniffer, 234
PartitionMagic (PowerQuest), 345–346
passwords
 creating, 319–320
 generating, 320
 logging on, 24–25
 policies, 238
 resetting, 245–246
 user accounts, 137, 238, 243, 245–246,
  318–319
patch cable, 87, 388
patch panels, 93–94
patches, 337–338
PatchLink program, 338
PC (personal computer), 17–18
peer-to-peer network, 14–15, 69
performance
 bottlenecks, 266–270
 counters, 273–274
 defined, 265
 hubs, 278
 logs, 275–277
 malfunctioning components, 270
 memory leak, 278
 monitoring, 272–275
 scheduled tasks, 278
 servers, 268–270
 spyware, 278
 switches, 278
 troubleshooting, 265–266
 tuning, 271
Performance Monitor tool (Windows
  Server 2003), 272–275
perimeter, 193, 329
permissions
 Access Control List (ACL), 253
 Change Permissions permission, 254
 Create Files/Write Data permission, 254
 Create Folders/Append Data
  permission, 254
 defined, 252
 Delete permission, 254

Delete Subfolders and Files permission, 254
Full control permission, 253
granting, 262–264
List Folder Contents permission, 253
List Folder/Read Data permission, 254
Modify permission, 253
Read & Execute permission, 253
Read Extended Attributes permission, 254
Read permission, 253
Read Permissions permission, 254
security, 323–324
special permissions, 253–254
Synchronize permission, 254
Take Ownership permission, 254
Traverse Folder/Execute File
    permission, 254
Write Attributes permission, 254
Write Extended Attributes permission, 254
Write permission, 253
personal computer (PC), 17–18
Physical Layer (OSI Model), 392
physical security, 315–317
pin connections for twisted-pair cable,
    90–91
ping command, 233
plan
  creating, 63–64
  diagrams, 72–73
  examples, 74–79
  infrastructure, 71–72
  inventory, 65–68
  purpose of, 64–65
  system information, 68–69
plenum cable, 86–87
plenum space, 86–87
policies
  passwords, 238
  security, 326
PowerQuest's PartitionMagic, 345–346
Presentation Layer (OSI Model), 395
print servers, 70, 153
print spooling, 34
printers
  adding, 35–37
  File and Printer Sharing feature
      (Windows Vista), 44–45
  File and Printer Sharing feature
      (Windows XP), 42–43

Macintosh network, 366–367
  printing, 34–39
  sharing, 42–45, 50–53
  troubleshooting printing problems, 376
private IP addresses, 118
Product Activation feature, 149–151
profile information for user accounts,
    244–245
programs
  antivirus programs, 335–336, 382
  antivirus software, 382
  backup programs, 303–304
  Baseline Security Analyzer, 234
  disks, 390
  Ethereal, 234
  Hotfix Checker, 234
  licenses, 384
  memory leak, 278
  Microsoft Office, 53–58
  network license, 13
  Network Monitor, 234
  network-discovery program, 231
  packet sniffers, 234
  PatchLink, 338
  protocol analyzers, 234
  sharing, 13
  Sniffer, 234
  StarOffice program suite (Linux), 342
  System Information, 234
properties of user accounts, 238, 241–245
protocol analyzer, 234
PSTN (public switched telephone
    network), 218
Public folder, 48–50
public IP addresses, 118
publishing applications, 208
purpose of a network plan, 64–65
PVC cable, 86

• R •

radio spectrum, 173–174
radio waves, 171–172
RAID (Redundant Array of Inexpensive
    Disks), 251–252
range of wireless networks, 175–176
Read & Execute permission, 253
Read Extended Attributes permission, 254

Read permission, 253
Read Permissions permission, 254
remote access/VPN server, 154
removing
  files, 375
  user accounts, 247
repeaters, 101–103
reservations, 123
resetting passwords, 245–246
resources
  local resources, 21–22
  network resources, 21–23, 29–30
  sharing, 12
restarting
  computer, 280, 285–287
  Linux networking services, 354–355
  network server, 280, 285, 288–290
  network services, 287–288
  servers, 374–375
ring topology, 82
RJ-45 connectors, 91–92
roaming, 179–180
route command, 233
routers, 104–105, 191, 394
routing, 394

• S •

Samba
  defined, 355–356
  installing, 357
  Samba Server Configuration tool, 358–361
  security, 359–360
  shares, 356, 360–361
  SMB (Server Message Block) protocol, 356
  starting, 357–358
  stopping, 357–358
scheduling
  downtime, 383
  tasks, 278
scopes, 121–122
script, 245, 249–250, 325–326
security
  administrator user account, 320
  antivirus programs, 335–336, 382
  backups, 312
  closed-door approach, 315
  digital certificates, 138

firewalls, 192–194, 327–334
group accounts, 324–325
hackers, 314, 330
importance of, 314
Internet, 376–377
IP spoofing, 330
network operating system (NOS), 137–138
open-door approach, 315
patches, 337–338
permissions, 323–324
physical security, 315–317
policies, 326
Trojan horse, 314, 335
user accounts, 137–138, 244, 317–322
user rights, 322–323
virtual private network (VPN), 138
viruses, 334–337, 382
worms, 335
server operating system, 143–144
server roles
  application server role, 154
  Configure Your Server Wizard, 152–153
  DHCP server role, 154
  DNS server role, 154
  domain controller server role, 154
  file server role, 153, 256–259
  mail server role, 154
  print server role, 153
  remote access/VPN server role, 154
  streaming media server role, 154
  terminal server role, 154
  WINS server role, 154
servers
  application server, 154
  backups, 376
  configuring server roles, 152–154
  database servers, 71
  dedicated servers, 14–15, 69
  defined, 13–14, 41–42
  DHCP servers, 120–126, 154, 183
  DNS servers, 130–131, 154
  domain controller server, 154
  file server, 70, 153, 251–252, 256–262
  firewalls, 192, 328
  free space, 378, 382
  Mac OS X Server, 364–365
  mail servers, 71, 154, 195–205
  network performance, 268–270

network server, 280, 285, 288–290
print servers, 70, 153
remote access/VPN server, 154
restarting, 374–375
streaming media server, 154
terminal server, 154
turning on/off, 374–375
Web servers, 70–71, 210–212
WINS server, 154
service accounts, 322
service packs, 152, 337
service set identifier (SSID), 170, 179
Session Layer (OSI Model), 395
setting up an intranet, 209–210
share name, 46–47, 255
shared folders
  defined, 26–28
  drive letters, 33
  mapping, 31–34
  Windows Vista, 47–48
  Windows XP, 45–47
shares, 254–255
sharing
  databases, 58
  File and Printer Sharing feature
    (Windows Vista), 44–45
  File and Printer Sharing feature
    (Windows XP), 42–43
  files, 12, 26–28, 42–45, 367
  Internet connection, 191
  printers, 42–45, 50–53
  programs, 13
  resources, 12
  user accounts, 326
shielded twisted-pair (STP) cable, 86
shutting down Linux operating system, 348
skimping on cables, 373–374
Skype software-only VoIP system, 218
Slackware Linux distribution, 344
Sleep feature on computers, 281
smart cards, 244
sneakernet, 10
Sniffer program (Sniffer Technologies), 234
software, 16. *See also* programs
software disks, 390
software patches, 337–338
software-only VoIP systems, 218

solid cable, 87
spare parts, 383, 387–389
special permissions, 253–254
spectrums, 173–174
SPI (stateful packet inspection), 331
spooling print jobs, 34
spyware, 278
SSID (service set identifier), 170, 179
stackable hubs, 98
standards for wireless networks, 174–175
star topology, 82
StarOffice program suite (Linux), 342
starter kit, 101
stateful packet inspection (SPI), 331
station cable, 87
storage
  disk space, 251
  file server, 251–252, 256–262
  permissions, 252–254, 262–264
  shares, 254–255
  storage appliances, 252
STP (shielded twisted-pair) cable, 86
stranded cable, 87
streaming media server, 154
subdomains, 129
subnet masks, 116–118
subnets, 115–116
subnetting, 114–116
surge protectors, 281
SuSE Linux distribution, 344
switches
  activity indicators, 96
  costs, 389
  daisy-chaining, 96–98
  Data Link Layer (OSI Model), 393
  defined, 16
  versus hubs, 95
  installing, 95
  network performance, 278
  ports, 95–96
Symantec
  Norton AntiVirus, 336
  Norton Utilities, 234
Synchronize permission, 254
system information, 68–69
System Information program, 234

• T •

Take Ownership permission, 254
tape backups, 302, 309–310
tape drives, 302, 310–311
tape rotation, 309–310
task scheduling, 278
TCP/IP
  DHCP (Dynamic Host Configuration
    Protocol), 119–123
  DNS (Domain Name System), 127–129
  IP addresses, 107, 110–123
TCP/IP diagnostic commands, 233
TCP/IP ports, 329–330
telephone network, 217–220
templates
  user templates, 56–57
  workgroup templates, 55–58
10Base2 cable, 96
10Base5 cable, 96
10BaseT cable, 96
terminal server, 154
testing network operating system (NOS)
    installation, 152
third-party utilities, 234
Token Ring, 82
T1 dedicated high-speed digital line, 191
tools
  computer tool kit, 89, 388
  crimp tool, 89
  duct tape, 387
  fish tape, 89
  wire cutters, 89
  wire strippers, 89
topologies, 82
trace logs, 275
`tracert` command, 233
training users, 293–294, 384
transaction applications, 208
Transport Layer (OSI Model), 394
Travan drives, 302, 310
Traverse Folder/Execute File
    permission, 254
Trend Micro's OfficeScan, 336
Trojan horse, 314, 335

troubleshooting
  basic steps, 280
  dead computer, 281–282
  documentation, 291–292
  error messages, 280, 283
  event logs, 290–291
  narrowing the cause of the problem, 284
  network connection, 282–283
  network performance, 265–266
  network server, 285, 288–290
  network services, 287–288
  network settings, 283–284
  printing problems, 376
T3 dedicated high-speed digital line, 191
tuning network performance, 271
turning on/off servers, 374–375
2600 (magazine), 235
twisted-pair cable
  categories, 85
  defined, 16, 83
  pairs, 85–86
  plenum, 86
  PVC, 86
  RJ-45 connectors, 90–91
  shielded twisted-pair (STP), 86
  unshielded twisted-pair (UTP), 84, 86

• U •

Unix, 71, 139
unshielded twisted-pair (UTP) cable, 86
up (defined), 11
updates, 337–338
upgrading the network operating system
    (NOS), 141
upper layers of the OSI Model, 391
user accounts
  Administrator account, 320–322
  backups, 312
  contact information, 242
  creating, 239–241
  delegation, 244
  deleting, 247
  disabling, 243, 246
  domain, 238

enabling, 246
encryption, 244
group membership, 238, 247–249
Guest account, 321–322
Linux operating system, 351–352
local, 238
logon name, 24, 243
logon script, 245, 249–250
passwords, 137, 238, 243, 245–246, 318–319
profile information, 244–245
properties, 238, 241–245
security, 137–138, 244, 317–322
service accounts, 322
sharing, 326
smart cards, 244
user IDs, 22–25
user profile, 325
user rights, 322–323
user templates, 56–57
username, 22–25, 238, 317
users
    downtime, 377–378, 383
    library, 294–295
    managing, 232–233
    network server, 285
    permissions, 252–254, 262–264
    security policies, 326
    shares, 254–255
    training, 293–294, 384
utilities, 234. *See also* programs
UTP (unshielded twisted-pair) cable, 86

● *V* ●

versions of Windows Server 2003, 138
virtual memory, 269
virtual private network (VPN), 138, 224
viruses, 334–337, 382
VirusScan (McAfee), 336
Visio (Microsoft), 72–73
VoIP (Voice over IP)
    advantages of, 219
    Analog Telephone Adapter (ATA), 218–220
    AT&T CallVantage VoIP services, 218
    cost of, 219
    defined, 217
    disadvantages of, 220
    features, 219

how it works, 217–218
Skype, 218
software-only VoIP systems, 218
Vonage VoIP services, 218
VoIP For Dummies (Kelly), 217
Vonage VoIP services, 218
VPN (virtual private network), 138, 224

● *W* ●

wall jacks, 93–94
WAP (wireless access point)
    ad hoc network, 180
    Basic Service Set (BSS), 179
    configuring, 180–182
    functions of, 177–178
    infrastructure mode network, 170, 179
    multifunction, 179
    roaming, 179–180
    security, 377
    Service Set Identifier (SSID), 179
    wireless bridge, 180
wavelength, 171–172
Web servers, 70–71, 210–212
WEP (wired equivalent privacy), 182
Wi-Fi, 170
Windows & .NET (magazine), 235
Windows Resource Kit (book), 295
Windows Server 2003
    Configure Your Server Wizard, 152–153
    costs, 139
    Event Viewer, 290–291
    features, 138
    Performance Monitor tool, 272–275
    popularity of, 15
    tweaking, 17, 71
    versions, 138–139
Windows Server 2007, 15, 71
Windows Update, 337
Windows Vista
    computer identification, 164–166
    File and Printer Sharing feature, 44–45
    firewall, 193–194, 333–334
    network connections, 160–162
    offline files, 59–60
    Public folder, 48–50
    shared folders, 47–48
    shared printers, 52–53

Windows XP
  computer identification, 163–164
  File and Printer Sharing feature, 42–43
  firewall, 193–194, 333–334
  network connections, 156–159
  offline files, 59–60
  shared folders, 45–47
  shared printers, 51–52
  wireless networks, 183–186
WINS server, 154
wire cutters, 89
wire strippers, 89
wired equivalent privacy (WEP), 182
wireless access point. *See* WAP
wireless bridge, 180
wireless local-area network (WLAN), 170
wireless network adapter, 176–177
wireless networks
  ad hoc mode network, 170, 180
  Alohanet, 174
  Basic Service Set (BSS), 179
  defined, 10, 169–170
  DHCP servers, 183
  how they work, 171–173
  Independent Basic Service Set (IBSS), 180
  infrastructure mode network, 170, 179
  range of, 175–176
  roaming, 179–180
  service set identifier (SSID), 170, 179

standards, 174–175
WAP (wireless access point), 170, 177–182, 377
Wi-Fi, 170
Windows XP, 183–186
wireless bridge, 180
WLAN (wireless local-area network), 170
workgroup name, 24
workgroup networks, 24
workgroup templates, 55–58
working from home
  Outlook Web Access, 199, 221–223
  virtual private network (VPN), 138, 224
worms, 335
Write Attributes permission, 254
Write Extended Attributes permission, 254
Write permission, 253

• X •

X Window System (Linux), 342
XOR logical operator, 109

• Y •

Yosemite Backup (Yosemite Technology), 303

BUSINESS, CAREERS & PERSONAL FINANCE

0-7645-9847-3

0-7645-2431-3

Also available:

- Business Plans Kit For Dummies
  0-7645-9794-9
- Economics For Dummies
  0-7645-5726-2
- Grant Writing For Dummies
  0-7645-8416-2
- Home Buying For Dummies
  0-7645-5331-3
- Managing For Dummies
  0-7645-1771-6
- Marketing For Dummies
  0-7645-5600-2

- Personal Finance For Dummies
  0-7645-2590-5*
- Resumes For Dummies
  0-7645-5471-9
- Selling For Dummies
  0-7645-5363-1
- Six Sigma For Dummies
  0-7645-6798-5
- Small Business Kit For Dummies
  0-7645-5984-2
- Starting an eBay Business For Dummies
  0-7645-6924-4
- Your Dream Career For Dummies
  0-7645-9795-7

HOME & BUSINESS COMPUTER BASICS

0-470-05432-8

0-471-75421-8

Also available:

- Cleaning Windows Vista For Dummies
  0-471-78293-9
- Excel 2007 For Dummies
  0-470-03737-7
- Mac OS X Tiger For Dummies
  0-7645-7675-5
- MacBook For Dummies
  0-470-04859-X
- Macs For Dummies
  0-470-04849-2
- Office 2007 For Dummies
  0-470-00923-3

- Outlook 2007 For Dummies
  0-470-03830-6
- PCs For Dummies
  0-7645-8958-X
- Salesforce.com For Dummies
  0-470-04893-X
- Upgrading & Fixing Laptops For Dummies
  0-7645-8959-8
- Word 2007 For Dummies
  0-470-03658-3
- Quicken 2007 For Dummies
  0-470-04600-7

FOOD, HOME, GARDEN, HOBBIES, MUSIC & PETS

0-7645-8404-9

0-7645-9904-6

Also available:

- Candy Making For Dummies
  0-7645-9734-5
- Card Games For Dummies
  0-7645-9910-0
- Crocheting For Dummies
  0-7645-4151-X
- Dog Training For Dummies
  0-7645-8418-9
- Healthy Carb Cookbook For Dummies
  0-7645-8476-6
- Home Maintenance For Dummies
  0-7645-5215-5

- Horses For Dummies
  0-7645-9797-3
- Jewelry Making & Beading For Dummies
  0-7645-2571-9
- Orchids For Dummies
  0-7645-6759-4
- Puppies For Dummies
  0-7645-5255-4
- Rock Guitar For Dummies
  0-7645-5356-9
- Sewing For Dummies
  0-7645-6847-7
- Singing For Dummies
  0-7645-2475-5

INTERNET & DIGITAL MEDIA

0-470-04529-9

0-470-04894-8

Also available:

- Blogging For Dummies
  0-471-77084-1
- Digital Photography For Dummies
  0-7645-9802-3
- Digital Photography All-in-One Desk Reference For Dummies
  0-470-03743-1
- Digital SLR Cameras and Photography For Dummies
  0-7645-9803-1
- eBay Business All-in-One Desk Reference For Dummies
  0-7645-8438-3
- HDTV For Dummies
  0-470-09673-X

- Home Entertainment PCs For Dummies
  0-470-05523-5
- MySpace For Dummies
  0-470-09529-6
- Search Engine Optimization For Dummies
  0-471-97998-8
- Skype For Dummies
  0-470-04891-3
- The Internet For Dummies
  0-7645-8996-2
- Wiring Your Digital Home For Dummies
  0-471-91830-X

* Separate Canadian edition also available
† Separate U.K. edition also available

Available wherever books are sold. For more information or to order direct: U.S. customers visit www.dummies.com or call 1-877-762-2974.
U.K. customers visit www.wileyeurope.com or call 0800 243407. Canadian customers visit www.wiley.ca or call 1-800-567-4797.

SPORTS, FITNESS, PARENTING, RELIGION & SPIRITUALITY

0-471-76871-5

0-7645-7841-3

Also available:
- Catholicism For Dummies
  0-7645-5391-7
- Exercise Balls For Dummies
  0-7645-5623-1
- Fitness For Dummies
  0-7645-7851-0
- Football For Dummies
  0-7645-3936-1
- Judaism For Dummies
  0-7645-5299-6
- Potty Training For Dummies
  0-7645-5417-4
- Buddhism For Dummies
  0-7645-5359-3

- Pregnancy For Dummies
  0-7645-4483-7 †
- Ten Minute Tone-Ups For Dummies
  0-7645-7207-5
- NASCAR For Dummies
  0-7645-7681-X
- Religion For Dummies
  0-7645-5264-3
- Soccer For Dummies
  0-7645-5229-5
- Women in the Bible For Dummies
  0-7645-8475-8

TRAVEL

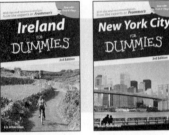

0-7645-7749-2

0-7645-6945-7

Also available:
- Alaska For Dummies
  0-7645-7746-8
- Cruise Vacations For Dummies
  0-7645-6941-4
- England For Dummies
  0-7645-4276-1
- Europe For Dummies
  0-7645-7529-5
- Germany For Dummies
  0-7645-7823-5
- Hawaii For Dummies
  0-7645-7402-7

- Italy For Dummies
  0-7645-7386-1
- Las Vegas For Dummies
  0-7645-7382-9
- London For Dummies
  0-7645-4277-X
- Paris For Dummies
  0-7645-7630-5
- RV Vacations For Dummies
  0-7645-4442-X
- Walt Disney World & Orlando
  For Dummies
  0-7645-9660-8

GRAPHICS, DESIGN & WEB DEVELOPMENT

0-7645-8815-X

0-7645-9571-7

Also available:
- 3D Game Animation For Dummies
  0-7645-8789-7
- AutoCAD 2006 For Dummies
  0-7645-8925-3
- Building a Web Site For Dummies
  0-7645-7144-3
- Creating Web Pages For Dummies
  0-470-08030-2
- Creating Web Pages All-in-One Desk
  Reference For Dummies
  0-7645-4345-8
- Dreamweaver 8 For Dummies
  0-7645-9649-7

- InDesign CS2 For Dummies
  0-7645-9572-5
- Macromedia Flash 8 For Dummies
  0-7645-9691-8
- Photoshop CS2 and Digital
  Photography For Dummies
  0-7645-9580-6
- Photoshop Elements 4 For Dummies
  0-471-77483-9
- Syndicating Web Sites with RSS Feeds
  For Dummies
  0-7645-8848-6
- Yahoo! SiteBuilder For Dummies
  0-7645-9800-7

NETWORKING, SECURITY, PROGRAMMING & DATABASES

0-7645-7728-X

0-471-74940-0

Also available:
- Access 2007 For Dummies
  0-470-04612-0
- ASP.NET 2 For Dummies
  0-7645-7907-X
- C# 2005 For Dummies
  0-7645-9704-3
- Hacking For Dummies
  0-470-05235-X
- Hacking Wireless Networks
  For Dummies
  0-7645-9730-2
- Java For Dummies
  0-470-08716-1

- Microsoft SQL Server 2005 For Dummies
  0-7645-7755-7
- Networking All-in-One Desk Reference
  For Dummies
  0-7645-9939-9
- Preventing Identity Theft For Dummies
  0-7645-7336-5
- Telecom For Dummies
  0-471-77085-X
- Visual Studio 2005 All-in-One Desk
  Reference For Dummies
  0-7645-9775-2
- XML For Dummies
  0-7645-8845-1

Networking For Dummies,® 8th Edition

Cheat Sheet

My Internet Connection

Provider

Company name: _____

Technical-support contact: _____

Tech-support phone number: _____

Web site: _____

E-mail address: _____

TCP/IP information

IP range: _____ to

_____

Subnet mask: _____

Default gateway: _____

Nameservers: _____—

_____—_____

Router information

Make and model: _____

Internal IP address (LAN): _____

External IP address (WAN): _____

Administrator username: _____

Password: DON'T WRITE IT HERE!

RJ-45 Pin Connections

- **Pin 1:** White/orange
- **Pin 2:** Orange
- **Pin 3:** White/green
- **Pin 6:** Green

Private IP Address Ranges

10.0.0.0	to	10.255.255.255
172.16.0.0	to	172.31.255.255
192.168.0.0	to	192.168.255.255

Useful Web Sites for Networking Information

TCP/IP and Internet information

To register domains:

www.internic.net

www.networksolutions.com

www.register.com

To check your TCP/IP configuration:

www.dnsreport.com

To see whether your e-mail server has been blacklisted:

www.ordb.org

Standards organizations

Institute of Electrical and Electronics Engineers:

www.ieee.org

International Organization for Standards:

www.iso.org

Internet Engineering Task Force:

www.ietf.org

Internet Society:

www.isoc.org

Networking For Dummies,®
8th Edition

Cheat Sheet

My Network and Welcome to It

Account information

My user ID: _____

My password: <u>DON'T WRITE IT HERE!</u> _____

Domain name: _____

Network administrator

Name: _____

Phone number: _____

E-mail name: _____

Favorite snack food: _____

My network drives

Drive Letter	Description
_____	_____
_____	_____
_____	_____
_____	_____
_____	_____

My network printers

Printer Name	IP Address	Description
_____	_____	_____
_____	_____	_____
_____	_____	_____
_____	_____	_____
_____	_____	_____
_____	_____	_____

My network servers

Server Name	IP Address	Description
_____	_____	_____
_____	_____	_____
_____	_____	_____
_____	_____	_____

For Dummies: Bestselling Book Series for Beginners